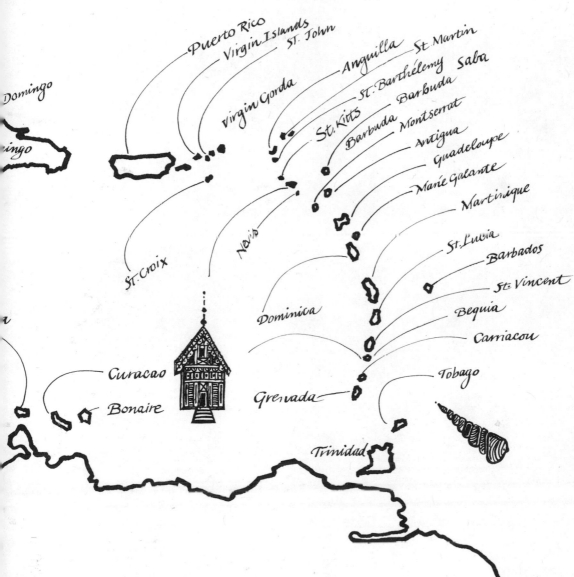

Domingo

Domingo

ingo

Puerto Rico

Virgin Islands

St. John

Virgin Gorda

Anguilla

St. Martin

St. Barthélemy

Saba

St. Kitts

Barbuda

Barbuda

Montserrat

Antigua

Guadeloupe

Marie Galante

Martinique

St. Croix

Nevis

St. Lucia

Barbados

St. Vincent

Dominica

Bequia

Curacao

Carriacou

Bonaire

Tobago

Grenada

Trinidad

THE CARIBBEAN

BOOKS BY SELDEN RODMAN

Verse

DEATH OF THE HERO
THE AMAZING YEAR
THE REVOLUTIONISTS
THE AIRMEN
LAWRENCE: THE LAST CRUSADE
MORTAL TRIUMPH AND OTHER POEMS

Art

THE FRESCOES OF OROZCO
THE INSIDERS
CONVERSATIONS WITH ARTISTS
THE EYE OF MAN
PORTRAIT OF THE ARTIST AS AN AMERICAN
RENAISSANCE IN HAITI
HORACE PIPPIN: A NEGRO ARTIST IN AMERICA

Music

THE HEART OF BEETHOVEN

History and Travel

THE CARIBBEAN
THE PERU TRAVELER
THE GUATEMALA TRAVELER
THE ROAD TO PANAMA
QUISQUEYA: A HISTORY OF THE DOMINICAN REPUBLIC
MEXICAN JOURNAL
HAITI: THE BLACK REPUBLIC

Anthologies

ONE HUNDRED MODERN POEMS
ONE HUNDRED AMERICAN POEMS
WAR AND THE POET (with Richard Eberhart)
THE POETRY OF FLIGHT
A NEW ANTHOLOGY OF MODERN POETRY

THE CARIBBEAN

by Selden Rodman

drawings by Bill Negron

Hawthorn Books, Inc.   Publishers   New York

First Edition: 1968

Designed by Gene Gordon

To
Patrick Leigh Fermor,
who at my home in Haiti in 1946 gave me
the distant vision of this book,
and to
Derek Walcott,
at whose home in Trinidad in 1966
it received its final illumination

CONTENTS

THE CARIBBEAN

ACKNOWLEDGMENTS

Between November 21 and December 24, 1966, accompanied by Bill Negron, the illustrator of this book and of *The Road to Panama*, with whom I had previously traveled in Central America and Peru, I visited Jamaica and Trinidad and all the major English- and French-speaking islands in between. From January 1 to April 1, 1967, I lived in Puerto Rico with my family, lecturing on art and visiting the Dominican Repub-lic (for the fifth time), all the Dutch islands, French-speaking St. Martin and St. Barthélémy (St. Barts), and the Virgins. On these shorter trips I was accompanied by my wife Carole. On a four-day visit to St. Croix my companion was my daughter Oriana. Toward the end of March I returned to Jamaica for several days with Seymour Leichman. On April 1 Bill Negron joined me in Haiti (my seventeenth visit), and we traveled there for a week. The following September we flew to the Bahamas, revisiting briefly the Dominican Republic and Haiti on the way back. Our passports were cleared by the Department of State for travel in Cuba, which I had visited often in pre-Castro days, but visas were denied to us. To Bill Negron, Seymour Leichman, and my wife and daughter, with each of whom travel is exciting, go my primary thanks.

Without the help of several airlines and hotel associations, which gave us tickets and accommodations without asking anything in return, these wide-ranging trips would have been economically impossible. As we were not putting out a guidebook and so had little or nothing to offer these benefactors by way of publishing information about schedules and rates, only visionaries who hoped that their favorite islands might be appreciated helped us. Among them were Bob McKinney, then public relations officer for British West Indies Airways, who made it feasible for us to fly (on a very complicated schedule) to Trinidad and back, touching at most of the islands along the way. Equally generous with their help were Marguerite Allen of the Robert Warner Agency; Virginia Radclytfe, Richard Hazlitt, and Jerry Mahoney of Sontheimer & Co.; Jack Waugh, Mike Segara, and Kal Wagenheim of the Aruba Information Agency; Ben Caruthers, William Kalis, and Oscar deMejo of Infoplan; William Wallace, public-relations officer for the Rockefeller hotels in the

1

Virgin Islands; Dennis Trigo, Vice-President for Public Relations of Caribair in San Juan, Puerto Rico; and the public-relations staff of Trans Caribbean Airways in the same city.

Fred Wilmot and Douglas Burke of the Jamaica Tourist Board took care of us royally during our two trips to Jamaica.

Our thanks go to Dan Darrow, manager of the Caribbean Beach Hotel, Frank Gilmore of LIAT airlines, and Felicia and Jerry Gomes in Antigua; to Jen Osborne of the Vue Pointe Hotel in Montserrat; to Helen Maingo, Campbell Evelyn, and Arthur Leamon of the Golden Lemon in Dieppe Bay, St. Christopher (St. Kitts); to Mary Pomeroy of the Nivet Plantation House in Nevis; to "Foxy" Gilette of Coco Point in Barbuda; to Roger Fortuné, Directeur de l'Office du Tourisme, at Point-à-Pitre in Guadeloupe; to Henri Joseph, Directeur du Tourisme, Alexandre Bertrand, Directeur du Centre d'Art at Fort-de-France, and Albert Veille, manager of the Bacoua Hotel at Trois-Îlets in Martinique; to Peter Brand, owner-manager of the Island House Hotel in Dominica; to Messrs. Milne-Marshall and Bergasse of the Tourist Board in Castries, St. Lucia, and the St. Lucia Beach Hotel, to which they sent us; to C. G. Huggins of the Tourist Board and Ken and Phyllis Punnet in St. Vincent; to Tom and Gladys Johnston of Moon Hole, Bequia; to Kenneth Coombs, managing director of Sam Lord's Castle, and Frank A. Collymore in Barbados; to Gertrude Protain of the Tourist Board, Allan Krassner of the Spice Island Inn, and Carl Schuster of the Nutmeg Bar and the sloop *ZigZag* in Grenada; and to Derek and Margaret Walcott in Trinidad.

We owe our thanks to Mike Kuiperi and W. Watti Chai of the Aruba Tourist Board and to Marcel Wortman, general manager of the Aruba Caribbean; to Boeli van Leeuwen, René de Rooy, and Herman Lichtveld of the Curaçao Tourist Board and to the manager of the Hotel Curaçao Intercontinental; to Tom Crawford of the U.S.I.S. and his wife Caroline in Santo Domingo, Dominican Republic, and to Tomás Pastoriza and his wife Claudina in Santiago de los Caballeros; to Julien Conner, chief of the Philipsburg Tourist Board, and to Hippolyte Ledée, José Dormoy, and Georges Greaux, pilot-proprietors of the Windward Islands Airways, all in St. Maarten; to Rémy de Haenen, veteran pilot and owner of the Eden Roc Hotel in St. Barthélemy (St. Barts); to Administrator Jan Lens in St. Eustatius; and to Gerard van der Val, Administrator of Saba.

Our thanks also go to Tram Coombs of St. Thomas, U.S. Virgin Islands; to Edward Sullivan and David Brewer of the Caneel Bay Plantation, St. Johns; to Andy Anderson, manager of the Beach Hotel of St. Croix, to its proprietor, Lon Southerland, and to Sally Kramer of the Tourist Board; to Ted Doyle of the Bahamas Government Information Services; to Robert and Tamara Baussan of the Ibo Lelé Hotel in Port-au-Prince, Haiti, to Harold Busenius of the Mont-Joli Hotel in Cap Haïti, to Mason Dobson of the U.S.I.S. in that city, to former Ambassador to Haiti Benson E. L. Timmons III and his wife Sanya, and to Ambassador Claude G. Ross and his wife Antigone, our gracious hosts.

INTRODUCTION

How lucky we are to have the West Indies in our "front yard"—and how meagerly we take advantage of the opportunity!

There may be particular islands in the South Pacific that are more beautiful to look at than St. Kitts or Saba. The jungles of Ceylon and Madagascar may be denser than those of Dominica and St. Lucia. A few hidden valleys on remote New Guinea still remain to be explored, and in them Stone Age savages still carve incomparable fetishes, but there are valleys in Haiti that are seen by no one but their inhabitants, and the country has a greater number of artists per capita than France. Sicily and the isles of Greece are eloquent with the ruins of antiquity, but Brimstone Hill and Christophe's palace echo thunderously too. The overcrowded Japanese and Indonesian archipelagoes have homogeneous cultures of their own; Trinidad's Hindu temples and Curaçao's baroque gables are almost as exotic. In short, where else within a few hours of our eastern seaboard is there such a variety of natural beauty, historical romance, and unspoiled, outgoing human beings? And how much of it do we even begin to sample?

Puerto Rico and the American Virgins, because they are "ours," are fairly well known to us; by the same token they tend to assume our familiar image and to hand it back to us shopworn or caricatured.

We touch gingerly those places that the British managed to endow with a trace of their tidy well-being—Barbados, Antigua, and the north coast of Jamaica—and in touching them remove imperceptibly the aristocratic polish lest it offend our democratic sensibilities.

In the French and Dutch islands, still maintained at great expense to soothe the wounded prides of the Netherlands and France, we savor only what is French or Dutch, not neglecting to display our sophistication by comparing the cuisine of Fort-de-France with that of Paris or Willemstad's waterways with those of Amsterdam.

On the big island of Hispaniola, politics has always been dirty, and the Great Powers (ourselves included) have taken advantage of it. In the Dominican Republic, the only remaining constitutional republic in the Caribbean with a Spanish background, our government has traditionally held aloof in times of the jackboot and the muffled scream, intervening only when American interests seemed threatened and sharing our bounty too little and too late. Those few visitors,with no desire to plunder stole quick looks, congratulated themselves on their superior institutions, and passed on. In Haiti, whose people are at once the most destitute and the most creative in the Indies, our smugness is compounded. For those who stay away either complain that they cannot bear to see the naked face of poverty or righteously spurn a government that our own is willing neither to aid nor to overthrow.

Which leaves about everything. All of Haiti, not just the politically tormented capital with its proliferation of artists and poets, dancers and drummers, but also the mysterious vales and wounded mountains, where hospitality never sleeps and the poorest are the most generous. The Dominican and Puerto Rican hinterlands, so rich by contrast and so empty, wait to be explored. And so does verdant, rolling Jamaica south and east of Montego Bay's gold coast—from the Cockpit country and the jungle-shouldered rivers of Ocho Rios through the Blue Mountains to the clapboard jungles of Kingston and Spanish Town, with their bearded world savers and world defiers. English Harbour in Antigua will not be brutalized, nor will St. John in Barbados. And the necklace of English-speaking islands in between—St. Kitts and Nevis, Montserrat, Dominica, St. Lucia, St. Vincent, Grenada, and the Grenadines—are still either too isloated or too proud of what they are to give up to blandness easily. The French and Dutch islands in between are just beginning to find their identities—identities neither French nor Dutch but blendings of each with the dominant African—and, if the floodtide of tourism spares them, they will suceed.

The African strain, in fact, dominates all the islands except Puerto Rico and Trinidad. Trinidad, liveliest and most polyglot of the lot, will very shortly have more people of East Indian than of African ancestry. The clash of cultures there has always been delirious and could become explosive, yet it is hard to imagine the calypso and the jump-up yielding to the sing-in and the sit-down.

Colonial history was ineluctably mercenary, but it had its glorious moments. The slave revolts were necessary, inevitable, and sublimely daring, yet the mindlessness and cruelty of the oppressors were mirrored, and sometimes exceeded, in the mindlessness and cruelty of the oppressed. And the heirs of revolt turn more often to the civilization of the masters in shaping their future than to the *laissez-faire* physicality of Caribbea or Africa. The ambivalence of this search for roots is part of the fascination. And so is the reaction of liberated serf, barely wakened and still idling in the dreamlike trance of his servitude, to the purposefulness of those who come to exploit or help him or to the indifference of those who come to play at any price.

Yet how dreary this book would be—how Calvinistic and willfully blind to the sensuality of the Caribbean's sun-drenched shingle, its jungles' bosky overripeness, its wine-dark reefs—if it took the form of a sociological tract! What kind of man would contemplate his (or the world's) navel in full view of the Pitons? write a political speech to the accompaniment of the *oiseau musicien*? analyze The Mighty Sparrow's grammar? compose a sermon at Trunk Bay? or plan a housing development to overlook Virgin Gorda's breast-shaped boulders? Yet *without* the age-old and ever-present accompaniment of what man has done (or not done) to accommodate himself to this earthly paradise, what would we have? The pursuit of happiness, detached from hows, whens, and whys, becomes no more than a pursuit. Without meaning or purpose, the "facts" of life add up to nothing. The hedonist becomes a voluptuary, the sunworshiper a beachcomber, the explorer a tourist.

And what is so wrong with that?

It was to answer this nagging question that Bill Negron and I set forth *as tourists* in November 1966 to make a season's circuit of all the islands described in this book. Could the word be divorced from its ugly associations? Because economy dictated stays of no more than a week each in the larger islands and often as little as one or two days each in the smaller ones, this trip would be a good way to find out. It might be an unfair test in the cases of Haiti, the Dominican Republic, and Puerto Rico, where I had made prolonged visits in the past; but for all the other islands, which we were seeing for the first time, how much could be absorbed in such lightning forays? Could pleasure and education be combined?

Had we been single-minded in our intent, the test would have been meaningless. An intellectual could talk to other intellectuals, a scholar to other scholars. A skindiver could commune with reefs and fish, a naturalist with the birds and the bees, an architect with colonial styles, an archaeologist with the Arawaks and Caribs, a gourmet with the bills of fare, a professional traveler with timetables and rates. Each of these people could escape, with little difficulty, the dread epithet "tourist." But neither of us was a specialist or wanted to be. All these activities appealed to us from time to time; others— like discovering beautiful places and faces; talking with artists, poets, and politicians; and playing tennis —appealed to us all the time. Furthermore, like the tourist, we enjoyed luxury hotels, wanted the planes and buses to run on schedule, railed not infrequently at the tropical propensity to put things off and let tomorrow take care of itself, even indulged now and and then in the snobbery of trying not to look or act like Americans.

If Americans, however, have any special virtue, historically speaking, it is their capacity to accept other people, other races, other religions, other customs, other climes, glorying in the diversity. This openness was the message of America's greatest poet, Walt Whitman, who was the first to express it. The typical American tourist may not be as disliked as the obtuse German or the arrogant Frenchman, but, when he forgets this national trait, he can be pretty obnoxious, escaping into the shell of a fancied superiority based on nothing but his material good fortune.

To recapture and celebrate the traditional appetite for diversity was the underlying hope with which Bill Negron and I embarked upon our voyage. But we had no intention of losing sight of the basic impulse of every traveler and tourist—*having fun*. To put the account in any tidier form than the day-to-day journal and quick sketches in which it was recorded would be dishonest: Part of the truth, as already noted, was our tendency to fall into some of the same temptations and intolerances as does the typical tourist. So, except for occasional interpolations from earlier journals kept while I was living in the Dominican Republic and Haiti and from books, here is the way to it was.

PROLOGUE: HOW NOT TO ARRIVE ANYWHERE

We made an almost fatal start. It was a Monday. For one of those incomprehensible reasons that only an airline understands, we had to fly from New York to Antigua (which isn't on the way at all) to get to Montego Bay, Jamaica—stopping at Kingston. This route isn't standard procedure, we were told, but as our flight plan was unusually complicated, that was the way it had to be. Because Antigua would be our second island anyway, we were not at all unhappy at the prospect of having a couple of hours to look at its capital city. I won't say anything at this juncture about what we saw, but I shall introduce the driver of our taxi, Eustace Samuel. He told us proudly that he had fourteen brothers and three sisters and that he wanted us to meet all of them. He had a disconcerting way of gesturing toward points of particular interest (all banks, just like the ones at home) as he rounded corners.

If you have never driven on the left side of the road and expect every car coming toward you to swerve and hit you head on, you'll understand why most of what happened during that circuit of St. Johns is a blur. Signs flashed by—"Joy Land Bar," "C. Percival's Petrol" "Happy Acres Guest House—and then, during a relaxed moment at a stop light, Bill Negron looked at his watch and said tensely, "The plane for Jamaica is taking off in fifteen minutes."

With Eustace now really pouring it on, we closed our eyes—and made it with five minutes to spare.

"So sorry," said the girl at the counter. "They've already boarded."

We gasped and turned hopefully to her superior behind her.

"Impossible," he said. "No exceptions . . . Next flight? Friday."

"*Friday!*" we gulped. "But that will eliminate all of Jamaica."

He turned away. I pleaded with him. I told him that we were guests of the airline, that without Jamaica we wouldn't be able to do our book at all. He couldn't have cared less. Why should he? As an Antiguan, he may even have thought that short-changing Jamaica wouldn't be a bad idea at all. We threw up our hands. We groaned. If he hadn't had his back to me and been facing the wall, I might have kneeled to him. I promised to give him special mention by name in our acknowledgments—"with your

7

whole family" (I was thinking of Eustace Samuel). Bill, who had given up, was beginning to see the humor of the situation. "Shall I do a quick portrait of him?" he said. But the imperturbable functionary, without raising his voice, murmured: "You see how impossible it is. Everyone is aboard. The ship is refueled. There goes the pilot."

"The *what?*" In a flash I was over the counter and through the door, pursuing a retreating figure in uniform as he trotted toward the plane. Two steps from the stairs the pilot stopped, and I explained everything once more. He nodded. "All right. Tell them to clear your luggage."

Finally, we sat down and fastened our seat belts—and waited a good half-hour for the jet to take off. We'd have been happy to sit in chains, with ashes on our heads. But our troubles were only beginning.

As the plane taxied into Kingston's Palisadoes Airport, Bill glanced at our tickets and rushed for the door.

"Take everything!" he shouted. "We've got to be rewritten for Montego. It may be a different ship."

I followed him out but never caught up with him. I ran head on into the President of Zambia; his full-bearded and braided retinue; a regiment of Jamaica honor guards in plum-colored tarbooshes, jeweled swords, pith helmets; and a brass band clad in canary-yellow frogged boleros and white spats. A dozen motorcycle policemen, as gaudily plumaged, were edging their way thunderously through all of this. By the time I'd fought my way through, I was in no mood to decelerate. I streaked past health, customs, and immigration authorities, without noticing them at all, coming to rest in a heap with my three bags in front of the B.W.I.A. couter.

A tall and beautiful Jamaican girl, the color of cinnamon, looked at me and at my ticket sympathetically.

"Our aircraft is about to depart, sir."

"But I have no ticket to Montego Bay," I said between pants.

"Let me see. You are Mr. Negron, sir?"

"No." In the shuffle at Antigua, Bill and I had evidently exchanged tickets.

"First, you'll have to find your luggage checks, sir."

"But—but they're on Mr. Rodman's—I mean Mr. Negron's ticket, sir—I mean, miss."

"Then, sir," she said, without a trace of contempt, condescension, or impatience, "it will be incumbent upon us to find your traveling companion, won't it? For we must clear your luggage through Kingston customs before we rewrite your tickets. But meanwhile," she added with a sweet smile, "I'll telephone them to hold the aircraft."

When Bill finally showed up, he said: "How did you get here ahead of me? I had to clear six different officials."

"Officials?" I said, "I never even opened my passport case, and you can thank the President of Zambia for that."

"Amazing," he said, "but never let's do this again—twice in the same day. We'll go home in strait jackets, yelling: 'Check me in! Check me out!' "

"Let our motto be," I said, "never get *off* a plane that's going in the right direction."

And it was all for nothing too, because no sooner had we arrived in "Mo' Bay" than an official waving a cablegram ran up to us and asked our names. "There's been a change of plans," he said. "You're to board a plane in ten minutes—for Kingston."

I

JAMAICA

Kapo I

Every nation on earth, except perhaps the big ones that lost their unique flavors, hides away in itself somewhere an individual who summarizes its national traits. Only a computer with eyes, wings, and a heart could find such an individual. But in Jamaica we stumbled upon him by accident. It was only later, much later, that it occurred to us that he was Mr. Jamaica.

Kapo is the shepherd of an ancient and local cult, called "Pocomania," that blends evangelical Protestantism with African voodoo. He is a hearty man—perhaps that word best describes him—hearty, earthy, natural, kind-hearted, self-assured. When he is not preaching, he carves wood and paints pictures. And all the time, without any conflicts of interest, his Kingston shanty, which serves as temple, studio, and home, is the "corner grocery," dispensing charcoal, firewood, matches, paper, dried fish, tea, and gossip.

But consider Kapo's other qualifications to local everymanship. Jamaican society is notoriously mother-oriented. Though dominantly masculine himself and with a voice like a bassoon, Kapo, whose given name is Mallicia, wears a toque and gaudy robes that sweep the ground, and is surrounded by priestesses as he shepherds his flock. Jamaica's history, from slave days to the present, has been notably mild. Kapo, operating in a fringe of society shrill with preachments of separatism and Black Power, advocates class integration and the union of all races under God. Like

11

most Jamaicans he is uninhibited, verbally imaginative, physically handsome, humorous. And, of course, he is black.

We had our first meeting with Kapo at the end of a long and wonderful
day. The morning had been spent exploring Port Royal and Spanish
Town, the afternoon chatting with pot-smoking Ras Tafarians in their
suburban crate jungle. Kapo's all-purpose dwelling is also constructed
of crates, but its façade is a labyrinth of signs. One is a shopping list.
Another reads: "Primitive Arts in Painting and Carving and Molding.
Buy Jamaica." The biggest sign includes everything:

King of Wood
No Weapon That Is Formed Against Thee
Shall Prosper. Whatever You Do Be
Careful—Kapo. Kapo's Snow-Cones: Cool
Off Here. Works of Kapo in Primitive Art:
Buy Jamaica. Brown Rice 9c. Fag 4. Small
Sardines. See the Afro-American Self-Taught
Artist.

Across the street is another sign: "Why Forget Boys in Trench-Town? We Human Too."

It was night when we arrived, and from an inner sanctuary came the voices of the "angels" singing and the alluring smell of salt beef and red peas. The narrow entrance passage was jammed with people coming and going. Shelves were loaded with Kapo's wooden figurines. Paintings were stacked on the floor, leaning against the baseboard in piles. As a sculptor Kapo produces imagery that is grotesque and inelegant, influenced perhaps by what passes for "African" in the tourist shops, and his figures are generally polished to a high yellow shine. But as a painter he has invented his own style. His bizarre self-portraits and deities are presented frontally, with arms and legs akimbo, against dense thickets or flowering mountains. Sometimes the landscape is diagramed with rectangles of impasto, and sometimes it is picked out with tiny spots of brilliant color. The effect is very much like that achieved by the late Hector Hippolyte, voodoo priest and *doyen* of the Haitian primitives, whose work made such an impression on André Breton, major-domo of Surrealism, in the 1940s. One picture was of a naked, smiling man sitting on the ground and holding his knees apart in such a way as to expose every part of his anatomy. It had been inspired by an incident in the recent elections; this man, accused by the police of carrying concealed weapons, had stripped in the street and cried: "There! You see everything I have in this world!" A more lyrical canvas, depicting three dusky graces with tubular arms and legs intertwined, carried its own explanation on the back:

> Three Sisters Ticklle
> Mamsel, Munsey & Maulin Are Three Loving Sisters
> The Love to Tickle Each Other The Have Work Eat
> Bath and Dress Together I Wonder What Is Going
> To Them When One Get Married

The chant was beginning. "The band of angels say good evenin'." Kapo, who had been attiring himself in his ceremonial robes and turban, emerged from behind a blue curtain. He is a magnificent figure of a man. His skin is black and shines like oiled ebony, the nose is flattened but sensitive; the eyes, in deep pockets of flesh, close to ecstatic slits when he chants the responses. When his thick lips open, his cavernous mouth reveals a treasure in gold. Seizing his seven-foot shepherd's crook in one hand and a knobby scepter in the other, he swept between the crowded benches and approached the oblong "altar," a table spread with a lacy cloth on which were candles, one for each disciple, a pile of corn kernels, bits of driftwood, a jug of water, maracas, and two vases of flowers. Biblical slogans adorned the crate wall behind him.

Ceremoniously Kapo invited me to light a candle. One of his female attendants had already dropped one, an episode that seemed to cause alarm. Kapo had been careful not to replace it, and I handled mine gingerly lest the bad luck be compounded. Like the Haitian *houngan*, Kapo now began to speak in mysterious "tongues." And, like the *hounsis* (attendants of the priest) in the neighboring island, the "angels" began to dance as they chanted, hips undulating, eyes rolling, bodies whirling like dervishes. When he isn't singing in his deep bass, Kapo makes a wheeze with his mouth closed, a sound like that of a caged lion or a locomotive. "Higher," was the way he described his sound to me later. "High-er, high-er, high-er! You know we all have something special from God. Kapo has this big throat and voice."

I asked him about those features of Pocomania that seemed to resemble voodoo. "I call the spirits in the African way," he told me, "but the candles are for those at the Last Supper. They are very important. If one is lighted from the last, that means destruction. They must be lighted alternately. This bunch of leaves with white on the green—you know what that is? We believe Mary after leaving the Manger squeeze some milk from her bust and it fall here. This may be sounding a little bit strange, but it been tested many time."

The climax of voodoo comes when the *serviteur* is "possessed" by the African deity he invokes. By losing his identity momentarily, the Haitian is physically released from whatever has been troubling him. In Pocomania "possessions" are not uncommon, but they are neither sought for any specific therapy nor controlled. H. P. Jacobs speculates that the gasping practice—common to groups other than Kapo's—contributes to dizziness by diminishing the residual carbon dioxide in the lungs and that it has an autohypnotic effect on the cultists. This practice is the counterpart of the drum rhythms in voodoo. In both religions those possessed "speak with tongues" when they fall to the ground. Jacobs suggests that this phenomenon has a Nigerian provenance. But the word "Pocomania" itself, he says, is derived from Pucku, the name the possession-god of the Bush Negroes in Surinam.[1]

The climax of Kapo's ceremony is the sermon. It is a rambling discourse delivered with great gusto, almost sensually. In this instance it covered everything from Kapo's conversion at the age of twelve, when he dreamed of Christ crucified and was "born aloft by seventy-two angels," to his arrest during the election disturbances, when the police found Molotov cocktails on the premises. (These bombs were later discovered to have been hidden there by direct actionists, unknown to him.) We suspected that his final injunction was directed to us as Americans: "We believe in all races and that God is colorless, but we must invoke the spirits to bring unity and peace and overcome Satan who wants the races to fight each other. Satan is a man, a woman, a human being. So be careful!"

[1] H. P. Jacobs, "Dialect, Magic and Religion," in Morris Cargill, ed., *Ian Fleming Introduces Jamaica* (New York: Hawthorn, 1965).

Glimpses of Port Royal and Spanish Town

Accompanied by an old Jamaican friend we set out for Port Royal early the first morning, stopping on the way to inspect Devon Great House, a stately, well-restored colonial mansion said to have been much admired by Kirk Douglas, who wanted to film a picture around it. Its unusual feature is louvered walls; the boards between the windows are hinged to admit the sea breeze. But the characteristic it shares with all great houses is a ponderous exclusivity. Dominant planters—the Beckords of Fonthill Abbey; the Hibberts, whose terminal heir in England received £131,120 in compensation for his 1,618 slaves in 1837 and the sale of whose library lasted forty-two days; the Longs, with their 14,000 acres; John Gladstone, father of the Victorian Prime Minister, whose slaves were worth twice as much as the Hibberts'—built elegant homes and lordly gardens in England with their Jamaican fortunes, but in Jamaica (to which they deigned to make occasional supervisory visits) they built for climatic comfort and security against insurrection alone. And the hypocrisy of their disclaimers of racial prejudice was notorious. Asked to confirm that the slaves were habitually happy, the wife of one planter replied that on her one visit they had appeared to be always smiling, though she had wondered why the cook had to be chained to the stove. And the novelist Anthony Trollope, reporting a typical conversation that he had overheard about a certain planter suspected of having a distant Negro ancestor, wrote: "The next time you see Jones, you observe him closely, and you can find no trace of the Ethiop. But should he presently descant on purity of blood, and the insupportable impudence of the coloured, then, and not till then, you will begin to doubt."

On the hillside above Devon is a gaudier pillared palace belonging to Pat Chung, an immigrant from British Guiana who became a merchant prince in Jamaica and is now said to be writing a history of religion and mankind.

I remarked to our friend on the apparent lack of intercourse (or even interest in one another) that characterizes the Caribbean peoples. He confirmed it in Jamaica's case: "We don't know or care anything about Haiti ninety miles to our east, but we know all about King Alfred and can tell you the exact distance between London and Oxford. There used to be some curiosity about Cuba, Costa Rica, and Panama," he added, "but this involved only those who had relatives picking bananas there."

Passing Palisadoes Airport halfway down the long spit of sand spiny with dildo cactus, we arrived at the peninsula's tip, Port Royal—or what was once Port Royal. For nothing remains today of the roistering buccaneer's metropolis, the wealth of which dwarfed that of London in the seventeenth century, except an agglomeration of barracks, warehouses, and crumbling gun ports. Not a soul was in sight. We passed through one cavernous derelict after another, hallooing but raising only echoes, till we came to the placid waters of the bay. It was there that an earthquake struck and that the "wicked city" sank at 11:43 on the morning of June 7, 1692. Two hundred yards out a deserted barge equipped with minimal diving equipment lay motionless. Our eyes strained to penetrate the murky waters at our feet for some trace of those submarine streets along which once had clanked pirates stoned with rum, waving their gold tankards embellished with "gems torn from half a hundred cathedrals," where the brilliant freebooter Henry Morgan had relaxed over a wine cask preparing to sack Panama or Portobelo between his raids on Spanish shipping and threatening to shoot any man who wouldn't drink with him. The bay was like an opaque mirror. Then suddenly, to our utter astonishment, there emerged from the deep a young man clad from neck to toes in black rubber and carrying a mask.

Stepping out, regarding us with no astonishment at all, and shaking the water from his hair, he introduced himself as Bob Marx. He was, he said, one of the team of marine archaeologists following up the operation of Ed Link, of Link Trainer fame, who first started to explore Port Royal systematically ten years ago. He handed me a coral-encrusted watch, and we followed him into the improvised museum.

"11:43?" I asked, looking at the lump of barnacles in my hand.

"Almost certainly," he said. "We'll X-ray this one like the other before scraping it. Link discovered the exact time of the 'quake on that original find, which was manufactured in Amsterdam in 1686. The hands were gone, but they'd left a faint impression on the coral shield facing the dial."

"Are you finding any of those millions of pieces of eight the buccaneers took from Spain?" Bill asked.

"Not many," he replied, "and very little of the movable wealth, though most of the buildings are still buried in the mud. The thing is that within a very short time of the disaster everything accessible—and the water was clear then—was removed by divers or grappling hooks. Whatever we find has to be under a crumbled wall."

We looked over the shelves of loot: bits of willow ware attesting to the rage of *chinoiserie* under James II, hundreds of clay pipes, German beer steins (even then!), petrified butter, and human turds. Ours, I reflected, is another age that is bound to be remembered by its ephemera and effluvia. Bob Marx shook his dripping head. "Our job will take at least thirty years to finish—if it ever is finished—and never by the three of us; but the scholars are right. It *is* the greatest seventeenth-century midden anywhere, and God knows what we may find." He went on to tell us of some of his more hair-raising experiences, like the time he wrenched an octopus off his face by fastening his airlift compressor to the back of its body and sucking it loose and the time his friend was enveloped for a full five minutes in the "arms" of a 12-foot manta ray. "The worst," he said, "was the time I returned alone at sundown for a last look and a wall fell on me, knocking me unconscious. When I came to and found myself under that wall I thought of religion for the first time. What saved me was that the button of my intake valve had struck bottom before I did and remained in the on position."

Port Royal and Spanish Town were the focal points of colonial Jamaica, and in both cities time has stopped. The history of Port Royal—that "gaudy brothel," as John Hearne calls it—is shorter and more flamboyant. Had the buccaneers from Haitian Tortuga and Île à Vache not banded together in "The Confederacy of the Brethren of the Coast" and offered England their piratical services, Jamaica—and probably Haiti and many of the smaller French and British islands as well—would have been retaken by Spain, and the Caribbean today might be as "Latin" as Latin America. England was reluctant to be saved. Because he had had the enterprise to seize Puerto Principe (now Camagüey) in Cuba, Maracaibo in Venezuela, Portobelo and Panama on the isthmus—and with these latter cities the gold and silver in transit from Mexico and Peru—Morgan was rebuked for exceeding orders. Like the Israelis of today, whose act of self-preservation has been called "the only war in history where the victors were asked to give up what they took and the vanquished demanded unconditional surrender," Morgan was a winner whom nobody congratulated. Worst of all, he was obliged to leave his beloved base, "The Babylon of the West," for dreary London. But the fame of his exploits—the ships he had burned to block retreat, the paths he had hacked through jungles to surprise professional armies outnumbering his starving marauders three to one, the stampeding bulls he had stopped, the wild revels that had followed every triumph—endeared him to the public. He received a hero's welcome in the London streets, and soon he was spending riotous nights with the nobility. King Charles reversed himself, knighted the pirate, and made him Lieutenant Governor of Jamaica. But, as Clinton Black put it, "the old sea-rovers by removing the Spanish threat to Jamaica so effectively had worked themselves out of a job." [2] Morgan settled down. The small proprietors, who couldn't afford to replace their indentured white workers with Negro slaves when the former joined the pirates gave way to the big planters, who could and did. Those, including the buccaneers, who couldn't understand that the Age of Sugar was dawning ended, in Black's words, "with a rope around their necks at Gallows Point on the Palisadoes (often on Morgan's orders) because they would not give up their way of life." Spanish Town, the sleepy little colonial capital under Spain and England alike, was about to enter upon its years of glory.

The city today, long-since superseded as Jamaica's capital by brassy, raffish, port-side Kingston, is as sleepily inglorious as it was in the years before Port Royal and its stews met the fate of Sodom. We entered the square, with its celebrated brick administrative buildings and the Rodney Memorial, which shows the great Admiral absurdly dressed in a Roman toga, and we were alone. The square was exactly as Patrick Leigh

---

[2] Clinton V. Black, *The Story of Jamaica* (London: Collins, 1965).

Fermor described it seventeen years earlier "full of sunlight and heavy with that late-afternoon atmosphere which is peculiar to towns that have lost their importance." Well, we were not *quite* alone, for presently a Ras Tafarian, with shoulder-length dusty braidlets like pipe cleaners, slouched out of a shady portico to join us on the Assembly steps. A few minutes later a colleague on a bicycle pulled up at the curb and invited us to converse with Haile Selassie's worshipers on the Dunghill.

We were aware that these picturesque dropouts from Western society—men whose refusal to fight, work, or be counted long predates the protests of our beatniks or hippies—swear allegiance to the Emperor of Ethiopia (Prince Ras Tafari before his coronation). We had also been told that the direct-actionist wing of the movement wear blue hats. As our braided friend, whose name was Ras Codey, was carrying a straw with a plaid band and smiled benignly, we had no hesitation in accepting his invitation. I asked him if allegiance to the Negus spread beyond his reputed 30,000 Jamaican followers. "Oh yes, man, we everywhere," he said. "Even New York. Twenty-Ninth Street and Tenth Avenue. Malcolm X was coming close to us when they killed him."

"But why did it all start here in Jamaica?"

" 'Cause it say, 'They shall come from the East, and ye shall bring them to the West.' "

"Where does it say that?"

"In the King James Bible, man, Fifth Chapter Revelations and Isaiah Chapter Seven."

"What will happen when Ras Tafari dies?" I asked.

"After? They is no after. He lives forever. He is returned Messiah."

"And if the papers report his death?" I persisted. "Isn't it true that when he visited Jamaica last year the Emperor denied publicly that he was God?"

He laughed uproariously. "The papers have to report that: they *have* to! We know what he really said. If they say he die, they lie. If history say so, history will be wrong. Will it be for the first time?"

We allowed that it wouldn't. "So we agree that they are wrong," he concluded happily, "and we agree that he is All Right!"

While Bill sketched the carefree brethren on the hot steps, I wandered into the Archives Building in search of Clinton Black. The chief archivist was at his desk, a British-type gentleman on the surface but a Jamaican patriot all the way through.

I asked him how he accounted for Jamaica's peaceful development. Did he think, for instance, that the 1738 treaty with the maroons had released the accumulating pressure for revolt that had exploded in nearby Haiti in 1791? He thought so, but he didn't agree with the theory that Governor Balcarres had expressed in 1795, when the Reign of Terror was at its apogee in Paris—the theory that the abortive Jamaican uprising in that year was inspired by *agents provocateurs*, slaves brought to Jamaica with their fleeing masters from the Haitian holocaust. "We were

Ras Tafarian Interlude

When Leigh Fermor visited the Dunghill (pronounced Dungle) in 1949, he found the followers of the Ethiopian Emperor outspokenly antiwhite, bearded, smoking marijuana, living in the half-buried chassis of junked cars. He also found these lotus eaters opinionated and unexpectedly friendly. Nothing has changed. Perhaps it is no longer true that "not one Ras Tafari, since the birth of the cult twenty-odd years ago, has ever undertaken the journey to Addis Ababa." I heard tell of a small delegation that did go and came back in a hurry. No adept today would be likely to chant "All for Manley and Communism"; Sir Norman Manley, who still heads the People's National Party, has tempered his tune to the times. But here murderers and philosophers, freewheelers and sweet singers, incendiaries and bums still have in common their unwashed independence. And he who might ask of a beardless one why he is out of step would not be surprised to hear the same sad, wonderful answer: "I can't grow no beard. But, boy! I'm beard minded!"

More than likely the prevalence of far-out cults in Jamaica goes back to colonial times, when the established church was characterized by the best of the governors as "corrupt and despicable to a degree which must appear almost incredible." The Church of England left the slaves to their own devices, but the Methodist, Baptist, Wesleyans, and Moravians were courageous enough to interpret Christianity as a revolutionary doctrine and to insist that before God all men are equals. Evangelism thus tended

to absorb the African tribal animism, perpetuating the belief in magic under Christian auspices. Morris Cargill suggests that Christian institutions may take credit for the fact that Jamaicans are a tolerant, kindly people, but he also says that the remarkably high church attendance here is "possibly due more to sociability, a need for emotional uplift mixed with a bit of entertainment and singing, and a good bit of superstitious awe, rather than to any deep understanding and conviction." And he also points out that Christian teachings on marriage and sexual morality are almost totally ignored; 70 per cent of Jamaica's children are born out of wedlock.[4]

While Bill drew three of the picturesque cult leaders in their knitted caps and derbies, a fourth suggested that I take notes on the tenets of his faith. As he rambled on and on, I did, and here are extracts from them, unedited:

> You can feel it when true love flow between man and man. Then come Mankind. . . .
>
> The Queen of Sheba journey to Jerusalem in 6500 B.C. She was Queen of Ethiopia. Their child, hers and Solomon's, was Ibn el Akim (Menelek 1). Haile Selassie is 225th in direct line of descent. But what make him special is that when he ascended the throne in 1930 he took many new titles: King of Kings, Conquering Lion of Judah, et cetera. Now, if you read Chapter 5 of the Book of Revelations, you see that all that was prophesied has come to pass. Sealed with the seven seals, it say! And in the nineteenth chapter it say, "He shall wage war with the lambs but the lambs shall overcome him."
>
> One of our predecessors was your Marcus Garvey, the greatest of all non-African liberators.

My informant quoted at this point a long passage, which he said was from Isaiah, and, as he finished, another bearded brother passed in front of him, puffing marijuana from a double-barreled pipe and without glancing our way, said mildly "Hebrews Eleven."

> Prester John was one of our early ones, but all culture comes from Africa; all religion; the smallest men, the Pygmies; the tallest men, the Nubians; the best diamonds; the most prolific people. Is it not so?

The others were beginning to chant, chiming in with "amens" from time to time, as in a Mississippi revival.

> Each race must develop according to its own ways. But only when they unite under we will there be Eden. ["Amen!"] if it weren't for our religion we'd be Castroites. ["Amen!"] We'd have to be! ["Amen!"]

4 Cargill, op. cit.

By this time someone had come with a basket containing bottles of beer and pop that Bill had paid for, and this final reasuring pronouncement was delivered:

People die only of diseases. If you are clean you will live forever. Senility and old age do not exist. ["Amen!"]

Squeezing as many of our friends into the car as we could, we moved on to a cluster of connecting shacks, where Count Ossie's Drummers performed for us in the yard. There were eight of them: four on bongos, one on bass, one on maraca, and two playing coconut strainers and steel plates tempered to give a variety of clanking notes. The Count gave a solo on a special drum, as good a performance as any I'd heard in Haiti, the world's undisputed drum citadel. In the fading light I could just make out this legend on the skin of the drum:

> *Even Aaron's Beards*: *That Went*
> *Down to the Skirts of His*
> *Garments as the Dew of Hebron and*
> *as the Dew That Descended*

John Hearne, the Jamaican novelist, calls steel-band music as monotonously arresting as a pulse beat—"the unworked rhythms of a people who have only realized music as a social adjunct, not yet as an art." I thought of this remark as we drove home and of Hearne's description of Kingston as ideal in size—"just large enough to foster those conceits and eccentricities that can develop only in a capital yet just small enough to make anonymity impossible." How true. Jamaica alone of the former British colonies has (we were soon to discover) this crazy social atavism that forces one to confront the hidden savageries under one's own skin.

Tourism: Montego Bay and the North Coast

Montego, or Lard, Bay ("montego" is a corruption of "manteca", the Spanish settlers of Jamaica made their candles by melting down cattle) has a lard-like look as you fly in. There's a brackish, shallow lake of yellow-brown water beside the strip at seaside. Amphibious bulldozers were wallowing in this sink as we landed beside it, so presumably it is being cleaned up to conform to Montego Bay's image. That image, as everyone knows, has nothing to do with reality. The image Montego Bay is successfully spending millions to project (and from which it receives in return an accelerating cascade of millions larger than any other resort in the Caribbean) is most unlard-like. It is compounded of cleanliness, colorlessness, Britishness, expensiveness, and exclusivity. The theory is that this five-layer cake is what the American tourist wants, provided it is topped with just enough icing of picturequeness to convince him that he's left home but not so much as to frighten him into thinking he's sacrificed any of the comforts of Squaresville. Cleanliness is achieved by going far beyond the elimination of the Anopheles mosquito and the Salmonella enteritis bacillus; every hedge and blade of grass is shorn clean with a knife, every crack in a wall filled with putty, every poor native given a uniform or gently pushed back into the off-limits countryside. Colornessness is neither legislated, enforced nor talked about: It simply happens that the executive (or responsible) face is white and that, when a black body is put into a white tunic in a paneled bar, you don't notice it. The British presence didn't have to be imported; it was always there, requiring only an exaggerated monicker or a touch of grease paint to seem alive. Well out of town or high in the cool hills back of Kingston the great families of colonial times in their great houses accepted slavery as a necessary evil and prudently refrained from imposing their taste (or their money) on anything Jamaican. The Duke of Marlborough and Noel Coward are equally unobtrusive today. Expensiveness and exclusivity go hand in hand. There are no inexpensive hotels or reasonably priced meals to be had anywhere on the north coast from Negril to Port Antonio. The theory seems to be that, when a secretary from Brooklyn or a schoolmarm from Kalamazoo reads a *New Yorker* ad about the $2,500 it costs to spend two weeks at Frenchman's Cove, she will blow five years' savings to come as close to duplicating this guaranteed incarceration in antiseptic tedium as possible—and it works!

John Pringle, the promotional genius more responsible than any other man for making it work, is sophisticated enough to regard this triumph of salesmanship and snobbery with ambivalence. In fact, he was retiring as director of the Tourist Board the day we met him and was flying to Haiti to stock up on that kind of uninhibited, inventive native self-expression in folk arts that tourist boards have no time for. Pringle is young, dynamic, blue-eyed, and white, and his sense of guilt is deeply rooted and honorable. His family, entrenched in the plantocracy for centuries, not long ago owned so much land that a Pringle was said to be able to journey from the north to the south coast without ever stepping on a neighbor's real estate. We asked John Pringle if the story was true, and he allowed with a laugh that it was—"but only by taking a very round about excursion via the eastern tip of the island, an excursion that no ancestor of mine would ever have undertaken." Pringle himself has revived the family fortunes, which had almost reached the vanishing point in this century, by his own efforts and by identifying himself with Jamaica's will to make itself a nation and a disciplined, prosperous one. But tourism is rapidly overtaking bauxite as the key to the island's lopsided boom, and Pringle's undisguisable guilt is caused by the nature of the image that he has done so much to create. His masterpiece, for example, is a pocket-sized five-color *Value Guide to the Hotels of Jamaica*, prepared and updated annually by faculty members of the Cornell School of Hotel Administration. It rates, with one, two, or three gold stars, every hotel on the island in terms of rooms, service, food, and outstanding features. Its annual appearance strikes cold chills into the hearts of hoteliers not on their toes, because its ratings can't be bought. But its visual symbols for "what's worth going out of your way to look into" provide a clue to the isolation of the whole tourist setup from Jamaican life—and to John Pringle's unease. These symbols stand for "fine restaurant," "exquisite beach," "excellent golf course," "good entertainment," "lavish cottages," "first class tennis courts," "beautiful gardens," "fabulous view," "lovely suites." There is nothing about people, nothing about culture, nothing mentioned (except the particular view) that is unduplicated in San Juan, Miami Beach, San Diego, or Honolulu.

What astonished me most about Pringle was that he offered no defense. He had a clear view of a viable alternative, yet he was making no plans to carry it out. Of our own beach resorts, I had seen San Juan's "strip" in all its horror most recently, so I asked him what was to prevent Montego Bay from plummeting to the same level.

"Not being under the American umbrella," he said. "We haven't found the money yet."

"I've seen pictures of Tryall, where your funds seem to have been unlimited," I said. "Do you consider that a step in the right direction?"

"Hell, no," he said. "It's a millionaires' Levittown, and Round Hill is only a little better. The whole area is horribly overpriced. Between the few tiny eight-or-ten room guest houses, like The Great House at Sign, where you're having dinner, and the typical Montego hotel, which charges $75 a day and has to be full three quarters of the time to break even, there's nothing. The north coast is pricing itself out of the market, and only lack of big money has prevented the erection of fifteen-story Hiltons—so far. The only serious alternative to the latter that I can see is to build *tourist villages*, twentieth-century casbahs, nests of houses one on top of another, with your roof your neighbor's garden, and so on, along the lines of the Israeli city at Expo 67 or the cliff villages, like waterfalls, in the Algaro district of Portugal. If these 500-house complexes were to be built of prefabricated units and then assembled imaginatively, so that every unit had its own character and originality, the unit cost could be reduced so drastically that we could charge $15 instead of $50 for a room in the off season—maybe even in the in season. I. M. Pei has proposed this solution for a development at White River that the Rothschilds are contemplating, but," he shook his head at our hopeful expressions, "I don't see much likelihood that Jamaica will develop along these lines."

And with John Pringle off to console himself with the creativity of a starving country that has more voodoo priests than tourists and then to settle down for two years of country squiredom in England, neither did we.

The best hope for Jamaica, we were already beginning to suspect, was that Jamaicans of African ancestry might impress their own flavorful personality on the façade, as well as on the heart, of Jamaica. Tourists

will appreciate the advantage in good time. John Pringle assigned one of his top operatives, Fred Wilmot, to drive us along the north coast. But we had other ideas.

"Well what would you like to do?" said Fred.

"Play tennis," we said, "up at Don Budge's courts."

"All afternoon?" He gave us a look of stunned disbelief.

"All afternoon."

"Then tonight we'll visit the night clubs?" he said hopefully.

"No. Tonight we'd like to visit Jerry Morrison and see what he's up to." Jerry Morrison, better known as 'Ti Barb from the days when he was riding high as President François Duvalier's right hand in Haiti, was reputed to be in town for the night. Fred shook his head glumly, and that night, when we met him for dinner at The Rum Barrel, he was still shaking it. We told him that we were going to scrub the beaches and drive directly to Ocho Rios the next afternoon.

"You don't like beaches?" he said.

"We like to swim," I said. "If we see a nice place we'll stop."

"What *are* you looking for?" he asked.

We told him about a disreputable character who had come up to us on the waterfront before breakfast that morning and introduced himself as Gerald Waters. When we asked him what his occupation was he said, "Fire-eater; wanna see how I do it?" Before we could answer he had whipped a pint bottle of kerosene out of his hip pocket, taken a deep swig, and blown two-foot clouds of flame all over the place, gesturing like a ballet dancer. He told us about how business is good only Christmas week, with the Band of the Jaw Bone and the John Canoe Dancers, and when we remarked on the condition of his lower lip, he had answered "Why, I've been doing this seventeen out of my twenty-eight years, and the only time I ever suffered was when a bloke poured out my kerosene and refilled the flask with petrol." He pulled up his dirty T shirt to show us the scars all over his belly.

'Ti Barb is just as complex a man as Fred, but he hides it under an invulnerable front. The pointed red beard helps. And so do the guileless, almost melting, blue eyes. He was in pajamas and bathrobe and said that he was blowing his third fortune promoting tourism in Jamaica. He is also writing a memoir of his glory days with Papa Doc but expects it to be filmed first in Hollywood, with James Coburn as 'Ti Barb—a characteristic touch. I asked him whether or not the newspaper story about the hijacked plane in which he had escaped from Haiti after his fall from favor with the dictator was true; according to the account I'd read, he had been met by a delegation of the F.B.I. which had removed a dozen submachine guns from the luggage. He laughed easily. "You'll be more surprised when you read the true story." He has fond memories of Clement Barbot, founder of the dreaded Tonton Macoutes, and of the days when Barbot and Papa Doc were hiding from Magloire's police in Kenscoff dressed as women. Morrison himself was taking messages from them to their followers in the underground. 'Ti Barb is of the opinion that there is no organized opposition to Duvalier in Haiti but that when he dies there will be a bloodbath touched off by his many would-be successors among the Tonton Macoutes. He blames "the Eisenhower-Dulles State Department" for Duvalier's entrenchment and survival.

'Ti Barb, whom I'd last seen at a champagne party in Port-au-Prince showing off his art collection—he'd wanted me to appraise the collection and was not at all offended when I told him he'd bought all the wrong painters—has always been an appealing person. He is generous and humorous and doesn't look at all capable of putting his enemies in sacks of cement, as his enemies charge. What he is doing in Jamaica and what he is living on are not clear. [At first he was running Jinny Simms' Reef Club, but after the last of several prolonged and mysterious absences from the island he came back to find nothing left—even the panes of glass had been taken out of the windows. Then he was running something called Breeze Point East. It folded, and now he has plans for a discothèque.]

Fred was not feeling well the next morning. He left word that he'd meet us at Rose Hall at noon for the drive to Ocho Rios and that he'd bring our bags in his car. Meanwhile we felt rather disloyal accompanyhis stand-in, Douglas Burke, on a tour of those hotels that we'd spurned the day before. The trip was thoroughly enjoyable and instructive. We drove west along the coast toward the great seven-mile-long beach at Negril, which has yet to be developed, passing the Duke of Marlborough's house high on wooded Tamarind Hill, and an architecturally fascinating wooden beach house at Flint River, with pediments painted pale blue under shingled gables and the intricate jigsaw work along the veranda roof in chartreuse. Tryall, which we'd discussed with Pringle, is a new 2,800-acre development built around Tryall Great House, a low-lying shingle-roofed building of considerable distinction and Oriental overtones, which dates from 1834. It has been restored in impeccable taste, with parquet floors of four precious hardwoods, each a different color. Everyone who builds must follow the style of the Great House, at least in the shingled roofs. The houses, on two-acre lots, vary in price from $85,000 to $125,000.

Continuing on through town, we drove another fifteen minutes to Rose Hall, another huge development in the same price range as Tryall, with 7.25 miles of beach front, an eighteen-hole golf course designed by Robert Trent Jones, and two watermills. An American named John Rollins is the owner and is said to have allocated $3.5 million to the restoration of the great house, which had been stripped of its interior grand staircase and paneling and was in danger of collapsing entirely. The house struck us as grim and prison-like, but perhaps when its interior furnishings are restored and the terraced gardens brought back to life it will be less forbidding, or were we only reacting to the Gothic horrors of Herbert G. de Lisser's novel which we'd read far into the night before? It's an enthralling romance, this tale of Annie Palmer's erotic bouts with a young idealist from England who looses his infatuation when he discovers the clever mixture of sadism and witchcraft with which she keeps her slaves in hand; Clinton Black had already told us that Annie Palmer's lurid history was a posthumous invention, but fiction is stronger than truth, and when we were shown the five palms under which the redoubtable temptress is supposed to have buried her five husbands, we shuddered involuntarily before we laughed.

After meeting Fred in the afternoon, we set out east, first passing Fisherman's Cove at Falmouth, where the water is more phosphorescent than anywhere in the world and where the U. S. Navy is making tests to develop light without heat.

Next came Joe James' attractive, pebble-carpeted gallery at Rio Bueno. James is a bearded young artist who paints blocky nudes like rocks in the landscape and charitably hangs dozens of other pictures by less talented native artists. Pringle wants to make an artists' colony of this little town, which became a "ghost" when the sugar industry declined.

Next came Columbus' landfall, Discovery Bay (Puerto Seco), with the arched ruin of its old stone wharf and, to the right of the road, Henry J. Kaiser's gigantic tin-roofed storage dome for bauxite. Kaiser is one of the big three who mine this world's largest deposit of bauxite, the base for aluminum, and Fred volunteered that his government makes them "bank" the topsoil and restore the land after stripping it—a policy we assured him, in which his government is far more sensible than ours.

Next came Runaway Cave, a moderately interesting series of underground caverns in the limestone, one with a brackish tidal "lake" eight feet deep, in which there are blind eels. Once used for "mining" bat guano, the caves were developed as a tourist attraction by Frank Kirkner of Coopertown, New York. The present owner conducts tours by the light of a kerosene lantern.

A sign, "A Night of Impeccable Ska," started us talking about place names in Jamaica. There is a village called Upya ("Where you, Tom?"; "Upya!"), another called Stretch-n Set. There are also Waitabit, Snow Hill, Put Together, Poor Man's Crime, Breast Works. The shopping woman of Jamaica is called a "higgler."

Fred informed us that the Spanish Agua Alta became corrupted into Wag Waters and Boca de Aguas into Bog Walk. The Jamaican's musical speech, he added, goes back to the Welsh, with whom Oliver Cromwell repopulated Jamaica after Penn and Venables had chased the Spaniards out. Morgan, who came as an indentured servant from Barbados, was one of them.

Playboys and Painters

East of St. Ann's Bay is the Jamaica Hilton, largest (365 beds) of Jamaica's hotels. Fred knew us well enough by now to know that we wouldn't be stopping, "but I assume that you *will* want to see the Play-boy Club up the road a way?"

"Wouldn't miss it for the world, nor this waterfall," we answered as we pulled up at the magnificent cascade splashing over rounded boulders into effervescent pools: Dunn's River Falls. These falls, which are a delight to climb, are in a setting of breadfruit, avocado ferns, and palms clustered around the sprayed rocks. There are dressing cabins just off the road, and one can half-walk, half-swim from the cool fresh waters into the warmer Caribbean. The rusty vats and tanks of Reynolds Metals' bauxite works come next and then, after Falcondip and before Oracabessa, Hugh Heffner's glossy unpleasure dome.

We walked through the glass doors and were instantly hooked. The lobby was empty and dark, but, as our eyes began to refocus, there leaning with one elbow on the counter was a tall, superbly limbed black "bunny" laced tightly into an abbreviated golden bikini that exposed all but a hairline of her bulging buttocks and breasts. True to the Heffnerian ethic, she gave us one long, dissolving, impassioned look and vanished. We staggered on through salons gaudy with noncommittal Neimans to the dining salon, in the center of which is an elevated blue-plush throne for the voyeur in chief and his court. We were too limp to give more than a hopeless glance at the bar with its blowups of semi-exposed models; we reeled out onto the patio with its Olympic pool and "Bunny Hutch." Hanging over the rail we wanly contemplated "Bunny Bay," then turned listlessly to the bills of fare, which an unseen hand had thrust upon us:

Each of the 204 air-conditioned rooms is a vacationer's dream. All have lavish nine-by-four-foot sunken Grecian bathtubs. Sleeping comfort is a certainty on king-size or twin beds. . . . Begin with breakfast. Are you daring? Try our Brandy Bracer. . . . Summon your Bunny to bring you a huge mug of Rabbit Punch. . . . The atmosphere is casual and friendly in the Playmate Bar. The Penthouse is intimate and late-nite offers a spectacular and moonlit view of the sea from the adjoining Bunny's Nest. . . . Neutral backgrounds are accented with touches of spicy colour. . . .

Nothing could spice the haggard, debauched couple whom we passed at poolside on the way back. The two were oiling themselves in their deck chairs, their skins stretched too tightly here and hanging too slackly there, death's-heads unconcealed, rheumy eyes wandering resentfully over the too-perfect bodies that they could pay to look at but could never possess. For it is the whim of Heffner that the bunnies cannot be touched—much less hutched. "What is this?" we thought as we fled this mirage of mirrors.

Jamaica, too close to nature to know, received us with a bolt of sunlight.

The flora became more and more lush as we passed on: poinsettias,

royal poincianas, African tulips with crimson bursts. But beyond Ocho Rios there is a bare stretch with windblown leafless almonds, and in this relative desolation live Parboo Singh, born at High Gate, and his wife, Seya, born at Allentown, Pennsylvania, two of Jamaica's best-known painters. Parboo, up until the time of our coming,[1] had received his government's only mural commission. The result is a well-concealed "12 x 10" casein decorating the approach to the Prime Minister's office, and it was done in 1956. Parboo had just returned from years of training abroad—study under Kunyoshi at the Art Students League in New York, apprenticeship with Fernand Léger and Georges Rouault in Paris, instruction from David Alfaro Siqueiros on a wall in Mexico—and was raring to go. As anyone in the circumstances would have done, he began tentatively. His mural, which we had already seen, was competently

[1] But no longer. In the spring of 1968, jointly sponsored by the Tourist Board and Edward Seaga's Ministry of Finance and Industry, the American painter Seymour Leichman arrived in Kingston to paint an outdoor mural synthesizing Jamaica's history for the capital's new waterfront development project. Dominated by a symbolic figure of Kapo, Leichman's mural has already sired some promising and ambitious experimental wall-painting among his young student-assistants.

Rivera-esque, with black peasants in white work clothes weaving through flowery foliage. Today, like most of the talented painters of his generation, Parboo is painting pictures for the tourists. And who is to say that, if Mexico had stopped commissioning its painters after the first Mexican mural (which was a dismal failure too), the great Mexicans wouldn't have turned into tourist painters? Well—perhaps not. In Jamaica neglect isn't countered with defiance. Nor does an artist join with his peers to demand his share of the state's largesse. Instead, he moves to the highway where the action is—the passing cars, the bargain hunters, the decorators who want their bars and lobbies to look different but not too different. Parboo and his wife, with their roadside showroom, where they hospitably served us rum-sodas under the tattered pergola with its forlorn view, are sweet people, not fighters. And Jamaican art, unless it fights hard and in some kind of unison, is never going to get off the ground.

Self-taught art is something else again. The next day we would be passing, near St. Margaretz Bay, a corner cantina (Pearl Savery's) embellished with some of the most freely brushed murals of diners, doxies, and dupies imaginable. In Kingston we had already picked up a glowing watercolor of a trolley car in a densely populated jungle by Benjamin Campbell; it stands up with the best of the early Haitians. But the dilemma of the sophisticated Jamaicans had been driven home to us that same day by two incidents. We had taken in a show by Eugene Hyde—semiabstract sunflowers tastefully magnified and elegantly brushed, which looked perfectly indigenous to Madison Avenue. And right after that there had been a startlingly original mural on an outside wall, which Bill noticed as we were threading our way to Port Royal: cricket players, bathing beauties, and Ras Tafarian copouts racing all over the façade of a grocery store. We located the seedy-looking artist with some difficulty and asked him who had defaced his mural with slashes and drips of paint à la Jackson Pollock.

"I did."

"Why?"

He scratched his dirty beard and mumbled some incomprehensible sentences laced with dictionary definitions of "design," "aerial perspective," and "composition." When he had wandered off, giggling, we asked the grocery woman who he was. She said he was quite mad and that several years earlier he had been given a scholarship by the British Council to study painting in London on a "cultural exchange" program. The British Council, Fred told us later, is allied with the PEN Clubs. "It skims the cream of our intellectual talent, and this is what happens. A gifted artist without any intellectual background is exposed to collage, cubism, abstract expressionism, pop, and op, and—well, you see the result."

Depressed by the gloomy thoughts our meeting with gentle Parboo Singhs had stirred in us, we drove on toward Port Antonio in the gathering dusk.

"Well, Fred," I said to break the mood, "when do we start sleeping in a standing-up position?" (Fred, after telling us that there were no rooms for us in the north coast's luxury hotels, had fallen into our mood when we told him we'd rather go without beds than miss this trip.)

"I'm ready," he said with a chuckle, "but let's try the Casa Maria at Port Maria first. They just might have room to stack us in horizontal position."

And they did, with a swim in their pool and an excellent meal too, for the hotel was empty in preparation for its apotheosis on April 1. On that Fools' Day, Metro-Goldwyn-Mayer was to take over for a month to start filming *Dark of the Sun*, and the hotel (pool included) was to double as the home of Moise Tschombe. Oh to be Lumumba, now that spring is here . . .

Rafting the Rio Grande

Passing through Errol Flynn's Port Antonio and Navy Island, where the somewhat more redoubtable Captain Bligh careened his ship after

bringing home the breadfruit, we drove off the road and up a hill to the boathouse, where rafts are to be rented for the descent of the Rio Grande. Our helmsman, Reggie Gay, was deservedly proud of his prowess—and of his passengers, Flynn and Princess Margaret among them. The trip down river to the ocean takes an hour and a quarter minimum—twice that with stop-offs for swimming, as we did it—and the raftsman's tariff is $7, out of which he must pay $2 to the young Hercules who brings the raft back, walking in the stream bed and pulling it against the current: a four-hour proposition, and 50 cents to the rafting station. Great skill is required to maneuver the twenty-foot tapered craft of tied bamboo around the bends and through the rapids. To prevent capsizing, the position of every submerged boulder must be known. A bamboo pole is the steering device, wielded end over end by the raftsman in the bow. The weight of the passengers must be evenly distributed. After heavy rains, when the river rises as much as five feet and the milky-green translucent waters turn brown, there is no traffic. The art developed in the days when bananas had to be brought to port from the Blue Mountains by this route. We asked Reggie about the fishing, and he said snook up to twenty-five pounds and mullet up to ten pounds could be taken on plugs or by trolling. He seemed startled (and pleased) when we suggested that he provide customers with tackle for another $3. He told us that replacing waterlogged rafts every few months is an expensive proposition and takes weeks. The curved bamboos must be straightened with weights in the sun.

All this northeast coast is jungle-rich from the 200 inches of annual rainfall it enjoys, and all along the seemingly uninhabited banks of the river are "tent cities" of bean vine and the parasitic strangler fig. Clusters of bamboo thirty to forty feet high have new growth waving delicately at the top like antennae, the old stalks red at the base, brilliant green and thickly leaved higher up. There are white-barked trumpet trees, ceibas, trailing lianas. Moss and orchids crowd the white limestone cliffs that rise precipitately from the right bank, accented here and there with the more voluptuous greens of banana and coco palms.

When we reached the river's mouth, where Fred, who had made the descent before, was waiting, women were hanging their black umbrellas under a mesquite. We had to pass through Port Antonio again to reach Frenchman's Cove, where we were expected for lunch. This installation is the poshest of the posh hotels, and exclusivity in its principal attraction. Guests no doubt never get over the glory of boasting about how much they have paid. Our lunch was very good, and perhaps I'd remember what we ate if I'd had to pay for it, but one has to be a seasoned gourmet to tell the difference between a $5 lunch and a $25 one, and we were just a couple of hungry rafters. There is a gem of a beach, no more than 100 yards of white sand nestling between two jungle-clad cliffs. A little stream of fresh, pure water meanders about the same distance from the hotel through the palms and beach chairs to the sea, and guests are carried back and forth along it in electric golfcarts. The strain of paying $175 a day must be telling.

Farther east along the coast is a wooded island, which, Fred told us, Fritz Thyssen, the munitions king who financed Hitler to power, had given to his daughter as a birthday present. Beyond that is the exquisite 180-foot-deep Blue Lagoon, recently bought by Robin Moore, author of *The Green Berets*. He wants to turn it into a marina, which would be a shame, but meanwhile he has given the community Boston Beach a mile or so to the east. The community, which has few swimmers, has built an unsightly bathhouse on this lovely beach; it looks like a tin urinal and has doors coyly marked "Adam" and "Eve." Abe Issa, a merchant, owns the woodland between these two properties.

Passing Flynn's house, high on the hill and now occasionally inhabited by his widow, we came to Priestman's River, beautiful at its mouth, with undercut lips of white stone and 100-foot-high banks of philodendron. From there the highway crosses a bridge, over to See No More Gully, from which the tops of the forest giants on either side can almost be touched, their trunks lost in Stygian darkness.

Manchioneal has a certain raffish charm, with its crumbling, balconied, gingerbread houses. The road continues past it, between stone walls hand laid two centuries ago, to the grand view of the eastern tip of Jamaica at Quaw Hill. The immense sugar and coconut plantations that cover this fertile plain 90 miles from Haitian Jérémie belong to the father of the late Ken Jones, for whom this stretch of white-marl highway has been named. But now the curves were becoming curvier, and we dozed past historic Morant Bay and the crocodile swamps, whose exciting pasts and present still lay ahead of us.

Novelists and Politicians

In Mexico the painter Siqueiros once told me of a remark that Jawaharlal Nehru had made to him. "In your country," the Indian leader had said, "painters are more important than politicians." In Jamaica painters and poets don't rate, but the novelties, though counting for less than the politicians, are very distinguished, and they know and care a great deal about politics. "There is no history in this country," one of them put it, "only politics." V. S. Reid, their forerunner, made the Morant Bay Rebellion of 1865 a familiar part of the national heritage as no speech maker ever could; and by experimenting with styles he freed those who followed him from the obligation to be conventionally unconventional. Roger Mais is dead, but his three richly colloquial novels of Rabelaisian bouts and tragic violence among Kingston's slum dwellers are very much alive; in fact, they had just been reissued in a single paperbound volume, with a glowing foreword by former Premier Sir Norman Manley, perennial leader of the People's National Party (P.N.P.) John Hearne is a mature, deep-thrusting and witty fictional commentator on the social scene.

His fictions are not confined to dropouts any more than they are to pace-makers. Victims of the Jazz Age, paralytics of the Lost Generation, dere-licts of the Deep South (or their counterparts) could pass through this busy terrain but never monopolize it, for Hearne writes of the whole of society, not only of its sick parts. Politics, in a Hearne novel, is not a pathological excrescence but the arena in which the community's ablest men, some idealistic and some ruthless in their appetites for power, forge the future. He writes as convincingly of *good* people as of bad, and his characters, of whatever class, are healthily articulate.

I had just read Hearne's wonderful story[5] about the young politicos who go through agonies of embarrassment trying to tell the grizzled Old Man of their party that he must retire, when John Hearne honored us with a too-brief call at our Kingston hotel. The symbolism of the story so obviously fitted the case of Sir Alexander Bustamente, the island's George Washington and perennial leader of the dominant Jamaica La-bour Party (J.L.P.), that I asked the novelist if he had ever considered writing a biography of "Busta" now that the old warhorse has become too feeble to rule.

"I'd like to," said Hearne, who reminded me of E. E. Cummings with his frizzled red hair, almost lashless darting blue eyes, and caustic man-ner, "if they'd open the archives to me. Busta is a master politician, quite like Lyndon Johnson: He twists your arm almost off, and then, just before it breaks, he slaps you on the back." I asked him if Sir Nor-man's counterpolicy of breaking up the big estates made sense. "Our population will double before the wear 2000," he rasped. "To break up the big estates wouldn't accomplish much. You can't get a Jamaican to farm even the available lands—not any more, and I can't blame him. The city has so much more to offer—cinemas, TV, cars, dancing, night life. He'll never go back to the simple, sweet, dull life on the farm. The action is here."

If we talked politics rather than literature with John Hearne it was because we had been doing so for days and couldn't stop. It began when driving through Morant Bay, with Fred, we passed Edna Manley's sculp-tured memorial to Paul Bogle. Bogle was the emancipated black slave insurrectionary of nearby Stony Gut, who has become since independence in 1962, Jamaica's national hero. The mulatto ("coloured" in Jamaican parlance) Assemblyman from Kingston, George William Gordon, de-serves at least an equal share of the title. For it was this converted Bap-tist man of substance who had everything to lose in assuming the role of people's advocate. Bogle, whose bloody uprising at Morant Bay took place October 11, 1865, had taken Gordon's words to heart. Both men were hanged, Gordon on trumped-up charges.

Those were the days when the Negroes were at long last technically free, when sugar had lost its protected market leaving Jamaica's econ-

[5] "The Wind in This Corner" in Barbara Howes, ed., *From The Green Antilles* (New York: Macmillan, 1966).

omy in chaos, and "Missis Queen" (Victoria) was being, in Gordon's words, "too noble-hearted to say anything unkind even to her most humble subjects." A ruthless proconsul, Edward John Eyre, did the job for her. There would be no Indian Mutiny in Jamaica, no "second Haiti ruled by Negroes who would expel the white people and destroy their property." But had Bogle's rebels in Morant Bay not counted too heavily on being joined by the maroons in the backlands, there might have been. And who is to say which outcome would have served Jamaica best? No one (not even the Queen's homeland subjects at that time) could condone the terrible whippings and drum-head hangings with which Eyre stamped out the spreading brushfire of insurrection. Eyre was ultimately recalled and censured, but Jamaica had lost its parliamentary self-rule and become a crown colony. Had Bogle's rebellion succeeded, the long, heart-breaking, but orderly march to parliamentary democracy would never have taken place. There would have been no need for it. Jamaica today, in all probability, would be another Haiti.

"What about Haiti?" I asked John Hearne, who had remarked that the West Indian Federation, knocked into a cocked hat by Busta's party five years earlier, was Jamaica's only salvation in the long run. "Will Haiti ever join it?"

"I think we'll have to send an army in there eventually to clean Haiti up, even if it costs a million lives."

He didn't make this remark altogether seriously, but it was clear that he thought the sore that is festering there would prove intolerable to the Caribbean sooner or later.

Gordon's heirs, the swashbuckling pragmatist Bustamente and his perennial opponent, doctrinaire left-liberal Manley, are a fascinating study in contrasts. Busta, before he became a labor leader-politician in the 1930s, knocked around the world. He was a policeman in Panama for a while and, by his own account, fought Spain with Abdel-el-Krim's Muslim separatists in Morocco. The worst his enemies accuse him of is "usury"—lending the dockworkers money at stiff terms during the Depression. The masses never doubted that this white-skinned "red man" with flying mane, who could drink any man under the table, was one of them. They loved his rabble-rousing oratory and his folksy sense of humor—especially the way he used to chide "my cousin Manley, whose laugh doesn't go any deeper than his larynx."

"Busta," as Fred put it, "is loved as a father; Manley is respected as a guardian." Guardians are not trusted, not for long anyway, especially when they are "cold-blooded lawyer types who think too long before acting." Manley equivocates when the chips are down, and Busta completely outfoxed him on federation when Manley was Premier. Busta rode back into power by telling the electorate that Jamaica would be outvoted by her smaller and weaker allies and forced to pay the bills.

Manley's high principles and sound reasoning counted for nothing. Federation was dead, and so was Manley.

Actually the two parties are essentially alike (as major political parties must be in a functioning democracy); each sits waiting to see which way the other will move before moving. Busta's party, though less popular than Manley's in Kingston, which contains a quarter of Jamaica's 1,760,000 citizens, is more popular in the countryside and is generally thought to be ruling well today, especially in education and housing—"so why rock the boat?" We heard some grumbling in Kingston over Premier Sangster's "whiteness," but then, as one Jamaican put it, "Look at Eddie Seaga, a white Syrian type elected from the blackest, poorest slum of Kingston over Dudley Thompson, who was Jomo Kenyatta's lawyer when the Mau Mau were butchering the whites." The electorate, it seems, thought Thompson too "middleclass." Does it follow that color and political leadership are unrelated in Jamaica?

We asked Peter Abrahams one morning to clarify this point for us. Abrahams is a gifted South African novelist who has settled in Jamaica and become thoroughly Jamaican. We visited him and his English wife and their children at their home on a steep hillside overlooking the capital. We told him about a Babbitt-type American druggist who has settled on the island of Grand Cayman—"where the racial distribution of one-third white, one-third mulatto, and one-third black is just perfect" —and who had been telling us at breakfast that "the big Amercian companies like Ford and General Motors will never risk capital in Jamaica the way it's heading."

Abrahams grinned wryly. "A racial posture is a luxury here," he said. "You talk one way to an African, another way to an American. But we *face* the United States, not Dakar. When it comes to an issue, a Jamaican votes for the better man, white or black. We're pragmatists, and we've come a long way from the time when Busta returned and impressed people by calling himself a Spanish grandee. Busta wouldn't assume that pose today.

"The corrupting factor in a society like ours," he went on, "is falling into the assumption that people exist to work for you. There's nothing wrong in itself about man serving man, but, when dependence and the English concept of 'the better classes' enters into it, as here, that's bad. You have to be on guard constantly. You say to a servant, 'All I can pay you is 12 shillings a day,' and then you remember that that's less than you pay for a good bottle of spirits. I'm not an equality monger, but I believe in inequalities created by responsibilities."

We walked into his library, and as if to emphasize his philosophy, Abrahams stumbled over a black girl scrubbing the floor and patted her on the shoulders with an airy, "Sorry, my sweet, for surprising you on your knees!"

"What is your impression of Jamaica?" he asked me when we had sat down again.

"It's too early to say," I equivocated. "Except that on your north coast I feel like a poor-white American who is never going to be able to afford all that luxury."

He laughed. "That's your dilemma. I'll tell you more about ours. A coal-black American A.I.D. representative finds himself being called a "white supremacist" here because he asks for equal rights for all regardless of skin color. You see, our government, in order to give Jamaicans at long last first call on jobs, gives precedence to those with the darkest skins."

"What about Seaga?" we asked.

"The paradox again! Though he is the whitest of the J.L.P. [Jamaica Labour Party] cabinet members, he's the furthest left and the closest to espousing black supremacy—no doubt as a means of establishing his own power base. The J.L.P., of course, has no ideology. As a matter of fact, both parties are opportunistic, and in both the 'Almighty I' is very important. When Manley came out with the slogan 'Have Faith in a Man with a Plan,' he was done for. Jamaicans are skeptics. Their answer was 'Have faith only in God!,' and they promptly voted for Busta. Manley's proposal to limit landholdings to 500 acres is a philosophical not a practical idea and so will never be enforced here. Muñoz Marín over in Puerto Rico had just such a law on his books and ignored it—being a good pragmatic politician. You see we have two types of land here. First, there are the very large sugar and bauxite holdings, which earn us foreign exchange and so can't be split up. Next come the medium-size farms cultivating up to 500 acres. Since Manley's Land Bonds Law of 1955, under which the government can compulsorily acquire unused lands, the absentee landlord is a dying breed."

Abrahams approved of this sensible law and its strict enforcement by officials of both parties, and he also applauded Pringle's approach to tourism. Pringle's predecessor, Abe Issa, he said, had kowtowed to tourists. "The symbol then was a black waiter in a white coat obsequiously carrying a tray of drinks. Pringle says, 'We're doing everything to make you happy, but you're coming to our country as guests and must observe our ways.' " If this injunction is really honored, it is all the more remarkable that tourism under Pringle has outdistanced sugar to take the number-two spot in Jamaica's economy—a £22,300,000 industry that may soon overtake bauxite.

There is a passage in John Hearne's novel *Land of the Living* that gave us a final illumination on the subject of Jamaica's racial merry-go-round. The mixed-up professor who is the protagonist has just come ashore from one of the south-island swamps, where he has been collecting specimens with his pupils. Suddenly a Ras Tafarian steps out of the bush and for no apparent reason proceeds to smash their portable aquarium:

In that heavy, expectant stillness, I could feel a tingle crawl damply across my skin; a miasmic projection denser than simple hate or even madness seemed to chill and darken the burning afternoon. Behind the inanely exultant face before us, I saw the haggard countenance of an antique, irremediable terror: something of itself, desolate and inaccessible, rising from the chaos that lurks at the centre of our small, decent achievements and from which we turn avidly into the factitious warmth of illusion, betrayal and sordid, desperate alliances of cruelty. . . . Looking at the impenetrable, fatuously exultant face before us, I was forced to acknowledge something pure, austere and dedicated: as if he were the solitary, indomitable witness to a persecuted but enduring truth. A wild and enigmatic dignity glared from his eyes and searched in my heart like a boathook. Behind the brimming challenge of that gaunt, crouched body in the patched, immaculate khaki shorts and open shirt, I could sense a sad, dumb need: the old unappeasable hunger for a lost grace that inspires our most profound hope, our pity and our awe. For a moment he was reflected in the light of selfless anguish. Then his lips parted vividly behind his beard and his private, desolate breath of laughter reduced him once more to a figure of compulsive mischief.

If the Negro, in Jamaica and everywhere, seems in Western eyes to act irrationally, to have an understanding of politics but not of history, of the music without its intellectual content, it may be because the Negro is discovering at last that the new "soul" he had thrust upon him in the slave ships and cane fields isn't his own but the white man's. When he lost his gods, he lost his pride, and his pride must be recovered first, Hearne seems to be saying. Between full assimilation and outright secession is no man's land.

Fred was at the airport when we took off for Antigua. We kidded him about leaving Jamaica to find better tennis courts and night spots. But, when we embraced at the gate, we felt we were losing a brother.

The Maroons at Accompong

It was four months later that I flew back to Montego Bay, this time accompanied by Seymour Leichman, to visit the Cockpit country and other parts of Jamaica that I had still not seen.

The Cockpits are a maze of limestone outcroppings that form depressions filled with almost impenetrable thickets. They lie on a plateau in the western corner of the island. It was there that the slaves of the Spanish escaped when the English took over, and there they have managed, to hold "white civilization" at bay, their ranks augmented by many subsequent waves of freedom lovers, over the centuries. The word "maroon," by which they and other ecapees in other parts of Jamaica (and the other islands) came to be known derives from the Spanish *cimarrones* (peak dwellers). Even before the English came, the maroons were a problem to the establishment. They would side with the English pirates, swooping down from the mountains to make their raids coincide with the sweeps from the sea. The retreating Spaniards, of course, gave them arms and encouraged them to murder the English. But very soon they were on their own; spearheaded by Gold Coast Koromantee tribesmen, renowned in Africa for their superior physiques and fanatically libertarian spirit, the maroons developed guerilla skills that time and again contributed to successsful ambushes of the redcoats. In 1732 their three principal towns were captured, but the following year they rallied and slaughtered a naval task force sent against them by Admirable Sir Chaloner Ogle. Mosquito Indians were recruited in Nicaragua to march against them, but the maroons held firm, and on March 1, 1739, articles of pacification were concluded with their leader, Captain Cudjoe; [6] the articles guaranteed them freedom and the possession "for themselves and posterity forever all the lands situate and lying between Trelawney Town and the Cockpits, to the amount of 1,500 acres." In return, the maroons at Trelawney Town, at Accompong, and at Crawford Town and Nanny Town to the east, were to return runaway slaves and aid the colonists in case of invasion. But fifty years later the truce was broken in Trelawney Town, when an unpopular white superintendent refused to permit reprisals for the flogging of two maroons in Montego Bay, and this time, because the outbreak of violence coincided with the French Revolution and the massacre of the white colonists in nearby Haiti, it was dealt with savagely. The old maroons who surrendered to Governor Balcarres' regulars were thrown into prison. But 300 of the young men held off 1,500 European regulars armed with cannon for five months; the end came only when a shipload of man-eating bloodhounds was brought over from Cuba. Panic seized the maroons, and they agreed to give up on the promise that they would not be executed or deported. On the flimsy excuse that they had not surrendered quickly enough, the entire Trelawney tribe, including even those members who had made peace before the fighting started, was packed onto transports and shipped to icy Nova Scotia. Shaken by the thought of a similar fate, the other maroon tribes withdrew to more isolated positions and, as already noted in the case of the Morant Bay uprising half a century later, avoided trouble. But in Accompong they are said to maintain a government of their own to this day, and we wanted to see it.

Our driver for the expedition was a brash young Tourist Board apprentice named Dennis Clunis. Higher education had gone to Dennis' head. He had learned such fascinating things as, for instance, that Edna St. Vincent Millay was the greatest American poet and Bernard Buffet the world's outstanding modern painter—and that Americans, though nice, were cultural barbarians. We listened to these and other doctrines expounded at length over rum punches on the terrace of Don Budge's Racquet Club, much too exhausted from playing tennis in the hot sun

[6] *Cudjoe* is the Ashanti word for Monday; *accompong* is the Akan word for God.

to demur; then we drove with Dennis to Sign Great House for dinner, up and down hill at breakneck speed, an experience that left us more shaken than his lecture did. But that evening at Sunset Lodge, with Dennis' superior Doug Burke as a sardonic and delighted observor, we gave Dennis an introductory seminar on modern poetry and painting and told him that, although it is true that we have our quota of cultural barbarians, *all* Americans prefer to take curves on four wheels with the foot held just a little bit above the floorboard. This news must have had a traumatic effect on Dennis, for he didn't show up at 6:00 in the morning for breakfast, and we had to call Doug to drag him out of bed. Doug was furious, of course, and, when Dennis appeared at 7:00, he was much chastened. He proved to be a delightful traveling companion from then on.

Hardly had we left Mo' Bay's scrubbed and shrubby blandeur and climbed over the cliff to the pastoral landscape that stretches south to the Cockpits than we found ourselves in irrepressible Jamaica again. By the dusty roadside, around what looked like a Maypole, several dozen chanting and writhing country folk were engaged in a ceremony that had all the trappings of Pocomania. It wasn't, we were soon told by Mother Katharine Clark, the imperious mistress of her possessed flock; this group was the one and only Church of the Living God Pillar and Ground of the Truth, and, if we would stay a little while, she would show us. With a commander's chin, a fanatic's eye, and a voice like a band saw, Mother Katharine was not one to be denied. For a few minutes more she continued to lead the Old Testament chants with convulsive bobs of her head, dispensing holy water from a rum bottle, and then she ushered us into the covered but unwalled nearby chapel. The most interesting feature of this wholly personal cult is that, in front of the altar, there is a black square of cardboard painted in the form of a clock dial, with cabalistic numerals and letters in the corners, the letters of the alphabet (*not* in the conventional order) in a ring, and a basin of water with a sprig of leaves floating on it at the center. It is precisely the Masonic *vever* that preceeds a voodoo ceremony in Haiti, without the abstract connecting lines and volutes! All the priestesses attending Mother Katharine had pencils stuck in their turbans, and during the responses they "wrote" frantically on strips of bamboo. One girl was possessed briefly, and all the heads jerked with her in approval. "We call down resurrection of the just and damnation to the unjust! He's going to reward *us!*—[in positively savage tones] *us*, his people. Those of us who lead the perfect life here will reap *our* rewards. Man was born to die. There is life, there is death, there is heaven, there is hell. Take your choice!"

"It sounds like Yom Kippur," Seymour said behind his hand.

But, as we were leaving, Mother Katharine adjured us to read carefully the words behind the altar:

Road Blocks in Christian Life

The Unconcerned	The Unprayerful
The Unconscious	The Uncontrolled
The Unco-operative	The Unconfessed
The Unprepared	The Unconquered

"With all of these out of the way," she said as we were leaving, "we shall reach our goal."

"We may be *concerned*," I said to Seymour and Dennis, "but she's got us on every other count."

Continuing on up through wide, fertile valleys, with yams staked out to give their leaf systems maximum sunlight, we finally reached the nubby plateau of the maroons and Accompong. There's a cynical saying among Jamaicans who deplore the "culture" the English "robbed" them of: "They exterminated the Arawaks, drove out the Spaniards, and sent the Africans to Accompong." Were we about to see this culture in pure form?

We were greeted by "Colonel" W. J. Robertson, the elected chief, and his "Secretary of State" Mann O. Rowe, who claims to be Cudjoe's great-grandson. Both are old men, the Colonel over ninety by his somewhat tentative estimate and very courtly. They ushered us into their headquarters, waiting while we stopped to inspect a low thornbush by the door; it was alive with a dozen small children, crouching in the branches and staring at us fixedly. The chief and his deputy told us that they had been waiting for us, by-passing the usual Saturday market in Maggotty, the area's shopping center six miles away. We thanked them, entered the modest shanty, and sat down in the tattered chairs that had been drawn up for us. While Seymour sketched the Colonel, I followed the Secretary out onto the veranda and asked him some questions.

"How many maroons are there in the whole Cockpit country, Mr. Secretary?"

"One thousand."

"How many are there in Accompong?"

"Fifteen hundred."

"How can that be?"

"It's a long way to Tipperary."

"Is it true that the Colonel still administers the cat o' nine tails?"

"Only he."

"For what crimes?"

"Crimes?"

"Murder, for instance?"

"There's never been a murder here in all history."

"For what, then?"

"Indecent language, things like that."

"Can we step down to see the river, Mr. Secretary?"

"Not now. It's rather tedious."

I asked him whether or not there were taxes in the maroon "state" and what salaries the Colonel, captains, and other officials received.

"That's a secret," he replied. "We look into the circumstances and then give enough. When one of us wants to go abroad, he has to become a Jamaican to get a passport and so ceases to be a maroon. We hold no title to these lands because they are all held in common. There can be no sale. Each family has boundaries within the common land, but we just remember where they be. We're not fussy about that, because we're all one family."

I asked whether or not there was much drinking among the maroons and whether or not there were any Ras Tafarians or Pocomaniacs.

"We have no drunken man. We accustom; we hold so much," he laughed. "No Ras Tafaris. We just can't stand them. We don't discourage Pocomania, but we don't encourage it either."

I didn't like to ask any overt questions about culture, African or otherwise, but I did ask as we were leaving whether or not there were any maroon artists. I was shown a photograph of an elongated and quite elegant ivory *Mother and Child* by a maroon named Namba Roy, which had been presented to the Queen. The artist—an old and sad West Indian story—had gone to London. He had written a novel, *Black Albino*, and he had died there three years earlier. "As for art, that's about it." In the

Colonel's living room a sign indicated how well the maroons have been assimilated by colonialism and its religions:

> *Christ Is the Head of This House*
> *The Unseen Guest at Every Meal*
> *The Silent Listener at Every Conversation*

Crocodile Hunt

Fred Wilmot met us at Palisadoes Airport at 6:30 in the evening, and by 9:00 we had left the Myrtle Bank Hotel, that wonderful, rambling relic of Old Jamaica, with "Alligator Hunter" Jim Gore and his entourage for a crocodile hunt in the swamps of the southeast coast. (Crocodiles are called "alligators" in Jamaica, just as frogs are called "toads" and moths "bats," but they're crocodiles for all that; why they are still so plentiful along the whole south coast and nonexistent in the north is a mystery.)

Our party consisted of Gore and his wife Veronica, a Negro assistant who has hunted with Gore for twenty years, Jim Holgate, and an eight-year-old with a real Ashanti face and sad eyes named Balfour. Gore has the build of a heavyweight wrestler and a face to match it. He is largely uneducated, though his father was Jamaica's first industrialist—a man who surrounded his properties with high walls and dogs to keep out thieves (and union organizers). Jim Gore carries a magnum pistol, and he remarked casually during the long drive east that he'd shot several maroons from the Moore Town Reserve for straying on his lands—"The police don't care." His lands lie back of the swamps toward which we were heading, between Morant Bay and the island's eastern tip. But at his home in Kingston, which doubles as a parking lot, he keeps between fifty and a hundred crocodiles captive, feeding them live guinea pigs, killing "those that cause trouble," and selling one from time to time to a zoo or a museum abroad.

Crocodiles are such an obsession with Jim Gore that it's difficult to distinguish fact from fantasy when he is talking about them. It certainly is sheer nonsense to say that the crocs were brought to Jamaica from Africa by the slavers "to torture the slaves and keep them from running away," and Seymour and I burst out laughing when he said with a straight face that a specimen "forty feet long" had been found in a New York sewer, but it may or may not be true, as he claims, that his own record catch was a thirty-footer in Kingston harbor.

His relationship with the huge saurians seems to be part love, part hate. His decision to hunt them, he says, dates from age fourteen, when he was swimming in Salt River and saw a grown man pulled down, never to reappear. He decided then and there "to wage a war of extermination," and he has, but the war is tempered by his obvious affection for the beasts, perhaps an unconscious expression of his admiration for their ruthless efficiency as killers. He talks to them, fondles them, even grunts like them. And, unlike the other hunters in Jamaica, he doesn't kill them —at least not during the hunt. Bernard Cridland, a well-known marksman, or Neil Andrade, a shark hunter and one of the original skindivers and water skiers (it was he who co-survived with Jim Gore a twenty-five-mile swim to shore from California Banks when their boat capsized some years ago), take visitors hunting with flash-beam-sight rifles, so that it's almost impossible to miss; their assistants then dive for the bodies in the roiled-up water, hoping that the crocs will be dead. But Gore gets close enough to plunge a harpoon or two or three into a nonfatal area. The harpoon's haft is attached to a length of nylon cord. The beast is "played" and finally pulled near enough to the rowboat so that Gore can slip a noose over the long snout.

Preparations for our hunt took place from about midnight to 2:00 in the morning on the beach at Rocky Point near Holland Bay. The preparations were at least as interesting as was the hunt itself. Gore has taken the likes of Lord Beaverbrook, Errol Flynn, and Steve Cochrane hunting, and his procedure is meticulous. First we all stripped to the waist and anointed ourselves with mosquito repellent. Then Gore insisted that we each take a methadrine pill to keep awake. Our two boats were carefully lowered from the specially constructed open pickup truck, the second to be towed behind the first to carry the disabled crocs in the event that we should capture more than one. Next, the outboard motor was attached to the lead skiff. Then the lines were soaked in salt water. Finally we had hot coffee from a flask and were ready to take off. Only Balfour was left behind to guard the cars on the dark deserted beach. He looked scared and protested feebly, but, when Gore seized him under the chin and swung him several times through the air, he subsided into the front seat. Veronica stroked his cheek and handed him a flashlight. We were off.

Our first stop, after idling a while to let the moon go down, was a swampy inlet of brackish water clogged with bone-white stumps and dead mangrove branches. After anchoring the second skiff out to sea, we threaded our way cautiously into this eerie web, Gore and Holgate sometimes wading alongside to pull the boat when the water became too shallow or tangled to paddle through. The smell of sulphur was overpowering. With our three electric torches wired to a storage battery, we picked out many pairs of eyes, which in the distance glow redly from the phosphorus in the water. But we never came close enough to harpoon one of the crocs. We were startled at one point when a two-foot needle-like wahoo jumped aboard.

Giving up, we went out to open sea, where the water is two to six feet deep, and there, after an hour of weaving up and down the barely visible black coast line, we bagged our only victim. He fought hard to get away after Gore first sighted him, working his way toward the beach, but to no avail; each time he broke surface we were a little closer, with his retreat cut off. Finally he came up inches from the boat, and Gore drove a harpoon into him. Five minutes later a second harpoon caught him, and he was exhausted enough to be pulled alongside. He was about eight and a half feet long and lavender in color, with a white underbelly. The first noose caught only his lower jaw, but that was enough to maneuver the sluggish monster up to the gunwale, where a second noose clamped both jaws together. Gore slugged him between the eyes with his machete, momentarily paralyzing the egg-sized brain. The croc's body was pulled up and his front feet secured. Then the back pair were hamstrung. And finally the armored tail, capable of breaking a leg or knocking one overboard, was trussed securely to the upper torso. He was aboard, and now very deliberately the flat luminous eyes the size of quarters, with pupils like black daggers, opened and regarded us unblinkingly. Gore, who waves his arms like an orchestra conductor when he is standing in the prow with the torch on his cap, slapped the lids shut and crooned to the croc about being a good baby: "We'll treat you right, if you treat us right," and so on. Then he gave the bloody forehead another playful whack with his cutlass. I thought of the old Jamaican in a Hearne novel, describing the businesslike way an American tycoon hunted: "Is like him an 'de alligator have quarrel, personal." A lovers' quarrel?

We took the stunned animal ashore to a small cove filled with conch shells and drove back for him in half an hour. Where Haiti lies just under the eastern rim of the ocean the first saffron streaks of sunrise were beginning to show.

The trip back to Kingston was a nightmare. The methadrine had begun to wear off even on the boat, where once, standing up to sweep the shore line with my torch, I'd gone to sleep on my feet and almost pitched overboard. But Gore had no intention of letting us sleep—or of getting us back at 8:00 as he'd promised so that we could get a few hours' sleep before a noon appointment. Perhaps he was annoyed because I had asked him several times to turn down his blasting car radio and, when he didn't, turned down the volume myself. At any rate, he began to think up ways of prolonging our discomfort, stopping six times at his St. Thomas marble quarry to give orders to various workers, then twice for coffee, twice for beer, and twice for gas, standing in the shade to watch us struggling between sleeping and waking with the sun beating on our exposed heads, driving as slowly as possible between stops. And so, arriving back at the Myrtle Bank at eleven, we parted unamicably, shaking hands with the kindly Veronica, giving Balfour and Holgate all the cash we had in our pockets, and staggering upstairs for one hour of blessed sleep. Had Jim Gore sneaked a second round of methadrine for himself when we weren't watching him? Or was it just the thought of feeding those hungry crocs at home that kept him going? We would never know.

Kapo II

"This world isn't all white!" ["No, man!"]
"This world isn't black neither!" ["No, man!"]

"This world isn't blue, and it isn't pink, and it isn't yellow. It's *all* colors. And it's beautiful 'cause it's all colors. We're *one family*." ["Yes, man!"]

Where else could we have been but at Kapo's?

Ah, if the Kapos could rule this world. But it's much too late. They never have ruled it. The very first family had its Cain, and Abel didn't have a chance. Most *illuminati* aren't even given the time to take their own poison, as Socrates was; they might talk, as he did. Kapo is permitted to talk because it's assumed that no one is listening. If he moved two steps out into the street, they'd have him in the paddy wagon before he could even mount the soapbox. Inside, he's "harmless." Pocomania has a funny ring; it sounds like something the Marx Brothers might have invented. Besides, he's a "primitive," isn't he? What do "primitives" know about statecraft or spacecraft, cybernetics or cosmetics, law or war?

A touching thing about Kapo is that he *calls himself a "primitive."* It is the ultimate proof of his innocence, the signature that can't be forged. The pure in heart don't know which side the organ is on or even if it exists; it takes a doctor to know that. An artist with even a trace of sophistication builds on what he can learn and never stops learning, but a great one knows that the most important things can never be learned, taught, or even consciously perceived. Kapo, with one of the wildest of his paintings in his hand, came over and looked at the portrait drawing of him that Seymour was completing over in the corner. He shook his head in admiration and disbelief.

"I could never do that," he said.

"And I could never do *that*," said Seymour, with as much truth and respect, pointing to the picture in the Jamaican's hand.

"It was exactly," he said to me as we walked home later on, "like a pretty good sax player talking to a pretty good trumpet player."

But it was in the sermon, already in progress when we entered, that Kapo had switched unobtrusively from the brotherhood of man to his calling as an artist. Nothing had changed from the night when Bill and I had been there except that Kapo had acquired a microphone, the wires of which led to a circular speaker in the rear neatly lettered "Kapo's Voice." Over the speaker was a small shelf containing a glass of water, a toothbrush, and a tube of Crest toothpaste. Under the speaker a four-year-old girl with eyes like full moons in a midnight sky was studying pictures of blond, blue-eyed children in a primer. The voice stopped vibrating with those organ tones of universal injunction and reminisced quietly:

> When I was a boy the red soil of St. Ann's Parish used to dirty the laundry something terrible, and we cursed it for being red, but it turned out to be bauxite. Then, later on, when there was no bread in the cupboard and I felt like cursing a preacher's hard lot, God came to me in a dream and said, "Kapo, I want you to be a primitive sculptor." And later on, when that wasn't enough, He came to me again and said, "Kapo, I want you to be a primitive painter." So now I'm fifty-six, but I never feel tired . . . to do the work of the Lord. It's not easy to paint. It's not easy to do anything. Don't you ever think that things will fall down from the sky. You must *work*. And work together. And talk it out. But it's better to express what you feel by singing and dancing than to talk *alone*.

Kapo bids you good night.

II

THE ENGLISH-SPEAKING
LEEWARDS

Part 1. Antigua

Antigua (pronounced An-*tee*-gah) is an island about the size of the City of Philadelphia, with a population of 65,000. Its dry, rolling hills and deeply cut inlets lie close to the top of the chain stretching between the Virgins and Trinidad. From the days of Columbus, who named it at a distance and passed on; to those of Horatio Nelson, who tarried three years but disliked it; to those of Jacqueline Kennedy, who comes to Mill Reef for privacy, Antigua has always had about it an air of detachment. It is the coolest hot island under the sun. The rich and celebrated who prize it for its barren beauty make a point of leaving it that way.

We arrived, appropriately, as the sun was setting and found Eustace Samuel standing precisely where we had left him on our way to Jamaica. As it was much too dark to point out any of the banks we might have missed on our first drive through St. Johns, he wasted no time in depositing us at our destination, the Caribbean Beach Club, with only a curt injunction to be ready to leave early in the morning if we wanted to take advantage of his "grand tour" of the island.

I awoke with the dawn to hear Bill asking the telephone operator what time the airline offices open. There was a pause. "Today? Oh."

"Are you thinking of leaving already?" I said.

"I don't know how much more of this I can take," he said, pointing in all directions.

Our beach house on the sugary coral sand had glass facing the sea and a back wall of earthenware planters alternately inverted and covered with telescoping mahogany strips to let the air in. It was furnished like a bridal suite, with a gathered canopy (mosquitoes pendant) hanging from a hook in the ceiling above our golden-sheeted beds. Dan Darrow, the manager, had already ticked off the islands we would be seeing. Left to right from our terrace, they were verdant Montserrat; steep, uninhabited Redonda; compact Nevis; the two dots of St. Eustatius and St. Christopher (St. Kitts); and, just out of sight to the north, Barbuda. The mouth of St. Johns' shallow harbor is visible to the south.

A unique feature of this hotel is that its main building at the top of the cliff is connected to the beach houses by a glass-enclosed funicular car. The trip takes four minutes each way; the car stops and starts with a jerk, and the waiting time for some reason is always eight minutes. Nobody really minds. There's nothing to hurry for in Antigua.

On the beach two fat white ladies in flowered bathing suits were observing four thin black native women, bottoms up, apparently clamming. When we approached the latter, they revealed their occupation and their faces. They were gathering tiny shells for necklaces, and they were so remarkably ugly in their rimless spectacles and gold teeth, with their harsh Anglo-Saxon diction accompanied by frowns and mirthless grimaces, that I could only think, involuntarily, "Protestant, Baptist, British."

I was generalizing just as irrationally eight minutes later on the breakfast patio, when four black grackles with beady eyes descended on our
table and told us in no uncertain terms that the toast we were rushing
to our mouths was theirs. In fact, it wasn't until an hour later, when we
stopped at a shop in St. Johns to buy sandals, that I regained my perspective. I had paid the cashier and was asking her to repeat for the third
time a sentence, which she accompanied by a suspicious look, that
sounded like "Get yo' purse, man," when she threw up her hands and
said with a smile, "You don' spik English?" I smiled ruefully and said,
"I guess not, only American," for it turned out that she was joking dead-
pan about the flaps on my Haitian shirt, into which I'd dropped my
change.

Around the Island

Fat goats, silk-cotton trees with trunks gnarled and spiked like rhinos'
heads, loblollies and tamarinds, fields of sugar cane dominated by the
truncated cones of ancient stone mills, clusters of well-dressed school
children repeating their lessons to teachers under flamboyant trees, fields
of pineapple and arrowroot, stands of bananas (called "figs"), papaya
and breadfruit, mango and soursop—all belie the descriptions of Antigua
as "arid." But it had been raining, for the first time in weeks, two days
before we arrived, and now it began to drizzle again.

We ducked into the Jolly Beach Hotel south of St. Johns and inspected
the open-air dancing pavilions surrounded by roofed tables. There's a
fine beach there, with a view of Montserrat to the west. It's equipped
with peddle boats and rafts, copper-sheathed spits, and towering coconut
palms. Behind the hotel rises the island's high point, 1,319-foot Boggy
Peak, capped with a television transmitter. There's another fine beach at
Pigeon's Point near Falmouth Harbour ("Princess Margaret swam here,"
Eustace said proudly), but we made a quick decision to find a beach of
our own alone on the north coast after completing the circuit of the
island. We would leave climactic English Harbour for a leisurely visit the
following afternoon; a re-creation of the whole Nelson episode was
scheduled at Shirley Heights that evening.

The Marmora Beach Hotel and Casino—to which planeloads of gamblers are flown from the United States almost daily, Eustace told us—is
across the peninsula formed by Falmouth Harbour and Willoughby Bay.
We continued east past it to the tip of the island and had our swim,
naked in the pouring rain, off a boggy cow pasture between Antigua's
poshest resorts, Half Moon Bay and Mill Reef Club. Because our search
for privacy had mired Eustace's car in the mud and we were splattered
with mud from head to foot pulling it out for him, we took a second
dip—this time in sunlight.

Half Moon Bay has as delectable a palm-fringed beach as has Jolly Bay
and its own golf course, tennis courts, kidney-shaped pool, and shuffle-

board deck as well. We had wheedled our way past the guards at Mill Reef to call on the poet, Archibald MacLeish, hoping to find out what attracts him to this headland, which has been called "a Tropical concentration camp for millionaires," but he was to arrive the day we were leaving Antigua, and we never found out.

We struck out at Devil's Bridge on the next peninsula for different reasons. Eustace took a wrong turn, but we didn't find that out until the next day. "Musta caved in," he said airily after we'd clambered up and down cliffs for an hour looking for the natural arch. The limestone cliff, which the sea, unimpeded by coral barrier reefs, undercut deeply during the glacial period, is covered with a mossy seaweed consisting of millions of tiny green and red "balloons"—a wonderful pneumatic couch cover upon which we relaxed without any regret that the notorious bridge had vanished.

Eustace, no doubt suffering from guilt over his little deception, became very talkative, and we took advantage of his volubility to find out as much as we could about Antigua's irascible politicians. We were already familiar with the calypso that goes

> *Independence is good for my country.*
> *We have no sugar, but we got tourism.*
> *Papa Bird is the Moses of Antigua.*

We knew that the only factory still manufacturing sugar in Antigua had just closed its gates and gone into receivership. We knew that Antigua's thirty-three hotels and one casino form the biggest tourist operation in any of the smaller sugar islands of the Caribbean—but not nearly enough to keep a fast-growing population of 65,000 solvent. And we knew that two months thence, when Antigua's centuries of dependence on Great Britain were to be terminated with fireworks and the raising of a gay red, blue, white, black, and yellow flag, it would be the six-foot four-inch mulatto Premier, Vere Cornell Bird, who would be expected to have the answers.

"Does he have the answer?" I asked Eustace.

"Papa Bird?" he laughed. "He say, 'The white part of the flag's for hope.' That his only answer—hope."

"But then why did you vote for him and for independence?" I asked.

"Who voted for him? I don't know any taxi driver voted for him. Or any sugar-cane cutter. Or any street vendor. Or any . . ."

"Then who did?"

"The big shots. It's politics, you have to understand, politics! Who'd vote for taxes and confusion under those people?"

But Vere C. Bird, the prophet of independence for two decades, was soon to tell us that independence isn't something you can wait for until you are "ready," that Antiguans, when they have achieved that freedom "which their sense of dignity entitles them to," will find the answers. "These people have been subjects all their lives. They've had a mother country. They've had security. Like children, they're frightened. But are you going to run off because you're independent?" He plans to build water services—reservoirs and wells for the drought-stricken island—and a deep-water harbor. He plans to spend $3 million for an automatic telephone system and $5 million for airport improvements. And he says, "Antigua will pay her own way for all this," and blames the rival Democratic and National Parties for sowing doubts about the ability of his own Labour Party, which has been in power twenty years, to make do. "After all," he says, "I remember this island when there were only footpaths; unskilled women were paid 12 cents a day. Today the unskilled get $30 a week and the skilled as much as $10 a day." He opposes federation, pointing out the disadvantages to English-speaking Antigua, with its heavy dependence on American tourism, if "integrated" with such "poor" French-speaking islands as St. Lucia and Dominica, though he does admit that "some day we'll have to get together."

"What about that?" I asked Eustace.

"The few down there as wants to work," he replied, gesturing vaguely with a sweep of his arm, "come here. You see how much of *us* you find in those other places! But after we cut loose February," he added gloomily, "I 'spect we all get lazy together."

English Harbour and Horatio Nelson

When Horatio Nelson, then a junior captain aged twenty-six, brought the *Boreas* into English Harbour in 1784, the little dockyard around the headland on the western inner slip must have looked much as it does today. But the tideless blue waters around it were so polluted with sullage that sailors were complaining of "putrid distempers" and "black vomit" for this harbor was the busiest anchorage in the cockpit of Empire. George Brydges Rodney's great victory at the Saints two years before had at last given Britain the upper hand in its struggle with France and Spain for world supremacy, but the ships of the newly independent United States were doing a thriving business as though nothing had happened to change their preferential trading privileges with the mother country. As there was temporary peace with France, Nelson could do nothing heroic to carry on where Rodney had left off; as a protégé and admirer of Lord Hood, who bitterly criticized Rodney for permitting De Grasse's defeated squadron to ecsape off Dominica in April 1782, Nelson himself had nothing so far to show for his patriotic fervor save an inconclusive land engagement with the Spanish in unhealthy Nicaragua. But in the minor matter of enforcing the Navigation Act and stopping the illegal American traffic, Captain Nelson was in a position to take a stand—and did, almost to the ruin of his promising career. To the easygoing and no doubt corrupt career officers ashore, the Nelson of those three years in English Harbour must have seemed a busybody, a martinet, and a prig; but men of genius, in times before their gifts have found the opportunity to flourish, have notoriously sickened upon the frustrations of inaction.

A vivid description of the young Nelson of that time came from Prince William Henry, Duke of Clarence, the future William IV, who one day in Portsmouth had his first glimpse of Nelson as the Captain came aboard Hood's *Barfleur*, on which the Duke was then serving as a midshipman:

> He appeared to be the merest boy of a Captain I ever beheld. . . . He had on a full laced uniform: his lank unpowdered hair was tied in a stiff Hessian tail, of an extraordinary length; the old-fashioned flaps of his waistcoat adding to the general quaintness of his figure, produced an appearance which particularly attracted my notice; for I had never seen anything like it before, nor could I imagine who he was, nor what he came about. My doubts were, however, removed when Lord Hood introduced me to him. There was something irresistibly pleasing in his address and conversation; and an enthusiasm, when speaking on professional subjects, that showed he was no common being.

One subject that they are known to have agreed upon was slavery; their contempt for the "hypocritical" Wilberforce and the other abolitionists was mutual. And it was a good thing for Nelson that he so impressed his future sovereign, for it was the Duke of Clarence who came to his defense when the conscientious Captain brought the lax officialdom at English Harbour to heel and who gave away the bride when the young officer married the widow Nisbet of nearby Nevis.

A year earlier, Nevis had failed to appreciate Nelson's strict interpretations of the law. In fact, when he seized four American ships that were trading there, the islanders claimed the enormous sum of £40,000 in damages and threatened to arrest Nelson and force him to stay aboard the *Boreas*, where he kept the ship's company amused with amateur theatricals, music, and cudgeling. To Governor Shirley of the Leeward, who had winked at the contraband and accused Nelson of youthful inexperience, the Captain replied that he was as old as Prime Minister William Pitt of England and was as capable of commanding one of George III's ships as Pitt was of governing the state. But probably Nelson survived his enemies' attacks because his political conservatism, dislike of Americans, and fierce hatred of everything French were in tune with official British viewpoints. "If once the Americans are admitted to any intercourse with these Islands," he wrote in 1785, "the views of the Loyalists are entirely done away. They will become first the Carriers, and next have possession of our Islands, are we ever again embroiled in a French war. . . . The residents of these islands are Americans by connexion and by interest, and are inimical to Great Britain. They are as great rebels as ever they were in America, had they the power to show it."

What Nelson thought of English Harbour's commander in chief, Sir Richard Hughes, a poor seaman who had been kicked upstairs and who had lost an eye (not in action, as Nelson was soon to lose his, but in an accident chasing a cockroach with a table fork), may be imagined. While Nelson was challenging the violations of the Navigation Act singlehanded, Hughes authorized Commissioner of the Navy Moutray to order the hoisting of the broad pendant of a commodore at English Harbour; Nelson, though half in love with Moutray's wife, had no hesitation in telling this civil servant with a nautical title that he had no such right—an action that led the Admiralty later on to place all commissioners on full pay and appoint them to nominal command of ships.

But Horatio Nelson's sojourn in this lovely yachtman's paradise, which he referred to as an "infernal hole," lends romantic luster to the surroundings in the reflected light of the glory he had yet to achieve. This glory is sadly served in the restored dockyard, where the great man's presence is reduced to a few curios, but splendidly given wings in the audio-visual tableau presented on Shirley Heights.

The *Boreas* is gone from the dockyard—was gone decades before the naval station itself was abandoned by the Royal Navy in 1899—and it is difficult to imagine the great ship from which Nelson wrote Mrs. Nisbet of the "hundreds of Mosquitoes . . . devouring me through my clothes."

Well, maybe only the names change. At the museum's door is a contribution box:

> *THIS IS OUR PROBLEM*
> *This lovely house is over-run*
> *by wood-eating termites. So far*
> *we have been able to repair only*
> *. . . this room. The uprights must*
> *be replaced. Please help us.*

Over the door there is a painted bust of the great hero, with his black patch, and there is a fine painted ship's figurehead inside, both good examples of folk art. The rest is period furniture and mementos—the Admiral's teacaddy, a photostat certifying his marriage to Frances Herbert Nisbet in 1787, and so on.

Nelson, who wrote Mrs. Nisbet after his first night in a French inn that "a clean pigsty is far preferable" and whose three injunctions to young seamen concluded, "You must hate a Frenchman as you do the devil," would certainly have cringed to hear the English Harbour spectacle called *son et lumière*. Christopher Ede, its producer-director apologizes that this form of entertainment originated on the Continent and proved as untranslatable into English as such British institutions as "week end" and "sandwich" have proved into French. Could the form— voices of character actors and a narrator on an amplified soundtrack timed to coincide with the illumination of the actual historical sites in which the action transpired—be anything but stuffy and static? We took our seats (almost alone) in the amphitheater across the road from Prince William Henry's Clarence House on Shirley Heights—and were pleasantly surprised.

The view almost straight down to the dockyard, on its narrow isthmus separating English Harbour from Falmouth Bay, is breathtaking enough in the sunlight. At night, with the aid of incandescent, fluorescent, and tungsten-iodine lamps, it is magical. And what a relief it is not to see over-upright Captain Nelson or the easygoing Prince or those brash American traders ("Money is the great object here," said Nelson once of New York. "Nothing else is attended to"). Sitting there in one's shirtsleeves with eyes half-closed, it is delightful to have to exercise visual imagination and to flesh out the picture of the lecherous Nelson contemplating Mrs. Moutray's lacy lap or of the blimp-like Hughes contemplating ways to get rid of this ambition-ridden little tyrant who stood officiously in the way of lucrative trade. There are a few jarring notes, like the screams when the Caribs descend on the peace-loving Arawaks—compared with the dead silence following the arrival of Columbus' murderous Spaniards. But, on the whole, scriptwriter Nesta Pain has handled the proceedings with admirable restraint, and the voices floating up from the spotlighted little naval base are convincing. One feels only that, in the beginning or at the end, a little more about the period that saw the real action would be in order. It seems not quite enough to say "came Trafalgar and the years when Captain Nelson became one of the greatest of Britain's naval heroes and Mrs. Nisbet one of a long line of dishonored wives." But that last clause, without overt reference to Emma Hamilton, *is* a nice touch!

Part 2. Montserrat

For almost three centuries after Columbus named this mountainous eleven-mile-long island after the famous monastery near Barcelona, Montserrat shifted back and forth between the English and French, becoming finally British the year after Nelson arrived in English Harbour. Or should one say it became Irish? There was a "joke"—in the days when the white colonists bolstered their fancied superiority with such badinage—about a true citizen of the Emerald Isle, who drove ashore, took one look at the inhabitants, and rowed quickly back exclaiming: "Bedad! They towld me Irishmen have been here only tin years, and by the powers they're already black as me hat!" The Irish did in fact come with the original settlers, by way of St. Kitts, in 1632; they were Catholic malcontents escaping the Protestant domination in St. Kitts, but they were mistrusted by the English, who tried to starve them out, and they left nothing to show for their presence but their names and a touch of the brogue. The Catholics became Protestants. O'Garras, Fentons, Cadogans, Sweeneys, and Fagans are everywhere, and in fact white letters across the black macadam of the first road we took proclaimed:

Fenton Made Wide
Road and Waste Lot of
Money Too

Fenton, it seems, was subsequently removed as road commissioner, but we applauded his generosity in making the highways just large enough so that cars can occasionally pass each other.

We had taken off from Antigua at 9:00 in the morning in a driving rainstorm. LIAT's twin-engine six-seater Beechcrafts make the hop to Montserrat in fifteen minutes. They fly onto a cliff on the lee side of the tiny island, sideslipping at the last moment to set down on an 800-foot sea-to-sea strip that occupies the only comparatively flat space on the island. As in almost all the islands (we were soon to discover) it's a long ride across the island from airport to hotels and an expensive one—$6 B.W.I. per person on Montserrat. Our destination was the Vue Pointe, and already, passing through Plymouth, the capital, we began to see signs of the real-estate boomlet that is Montserrat's answer to the failure of agriculture.

Sugar, of course, began to decline as soon as slavery was abolished,

and later on the sugar beet dealt Montserrat the *coup-de-grâce*. The planters packed up and left after the first blow, their managers after the second. Nothing remains of that unshared prosperity but the empty great
houses of brown stone, which the planters built on the heights in order
to leave every square inch of the relatively flat valleys available for cul-
tivation. Their slaves built the villages. Toward the end of the nineteenth
century, the export of lime juice for the London clubs took up the economic slack, but lime groves fared better in Dominica it seems. There was
a period of migration to England, stopped only when England imposed
racial quotas—and moderated its "official" criticism of racial prejudice in
the United States. Until the Canadian and American builders came, those
who couldn't afford to move away looked enviously at the rising tide of
tourism all around. Montserrat could never compete with Antigua in
beaches, and Montserrat's Soufrière—a dormant volcano with smoking
sulphur pools—is less accessible than are other such sights in the neighboring islands.

Montserrat's two tourist hotels, the Vue Pointe and the Emerald Isle,
were built in 1962, when real-estate interests came to the rescue. A sign,
as we drove into the former, told us what to expect: "We Build Your
Dream House." Burl Johnson of Washington, D. C., was at one of the
bungalow clusters putting aluminum window frames and louvers into
newly cemented walls. "This vacation-house operation," says one of the
brochures he gave us, "provides the opportunity to enjoy an exceedingly
pleasant climate surrounded by interesting retirees." The inception of
the American social-security system brought about the flight from fuel
bills and snow shoveling, Johnson told us—and where better to flee than
to this island, where the winter temperature in the mountains never falls
below 58 degrees, the summer temperature on the beaches never rises
above 92 degrees, and the mean humidity is 62 per cent? We had met one
of these "retirees" on the shuttle plane, a Mrs. Freda Wiegericht of
Michigan, elderly but remarkably spry. She proudly showed us her future home, a "modest" $18,000 house on a $3,000 quarter-acre lot overlooking nothing but a patch of open sea across the treetops. One reason
that everything is so expensive in Montserrat, complained Jen Osborne,
the Vue Pointe's manager, is that "every blessed piece of building material, including even the wood and the cement, has to be imported." There
used to be a lot of cedar and mahogany in the hills (which are still
thickly wooded), but once cut out it was never replaced.

The Vue Pointe is on a hillside overlooking one of the black sand
beaches in a curve of the rocky coast. It has a golf course with many
water hazards, salt and fresh. Its glass-walled restaurant overlooks the
swimming pool. Its hexagonal bungalows on a sloping lawn were designed by Osborne, a very talented Negro gentleman of Irish descent,
who represented the crown colony—Montserrat wants no part of Antigua's unsubsidized independence—at the coronation of Elizabeth II.
His bungalows are attractive from the outside, but inside the spacious-

ness of beamed ceilings seems fatally interrupted by bathrooms like slices of pie with flat ceilings; Osborne argues that "two-room privacy" is thus obtained.

The Emerald Isle is more conventional. Its low-lying blue-and-white walls blend better with the landscape, but there is no pool (a nearby beach is ten minute walk through the scrub), and there seemed to be no other guests when we visited it. There was one glorious compensation, however. The mountainside behind was framed in a perfect rainbow five miles long from end to end. This poetic by-product of the low cloud drifting west is a daily feature, we were told, of this 3,000-foot-high island with its abundant sixty inches of rainfall and three crops annually.

Driving north to where the road ends at St. Johns, we passed many of those impassive, abandoned sugar mansions—a sight even more disturbing than Antigua's cane-like mills, which could be incorporated so effectively into hilltop homes but never are. Beyond Cudjoe Head we came to Carr's Bay, where there is a fine beach, probably the best on the island. No homes are near it. Fisherman were stringing their huge nets, with cork floats, from tree to tree; dories and fishtraps were scattered below in pictureque disarray. The old salts seemed busier than the young ones. Perhaps in Montserrat's perfectly balanced climate age is not a handicap. Of eight tombstones facing the Anglican church of St. John's, Bill noticed that five of their dead had lived to be eighty years old or more and one to be ninety.

Our "Dutch Aunt" Freda, whom we'd invited to accompany us on this trip, showed us a pamphlet written by one Dolores Somerville, which contains some delightful bits of local lore.

For instance, Montserrat prides itself on being the cleanest island in the Caribbean. "Our police department is very vigilant. . . . Her Majesty's prison is complete with execution chamber."

Gin costs $1.59 (U.S.) a bottle, and Montserrat is "a dangerous place for anyone with a drinking problem."

After noting the availability of "Cheer, Lux Liquid, Clorox, Brillo, Campbell's Soup, French Seasonings, Carnation Milk, and Dream Whip," Miss Somerville adds: "This is how meat is obtained. . . . Late Friday night she is killed, and while still warm is chopped up with a cutlass. . . . The beef is hacked up any old way, with sublime disregard for the meat chart hanging in full sight." The scene, she concludes, "is one of mass hysteria."

The native dish for special occasions is "goh-at wattah" (goat water) washed down with "plastic" (raw rum). "A wonderful time will be had by all, what with food, music, dancing, girls and boys, and plastic—why not?"

As for death and burial, ". . . in this island you are literally here today, gone tomorrow. As there is no embalming service, a body must be interred within 24 hours. . . . The doctor writes the death certificate, the undertaker produces the beautiful red-cedar coffin (insects don't like this wood), the deceased is laid out, everyone brings masses of flowers, the service is held, and it is all over and done with by tomorrow night. . . . We ourselves have been closely concerned with this custom in the last two years, and each time the total cash outlay, including the cemetery lot (at £8.24 BWI) came to around $100 (US). Here they consider death a natural occurrence . . . no disrespect for their dead; it is just their particular way of dealing with the inevitable."

Back in Antigua, we checked in with Frank Delisle. The friendly manager of LIAT first came to Montserrat after World War II. Starting with one Piper Apache (and *no* landing strip), he put together one of the most efficient small-plane operations in the world. He was prepared to fly us anywhere in the vicinity—including nearby Barbuda, which we knew nothing about at all but were determined, once Frank mentioned wild horses and pigs, to see at any cost. Frank's pretty American secretary, Felicia, invited us to meet her Antiguan husband, Jerry Gomes, a local tennis champ, and he took us to his club for doubles. We all had dinner together afterward and listened to Antigua lore, enjoying especially one story of an early governor, whose wife had been kidnaped by a band of marauding Caribs. They took her to Guadeloupe by way of Bat's Cave near English Harbour, from which a tunnel then led, so the story goes, to the French island sixty miles south. When the Governor finally got his wife back, he put her in fetters on Blake Island in Falmouth Harbour (where the fetters are still to be seen) for "misbehaving." Driving in to the Caribbean Beach Club, they also told us of being trapped once in the funicular car for forty minutes with four guests and 4,000 hungry mosquitoes. When we arrived, our friend Dan Darrow was taking no chances; he was having the tracks, the cab, and the whole beach area "fogged" with D.D.T. He promised to wake us at dawn for the flight to St. Kitts.

Part 3. St. Christopher (St. Kitts), Nevis, and Barbuda

Basseterre, the capital, which holds 32,000 of St. Kitts' 48,000 embattled citizens, is a port and market town of aristocratic antecedents, proletarian politics, and indefinable charm. Two minutes' walk from the quay is the square that Patrick Leigh Fermor described so memorably as "filled with great weeping trees whose tasselled branches all swayed together with the least breath of wind" and the noble Georgian houses "weathered and time-nibbled to a state of infinite mellowness." But times have changed since 1946, when a white lady of St. Kitts could still remember the great receptions and balls given by the remnants of the plantocracy. St. Kitts is now in the grip of wily trade unionists who come as close to practicing the doctrine of Black Power as does any government in the Caribbean. A diminishing contingent of white businessmen is holding on desperately, with little hope for survival. And tourism exists only in an isolated enclave or two, smiling bravely and waiting for the ax to fall. (The first sign we saw at the airport read, "Nice Seeing You, Goodbye.")

From our balcony at the Seaside—a pension for seamen and traveling

salesmen but immaculately clean—we could see the market women stacking their neat piles of yams and the fishermen hawking their crabs and turtles. Our lunch, from which we were soon staggering about in a daze, consisted of pumpkin soup, giant crabs, fried blue-marlin steaks, spaghetti, French-fried potatoes, yams, string beans, breadfruit, tomatoes and lettuce with onion rings, *vin rosé*, two bottles of the local Carib lager, and some wafer-thin pumpkin pancakes with molasses sauce. While a St. Kitts belle was explaining to Bill how arrowroot cleanses the intestinal tract, I made notes of the room's remarkable *décor*: frosted-glass balcony doors ringed with lavender; a glass partition to the bar hung with floral-patterned imitation lace; a black-and-gold tapestry of lion hunting zebras; and, in the place of honor, over perfunctory mural still lifes, *two* official framed photographs of John F. Kennedy flanked by smaller koda-chromes of Her Majesty the Queen and the Prince Consort.

From sources of varying color, at the bar and behind it, we were beginning to piece together an impression of the Bradshaw government and its role in St. Kitts' dilemma; the once-richest island in the Leewards now the poorest, the island with everything to offer tourists and not a single operational tourist hotel in sight.

Black Whitelash

Robert Bradshaw, the First Minister of St. Kitts-Nevis-Anguilla, who was to become Premier in February and to lose one of his three islands for a while in June, is a black nationalist; he was in Trinidad at the time that the West Indian Federation collapsed, but he had already organized the sugar workers in St. Kitts. His enemies say that he deliberately turns tourists away, lest the unemployed union members, who constitutes half his political machine, seek jobs in the hotels, and the employed union members, who constitute the other half, leave the island for higher wages elsewhere. Bradshaw constantly threatens to nationalize land, but, perhaps remembering the near bankruptcy that came to Antigua when it bought into 40 percent of the sugar industry, he hasn't yet. His henchmen justify his extremism on the ground that thirty white families—"the kind that stop work every afternoon at five for tea and tennis"—still own all the sugar estates. Those on the fence, and there aren't many, say that one bunch of extremists begets another. But the British government backs Bradshaw without enthusiasm. When the first uprising against him took place in Anguilla this year, it sent a frigate with a load of marines to put down the rebellion; the Anguillians, ironically, wanted to stay with the Empire. There was a telephone system in Anguilla under the British, an Anguillan at the hotel told us, but as soon as Bradshaw took over every phone on the island disappeared.

Too late, Bradshaw's critics say, the government is beginning to realize that the sugar industry (which is wholly dependent on having its product bought by Britain at prices in excess of those on the world market)

has no future and is making motions to capture some of the influx of spending visitors who are giving Antigua, and even tiny Montserrat, their booms. Bradshaw isn't giving bar licenses to anyone, however, and television sets can't be sold in Basseterre unless they are "adjusted" to receive only from Bradshaw's low-frequency transmitter. But a British combine called INDELCO is being encouraged to sign a contract under which £20 million would be invested in a development at Frigate Bay. Gradually over ten or fifteen years, three resort hotels, a racecourse, a marina, a golf course and tennis courts, a gambling casino, and hundreds of rentable or salable cottages would be included. This project would be one that the Tourist Board would want us to see.

St. Kitts is shaped like a flask with a very long neck and a triangular stopper. We had flown over the stopper coming from Antigua and were dazzled by its beautiful green hills, salt ponds, and white beaches, but we were puzzled to observe that the one hotel in the area, quite evidently a luxury layout, had no road connecting it to the rest of the island. This hotel, we discovered, is the small but hopelessly marooned Cockle Shell Bay, whose American proprietor, N. F. Bowers, has to ferry his guests from Basseterre. The road ends at Frigate Bay, where the narrow peninsula begins. Mr. Morton of the Tourist Board drove us there to show us what INDELCO has in mind. So far there is only the road (built with American aid) and a storage reservoir. The beach is only adequate; it has no reef and no potential for snorkeling. Yet INDELCO'S contract specifies that no other new hotels will be permitted to open in St. Kitts once it is signed. Ballpoints are dragging because the British say, "Put in a jet strip, and we'll sign," whereas Bradshaw replies, "Start building and we'll put in a jet strip."

But Cockle Shell Bay is not alone in its splendid isolation. At the extreme northern tip of the island (the base of the "flask") is The Golden Lemon, equally isolated, equally splendid in its appointments and situations, equally harassed by the powers that be—and also the creation of a hardy American "capitalist" who is holding on for dear life. We came upon it by accident at the end of a long day's drive to Brimstone Hill.

Our driver was Campbell Evelyn, brother of Helen Maingot, our gracious LIAT contact in Basseterre. Evelyn, like Gomes in Antigua, is one of those sturdy colonial Britishers—level-headed, well-educated, high-principled—who make one wonder how the Empire was ever lost. No doubt there weren't enough of them, and perhaps they were left behind when the martinets and Blimps deserted the foundering ship to retire on pensions. I asked him if he would show us first one of the stones with pictographs that are the island's only memorial to the pre-Columbian period.

Background of Violence: Brimstone Hill to Dieppe Bay

The peaceful Arawaks had already been driven off in 1493 when Columbus discovered and named St. Kitts. The island was known by its Carib name, Liamigua (Isle of Good Waters). Thomas Warner, Captain John Smith, and a dozen other intrepid adventurers from Virginia, with their wives and children, landed a century later and began to dispute possession of the island with the first of many Frenchmen to come. One of these would-be tobacco planters described lianas and withes then "running about like roaps which soe entangle ye trees ye one with ye other, as we could not deuide them without cuttinge downe 4 or 5 together." The Caribs must have been friendly at first, or the little band, with no food of its own, would never have survived. But in November 1625 several hundred Caribs from other islands in war canoes had to be driven off, and two years later the French and English colonists, perhaps fearing a "fifth column" in their midst, combined to surprise the local chief, Tegremond, in his hammock and massacred all the remaining native inhabitants.

The large volcanic boulder we inspected is on Wingfield Estate, once owned by Governor Warner's son; it lies in a field off the road about halfway between Basseterre and Brimstone Hill. Two incised symbolic figures, one male and one (very pregnant) female with tiny face and sticklike limbs, are clearly discernible. There are more of these figures up

Bloody Ghout, where the 1627 raid took place. The excuse given for the massacre at the time was that a Carib mistress of one of the officers had tipped them off to a "rebellion" that was supposed to emanate from this gulch. (Hernando Cortés had brought this ploy to the New World a century before in Mexico.)

St. Kitts was never wholly French for more than a few months at a time. But for almost 100 years the French occupied the two extremities of the island, leaving the English in uneasy possession of the center. This portion was not only less fertile than the extremities were, but it was so subdivided by Mt. Misery and the Southeast Range that the colonists could only go back and forth by passing through French territory. Basseterre and Brimstone Hill were finally seized from the French in 1690 and, except for a brief capitulation in 1782 just before Rodney and Hood defeated De Grasse's fleet at the Saints, they remained in English hands.

As we drove on up the south coast toward "the Gibraltar of the Antilles," Mt. Misery loomed out of the clouds on our right, its slopes billowing with white flowers of sugar cane like sea foam. It rises almost 4,000 feet, and there is a crater on top that had a cold lake 800 feet below the lip until a recent avalanche filled most of it in. On the north slope there are hot sulphur springs. I had read Père Labat's account of a monkeyshoot on these slopes and of how quickly the good traveler-priest-gourmet had conquered his shock when four heads "like little children" stared up at him from the platter afterward. I asked Evelyn whether or not these simian predators were still to be seen and eaten, and whether or not they were native to the island. "They're still so much a menace to sugar and other crops," he said, "that there's a bounty of 12 cents on every head. But the natives hunt them for the meat, which is considered a great delicacy and sells in the Basseterre market for as much as 50 cents a pound. Some of the monkeys grow to twenty-five pounds or more. They're West African greens," he added, "with no relation to the indigenous howlers and spiders on Trinidad that came there from the South American mainland. Ours and those in Barbados and St. Lucia must have escaped from cages after being brought over as pets by the slaves from West Africa." I asked him whether or not the mountain's dense forests, in which the monkeys hide between raids, contain any virgin wood. The answer was the usual story: The precious woods were cut out long ago and never replanted.

Brimstone Hill is the largest, most picturesque, and best preserved reminder of the days when the world's balance of power was being decided in these waters. There is a commanding view from the summit, still bristling with twenty-four-pound guns. The Dutch constellation of St. Eustatius, Saba, and St. Maarten lie simmering in the north foreground, with St. Kitts' sister island, Anguilla, just a little too low on the horizon beyond them to be seen. Nevis dominates the sea to the south, screening tiny Montserrat. Perhaps in ideal weather conditions Guadelope's *soufrière* might be distinguished in the background. A little to the north up the coast the village of Sandy Point, once the English capital, may be seen.

Beautiful little ferns grace the black-and-white stones of Brimstone Hill, but the donjon is filled with bat dung, like screened brown sand, which stinks and is crawling with tiny insects. We made out the name "George Swale 3 Bucs 1798" scratched on one support, and Campbell Evelyn told us that the name, regiment, and date had been authenticated by the War Office in London. He himself had picked up dozens of regimental buttons in the surrounding fields, and as a child he had explored the underground escape tunnels leading to the shore below.

I asked him what the big, ugly railroad markers with numbers signified.

"They were put up during Her Majesty's recent visit to help her identify the points of interest."

"And over there in Sandy Point—why so many churches?"

"We have almost as many churches as Negroes here," he said. "Mostly Protestant, but the Catholics are catching up. They have more to offer in indulgences and much easier attendance requirements."

Driving around the northern end of the island to Dieppe Bay, we stopped in front of one of the handsomest buildings I have ever seen in the West Indies. It sits behind a high stone wall with a *cheval de frise* iron gate just across the road from a palm-fringed beach. Its long stone façade is two stories high, the ground floor pierced with arched stone doors flanked by iron shutters painted lemon-yellow and shaded by a railed wooden balcony cantilevered on white posts to give the second story its own protection from the sun. This great house, probably the finest on the island, was in ruins until 1962, when an enterprising American bought it and began restoring it inside and out. It had opened officially as a tourist hotel the week before we arrived, and, when we pulled the bell, its owner-proprietor came out to greet us. He introduced himself as Arthur Leamon.

"I know your books on Haiti," he said to me. "Come in, and you'll feel at home."

He was right. The stairwell was dominated by a magnificent life-sized figure in sheet metal, the work of the great Haitian sculptor, Georges Liautaud; along the far wall hung half a dozen exuberantly painted scenes of Haitian life by some of the artists I knew so well. But the real miracle achieved by this former art editor for *House and Garden* was in the restoration of this handsome building, in furnishing it with antiques lovingly gathered from junk yards and attics all over St. Kitts, and in the air of sunny splendor given to everything by a most sophisticated use of primary colors. Against the whitewashed walls of the high-ceilinged entrance chamber, with its original beams of Guiana Pitch Pine, stand polished hardwood cabinets. The new floor of bleached planks is accented on one side with a long mahogany stripe. The ground floor with its two-foot-thick walls of volcanic facing stone and Roman-arched doors is French from the period 1740—50. The wooden second story with beamed, open-gabled ceilings and high, half-timbered walls, is British and dates from 1790-1800. The six double rooms, featuring richly carved four posters open onto the balcony or overlook the patio, with its fruit trees and yellow-leafed crotons. I assumed that it was from these shrubs or from the lemon-yellow shutters (even the towels and face-cloths on the line were of this dazzling hue) that the young proprietor had taken his hotel's name (which sidesteps his own so tantalizingly by one letter), but no.

"It was named The Golden Lemon inadvertently," Arthur Leamon explained, "when a friend who had watched me buy the ruin for $25,000 came to the opening-day party for the island's surly top brass. 'Well,' said my friend, as we toasted each other entirely alone in the foyer, "It looks like you got yourself a lemon.'"

Arthur Leamon was born in Plainfield, New Jersey, educated at Haverford College in Pennsylvania, and "escaped" to St. Kitts after a thorough survey of all the Leewards and Windwards. "Only Dominica was cheaper than St. Kitts," he told us, "but Dominica didn't have such fine houses—or shells of houses—as this was in 1962 when I stumbled onto it. Or fine beaches," he added, "pointing to the fringe of white sand beyond the seventy-foot-high coconut palms, under which naked Negro urchins were chasing one another, tumbling, and standing on their heads.

He laughed ruefully as he watched this happy scene from the balcony. "This is the way its always is—except that, when I bring guests out for a swim, these kids retreat a little shyly to the background and have to be coaxed out—and I wouldn't want it any other way; but Bradshaw and his henchmen are now challenging my right to use the beach on the grounds that I've 'segregated' it! That, on top of fighting me with legal chicanery, innuendo and gossip ever since I moved in. But I don't care. I'll make a go of it in spite of them, unless they deport me. For this island, this town, and this house have everything. Even a ghost. Want to try your luck?"

We walked downstairs with him and took turns standing in a spot between two of the rooms. "I noticed it as soon as I moved in, and so do those of my friends who are psychically susceptible to such presences. It's eerily *cold*. Look at my forearm!" Sure enough, there was gooseflesh. But, although Bill, Campbell, and I tried it several times, we were unable to notice the slightest change in temperature.

"It must be Bradshaw's secret weapon against *you*, Arthur," I said.

"Well, it's not going to work," he replied, "because I like it!"

Nevis: M. Pomeroy, A. Hamilton, and H. Nelson

We had to make a difficult choice between Nevis and Barbuda the following morning. The LIAT plane that would have made connections with our scheduled flight to Barbuda was filled, and if we waited until the following day there would be no chance of returning and seeing Nevis. We weighed a return engagement with Jerry Gomes; an invitation to dine with Archibald MacLeish; and a promised meeting with Antigua's savant, Charlesworth Ross, against the ghost of Alexander Hamilton, and this time the ghost had his way with us.

Once more we were flying south over Cockle Shell Bay's roadless, pondy paradise, and ten minutes later we were sideslipping into an airstrip almost as cozy as the one on Montserrat. Half an hour later we were having breakfast with Mary Pomeroy. And half an hour after that our dynamic hostess at the Nivel Plantation House was assuring us that *she'd* fly us to Antigua the next day in time to make our Barbuda connection if we didn't mind returning to St. Kitts for the night. Mary Pomeroy is that kind of woman. Rumors of her prowess in the air, on the ground, and even at sea had been buzzing about our heads for a week.

On the plane coming over, for instance, an old Nevis hand had assured us that, when a cow strays onto Mary's plantation, she shoots it. I suggested to Bill that we go in with our hands over our heads. "Don't," he said, "she might take you for a reindeer." Then there was the story of how her sharp tongue had once so inflamed the skipper of an inter-island sloop that he threw her overboard; after swimming some miles to shore, she brought suit against the line and used the money she collected to buy her single-engine Cessna.

She is a small, wiry woman with good features, boundless energy, little humor but infectious warmth. Before the war she had been an interior decorator in England but it was while training for parachute jumps into Yugoslavia that she had decided to live anywhere but in her comfortable homeland. After acquiring her Nevis property a few miles north of Charlestown on the east coast of this almost circular island, she had managed the sugar lands and the coconut groves for the first ten years. It was when she decided to open a hotel seven years ago that things really began to happen. Alexis Saint-Leger (St. John Perse), the celebrated French poet of colonial nirvana had been among her first party of guests, and she had amused them by taking them on a monkey hunt—the forest surrounding 3,232-foot Nevis Peak has monkeys too. Then came the plane and adventures all over the Caribbean. I complimented her on her Haitian pictures, and she said she had flown into Duvalier land unannounced for a hotel owners' conference at El Rancho in Pétionville the previous year and then on to Cap Haïtien where everybody got saddle burns from those spavined horses that take visitors up to the Citadelle. Currently, she is up in arms over what she calls "this drunken, racist show of power" in the free islands, especially in St. Kitts. She encouraged me to take notes from a memo she had just sent to a tourist association in the United States. The English manager at Montpelier and his wife had had their work permits taken away the previous week for their allegedly "patronizing" attitude toward the work staff. Not a single invitee had showed up at the Golden Lemon's opening, she confirmed; one minister had written to Arthur Leamon loftily, "I do not recall having met you." She characterized INDELCO'S Frigate Bay project as "a real-estate speculation." The new head of Bradshaw's Tourist Board was "being sued for embezzlement." The Bowers' Cockle Shell Bay was "under constant harassment."

So, apparently, is Nevis' largest tourist hotel, The Cliff Dwellers, which we went to visit before lunch. Stewart Greene and his wife, Geraldine, took us up from shore level, where the pool and tennis courts are located to the main building in a reasonable facsimile of the Caribbean Beach Club's funicular. (The car was at the top as we arrived too.) They have six lavish double-room cottages ready for occupancy, but their license to operate a forty-eight-guest hotel is being withheld. The backer, an American named Welles McCormick, must have sunk $1 million into this luxury layout, with its pagoda-like shingle roofs hugging the cliff's edge.

Charlestown, the capital, is a picturesque but seemingly underpopulated antique town, with Chippendale balconies supported by wooden buttresses. The ruin of Alexander Hamilton's birthplace is a few feet from the beach and two blocks north of the dock. Hamilton was born there on January 11, 1757, the illegitimate son of James Hamilton, a charming but indigent Scot, and Rachel Fawcet of Nevis' Gingerland Plantation, who had already married at sixteen a dour Dane from St. Croix by the name of John Michael Levine (or Lawien), at the insistence of her mother. Mary Pomeroy, who had gone into Hamilton's complex genealogy in some depth, says that Rachel's rebelliousness repeated the pattern of her mother's life; the latter had broken away from a sick father in her youth. Rachel returned from a very unhappy trip to Cophenhagen and St. Croix with her husband and in a delirium gave birth to a child, Peter, whom she promptly packed off to St. Croix in the company of his grandmother. It was while recuperating from this trauma that Rachel met and fell in love with Hamilton. She was only nineteen and was unable to obtain a divorce. She didn't care; one experience of matrimony had been enough. Unions like hers with Hamilton, based on love and intended permanency, were not uncommon at the time. In the morally self-governing society of the island plantocracies, little or no stigma was attached to birth out of wedlock. Levine eventually obtained a divorce for "abandonment" in the St. Croix courts, but Rachel, as the defendant, was not permitted to marry again.

The love match with James Hamilton was ill fated. Hamilton blew his considerable fortune, and Rachel had to sell her estate in St. Kitts to bail him out and start off again in a salt project; by 1762 he was bankrupt again. This time Rachel's brother-in-law, Peter Lytton, came to the rescue and offered Hamilton the management of one of his St. Croix sugar estates. (John Levine and their son Peter had returned to Europe by that time). Alexander Hamilton was only five that April of 1762, when he left Nevis forever to sail with his mother for Frederiksted in the Virgin Islands. The story of what happened to this prodigious youth there dur-

ing the next ten years, including his premonitory account of the St. Kitts hurricane of 1772, belongs properly in our account of St. Croix. But it is interesting that the future Secretary of the Treasury kept in touch with his father from the time the latter abandoned poor Rachel, soon after reaching St. Croix, until the time he was killed in a duel in St. Vincent in 1799—just five years before his famous son met the same fate in New Jersey.

Nisbet Plantation House inevitably recalled memories of the other great man associated with Nevis, for it was at Montpelier House that Nelson took the widow Nisbet to wife, and the record of their marriage is still preserved at the Fig Tree Church there. C. S. Forester's biography of the great captain was in Mary Pomeroy's library, and we had several hours to scan it while waiting for our hostess to return from an afternoon flight and take us to Charlestown. Nelson had made a profound impression on his bride's family, Forester says, "partly by the manner in which he went out of his way to do his duty" [an officiousness that, as we have already seen did not endear him to the rest of the Nevis plantocracy] and partly by his extraordinary habit of not drinking more than was good for him at dinner." Nelson's official reports to the Admiralty, Forester notes "breathe more fire and life" than do his love letters. It is on record that a salient feature of Frances Nisbet's opinions was her belief "in the efficacy of flannel worn next to the skin;" their best man, Prince William Henry, may have been aware of this fact when he told Nelson that his esteem for his bride did not seem to be "what is vulgarly called love." Forester goes on to speculate as to why the ardor that Nelson was to lavish upon Lady Hamilton was never visited upon his wife: "Conceivably flannel next to the skin may convey part of the explanation; there are some women whom one cannot idealize."

Nisbet Plantation House is a rambling bungalow built in the Nelson decade, a perfect setting for Mary Pomeroy's very informal hotel operation. Spacious screened verandas and book-lined salons flow into one another, and in the back two imperial rows of palms flank the gently descending path to the beach. There, among piles of rocks to keep the sand from being sucked out to sea and tangles of bleached driftwood, everything is as informal as the house—and as delightful. There is also a tennis court, for Mary is reputed to play with as fierce a determination as she does everything else, and we regretted that rain made it impossible to pit ours against hers. Too soon, alas, she was driving us to the sulphur springs and the dock, from which Bill was catching the *Bahama Mama* for the 110-mile sail back to St. Kitts, and then on to the airport, from which I was taking off for a night at The Golden Lemon. On the way she gave us a résumé of Nevis' history and the attractions we'd have to come back to enjoy.

The island was given its name (which comes from the Spanish *nieve*, snow) because of the appearance of the cloud that almost always hovers over its perfectly symmetrical peak. (There is some doubt about this story, for Admiral Samuel Eliot Morison, Columbus' biographer, says that the island was originally called San Martin but that when this name was transferred to the nearby Dutch island, Nevis was renamed in honor of Nuestra Señora de las Nieves.) The Caribs were in occupation in 1493, but they fled to Dominica and St. Vincent after the massacre in St. Kitts. There were peace and great prosperity—and a flourishing slave market—in Nevis during the century after the Spanish raid of 1629. In 1677 the population totaled 1,534 whites and 1,422 Negro *men*. But for the next century, until Nelson arrived in English Harbour, the island was a battleground in the French-English wars. The final French invasion was repelled in 1805, and prosperity returned—very briefly. In 1834 slavery was abolished. The curse of absentee ownership descended on Nevis. Plantations were abandoned. (Today there are only seven resident planters left, and the Bradshaw government is slowly acquiring the abandoned estates.) The Bath House, built in 1778 for fifty boarders at a cost of £40,000, was described in 1825 by Coleridge, the traveler: "An invalid, with a good servant, might take up his quarters here with more comfort than in any other house of public reception in the West Indies." But in 1890 William Agnew Patton, another traveler, described the hotel as "a picture of desolation and decay . . . the abode of bats and owls . . . the resort of ghosts." Today there is talk that its present owner, the Swiss Bank Corporation, will restore it to its original grandeur—Bradshaw permitting. In all fairness to Bradshaw, though, the remnants of the plantocracy who still own the largest estates in Nevis, St. Kitts, and Anguilla will have to do more than beguile tourists to justify their survival. Few Negroes in any of the three islands own large enough pieces of land to provide vegetables for their own families. In Nevis, grandiloquently advertised as "essentially a beachomber's island," old sugar mills "with their blades still intact" are up for sale, pigeons are multiplying faster than the hunters invited to shoot them, and the monkeys up Fountain Gout must be laughing at the menus that falsely offer to serve them "cooked like wild hare."

Barbuda: Foxy Gilette and Charlesworth Ross

Arthur Leamon's driver made the trip from Dieppe Bay to the St. Kitts airport in forty minutes the following morning, picking up Bill in Basseterre en route. Mary Pomeroy flew in from Nevis at 9:00 as promised, and we piled into her single-engine Cessna. I didn't tell Bill what the LIAT pilot had said to me in Nevis the day before. "I wouldn't fly one of these crates over water for love or money. The nearest sea-air rescue base is Puerto Rico, two and a half hours away. You'd have no chance at all if she ditched between here and Antigua." But Mary handled the controls with aplomb. We flitted across the channel under a thunderstorm and circled the field at Antigua while the control tower rasped on the intercom: "Better let that jet land ahead of you, Mary. Give him plenty of time."

She did. Thanking her, we grabbed our bags and rushed across the tarmac to the LIAT Twin Bonanza waiting to take us to Barbuda. Charlesworth Ross, a pipe-smoking colonial-officer type in plaid Bermuda shorts and knee-length stockings, was already aboard. He wasted no time in handing us a mimeographed biography and pointing to passages in two books that he carries with him (one by Alec Waugh), both of which cite him as the most knowledgeable Antiguan. Quite possibly he is. He had been Colonial Secretary of the Leewards in 1948-1950, the biography said, Commissioner of Montserrat in 1949-1956—"when retired on pension at own request. Recreations: good conversations, reading, travel . . . " I looked at a wicked drawing of him, paunch in profile, that Bill was making and whispered, "Your first book of drawings will have to be *Drawn and Quartered*."

We set down first at Codrington, named after two governors of the Leewards, Christopher Codrington the Elder and Younger, both chosen for that august but low-paying post because of their wealth in salves and islands. "As for this Government," wrote the younger Codrington in 1701, " 'tis a charge and trouble to me; all the advantages of it don't pay for the wine the Masters of ships drink who come to report to me." And, while this state of affairs continued, he added darkly, "there will be illegal indulgences in point of Trade, Justice will be bought and sold, Chancery suits protracted, and the poor opprest." Smuggling was off to a good start. Then as now Barbuda was confused with Barbados. The Earl of Carlisle's second grant to the two islands described the first as "Barbido alias Barbado alias Barbuda" and the second as "Barbadas alias Barbudos alias Barbadus."

"There are more Barbudians in New York," Charlesworth Ross remarked as we walked away from the plane, "than in Barbuda." But like most other statements about this island, we were soon to discover, its was subject to challenge. "The highlands," he went on, "are 150 feet high, and during the war the United States considered bulldozing the whole flat island into a single airstrip. This is the only island with *pink* between waves and sand." The pink, we discovered, is caused by masses of crushed sea shells, and even the brackish ponds take on this lovely color.

Codrington is where everyone lives by law—a carryover from the days when the Codringtons made their barren possession a stud farm for slaves, keeping only the finest male specimens here and bringing in boat-loads of girls to be impregnated. It's a miserable village today, its only features being a martello tower, a circular vat in which to cool beef, and several large stone-walled enclosures contains basins of fresh water, which are supposed to lure wild cattle and goats into captivity. We saw several of both species drop in for a drink and leave; there was no one around to close the gates, and the crumbling walls would not have held them in any case.

Ross told us that the hunting is poor. He'd hunted all day recently for one of the cottontail deer imported from Virginia, but had bagged nothing. A local official had had "a scent of a deer."

Albert Lewis, Warden of Barbuda, joined us, and we had whiskey-sodas in his parlor at the Administration Building. We sat in front of his television set, one of five on Barbuda. He said that there was good reception from Antigua, and Ross promised to describe the day's proceedings on his next regular program.

Barbuda is composed of coral on limestone, thinly covered with thickets of chaparral, and of course there are no springs or rivers. There are deep clefts filled with fresh water in the highlands, but they are too far away, apparently, to be tapped. I asked Mr. Lewis where the drinking water is obtained, and he pointed to the rusty tin roofs, only a few of which seemed to have small gutters attached to metal barrels. There are doves, pigeons, plover, guinea fowl, and ducks in abundance on Barbuda, and the fishing in the waters between the shore and the coral reef that completely surrounds the island is very good.

We climbed back into the plane and flew on to Coco Point, an establishment for well-heeled tourists run by William Cody Kelly of Cincinnati, a descendent of Buffalo Bill. It is in its sixth year, and its twenty double rooms go for $120 U.S. a couple in or out of season. "We provide everything except LIAT's $30 round trip from Antigua," said Mrs. "Foxy" Gilette, the resident manager who received us, "and we lose money." Foxy is a tall, handsome, blond Britisher, born on the Isle of Man. She has a reputation for losing her help, but we saw no sign of unhappy servants. She has charm and a good sense of humor and was wearing a blue gingham dustcap that looked rather like a nightcap. "We provide privacy, tranquillity, informality," she said, "and the best beaches anywhere."

We sampled Coco Point's beach forthwith and were inclined to agree with her. Every West Indian island claims that its beaches are the best. Jamaica is high on Doctor's Cave or Frenchman's Cove, but the garrulous druggist from Grand Cayman whom we had met in Kingston had insisted that they were far surpassed by his own—"or even by Grand Turk." Dan Darrow had seen them all and found nothing to compare with those on Antigua. Only Campbell Evelyn went a little afield, assuring us that Anguilla's sands were finer and purer and whiter than were those of any other island. But Barbuda's immense beaches can hardly be improved upon, and the incredibly translucent blue waters we waded into invited all-day swimming. The coral reef in eight feet of water is alive with bonefish, for which guests sometimes cast from shore, and lobsters up to fourteen pounds lurk in its "caves." We drifted over the reef in a rowboat, watching two agile native skindivers at work. A pole with a wire noose is held over the opening in the coral, and when the lobster pokes his head out the noose snaps tight. Bill came up with an eighteen-inch turtle, which he pursued underwater and brought ashore bare-handed.

The main house and connecting individual cabins are chicken-house modern, with corrugated asbestos roofs and white paint inside. "We serve lobster salad and champagne on the fishing launch," said Foxy as we sat down to lunch. "The guests find it sporting to cast into the mangroves in the inlet behind the hotel. We're a tiny country club, I guess you could say. We comb the beach every morning."

We'd already had an account in Codrington of the wild pigs, how savage they can be when cornered (where are there corners on Barbuda?) and how the natives hunt them with machetes. Foxy snorted. "They are *sweet* creatures. With tabby faces. And the deer are also very small and very lovely—but we eat them. Marinated in red wine and olive oil. Wild horses? No, no. They're *liberated* horses." We were drinking our delicious

Senegalese soup, a chicken broth with curry and peeled grapes. The talk turned to sharks. Foxy said that diamond rings attract their attention. "And don't smile at them," said Bill, "if you have gold teeth." I thought I knew Foxy well enough by now to make a facetious reference to the "Cincinnati girls" reputedly flown in at one time for entertainment.

"Cincinnati girls?" said Foxy with her arch smile. "Sir! This is an orderly house."

It's so orderly, in fact, that two Jewish journalists wrote a scathing piece about Coco Point last year, charging it with "selective prejudice." All that we saw was delicious, delightful, and a little dull, except for Foxy. Nothing dull there.

That night we put ourselves to sleep back at Dan Darrow's reading Charlesworth Ross's *From an Antiguan's Notebook*. There are spirited accounts of early island shipwrecks and hurricanes; and a memoir of Antigua Grammar School in the 1920s has its moments:

> There was almost no homosexuality at our school, no "pashes" between the pupils and only rarely a suspected *alliance* between boy and master. There was a good deal of ragging and bullying but nothing so serious as appears to have been current at many English public schools about the same time, thereby warping the lives of future distinguished Englishmen and causing them to write a public school novel at an early age.

As a literary critic, Charlesworth Ross had just what we needed. Introducing what he calls "one of the greatest love poems in English or any other language," he leads off:

> Well, Mr. Business Executive from Duluth, Minnesota, you with the well-lined pocket-book and the incipient paunch, permit me to offer you a bit of advice. It is a January evening in Antigua and you sit, not unaccompanied, by the window of the bar of Peter Deeth's Inn on Shirley Heights. . . . You and the tall voluptuous blonde in the G-string bikini have spent the day snorkelling in the colourful movemented submarine Caribbean. . . . It is the moment for invitation. Take my tip and murmur "Oeillades" softly in her ear. You will find it far more efficacious than three dry Martinis at the Four Seasons in New York.

> ### OEILLADES
> *Looking in your eyes I see*
> *Beauty, truth and mystery. . . .*

Zzzzzzz . . .

Part 4. Dominica

Dominica (pronounced Do-min-*ee*-ca) lies in plain sight of the two larger French islands, Guadeloupe and Martinique, which will be described in the next chapter, and half way between them. Guadeloupe, in turn, is in sight of Montserrat and Antigua and, on a very clear day, of Nevis and St. Kitts as well. South of Dominica the Windwards (Barbados excepted) stretch in an almost straight line to Trinidad. Dominica is gourd-shaped, twenty-nine miles long, and close to a mile high. So much for geography.

We found ourselves, after the usual hour's expensive ride from the airport, enmeshed, embedded, and embowered in the Caribbean counterpart of Santa Maria de Ostuma.[1] It is Peter Brand's Island House Hotel, a hostelry put together with genius in this most lush of the Caribbees. The vegetation on this island is indescribably dense, almost oppressively fecund. Everything is jungle, jungle, jungle, from the rocky coast with few harbors or beaches to the high peak of Morne Diablotin near the airport and Morne Trois Pitons, 1,000 feet lower, back of the hotel. The sight from one of the balconies of this rustic retreat was indeed so overpowering—sheer mountainsides of mangoes, breadfruit, giant fern, cedars, avocados, and almonds, with grapes and myriad flowering vines glistening a dozen shades of green in the dripping sunlight—that Bill, gasping for words, came up with the right ones:

"It's like—green whipped cream!"

In high places, and most of Dominica is high, there is an incredible 300 inches of rain annually. It rains, off and on, every day but briefly, and the sun dries everything again in minutes. There are reputed to be 365 rivers, but this figure, though now so commonly accepted through repetition that it is taught in the schools, is a tourist agent's estimate. One hundred and twenty rivers that actually empty into the sea make Dominica the best-watered island of the West Indies; the other rivers are tributaries, each with its own name, and of course none of them is navigable. There is an abundance of waterfalls too. One of them, Trafalgar, not far from the hotel, has been usurped by a hydroelectric pipe that is visible from the road to Roseau, the capital; before it rusted, hundreds of feet of silvery pipe knifed vertically through the jungle in the sunlight, and Brand's guests invariably mistook it for a cataract and exclaimed "How beautiful!" Another cataract, Laudat, is nearby and still intact.

The island's fauna include no poisonous snakes, but there is a boa

[1] Central America's most unforgettable inn is perched on a Nicaraguan mountaintop with its back to the jungles of Honduras; it was visited by Bill Negron and me in 1965 and described in *The Road to Panama* (New York: Hawthorn Books, 1966).

constrictor, the *têtechien*, which grows up to eight feet in length and has been known to go after chickens. Iguanas, wild pigs, and agoutis abound, and so does the *manecui*, a small possum-like creature that is good to eat. The wild pigs are sometimes hunted in the Glow Gomier section between Roseau and the airport. Birds include the Amazonian parrot (called *sisserous* locally), the whistling solitaire, and many other exotic birds. Mullet were introduced into the rivers but have been virtually exterminated by the native practice of "fishing" with dynamite and bark poison.

They say that the one monkey that got loose in Dominica was quickly killed by a farmer and that so were several imported deer—both having been considered menaces to agriculture.

The island's major "industries" and only exports are bananas, copra, and citrus fruits. Lime juice (origin of the term "limey," we were told) is squeezed into barrels between acid-impervious granite rollers at Rose's Plantation factory in Roseau. The lime trees are planted between rows of bananas, for shade and nourishment in their early growth, and both trees receive additional protection from rows of *galba* trees fifty or more feet in height.

We heard at the airport that Dominica's chronic unemployment problem is going to be exacerbated soon when amphibious plane connections will eliminate the hour's drive to Roseau. But our taxi driver, Ashworth Shillingford, seemed more inclined to ascribe all troubles to local self-government by the Labour Party, which has been in power for six years and resembles Bradshaw's regime in several respects. "We were much better off before," said Ashworth, a knowledgeable Dominican who answers all questions precisely with a "sir" attached to each subordinate clause. "They don't provide enough jobs, nor do they keep up the roads properly."

The road we were traveling was very good. We stopped once while Bill drew some banana sprayers with yellow compression tanks and long

blue tubes on their backs. One of them asked for money, and I noticed that Ashworth snapped at him in something resembling Haitian Creole. The patois, in fact, is identical:

Moin ké mané ou à hotel ou. "I am going to drive you to your hotel."
Common ou yé? "How are you?"
I coaxed Ashworth into giving me the following peasant saws:
Quan ou fé cabane-ou, c'est comme ça ou ké couché. "The way you make your bed, that's the way you're going to lie down."
Si ou plante casave, m'pas ké fé fig. "If you plant cassava, you won't get bananas."
Lé ou en bon caille, mauvais caille ça cri ou. "When you're in a good house, a bad one is calling you." (This last one is said to daughters who go out too much at night.)

The peasant huts, some palm-thatched and some with tin roofs, are invariably walled with dried banana leaves.

Rusty tin defaces Roseau too, though there are a few fine buildings with old ironwork or jigsaw-carved balconies. Still, the appearance of the capital hasn't improved much since 1908, when a traveler described it as a "collection of shanties and a squalid antidote to the Dominican traveler's conviction that he has been dropped directly into the bosom of paradise. . . . A good fire, judiciously directed, would vastly improve its appearance." [2] There is a splendid botanical garden in Roseau with cluster-palms and spreading bayans, but hardly an indigenous species to be found in it. The British were wonderful at cross-breeding cultures—on the botanical level.

Peter Brand's Island House

Peter Brand has done some of his own botanical crossbreeding. He has a stand of nonfruit-bearing plantains with lavender leaves and a beautiful purple-leafed ground cover, *Hemigiafis colorado*, which he has imported from Java. He told us that Honduras pines are being planted experimentally in Dominica, as well as some mahogany. One native tree, the gomier, whose trunks grow to three feet and more in diameter, Peter uses most effectively in his *décor*, which is original throughout and, wherever possible, created from indigenous materials. The closet in my room, for instance, was a cabinet set two feet off the floor on bamboo stilts, its doors made of fine matting of dried pandanus leaves. The same leaf, crisscrossed, makes the bed-lamp bases. Hanging spotlights are concealed in bamboo tubes. The black-and-white wood of the tree fern, never thitherto used for anything except firewood, provides the dining room's

[2] F. A. Ober, *A Guide to the West Indies and Panama* (New York: Dodd, Mead, 1908).

very elegant panelling. Hanging from the beamed ceiling in counterpoint are foot-wide pandanus mats. The locks of the massive *gomier* doors are most ingeniously opened by wooden keys attached to the latches by concealed gut cords. The door handles are of bamboo in leather clamps. One side wall of Bill's room was made of rough field stone. The other was pierced by four delicate Gothic arches giving out onto a narrow gallery with tables and chairs, screened from the outside by cinder blocks (locally made) cunningly split and fitted together to form a diamond grill. The ceiling was pitched slightly and beamed. The floor was covered by one of those magnificent rugs of woven *vetiver* grass; this weaving is Dominica's only folk export and an art that didn't exist twenty-three years ago.

We drove into Roseau in the afternoon to see the "factory" where the rugs are made: the Convent of the Missionary Sisters of the Immaculate Heart of Mary. The unsung innovator of this operation was Sister Mary Bertine, but the weaving is presently under the direction of Sisters Mary Camille and Mary Magdalen, who received us graciously. Under their direction, sixty-two Dominican girls work six and a half hours a day in the convent's stone common rooms and galleries weaving the squares, splicing them together, and shipping them at good (but reasonable) prices all over the world. We watched them in fascination, as they sat on the floor with legs crossed, their callused fingers plying the heavy steel needles—for the grass, which they call *khus-khus*, becomes very resistant when dried. Sister Bertine had no more than the simple patterns of native hats, door mats, and pig-tying ropes to begin with. But today the patterns of the large circular and square rugs are very complex indeed. Most are abstract. A few incorporate such Christian symbols as the fish very ingeniously.

Peter Brand drove us, at my request, to see Gilda Assief, a Haitian mulatto *émigré*, who has married a Syrian and paints under the name of Thébaud. We remarked on the way on the wonderfully peaceful atmosphere in the convent. "All Dominicans are peaceable," he said. "No matter what goes wrong, nobody here curses or gets mad because the man who is upsetting you may turn out to be your best friend's cousin. Everybody in Dominica is related, and knows everybody else."

In Assief's house I noted a copy of the Dominica coat of arms, rampant parrots with this curious legend in Creole:

Apres Bondie Cest Later.

I finally deciphered it: "Après (le) bon dieu, c'est la terre."

The Assiefs told us that the Labour government isn't hostile to tourism but encourages it only verbally. "All the available funds go to building roads to the isolated mountain villages." Not a bad idea! As long as they don't discourage the Peter Brands.

Back at Island House we marveled again at the artistry of Peter Brand. Here is a man Frank Lloyd Wright would surely have applauded, for his work is "organic" architecture, carried out as the Master himself did, down to the last wall fixture, chair, trash basket, shower stall, and place mat. Each bedroom, each bathroom, is different in every detail. Yet the details harmonize as the work of a single vision, carefully crafted. In one bedroom for example, the supporting beams of the ceiling meet in the eave; in another they cross in midair and are bolted together. In one, the indirect lighting fixtures are concealed behind a miniature balcony; in another they are out on the gallery throwing their light through the pointed arches. In one bathroom the deeply sunken shower pit is approached by circular steps, in another by a ramp. In the living room there are two ceilings of woven rushes, suspended at the corners by chains.

The "outdoors" is handled with equal brilliance. The bedrooms give onto a narrow concrete walk terminating in a gutter through which water runs in and out among clumps of papyrus. Then comes a two-foot wall of loose field stones surmounted by delicate, drooping ferns, then a solid planting of yellow *roseau* reeds eighteen feet high up to and beyond the walk's overhang. Where the walk turns to meet another building, there are little platforms and circular pools filled with green water-lily pads. The jungle swimming pool, with recessed steps at various angles and a miniature waterfall feeding it in a single glass-like sheet, is very beautiful.

A Day with the Caribs

We roused ourselves at 8:00 in the morning for the long day's trip to the Carib Reservation. There was to be a Sunday fair at Salybia, and we were lucky because it occurs only once a year. On any weekday the Carib "capital" is likely to be deserted, and to walk to any of the other Carib villages—Snakecoe, Gaulette, Bataca, Antwistle—in the 3,700-acre reservation takes hours from this road's end.

The Caribs have an interesting but tragic history, most but not all of it in association with Dominica. Though they did eat human flesh on occasion, the derivation of the word "cannibal" from the French version of their name hardly encompasses their character. A fiercely independent sea-going people from the South American continent, they turned upon the European marauders only when the atrocities visited upon the peaceful Arawaks in Hispaniola by Columbus and his Spaniards taught them what to expect. Even then they were friendly to the English and French, when not molested. But, unlike the Arawaks, they refused to submit to slavery. Driven from St. Kitts, as already noted, by Thomas Warner's massacre in 1626, they settled in Dominica, St. Lucia, and St. Vincent. In 1640 they executed a reprisal raid on St. Kitts, carrying off Warner's son, Edward, and his wife. In 1674 they raided Antigua, whereupon another of Warner's sons, Philip, led a punitive expedition to Dominica, killing eighty of the Indians, including Thomas "Indian" Warner, one of the old Governor's children by a Carib woman, who was reported to have led the Antigua raid. Philip Warner was subsequently imprisoned in the Tower of London for this massacre, there having been some suspicion that he had invited his half-brother aboard ship for a drink and had murdered him there and his Carib followers in the aftermath. But he was acquitted of this crime by a Barbados jury in 1676. Charging that the Caribs were being supplied with firearms by the French, the English mounted a larger campaign against them in all three of their island retreats. But, as late as 1796, in response to the inflammatory propaganda of the French Revolution, the Caribs came close to expelling the English from St. Vincent and had finally to be deported from there to the coast of Central America, where their descendants (intermarried with the Negroes) survive as the "Black Caribs" to this day. Only in Dominica, in this reservation set aside "in perpetuity" for their independant occupancy, did their descendants in the island homeland manage to straggle on into our century.

The road to the reservation—all but five of the forty-odd miles back to the airport and then five more sharply to the right over an "unimproved" road to Salybia—was uneventful. There was rain in the sun, a pleasant warm rain with many rainbows. The few fields were thickly matted with the lavender flowers called *kapi*. The only evidences of man were the Coca-Cola markers with their ironical "Sign of Good Taste" slogan, and a few posters lettered by hand:

> *Courtesy Week*
> *Be Courteous in Your Speech*
> *Can I Help You, Lady or Sir?*

Where the road turns, a fine stretch of coast with many volcanic black beaches is to be seen. Far in the distance one can make out Guadeloupe's satellites, Marie-Galante and the Iles des Saintes.

Salybia, an unpaved village with a few shacks and a tiny church, is at the head of a gully opening seaward. It was filled with parked buses and trucks, and people streamed down between two rows of booths connected with red and white pennons on clotheslines. The booths were marked "Bar," "Games Stall" "Snack Bar," and the like. At the games stall people were paying 10 cents to grab for packages wrapped in old newspaper. I watched a little girl open one. It contained a balloon and three jawbreakers that couldn't have cost more than a cent. Another booth sold native crafts: undistinguished baskets and place mats woven in light-and-dark patterns out of the *larouman* plant and walking sticks (for $1 apiece) covered with the same crisscrossed reeds. The church is attractive inside, with a spreading purple stripe on each side wall and an altar consisting of an unhollowed Carib dugout supported by a low cement arch studded with beach stones.

On a bluff overlooking the church I chatted with the Carib Chief (or *cacique*), Jerman-dois Francis, and with Edward O. LeBlanc, a Negro who introduced himself to me as Dominica's Chief Minister and Minister of Finance. The Carib chief, who wore an elaborately tapestried sash over one shoulder and carried a silver-headed staff, looked like a Spaniard with some Chinese blood. Very few of those who were pointed out to us as Caribs, in fact, looked like Indians, though I did photograph one who had distinctly Mongolian features and straight black hair. No Carib women were in evidence, and we were told that there are no more than a dozen "pure" Caribs left.

LeBlanc told me that his Labour government is "strongly tinged with socialism" and devotes all of its B.W.I. $8 million budget to social services, education, hospitals, and roads. "We encourage tourism, but we wouldn't like to see it become Dominica's number-one industry. Our intention is to bring in light manufacturing, like pumice, canning, concrete blocks. Tourists come to these islands mainly to be seen in their bikinis by a pool, which is all right, but we haven't the beaches to attract many of them." He added that the budget for tourism came to B.W.I. $500 annually—a sum that hardly pays for the postage to answer letters from would-be visitors and investors.

When he had walked away, the Carib chief drew me aside. "We don't agree *at all*—this gentleman that you photographed me with, and I. His government wants to break up our reservation and give us little parcels of land in return. We've written the Secretary of State for the Colonies asking to be saved. We want to continue to hold our 3,700 acres in common. We want the borders of the reservation defined and reconfirmed. We want this government to leave us alone."

I had been surprised to read once, in Sir Alan Burns' *History of the British West Indies*, how many Carib words survive in English, many in everyday use: for instance, "barbecue," "buccaneer," "canoe," "cannibal," "cassava," "guava," "hammock," "hurricane," "iguana," "maize," "manatee," "piragua," "potato," and "tobacco." Some are of Arawak derivation, no doubt, as are many place names in Haiti, Cuba, and Saba. I asked Chief Francis if any of the Carib tongue was still remembered here.

"A little. I'll give you some examples," he said. "If you want to say 'Good afternoon, white man, how are you?' you say 'Mabrica,' which means 'I meet you' three times and then 'Cuman noti'—'how are you?' If you want to offer a toast, you say 'Alaqua butu aneecay a moulin quat,' which means: 'Drink! Good health and prosperity!' If someone says to you 'Cai uma ou buca,' which means 'Let's go,' you reply 'En heu cai uma,' which means 'Okay, I'm ready.' The word for Dominica," he concluded, "is 'Ou ai tu cu buli.'"

We drove out of this depressed backwash of history to eat our sandwiches by the seaside. Even the red earth in this part of the island has rebelled against civilization's ways. The previous month an avalanche caused by roadside erosion buried the airport-Roseau road in one steep cutout. It took six days to clear the way. Bill told me that one of the Carib boys had called Dominica "an island of doom from which there is no escape without money." The Caribs traditionally spend their money on rum, or at least they have since that terrible night when they trooped aboard ship to drink toasts with the Warner brothers. We asked our driver, who claimed to be part Carib, whether or not he put his savings into land. He said no; he was saving up to get out—and forever.

"I may go to the Virgins next year. I hear there's plenty jobs there. There's none here. I'd even go to Guadeloupe!" But the peasant masses who vote Labour think otherwise. They buy land, and, as there are no land taxes they are reluctant to sell it. Once Dominica lost its grants-in-aid from Britain, it voted for independence.

From our Carib driver, from Ashworth the day before, and from Peter Brand we collected an anthology of other places in Dominica worth visiting. One is Boiling Lake, which is only about two miles east of the hotel as the parrot flies, but until a trail for horses is hacked out it is an all day hike with boots and machete. The approach to it is by way of the Valley of Desolation, where steam issues from vents in the lichen-covered rocks. You look down, and, when the wind occasionally blows the steam away, there is revealed an oval body of sulphurous white water perhaps 200 by 400 yards, its surface everlastingly agitated in a rolling boil.

More "usable" is Emerald Pool, where a waterfall drops into a natural swimming hole of pure green water with a sandy bottom. It is surrounded by jungle plants, those "shrouds of lianas," in St. John Perse's line, "where too-long flowers end in parrot cries." But the lianas are strong enough to swing out on and drop from. It is only a three-minute walk off the road that leads to Castle Bruce.

Jocko's Steps, halfway between Roseau and the airport, were cut into the solid rock, all seventy of them, by Jocko, a renegade slave, who thus ascended to an inaccessible hideway and was never captured.

The reef at Scott's Head offers snorkelling and underwater spearfishing as good as any in the Indies. Caves in a perpendicular underwater cliff remain to be explored. No sharks and "only one barracuda" have been observed there recently.

Rodney's Rock is the site that the ingenious eighteenth-century English Admiral camouflaged to look like a warship. He did it so well that the French stopped to bombard the rock. With the tactical advantage of being upwind, he then defeated them at the Saints, the victory that gave Britain control of the Caribbean.

Farewell to Peter Brand

We had dinner at the pool-side grill: fried chicken and the usual eight vegetables, topped off with frozen strawberries, a local orange cordial, coffee, and Dominican cigars. Then Peter took us down to his Loup-Garou Room, and on the way I asked him whether or not one could infer from this Creole term for the Haitian werewolf that voodoo is practiced in Dominica too.

"There is no voodoo mixed with Catholicism here," he said, "but there is plenty of belief in African witchcraft. There's the local legend, for instance, of the *su-quion*, a woman who sheds her skin and passes by in the night as a 'fireball.' How does one exorcise this troublesome witch? Quite simple. You find the skin she shed, fill it with salt and pepper, and, the next time you see a woman scratching herself, you seize her, and you have yourself a *su-quion*."

The Loup-Garou Room, with its massive open fireplace, dance floor,

orchestra stage, and bar is another Brand winner. The polished hardwood and terrazzo floor has wedges set into it in clusters, diamond-
shaped ("my module," Peter said). The walls are of woven bamboo. The
only decoration, aside from the lozenges in the floor, is supplied by the
glasses of various shapes that hang by their stems from a concealed slot
above the bar. Cross-ventilation is supplied by screened louvers just
below the ceiling. It was cold enough to sit by a fire of crackling logs—in
a sweater.

It was a good opportunity to draw Peter out a little. He is a short man
with delicate features and an elegantly pointed black beard. His eyes are
blue, alert, curious, twinkling, and sometimes far away. His mood is
generally gregarious, however; he'd be in the wrong business, were it not
so. He was trained to be a lawyer but quickly tired of it—partly, perhaps,
because his experiences as a navy pilot in World War II gave him a taste
for adventure. He won a commendation for pulling a burning comrade
out of a flying boat that plummeted into deep water after hitting an invisible oil slick. With his seat belt and harness broken, he had shot
through the tiny windshield head first and come to on the bottom. After
that, writing briefs, torts, and wills must have seemed pretty dull.

Six years ago Peter made a survey of the less-known Lesser Antilles
and picked Dominica. His wife agreed. They bought a seventy-six-foot
gaff-rigged ketch—and one of his crew promptly ran it aground in the
Bahamas, losing the ship and everything of value aboard.

"No, we weren't carrying a cent of insurance. Even now when I think
of it I get all tightened up inside, and tears come to my eyes."

"What did you say to the skipper?" Bill asked.

"I handed him a $20 bill. You've got to find another job, don't you?"

He flew back to his native Florida after that, picked up more money
designing and contracting 1,500 homes—"most of them, necessarily,
alike, a further incentive to building something like this! And then I
took off for Dominica again, this time by plane."

The first six months of the five years he'd been there, Peter spent finding the right piece of land and negotiating for it. For this delectable 7 1/3
acres, which look like 700 acres, he paid B.W.I. $500. I asked him how
much he has put into Island House since. It was a staggering sum, but he
didn't want it quoted. "I've been open two years, and I'm still losing
money on these six doubles, which few people know about. I'll break
even with sixteen. Then, when I've expanded to twenty-eight, I'll make
enough to do everything I want, including traveling half the year and
putting my three sons through prep school and college. But for that
many rooms I'll need a manager. I have lots of ideas, like closed-circuit
TV with selected tapes for every room, a horse trail to Boiling Lake, and
so on. If I just wanted to make money, of course, I wouldn't be here.
I'd be in Antigua, Barbados, or the Virgins, where masses of tourists
pour through, and I couldn't fail. But what challenge—or fun—would
that be? Meanwhile I keep afloat by operating the island's only freezer

business in Roseau. If I didn't have a little private income of my own, I'd never make it."

I asked him if labor was a problem. "Everything is a problem. But this island's carpenters and cabinet makers, once you can find them and induce them to work, are very good. You have to supply all the specifications and style, of course. Even now," he added, "the bar bill is my only extra. Guests are driven to and from the airport—you weren't because I didn't know you were coming—have their own room servant, guide to Boiling Lake, etcetera. I want it to succeed only so that I can make it the 'perfect place' everyone would like to visit. My pleasure is in seeing them enjoy it and talking to them."

To prepare for our rising, which seemed to get earlier and earlier with each island, we went to bed at 10:30. At least we were *about* to go to bed when Bill rapped on my door and said:

"Have you got the airline tickets?"

"No," I said, "Haven't you?"

Then we remembered that Peter had them—he'd taken them into Roseau to reconfirm them, as there was no phone at the hotel. And now he'd left by jeep for his own home, which is a mile or so down the road. We searched the hotel high and low for one of the boys. There was no sign of one. Finally we stood in the driveway and yelled alternately into the starlit night: "Haloo! Hey! Yo! Hi, there! Anybody home?" After about five minutes, one of the young Negroes appeared out of the bushes, barefoot, his shirt flapping. "Wha-what is, Sir?" He was shaking like a banana leaf. We'd awakened him from a sound sleep, and he'd had a nightmare of *loup-garous*. We explained our predicament and the early-morning start. He was about to take off down the road to Brand's house when Bill found the tickets in one of the tilted board slots that Peter had built behind the desk to eliminate the cliché of mailboxes.

The new Hotel Bacoua, named for the conical straw fishing hat worn in Martinique, is to be dwarfed by a Hilton opening on a point north of the city two years hence, but the Bacoua's site and luxurious appurtenances will be hard to beat. Its two arms embrace a little promontory looking straight across the great harbor to Fort-de-France. One arm contains the fifty-six double rooms with balconies in two strips; the other under peaked, tiled pavilions, houses the glassed-in dining room and salons. On the promontory itself is the pool, and below it to one side a few hundred yards of white sand beach. We had an excellent lunch of fish soup with capers, broiled lobster, and muscatel wine with Albert Veille, the co-manager, and then set out to have a look at *H.M.S. Diamond Rock* off Martinique's south coast.

Commodore Samuel Hood,[5] who captured all of the surrounding is-

[5] Leigh Fermor and other knowledgeable writers on the West Indies whose works I have consulted confuse this officer with his older cousin, Admiral Sir Samuel Hood, the co-victor of the Saints, who had earlier tried unsuccessfully to relieve Cornwallis at Yorktown. The elder Hood was still alive at the time but not on active duty.

III

THE FRENCH WEST INDIES

The city, by way of the river, drains into the sea like an abscess. . . .
The bats cut the soft evening up with little cries
Where fruits rot in the rainspouts,
Where time is nibbled away like the dry weeds a donkey grazes. . . .[1]

Part 1. Guadeloupe

When the Treaty of Paris was signed in 1763, there was much grumbling in London over the clause restoring Guadeloupe and Martinique to France in return for Canada. How could those sugar tarts flambés, with their bonus in coffee, indigo, slaves, and beautiful women, be "given away" for such a frozen wilderness? Hadn't the imports from Guadeloupe alone amounted to £2,004,993 between 1759 and 1762, compared to a piddling £48,000 from "Quebec"? But the sensible grumblers were overruled in the councils of Empire by West Indian planters from St. Kitts, Antigua, and Barbados, who were not anxious to have their monopoly challenged by competition within the establishment. The canny British thus concluded the greatest bargain in islands since the Dutch bought Manhattan from the Indians for $24, and the French were left with a

[1] St. John Perse, *Éloges*, translated by Louise Varèse (Princeton University Press, 1956).

problem that still plagues them—what to do with Guadeloupe?

The largest of all the Antilles between Puerto Rico and Trinidad has been a problem to the white man from the day Columbus first anchored off its southern promontory on November 4, 1493. The Admiral's first landfall of the second voyage, on November 3, had been Dominica, but he had continued to sail north to Marie-Galante in search of a decent harbor and then west between the Saints to the tip of the mountainous half of the the big island shaped like a butterfly. The Spanish sailors at the rail must have looked up open-mouthed. High above them hung the falls of the Grand Carbet River like an overflow from the cloud that sits eternally on Soufrière's cone. Caribs on the beaches of what is now Capesterre village fled into the jungle pursued ("for purpose of plunder," Columbus' scribe reported) by a landing party that promptly got lost. Partly to justify their own aggression and partly no doubt to ease their frustration at finding none of the gold that motivated all Spanish colonization and missionary rhetoric, they began at once to pin the word "cannibal" on the aborigines. Though the landing party, which was lost for four days, returned intact, joints of human flesh were alleged to have been found in the deserted Carib kitchens. "Lest they be eaten," Columbus took aboard his fleet "twelve very beautiful and plump girls from 15 to 16 years old," without disclosing what happened to them thereafter. Père Labat, the "Bellicose White Father" who left such an engaging account of his travels through the islands a century later, confirmed that the Caribs' taste for human flesh lingered on but that the European plunderers were then sending priests (or soldiers dressed and shaved to resemble priests) ashore first—it seems that a roast Dominican friar had once poisoned a whole tribe of feasting Indians.

The French had already been in Guadeloupe 100 years when the English enjoyed their brief occupation and the trade for Canada was masterminded. Voltaire had described the island as "small and prosperous, where the best sugar is produced," but, when the French Revolution broke out in 1789, the inequity in the distribution of Guadeloupe's wealth soon made the island the focal point for slave revolts throughout the Lesser Antilles. The Commissaire of the Terror, Victor Hugues, landed at Pointe-à-Pitre on February 4, 1794, and proclaimed the abolition of slavery. A guillotine was set up in the Place de la Victore, and Royalist heads began to roll. Hugues, as we shall see later, expanded his bloody ministrations to Martinique, St. Lucia, and St. Vincent but without conferring any positive social benefits. As a result, when the Bonapartist reaction swept France, Hugue's seamen mutinied rather than face the English, and British landing parties had little difficulty recruiting soldiers among the ex-slaves. It took another pawn-trading peace treaty (Vienna, 1815) to restore Guadeloupe and Martinique to the French, but more than a century was to pass before Charles de Gaulle finally managed to make the Negro islanders accept France with more than sullen apathy.

When Patrick Leigh Fermor visited Guadeloupe in 1946, this process had hardly begun. He found the island politically divided. There were the families of the conservative, ultra-Catholic plantocracy, who had backed Admiral Robert and Marshal Henri Pétain and were still holding out desperately against what they called "a band of free-masons, sir, whose only interest is to fill their own pockets and destroy the state! *La Dissidence a fait beaucoup de mal dans les îles.*" *La Dissidence* (Gaullism) was then an unruly alliance of patriots, adventurers, and communists struggling to consolidate their newly-found domination through integration of the French islands into the Paris Chamber of Deputies. Pointe-à-Pitre was a loathsome, malarial agglomeration of wooden shacks. The Saints were overrun with lepers, syphilitics, and victims of elephantiasis. Only the peak of Soufrière, with its "reek of brimstone" like a "backwater of hell," seemed worth visiting. Without a backward glance, Leigh Fermor and his party fled to Martinique, which had ridden out the war in amiable gentility.

From Pointe-à-Pitre to the Fort Royal

Guadeloupe has changed since 1946, but only a Francophile, a vulcanologist, or a gourmet could find it attractive.

Pointe-à-Pitre, named for a Dutch fisherman called Peter, who erected his shelter on the point in the 1650s, has been cleaned up. In fact it is the showcase of De Gaulle's effort to integrate the islands into metropolitan France. Outwardly the effort has succeeded. "More money is being pumped into Guadeloupe alone,"an English visitor told us sadly, "than the British are putting into all their West Indian islands together." The city is dominated by a dozen superb modern housing developments. There are more original architecturally and more colorful, with their blue-and-orange louvers, tinted glass, concrete grills, and walls pierced with clusters of portholes, than is anything in Miami Beach or Los Angeles. And there is the Ma Sabiel skyscraper, an office building put up by refugees from Algiers.

The French colonists were always more generous than the English with roads. Today Guadeloupe's roads, crisscrossing the flat eastern "wing" of Grande-Terre, with its immense cane fields; vaulting the Rivière Salée at the "butterfly's" spine; and slicing around Soufrière's steep shoulder to girdle inappropriately named Basse-Terre, with its small capital city of the same name, are better than ever. But, as for facilities for the tourist trade, De Gaulle's prideful largesse—he gives the islands more money proportionately than he gives any of the eighty-nine departments of continental France—does not result at all in what a tourist would like to find. French Canadians, who apparently come for the familiar language and the food alone, are well if expensively served. All others are unceremoniously dumped into one of the two absurdly isolated luxury establishments, the Fort Royal and the Caravelle. The Caravelle has earned a certain Gallic notoriety for its twin beds, double-tracked to provide togetherness. The Fort Royal is the brainchild of a ship's engineer, who designed it to look like a nautical hospital. Both hotels pride themselves on having staffs who don't speak a word of English.

We arrived at Pointe-à-Pitre at 8:30 in the morning, and, had we known better, we would have stayed there. Having no idea where we were being taken, but assuming that the hotel to which we had been assigned would be at most a quarter-hour's drive from the airport, we jumped into a taxi and said "Le Fort Royal, s'il vous plaît." One driver, Alexander Racine, nodded knowingly, and we were off. *One hour later* we pulled up at what Bill was quick to tag "The White Elephant of the Caribbean," one of those enormous stainless steel, air-conditioned nightmares that cost millions; it was entirely empty but for ourselves and a Junker businessman from West Germany, who had also arrived in a daze. "Dix dollars, U. S., messieurs," said Alexandre Racine. "Je suis toujours ici à votre service." We had a third breakfast, tried unsuccessfully to reach everyone on our Guadeloupe contact list, including the manager of the hotel, who had no knowledge of our reservations, and fell into two of the four beds in our preternaturally frigid suite. In no time at all I had my first and only attack of dysentery—an obviously psychosomatic case.

By 1:00 in the afternoon the operator was still unable to contact either Roger Fortuné, Directeur de l'Office du Tourisme in the Place de la Victoire, Pointe-à-Pitre, or Mario Petrelluzzi, owner of La Pergola in Gosier— the two gentlemen who were reputed to know Guadeloupe best. We were having $5 sandwiches with our fellow maroonee, whom I shall call Oberst Count Gerhardt Friedrich von Welcweck. He regaled us with a vivid account of being flown out of Stalingrad just before Von Paulus' surrender and of his escape two years later into Helgoland ahead of Marshall Malinowski's army crossing his native East Prussia. If Welcweck bears the mark of Cain, it may be in a too-great readiness to agree with one on the subject of Germany's war guilt and the United States' superior political institutions. Bill said later that he was a Nazi-type under the skin because he had remarked at one point that "The Negroes are only 12% of your country—why should they rule?" but I pointed out that this opinion must be held by at least a majority of Americans. The Count has an ineffable way of punctuating things that are just dandy; with his hands in front of his pale blue eyes in the formation one is supposed to use when ordering Ballantine Beer, he lifts them elegantly up—an expressive gesture we found ourselves involuntarily falling into for the first of many times when Alexandre Racine appeared at the table and asked us whether or not we would like to drive back into Pointe-à-Pitre for a bargain $10 round trip.

Two decisions confronted us. We could continue on around rock-bound Basse-Terre to the tiny capital, which every traveler seems to have avoided, and attempt to climb the semidormant volcano in its shroud of rain forests, leaving Grand-Terre, Roger Fortuné, and Mario Petreluzzi until the next day. Or we could accept Alexandre's bargain, visit Pointe-à-Pitre now, and fly out the next day, thus having an extra day in Martinique. The weather dictated our choice. Soufrière was entirely swaddled in clouds and might remain so for a week, we were told. From a safe distance we could speculate that the volcano, which played dead when Montagne Pelée destroyed Martinique's capital in 1902 and touched off sympathetic cataclysms in St. Vincent and other islands, was building up steam. Martinique's well-known charms seemed as irresistible as they must have been to Napoleon the first time he confronted the sultry Josephine.

From Victor Hugues to Mario Petreluzzi

Roger Fortuné was in his office—had been, in fact, all morning, so he said. "The phone never rang." I was intrigued by some two-inch mahogany figurines on his desk: *poilus* and mulatto beauties in Madras turbans, the work of a primitive sculptor, Flabbernot Télémaque, whom Fortuné has commissioned to do a large relief with many figures on a theme from the Victor Hugues period. He also showed me decorated gourds resembling the Peruvian *matés* of Huancayo, which he confessed to having carved himself.

"Then you are a primitive too?" I asked with a smile.

"A naïve savant," he answered.

"And Victor Hugues," I asked, "is he a hero here today?"

"Much less of a one than Victor Schoelcher, the mild reformer who abolished slavery in the French colonies in 1848, fifty-four years after Hugues had brought this island's white planters to the guillotine. Hugues's activism is the main reason why Martinique retains (outwardly) the culture of the plantocracy. Guadeloupe's sugar industry fell at once into the anonymous hands of institutional corporate capitalism."

"Is sugar yielding to tourism today?" I asked Fortuné.

"Sugar is still number one, followed by bananas, but sugar wouldn't survive at all unless De Gaulle chose to buy it—that is, subsidize its purchase—in order to give France a protected overseas market for its manufactured goods and even its foodstuffs. Do you wonder that our restaurants are expensive? Tourism has no rank at all yet, but it may have when our present 400 rooms are expanded to 1,500 in 1970."

"Is De Gaulle popular in Guadeloupe?" I asked.

"Well, yes. But not as popular as the De Gaulle of 1940."

"And who lives in his superb housing developments," I asked, pointing toward Raizet Airport, "the middle classes?"

"Absolutely not," Fortuné replied. "The proletariat." And he was right, for, walking through one of them later on and viewing the wash strung up in the living rooms and out on the balconies, we discovered that a single room rents for $12 a month and a four-room family unit for $26. The new normal school is a veritable Hilton.

I asked Fortuné where I could find out more about Hugues, whose life has always intrigued me but has proved elusive. He referred me to Petreluzzi, who in turn referred me to a researcher at the Smithsonian Institution in Washington, D. C. Hugues remained as elusive as ever.

Petreluzzi himself was anything but elusive. In fact he is so conscious of the values of publicity that he has a telescope, with which his staff can follow his movement from the sundeck as he threads his way among "his" islands, and a two-way radio to summon his home. One of the Saints, which lie directly off La Pergola's cliffside, is indubitably his, for he has rented Îlet à Cabris from the Guadeloupe government for 100 years. "I don't think I'll renew," the gingery, grizzled hotel man said to us after pointing out through his glass eight cottages that he has built on the islet, but there was nothing in his tone of voice to suggest that mere age would stop him. He is rightfully proud of this view, which embraces La Désirade and Marie-Galante, as well as the Îles des Saintes. He is as justifiably proud of his restaurant, the Corsair. He is also proud of his unique communication with the smaller islands. And he is inordinately proud of his somewhat frumpy La Pergola, and its eight tattered pergolettes.

"We have only one rule here," said Petreluzzi, whose father migrated from Sorrento but whose mother came of an ancient island family. "No transistors, no newspapers. We supply *peace*."

"Does the Fort Royal give you any competition?" I asked.

He snorted. "The Fort Royal was the idea of a savant who is a cretin. It will destroy tourism in Guadeloupe for a generation."

He took us out onto the gallery, where he has built rusty-metal relief maps of the islands in his panorama, each bolted to a jigsaw table a couple of feet off the floor. I looked at the nearest island, a few hundred yards offshore, and asked him if he owned it.

"Not yet," he replied dryly.

I pointed to Marie-Galante and asked him what the people do there.

"They cultivate sugar—the sickness of the Antilles."

"And in the Saints?"

"They cultivate Rodney, whose victory saved your Revolution, the propaganda says."

I'd seen pictures of the wonderful straw hats woven by the Norman-Breton "poor whites" of the Saints—the broad shallow brims sprouting like mushrooms from intricately plaited split-bamboo webs that hug the crown of the head tightly. Why were these hats not for sale in Guadeloupe? I asked Petreluzzi.

"Maybe they're ashamed to admit that the prototype came from Indo-China. Try the shops in Martinique. They don't have our forests or fertile plains; maybe they have our hats."

"I've heard they have everything," I said, hoping to needle him into a further pronouncement.

"I'll revise that," he said, glaring at me. "Martinique has two things, and only two, that we don't have: Josephine's bottom and 30,000 people who vanished in ten seconds."

Part 2. Martinique

Having once gone through a teen-age rage for everything pertaining to Napoleon, I was well enough prepared to pursue traces of his Martiniqaine Empress Josephine to Trois-Îlets and beyond; having retained much more vivid earlier memories of St. Pierre's destruction, as related to me countless times by a nurse who had witnessed the distant cataclysm and its aftermath as a little girl in Fort-de-France, I knew what I hoped to see under the slopes of the slumbering volcano. What I was not prepared for was Fort-de-France and the beauty of the island and its people.

Artistry, Hypocrisy, Gastronomy

Just off the capital's clamorous quais is the very large Savane, from which the city's narrow streets debouch. Happily, the Gaullist building boom has left most of the ramshackle balconied shops, with their mansard roofs and clamped walls intact; for, together with the agglomeration of neon signs, pennons, traffic, turbaned market women and bereted sailors with red pompon, it is these streets which give Fort-de-France an exoticism quite lacking in Pointe-à-Pitre. The Schoelcher Library on the Savane fits into this scene perfectly. It is a cast-iron *art nouveau* extravaganza out of the 1918 Paris Exhibition; its red-and-blue Romanesque portal, Egyptian lotus-petal columns, and turquoise majolica tiles were imported piece by piece and put together in their appropriate setting of royal palms and tamarinds. It seemed somehow appropriate also that the Mayor of this city has been for a generation the Communist-Surrealist poet, Aimé Césaire:

> *From here I see Kivu descend towards*
> *Tanganyika by the silver stairway of Riuzuzi*
> *(a big girl at each step*
> *bathing the night with the rustling of her hair) . . . .*
> *And Africa, multiple and one*
> *vertical in the thunderstorm's change of fortune*
> *with its swellings and nodules*
> *slightly apart, but within reach*
> *of the century, like a heart in reserve.*

It seems just as appropriate and in no way surprising that Senator Césaire prefers to live in Paris and that the only sign of Communism that we could detect in his absentee bailiwick of 200,000 foot-loose souls was a street sign, which we passed on our way in from the airport:

"Lunick Bar." I recalled Camus' bitter observation: "The Frenchman has preserved the habits and traditions of revolution. The only thing he lacks is guts: he has become civil servant, Philistine, *midinette*. It was a stroke of genius to make him a legal revolutionary. He indulges in plots with official approval. He reshapes a world without stirring from his chair."

We walked over to the Centre d'Art and made a quick survey of the island's folk arts and high arts—not much. An exhibit of tapestries with figures or abstractions embroidered on them "by a dozen artists working in common" was featured. They were gay. I was impressed only by a group of two-inch-high molded clay figures around a crèche made from a hairy coconut; these figures alone were imaginatively conceived in flat planes and brilliantly colored in primary hues. I asked the director, Alexandré Bertrand, who turned out to be familiar with Haitian art and my role in its development, why the painters here couldn't use such colors in their canvases. It was the old story. They go to Paris and become "confused," or if they don't make that scene they try to emulate its fashions with the same result.

Bertrand closed the Centre for the siesta between noon and 3:00 and drove us to his home. In his studio he showed us his own work. Some oils were figurative, some abstract. I asked why.

"I go to Paris for a few months every year myself," he said. "While I am there I paint abstractions. But as soon as I return I feel compelled to paint what I see around me."

I asked why again.

"Surely," he replied, "it is impossible to paint in the old way or to paint figuratively in our modern civilization. I am always stimulated by New York. But the only way to paint New York is in terms of the machines and impersonal forces that have taken over. Only here are the problems still of the earth, of human beings struggling to make a living, and one cannot observe that without wanting to return to a humanistic art. Don't you agree?"

"Certainly not," I said. "There are just as many—in fact, more— human beings in New York, and their struggles to make a living are just as desperate. To paint abstractions is merely to close one's eyes to this, to escape from it into an art that appeals mainly to intellectuals and collectors."

Bertrand shook his head, opening a volume on the table. "I love Brueghel," he said, "but can one paint like that in a big city today?"

"Not precisely," I said, "but it may be significant that the artist whose work is touching the greatest number of people in Philadelphia at this moment, Andrew Wyeth, ignores the city completely, concerning himself only with nature and man resistant to change."

He showed us some of his notebooks, and they were filled with sparkling squarelles of palm trees lacing the sunlight, of market women and portrait heads.

"Why don't you paint like this," I asked, "instead of like that?" pointing to one of the murky, labored oils.

"You think I should?"

"Absolutely."

Passing back to La Savane through the Rue Lamartine, I expressed surprise that the poet was a Martinican.

"He wasn't," said Bertrand. "He never even visited us," he added, as we swung through the Rue Renan to the Avenue Victor Hugo.

"La même chose?" I asked.

"Le même chose. We have a passion here for naming our streets after famous folk from metropolitan France who would never have deigned to visit us—as though hoping to capture their glory."

As he said it, the name Apollinaire flashed by, Apollinaire who had never seen the chaplet of isles off La Pergola's gallery but who had written "Quand bleuira sur l'horizon la Désirade?"

"Voyez?"

Back at our hotel we were less saddened to see French culture filling the colonial vacuum in its crasser manifestations. Where else could one find such a slogan as the one that confronted us from our bedroom window—"Lieu d'Intérêt Touristique-Gastronomique"—or such bedspreads as the cheap Louis XV pastoral prints that covered our five-foot 8-inch beds: *la vue*, a courtier craning his neck over the décolletage of a milkmaid; *l'ordorât*, the same courtier fondling the same breasts; *le gout*, the courtier handing her a plate of fruit with one hand in order to put his other in her lap. And what is most French is that in each scene a third person is looking on from behind a tree.

The "Frenchness" of Martinique is a *fait accompli* certainly, but it is beset by certain hypocrisies and may turn out to be only skin deep. Or not even skin deep. For the vaunted French tolerance of race appears to be used in Martinique to cover a shameless economic exploitation of the black majority by white merchants, and on the social level there is a snobbery of the white or mulatto élite in which integration is but a principle on which they compliment each other. Gradations of skin color, frozen in a set of uniquely cruel laws by the French in colonial times, are not forgotten—either by the light-skinned élite or by those, less light, whom they push around with the subterfuge of money. Martiniquain song and dance, compared to Haiti's wild improvisation and violence, are reduced by class-conscious French propriety to a travesty of the African originals, and Aimé Césaire's Martinique poems are as neurotically obsessed by his blackness as are St. John Perse's poems of his Guadeloupe childhood by the ghost of his whiteness.

We had a memorable dinner at the Royal (Fort Royal) Restaurant, tucked away in an alley behind La Savane; oysters, red snapper in a golden cream sauce of exquisite flavor, hearts of lamb chop with tiny onions and fried potato balls, and crêpes suzettes, for $8 apiece, including

wines, negronis, and coffee—about standard for any good meal in a restaurant in Martinique, we were soon to discover. Obviously, the poorer
classes must eat at home; the poorer tourists, if there are any, are
hooked. The other side of French civilization we savored on the way
home: the stench from the foot-deep open sewers that border every sidewalk in the city.

Montagne Pelée and Grande-Rivière

One celebrated French artist did visit Martinique, and I thought of him
the following morning as we set forth up the west coast. There is no
memorial to Paul Gauguin, and he left not a picture behind him. One
theory is that he spent most of his time in St. Pierre—one of his pictures
in Europe show Mt. Pelée—and that most of the pictures he painted during his four-month visit were destroyed in the volcanic eruption on St.
Pierre fifteen years later. Before he arrived, Gaugin called Martinique "a
magnificent country, where life is cheap and pleasant," but, though he
was overwhelmed by the charms of the Negro women and learned to paint
the deep shadows cast by the sun with black, he soon succumbed to mala-
ria and dysentery and signed on as a seaman aboard a ship sailing for
Brest, never to return.

Even on this dry side of the island, there is no sign of the terrible poverty that almost sank Martinique during the war. Twenty-dollar-a-month
apartments above the capital, though more modest than these in Guadeloupe, nevertheless seem to have stilled the rebelliousness that seethed
in the Volga Plage slums six years ago; they no doubt also account for
the 86 percent "yes" vote for De Gaulle in the 1966 Presidential elections. Everything else on the island may be expensive, but there is
no sign of begging—except for the church with the gentle hint in
English over its collection box "God Bless America!" Beyond the
scrubby hills we came to fields of citronella and in the distance over them
the heavily wooded Pitons du Carbet, source of all the rivers north of
Fort-de-France. There is a fishing village, Belle-Fontaine, with, high above
the beach, a house shaped like a cruiser and at Fond Capot a monument
commemorating the governorship under Louis XIV of the Marquis de
Baas, whom our driver, Paul Thomert, identified most implausibly as a
brother of D'Artagnan. Cabet, at whose beach Columbus is supposed to
have landed on his fourth voyage, is only two miles from St. Pierre but
somehow miraculously escaped the holocaust.

Rounding a curve, we were in the famous destroyed capital, which has
now been rebuilt on a modest scale. There are a great many accounts of
St. Pierre's brilliance before the fireball struck in 1902: stories of the
eighteenth century, when the city was the sugar capital of the Antilles
and its square was the scene of mass hangings and agonies on the wheel,
and of the nineteenth century when its fireworks, carnivals, and masked

balls were memorialized in the pages of Lafcadio Hearn. Only Hearn seems to have had a poet's presentiment of the city's fate. "Some day there will be a great change in the city of St. Pierre," he wrote. "The green host will move down unopposed; creepers will prepare the way, dislocating the tombs, pulling away the checkered tiling; then will come the giants rooting deeper, feeling for the dust of hearts, groping among the bones; and all that Love has hidden away shall be restored to Nature, absorbed into the rich juices of her verdure, revitalized in her bursts of color, resurrected in her upliftings of emerald and gold to the great sun." Without knowing the city's tragic history, one would never guess that the scattered ruins visible here and there had any special significance. In fact, the figure of an agonized recumbent nude on a pedestal atop the broken stairway to the stone theater could be taken for a piece of neo-Roman garden sculpture in an abandoned villa, for no tablet tells the story.

The little museum near the shore is perhaps more impressive because of its sad state of decay than it would be if the exhibits were well arranged and comprehensibly marked—impressive in the sense of shocking. For what a pitiful memorial to those who perished! And how keenly one comes to suspect, for that reason, that holocausts teach no lessons to survivors and that the greater one toward which we may be moving will be as easily disregarded—if there is anyone left to disregard it. There were warnings in St. Pierre too, all blithely ignored. A photograph taken the week before the two final claps of doom shows the whole mountainside behind the city a river of fire. But the Governor came from Fort-de-France to reassure the people. Everyone said to his neighbor: "It can't happen here. Not to us." No one took warning. No one moved. No one survived. Except Cyparis.

In every dusty cabinet of the museum the evidence of this heat death, so perfectly prefiguring that in Hiroshima, is at hand: Singer sewing machines leprous with rust; a headless Christ with arms outstretched in benediction; piles of fused screws; a blackened flute with melted keys and a horribly twisted trumpet; six melted glasses nesting one within another; spaghetti, rice, and coffee carbonized in the bowls from which they were about to be served; books with blackened leaves (only the words "L'Exposition de Paris 1883" visible); checks on the Banque de France, never cashed; a melded knot of blue dying balls; a molten iron spiked fence; the smoky playbill of a forgotten drama entitled *Les Cloches de Cornville*, which never opened; keys to doors that were blown out; blackened wedding rings; watches that stopped at the decisive moment.

Most ironical is the story of Cyparis, the murderer who escaped from his cell a few days before the calamity, only to have pangs of conscience and return, thus becoming the lone survivor. There is a photograph of this bearded young Negro exhibiting his severely burned back. It seems that in the desolation he escaped again, or perhaps it seemed insane to

lock him up once more. At any rate he went to Dominica, where he lived for many years and finally wound up as an exhibit in Barnum & Bailey's freak circus in the United States.

Just as we were leaving, an aged blind man with snowy-white hair and red, rheumy eye sockets tottered up to me and said: "I was eleven when it happened; I am the last to remember exactly what happened." He rambled on for fifteen minutes like a cracked phonograph record. It was too much. I pressed a 10-franc note into his withered hand and rushed out into the sunlight, feeling guilty for being unable either to stop his monologue or to continue listening to it. Had he been Cyparis himself, I would have left him there. I didn't want any part of this holocaust—or the next one. Within five minutes we were peeling bananas, joking, and looking for a place to swim in the sunny Caribbean.

We drove on up the hill past the dormant volcano, wreathed in clouds at this time of the year and too slippery to climb, and on to Morne-Rouge and the lush gullies sloping to the Atlantic on the other side of the northern peninsula. Waves of pale-blue pineapple plants rolled by on either side, and further on there were bananas, the fruit encased in multicolored celophane sacks to protect it from the sun. From Basse-Pointe we had our first view of Dominica. A woman passed us on the road carrying a small red carcass on her head—*manicou* (opossum), Paul said. Mongooses crossed in front of us frequently but he told us that they are never eaten, for it is their job to keep the deadly fer-de-lance in check. Why this fearsome serpent of the South American jungles is found on Martinique is the subject of much conjecture, but the British explanation——that it was imported to keep the slaves from taking to the hills—is certainly an anti-French canard.

We had intended to swim in one of the rivers, but they turned out to be muddy and shallow, fortunately, or we would never have discovered the fishing village of Grande-Rivière at the island's extreme northern tip. When we drove down the cliff into it, a big catch of wicked-looking needle-billed *orphies* were being brought ashore. The steep part of the beach was crowded with sailing dories in various shades of pink, lavender, and yellow: *Ste. Marie Bernard, Gloire à Dieu, Grand-Père, Misère,* and so on. We swam where the rattling boulders gave way to a patch of black sand, and while Bill sketched the scene (with a boy holding a plank over his head for shade) I helped the fishermen to fold their heavy *filets* and pull incoming craft out of the surf. We had noticed two black heads bobbing about, half a mile toward Dominica; presently they merged, and a few minutes later an eight-foot log with two riders knifed up the shingle. These boys had been fishing for red snapper and a more startlingly red fish with moles, and their catch was ingeniously spliced to the "bow" of the log with long strands of stapled gut leader. We bought the entire catch of eight fish (for 7 francs, or $1.40) for Paul, who said it would provide one meal for his family of five. We had our own lunch of peppery lentil soup, stale French bread, cheese, and two bottles of local beer up the road a mile; by the time we'd translated the 20-franc tab to $4, we concluded that we'd been had. There were better beaches at Lorrain and St-Jacques on the way back, but we didn't regret having settled for Grande-Rivière.

One thing impressed us about Paul in retrospect: his camaraderie with the countryfolk. Once he stopped the car to take a piece of string out of his trunk for a peasant who was having trouble tethering a goat. We asked him if he had any plans to see the world, but he said he would settle for Canada. Why? "Because we enjoy visiting people with our own culture and language, our kind of people. They visit us and like us, so we like them. Most Americans come to stare at us because we're different."

We spent the evening looking for *doudous* but found none to match that Eugénie described in Pierre Duprey's story:

> Her hair . . . clearly East Indian, straight, black, shiny and luxuriant. Her eyes were distinctly Asian, tilted upward at the temples. Her Minervan brow and classical nose were a direct inheritance from some Sicilian peddler. Her full lips opened upon gleaming teeth in a wide African smile, and from Africa, too, came her firm, high and insolent bosom.
>
> It had taken nature perhaps a century to shape such a masterpiece as Eugénie. The same ingredients, combined in a more slapdash manner, might have resulted in a caricature, a grinning monstrosity.[4]

For that matter, we found no one to match even Eugénie's ample Madame who had no need to feel envy or "covet her neighbor" because her digesttion was so good, and who "slept the deep instantaneous sleep of the innocent."

"The French Select Our Heroes for Us"

Bertrand drove us to Trois-Îlets the next morning in a driving rainstorm. We drifted back to the subject of street names while stalled in the heavy traffic. "You have an Avenue Victor Hugo," I observed, "but where is your Avenue Victor Hugues?"

He laughted. "The French select our heroes for us. The Alsatian Schoelcher liberated the slaves according to the French rules. Josephine is one of their heroes, not ours. We are more than ever under their thumb— more so now than when we were a colony."

I told him about the $4 lentil soup the day before.

"They saw you coming. It was not always so. There was a time when a visitor was treated as a guest. That was before the French taught everyone in Martinique to steal."

Was he referring, I wondered, to the cunning system under which the French have made Martinique and Guadeloupe dumping grounds for their products? For, apart from their sugar and bananas, these "liberated"

[4] Pierre Duprey, "Elisa the Hustler," in Barbara Howes, ed., *From the Green Antilles, op. cit.*

black Frenchmen are permitted to produce nothing—not even *milk*, which is flown in by Air France from the mother country. Not even newspapers—for Fort-de-France is obliged to read the venal and chauvinistic dailies of Paris and to wrap its bananas in them. Not even coconut oil!

By the time we arrived at the famous plantation across the harbor, the rain had subsided. We were disappointed to learn that the remarkable mulatto Mayor, who doubles as the island's veterinarian-in-chief, was away attending to an outbreak of fever among the cattle. For Dr. Rose-Rosette is reputed to be the philosophical architect of Martinique's alleged "racial integration," and we would have liked to ask him about the economic exploitation and class snobbery that it appears to camouflage. He is also owner and founder of the little museum on the former Tascher de la Pagerie plantation. The compound is in a depression with no view of either the village of Trois-Îlets or the bay of Fort-de-France. Of the original buildings only the old sugar mill still stands. The museum contains copies of well-known portraits of the abandoned Empress, contemporary furniture, and one interesting exhibit, a love letter written by General Buonaparte from Milan on July 21, 1796, which was purchased at auction in 1934 for 46,000 francs and presented to the museum. Its final paragraph reads:

> Que fais-tu à cette heure? Tu dors n'est-ce pas et je ne suis pas là pour respirer ton haleine, contempler tes grâces et t'accaber de mes caresses. Loin de tois les nuits son longues, fades et tristes. Près de toi l'on regrette qu'il ne soit pas toujours nuit.
>
> Adieu, belle et bonne, tant incomparable, toute divine. Milles basiers amoureaux partout, partout.

There is some doubt that the *jolie laide* with the bad teeth was actually born in Martininque but none at all that she spent her childhood at Trois-Îlets. Mario Petreluzzi insists that she first opened those soulful eyes in a shop at Ste. Anne in Guadeloupe. She was only the most celebrated of four "queens" the area produced. Madame de Maintenon, Louis XIV's last mistress, whom he married in his old age, was brought up on Marie-Galante. Josephine's daughter Hortense became Queen of Holland and mother of Napoleon III. Aimée Dubucq de Rivry was kidnapped by Barbary pirates and became the influential slave and consort of the pacific Sultan Abdul-Hamid I of Turkey, who lost the Crimea to Catherine the Great. There is a legend that when Aimée as a young girl was walking in the *mornes* with her cousin Josephine, they were accosted under a mango tree by an old Negro witch, who told their fortunes. "You," she said to Josephine, will be an empress and you," pointing at Aimée, "more than an empress." Josephine's imperial career reflected a combination of Creole frivolity and common sense. As mistrees and wife she was a fickle spendthrift who deserved what she got, but, after the divorce, Napoleon regretted not having taken her shrewd political advice, and drifted into disaster.

lands save Martinique from the French during the Napoleonic wars, observed that French shipping was evading the guns of St. Lucia to the south by passing between the Martinican coast and the precipitous 600-foot rock lying off-shore. A hawser was therefore rigged from the deck of the *Centaur* to the faceted summit. Five naval cannon and a party of 120 men and boys were hoisted to the top, where, for seventeen months, they commanded the passage, living on hardtack, rainwater, and an occasional bird. The mile-round bastion was promptly commissioned as a sloop of war, *H.M.S. Diamond Rock*, and so it has remained—at least in British naval records.

Shaped like a plum pudding, framed by the swaying palms on the lovely beach of Diamant, Diamond Rock faded away in the sunset—and with it the peaks far beyond of St. Lucia, our next destination.

Part 3. St. Martin and St. Barthélemy (St. Barts)

An island and a half of the French West Indies remained, and although we visited them several months later, the description of them belongs in this chapter.

The half-island is St. Martin, lying between St. Croix and Anguilla, which the French have shared amicably with the Dutch since 1648. Actually the French have twenty of the island's twenty-four square miles, which led to the legend of the partition having been accomplished by a Frenchman and a Dutchman starting back-to-back on the beach and walking around the island until they met, with the Dutchman drinking Holland gin along the way and thus slowed down to a staggering walk. But there is no historical basis for the legend at all. The Dutch came first in 1631; were driven out by the Spaniards; came back in 1644 under Peter Stuyvesant, who gained nothing but the pegleg that was to be his trade-mark later on in New York; and, finally for good returned from St. Eustatius along with a French party from St. Kitts, four years later.

Marigot, Where the French Speak English

French St. Martin has doubled in population and changed in many other ways since Leigh Fermor and his party were marooned in its "odious'" capital twenty years ago for four days of almost insupportable boredom. "Listlessness, we were to learn, was the essential characteristic of the town; that, and an absolute characterlessness that was so extreme that it contrived to develop from a negative attribute into something destructively positive." Marigot has changed—but not enough.

Classes in the schools are conducted in French, though the Negroes, who make up 90 percent of the population, speak nothing but English; and the colony's whole future, if it has one, will depend on American tourism. What is particularly ironic is that hardly any of the largesse that De Gaulle showers on Guadeloupe and Martinique comes to St. Martin— though during the war St. Martin backed De Gaulle and the Free French solidly, whereas the two larger islands sided with Vichy. For a long time the French wouldn't agree to make the whole island a free port, and until they finally did, in the 1930s, such absurdities as evading the prohibition to "carry" liquor over the border by *tossing* demijohns of cognac across went on. That situation left the French with only one way of topping the Dutch who were (and still are) getting the lion's share of the island's tourism. The Dutch had 120-volt electric current, so the French put in 220. It didn't work though. The French plant promptly broke down; the French part of the island is now buying current from the Dutch. I asked a Frenchwoman in Marigot about this problem, and she threw up her hands philosophically: "Alors, ça ne fait rien; we both get our drinking water from Guadeloupe, n'est-ce pas?"

Marigot lies on the big protected bay due north of Simpson's Pond, which fills most of the triangular island's western peninsula. Anguilla, with those matchless beaches and spirited liberty lovers we'd heard about in St. Kitts, is fifteen minutes (or three hours' swimming time) to the north, but the beaches all along St. Martin's coast, from Marigot clear around the point to Philipsburg, the Dutch capital, can hardly be improved upon. The sand is powder white, and the blue-green water shelves off very gradually without any breakers or undertow. On a hill overlooking the harbor is the ruin of Fort Louis XVI, named after that ruinous king, and below it the new forty-room Hôtel de Paris is going up; it too is ruinously expensive, from all the signs, and across the bay an even bigger and costlier monstrosity, La France, with 200 rooms, is rising, in a frantic bid to catch up with the enterprising Dutch, whose *yanquis, si!* policy is so far attracting all the local tourist trade.

French St. Martin, withal, has much to offer. The food, especially at Le Pirate and Le Tropical, is superior. Marigot's architecture, with its gingerbread wooden balconies, supported on spring-like iron brackets, has charm, and there are good shops along the waterfront. As all the higher terrain on the island is on the French side, there is more rainfall, and everything looks much greener. [The French were given their half, it seems, when St. Kitts was French, and the Dutch hoped that they would keep an eye on the British across the bay in Anguilla.] Today, with the Anguillans clamoring for independence, or even American citizenship, such proximity may prove dangerous.

St. Barts: Pirates to Pilots

St. Barthélemy, better known as St. Barts, is the least French of the French Antilles and probably the most alienated from the mother country. It was settled by the French a few years before St. Martin was, but Gustavia (then known as Carénnage) was never more than a pirates' and smugglers' haven. At the end of the eighteenth century the island was ceded to Sweden in exchange for 6 million francs and French commercial privileges in the port of Göteborg. For the hundred years that the Swedes held sway the island enjoyed great prosperity. It was declared a free port almost at once. The trim stone houses that ring Gustavia's square harbor went up. But, from 1878, when St. Barts again became a colony of France, to the post-World War II period, when the present modest tourist boom began, the tiny island's economy steadily declined. The last Swede, we were told, died in 1966.

We had been talking in the St. Maarten airport to Hippolyte Ledée and Georges Greaux, two of the three pilot-proprietors of the Windward Islands Airways. Would they fly us to the Dutch islands of Saba and St. Eustatius? They would be very glad to arrange our schedule in such a way that we could spend a day and a night in St. Barts as well, they said, and they were quite frank to add that they both operated export-import businesses there and wanted as many people as possible to discover "this little paradise with the best beaches in the Caribbean." We accepted their generous offer and didn't regret it, though we wondered later whether or not they would have steered us directly to the French island had they known that we'd be bedding down at the hotel operated by a rival pilot, Rémy de Haenan.

Crossing directly over Philipsburg's half-moon harbor, we flew south, with Saba and 'Statia off our west wingtip, and then banked sharply eastward to St. Barts' six-year-old strip, which must be approached "blind" over a ridge connecting two hills. Eden Roc and Autour du Rocher are the only two of St. Barts' five little guesthouses that are near beaches. We chose the former, and in a few minutes Madame de Haenen was serving us another of those irresistible French lunches from which one recovers after nothing less than a two-hour siesta. At 3:00 Madame Henri Querrard (we hadn't seen a man since we landed) was driving us northwest in her taxi to untouched Plage de Flamands facing the mountainous satellite of Bonhomme Island and inhabited by wild goats. A little beyond, at Pointe de Colombier, St. Barts' western tip, is Anse Rockefeller; David Rockefeller, the family banker, has his $200,000 cottage there, accessible only by boat. St. Barts' 2,200 inhabitants (2,000 Catholics and 200 Protestants, according to the official count) are 95 per cent French of Norman-Breton descent. Blond, blue-eyed Celts, they still speak the Norman dialect, and the elders still dress in the traditional costume. We saw several crones in the *kichnottes* (white coifed bonnet) and ankle-length skirts cultivating their sweet-potato patches enclosed by stone walls or plaiting latania for the island's only folk product: hats, flask covers, and bread servers of woven palm.

It hadn't rained for thirty days, and the rugged little island, which depends for its drinking water on run-off barrels and twenty small wells, was dun brown. A scattering of sapodillas and stunted mangoes vie with the cactus in the lee of the pitted black boulders, but St. Barts is virtually treeless. Turning south to Gustavia, we sampled the dozen free-port stores on the waterfront; they make St. Barts, together with French-Dutch St. Martin, the cheapest place on earth to buy perfumes and liquor. Other free ports, like St. Thomas, have a 6-10 percent tax, but in St. Barts and St. Martin all the world's luxury exports, Russian included, are available 100 per cent duty-free and untaxed. What impressed us more was the uncommercial spirit of these merchants. We tried to buy a bottle of Trinidad Old Oak rum that we saw in one shop, only to have the salesgirl, after searching in her ledgers for fifteen minutes for the price, direct us across the street to a rival shop. We offered a drink to a black seaman on a fishing boat at the wharf and asked him where the best beach was to be found. "Edinburgh, Scotland, man!" he said.

St. Barts' roads have no hairpin turns. They go straight up and down, whatever the grade, and so did the concrete ramp connecting the Eden Roc and its annex, to which we now returned to dress for dinner. Suddenly the rains came, and, when they come in St. Barts, they don't fool around. As soon as the cloudburst was over, we slid down the ramp in total darkness, sloshed across the road ankle-deep in water to the slippery ramp on the other side that leads up to the main building. Standing in the doorway was a waiter with a flashlight and an umbrella.

We had breakfast the following morning with Rémy de Haenan, the embittered pilot who was our host. Tall, lean, bronzed, and sandy-haired, he has a face like a Stone Age hatchet, with his nose as the cutting edge. Born of Dutch parents in London, he was brought up in Brittany, captained an expeditionary fishing boat to St. Barts in 1938, joined the French navy in St. Martin, and after France's collapse settled on the island rather than serve the collaborators under Admiral Robert. He now divides his antipathies among France, De Gaulle, Guadeloupe, and the Windward Islands Airways. The last, he assured us, monopolizes the inter-island trade by cunningly playing off the four nationalities involved against one another. He himself had opened the airstrip on St. Barts in 1947, after learning to fly in Miami and Puerto Rico. His pioneer plane was a Rearwin Sporter with an eighty-five horsepower Leblond engine and nicknamed "La Cucaracha." The hoteliers have to be pilots, he pointed out, because, unless one flies in one's supplies, "one starves or goes broke." He'd lost the inter-island concession to Windward, but he continues to fly charters.

De Haenen thinks St. Barts has a very limited future both as a resort and as a real-estate bonanza. "With 2,200 people already occupying 8,000 acres, how much room for expansion is there? So many people claim ownership of any given plot that it's almost impossible to establish clear title. Six thousand dollars an acre is the average price now. Rockefeller got his 140 acres ten years ago when land was cheap. What the island needs most is a deep-water pier and a distilling plant for fresh water. De Gaulle's policy is disastrous for us. Everything is centralized in Paris. He wants to make Martinique and Guadeloupe showpieces, and since we're under Guadeloupe they get—how you say?—the big money. There's a strong independence movement over there, goodness knows why. But if they secede from France, we'll secede from them. Who wants to be run by Guadeloupe's blacks?"

IV

THE ENGLISH-SPEAKING
WINDWARDS

Part 1. St. Lucia

It may be bad strategy in war to acknowledge a tactical defeat. A reversal in the field, especially when it comes at the very opening of a campaign to establish a new beachhead, may discourage the troops, as well as the public. But, in writing a book, the commander has no troops, and the public cannot be kept in the dark without censorship. St. Lucia did not eliminate itself from our itinerary as Cuba did, and it is too big to sweep under the map. The failure was ours—with generous assists from the weather and our diminishing funds, which precluded sitting out the downpour. We have no doubt that there are as many omniscient citizens, critical intellectuals, and plain characters on St. Lucia as on the other islands, but we didn't find them. We have even less doubt that the island's natural beauty matches that of the others, but when we were there it was barely visible. The hotels were par for the course. We did our best, cursed time and the weather, and passed on.

Fires, a Volcano, and Doctor Dolittle

Castries, St. Lucia's capital, is no help to a traveler with a will to be pleased. It has been ravaged by fires as many times as the island has been torn by revolutionary conflagrations. The fire of 1948 was the worst. It leveled the little that was left of the old city. As a result, Castries' graceless concrete, tin-roofed houses in no way conform to the beauty of the harbor—one of the deepest, most sheltered, and, because of its

117

ring of steep hills, most easily fortifiable in the West Indies. This last fact alone probably explains the unusual violence of St. Lucia's history. The Caribs, in their retreat southward, had tried desperately to hang on. So, with their superior weapons (and as little luck) had their successors the French and the British. It was from his anchorage here at Gros Islet that Admiral George Brydges Rodney had sallied forth in 1783 to defeat François Joseph Paul, Comte de Grasse, at the Saints, after his lookout on Pigeon Island had apprised him that the French were quitting Martinique. But it wasn't until 1814 that the English dug in to stay, and, in the years between, successive bloody assaults on Morne Fortuné above Castries made St. Lucia a shuttlecock in the imperialist game being played by the two powers.

Victor Hugues appeared in his familiar role, with his deputy Goyrand setting up the guillotine in the town of Soufrière to the south. Castries belles took to wearing skirts with pictures of the ghoulish engine printed on them in red to prove their revolutionary fidelity. Those romantic captains of the Napoleonic wars, Ralph Abercromby and John Moore of La Coruña, led successful charges only to have this "Helen of the West," with her fatal gift of beauty, restored to France as "expendable" in the diplomatic games being played at Amiens and Versailles. Between 1800 and 1834 there were no fewer than thirty-three governors; most of them succumbed to yellow fever. Black guerrillas ranged the high mountain jungles from the Pitons to Dennery. Small wonder that St. Lucia never developed a stable plantocracy or a docile labor force, that it remains untamed and unpredictable to this day, and that it gave birth to the best West Indian poet:

> . . . *here where the summer never ends . . .*
> *To change your language you must change your life.*[1]

At the rain-swept airport we were welcomed by Mr. Milne-Marshall of the Tourist Board, who drove us to the office of his chief, Mr. Bergasse, who in turn found us accommodations for the night at the St. Lucia Beach Hotel, set behind a splendid palm-fringed beach overlooking Pigeon Island. It was nice to be among friends again and not to have the feeling that we were merely being tolerated—tourism being something that De Gaulle needs at the moment, even though its participants (ourselves and all Americans) are carriers of a subculture that must not be permitted to contaminate Marianne.

The rain was coming down in sheets, but it was now or never: The Pitons might be invisible, but Soufrière's sulphur pits we could find with our eyes closed. Driving back through Castries, we detoured a bit, look-

---

[1] Derek Walcott, whom we were about to meet in Trinidad, taught school in St. Lucia for a few years and wrote a widely reprinted poem about his childhood memory of the fire that destroyed Castries, but as the poem is an early piece and leans heavily on Dylan Thomas and Robert Lowell, I prefer (as I'm sure he would) to quote from his mature work in this book.

ing for anything to certify that the town wasn't really Jersey City. A sign reading "Stop Here for Medical Gymnastics" could have been in Los Angeles. Another, "Hand in Hand Bar: Licensed to Sell Intoxicating Liquors," was more reassuring. Passing through groves of coconut palms banded with tin to keep the rats grounded, we hairpinned up the steep hill from which (weather permitting) there is said to be a fine view of the capital, the Vegie peninsula, Rat Island, and, farther north Pigeon Island. The houses on the hill gave us some idea of what Castries must have been like before the five fires. Some have rosette windows of jigsaw, and the ancient stone Government House sports a lacy wooden crown.

Vernon, our driver, pointed out the few big sugar estates, now converted to banana growing. There were originally four mills. The Americans dismantled one to build their World War II base at Vieux Fort. One belongs to Dennis Bernard, the island's largest landowner. The Dutch-English Geest Industries owns the other two. I asked Vernon if there was any agitation to expropriate these large holdings.

"No, sir."

"Would it be a good thing if they were divided up?"

He smiled. "I wouldn't say that, sir."

I asked him if there was any lumbering on the forest-clad Mt. Gimie and its surrounding peaks, which stretched away into the clouds as far as we could see.

"St. Lucians no longer like to cut wood," he said, "so houses in the countryside are now made of imported pitch pine." Food is imported too, judging by prices we sampled in a local grocery.

We passed Anse la Raye and Canaries and, after about an hour's driving, caught a distant view of the Pitons, two almost identically shaped conical mountains, thickly wooded, that rise half a mile steeply out of the shoreline beyond the town of Soufrière. In the rain these volcanic extrusions of a submerged mountain range look like sheeted ghosts. All climbers, until quite recently, were defeated by the combination of crumbling steps and deadly serpents.

The smoke of the low-lying crater came into view on the other side of the town. We drove into it and then walked through several acres of yellow-gray hillocks that look like slag and smell like rotten eggs. The ground is too hot to stand still on, and among the hillocks are dark-gray boiling pools with temperatures ranging from 214 to 350 degrees Fahrenheit. It's an impressive spectacle but has none of the beauty of the irridescent hot springs and silvery geysers of Yellowstone. There was no trace of the therapeutic "Louis XVI Baths," in which earlier travelers languished. High red immortelles and a low bush with shiny green leaves, which the self-appointed guide called *a-ou-li* in his Creole patois, form the background.

The patois reminded me of Haiti, and so did the identical names of towns along the coast: Anse à Galette, La Tortue, Anse Cochon, Frégate, Cul de Sac, La Voutte, Marigot. So did the avalanches threatening to cover the road and the half-naked peasants with their machetes—but not the cellophane banana bags with which they protected themselves against the downpour. Just beyond Soufrière, where, the previous year, Elizabeth II had come ashore from her yacht to drive to Castries, we observed, across a cemetery of black crosses and graves heaped with camellias, a row of twenty-five aluminum gas tanks, each containing one letter; together they read, "Au Revoir * God Bless Our Queen."

We stopped at Marigot, a lovely little harbor nestled in the hills just south of Castries, to see the Yacht Haven Hotel, where Twentieth Century-Fox had set up headquarters to film *Doctor Dolittle*.

Vernon had been filling us in on the most talked-about event in St. Lucia since the fire of 1948. The philosophy of Hugh Lofting's hero— "What does money matter, as long as we are happy? We'd be much better off if it hadn't been invented"—seems to have been wildly at variance with that of the advance agent for the shooting of the $15 million picture. The agent was nicknamed "Nervous" as soon as he arrived in Castries. "Why am I nervous?" he had responded to an American yachtsman solicitous for his health. "You'd be nervous if there were 500 people bucking for your job! But I've got what it takes here to open the doors on this li'l ole island," he added, opening his briefcase and showing his astonished acquaintance $50,000 in United States currency.

"No beads?" I asked Vernon.

"No beads," he replied, "but they pinned plastic leaves all over our trees."

I didn't find out why until we ran into the yachtsman Carl Schuster later on in Grenada. "I asked 'Nervous' the same question," he told us, "and he said, 'To make the leaves shine better—just like God would've done if he'd had the money.'"

We were disappointed to learn, when we reached the Yacht Haven Hotel, that "Nervous," Rex Harrison, and most of the company had already departed. "How did they ever make Harrison up to look like the little old bald-headed doctor?" I asked Vernon.

"That wasn't the problem," he replied astutely. "The problem was to make the little old bald-headed doctor look like Rex Harrison."

Morne Fortuné: Unlucky Hill

Eight miles from both Marigot and Castries, on a commanding hilltop, are the ruins of Morne Fortuné, the ironically named "Lucky Hill," which has changed hands in so many bloody encounters. The hill is surrounded by massive brick barracks, ugly and empty, which served as a regimental headquarters during World War I, and it is hard to believe that age will ever make their offensive practicality seem romantic as it has the graceful bastions of less utilitarian times. The stubby monuments don't help much either. One commemorates a charge led by the Duke of Kent, Queen Victoria's father, in 1794, just a year before Goyrand and his French

Revolutionaries seized the island. Another cites the Royal Inniskilling Fusiliers, who took the island back briefly in the following year. There are no monuments, of course, to Goyrand or Hugues, though their claims to have acted in behalf of the people of St. Lucia are at least as good. But it may be in tacit recognition of the spurious motives of both nations that the St. Lucians have let the site of these heroics fall into decay. For the visitor an aura of shabby futility pervades Morne Fortuné —at least that was how we felt as we climbed down the hill. The cannon-ball trees still bear their suggestively lumpish fruit. But it is as hard to imagine the sense of purpose that drove the redcoats to lay down their lives as it is to re-create the idealism of the French whose bodies were dumped into unmarked graves—or for that matter to visualize the re-puted brilliance of nineteenth-century social life among the upper classes in the drab, jerry-built oven that is Castries today.

Vox Populi

St. Lucia, like the rest of the once-British Windwards and Leewards, is now on its own, and it doesn't take any perspicacity to predict that its personality from now on will be of its own making and that it will be a happy or embittered personality in accordance with its people's capacity to govern themselves. The natural verve and potential creativity of these 100,000 Negroes, emerging from so many centuries of foreign harass-ment, are already beginning to assert themselves in small ways. The split personality is beginning to coalesce. Carnival is no longer overloaded with such obsequiously Anglican tableaux as Victoria mourning Prince Albert and Raleigh mopping up for Elizabeth I; and the carousers no longer carry "Drink Less Rum" signs. There is a lively theater, inspired and directed by Derek Walcott's twin brother, Roderick. There are also four newspapers, which carry on a spirited political debate, in sharp contrast to the moribund press in most of the other small islands.

I was still carrying with me copies of the St. Kitts *Democrat* and the St. Kitts–Nevis *Daily Bulletin*. The first featured a pretentious speech by Robert Bradshaw to the Arts Festival, which aired his familiarity with such cultural phenomena as Leonardo, Schubert, Beethoven, and the Bible, not neglecting "the Gobelin and the other great tapestries, the knitting of the late Queen Mary, and the crocheting of the great Mahat-ma Gandhi." The second presented on the front page this item of veiled political significance, quoted here in its entirety:

A decomposed carcass of an animal, partly wrapped up in a circus bag, was seen early this morning in front of the entrance of the Government Headquarters in Church Street, Basseterre. It appears that some miscreants are responsible for this act. Passersby were attracted by the smell.

Journalism in St. Lucia is far from sophisticated, but it is at least free and *engagé*. We spent part of the following morning with Mr. W. St. Clair Daniel, the intelligent editor of *The Voice of St. Lucia*, and the rest of it reading the uninhibited political exchanges carried on in his and the other three Castries papers. Daniel told us that he had just been "nominated" to the ten-man governing council of the island to "supply balance," as he put it, vis-à-vis the eight elected members of the (liberal) United Workers Party and the two from the more socialist "outs" the Labour Party. The lead article in his well-printed paper that morning was by Maurice Laurencin, a graduate of Tuskegee Institute; it began as follows:

> I have said enough on the question of necessity and inevitability of unification. And I am beginning to bore myself. It has been a religious thing with me to express myself on the matter with a religious lack of guise or polish only to discover that my deficiencies may have insulted the intelligence of you gentle people, my people. I have never lost sight of my severe limitations and need of learning. And I don't think my style, though painful, has been unsuccessful.

Laurencin went on to say that bananas, no matter how much they may go up in price, will never equal the high prices of imports and that St. Lucia will never escape from this economic dilemma until it starts making "toothpaste" and the other prosaic products that its people must use daily. But, above all, his article concluded, St. Lucia must federate *politically* with the other islands and not follow the divisive counsels of "those who give a posture of primordiality to economics in their philosophic discourses."

There was none of this humility and long-range thinking in the opposition's *Crusader*, a gritty sheet printed on a hand press, barely legible, but with plenty of spark:

> It appears that the Honorable Chief Minister is determined to knock out every simple St. Lucian who is likely to pose a challenge to him. . . . Persons of responsibility and those professing dignity should also practice it. We have always regarded as a mockery and a farce the proclamation of those who shout "Holier than Thou" when in a testing period their Satanic qualities reach the surface faster than the speed of sound or light. The UWP profess to be an aristocratic party of this island, although they call themselves a Workers party, but their aristocracy is only veneer when they leave their Ministries, their Legislative Council, and Government House, the sum total of their aristocracy. What do we see out in the fields? A veritable reversion to type. Scandalous, crude and savage. We witness the breaking up of a Labour Party meeting by children who are given 500 "SOUFLET BLAD" to blow while the meeting was in progress. . . . Men are born great, they cannot have greatness thrust upon them. They will always revert to type. And so it is with the UWP.

A letter deploring work permits, the brain child of a UWP minister who during the war had had three merchant ships torpedoed under him, appealed to the minister in these terms: "The true blood of St. Lucia flows in your veins. And it is the truth that St. Lucia has produced few heroes. But once a St. Lucian becomes a hero he must learn to *die* a Hero."

The final letter surely represented the Voice of the People:

Sir: I was in Castries last week and I hear the UWP boasting that even if they put up a "Mornshe Pilop" the UWP bound to win the Dennery seat. Man, that make me see "Blue Murdee"!
Yours truly,
Furious

Part 2. St. Vincent and Bequia

What emerald couched in a star-sapphire sea, upper pendant of that Grenadine chain whose nether diadem is Grenada, shaped like a teardrop, capped by a benign volcano, jealous of its hidden falls and lakes, ringed by scimitars of sand—but it's no use. Everyone makes as good a case for his favorite island with an almost identical catalogue of attractions. And St. Vincent's shadier aspects—its routed Caribs and abortive revolts, its wobbly shift from sugar to bananas, its current Black Power regime, its roads that go everywhere except to the major sights, and its hotels that cater only to the very rich or the very poor—are typical enough too.

Everything is jammed on the south coast at the teardrop's heavy end: Kingstown, the capital, with its daily schooner service to Bequia; the airport; the hotels. Everything, that is, except Baleine, the great cascade with its natural fresh-water swimming pool, which lies a mile from the sea at the northern tip of the island and can be reached only by chartering a launch for the day, swimming ashore, and ascending the river; and Soufrière's crater lake, many hours' hike from the road's end at Orange Hill and then a hazardous scramble down the crater's lip and up again, 1,000 feet each way.

An old island handbook that we discovered browsing through the library of friends in Kingstown contained a vivid eyewitness account of what happened at Soufrière on May 7, 1902. Though there had been an eruption of the volcano in 1812, "our generation had seen nothing but beauty and loveliness in the pearly green sheet of placid water which perpetually lay in the crater . . . the most beautiful sight in the West Indies." On May 2 Montagne Pelée, 100 miles to the north beyond St. Lucia at Martinique's southern tip, exploded. The terrible news of St.

Pierre's destruction arrived on May 3, and at the same time the earth in St. Vincent began to tremble sympathetically, and the small remnant of Caribs in the neighborhood began to flee. At 6:00 in the morning on May 7, a vapor cloud that had built up 30,000 feet high above the lake "began to yield to solid matter." At 1:55 in the afternoon "a terrific huge purplish and reddish curtain advanced up to and over Richmond Estate." By 4:00 lights had to be lighted in Kingstown, but already a climactic burst had been observed by vessels at sea. "In bright daylight the whole atmosphere quivered and shimmered with wavy lines intersecting each other like trellis work. We were encircled in a bristling ring of fiery bayonets. A mighty bank of sulphurous vapor and smoke at one time assumed the shape of a gigantic promontory, then a collection of twirling, revolving whorls . . . cauliflowers efflorescing into beautiful flower shapes, some dark, some effulgent, some bronze, others pearly white, and all brilliantly illumined by electric flashes. . . ." Fortunately there was no city, and very few settlements, in the vicinity. The disaster couldn't be compared to the hurricane three years earlier, which had killed 300 people, destroyed the whole sugar crop, and leveled half the buildings on the island. The flames in Soufrière's belly subsided. Miraculously, the lake resumed its original position.

The man-made conflagration that seared St. Vincent in the late eighteenth century was less benign. The planters had descended upon St. Vincent in the 1760s by way of Barbados, Antigua, and the American colonies. But the Caribs, pushed farther and farther south from St. Kitts, Dominica, and St. Lucia, as we have seen, were by that time firmly entrenched in St. Vincent and prepared to fight for the fertile little island.

In the beginning, they were no match for the English, who proceeded to parcel out the best orchards and grazing lands into enormous sugar grants. There was a brief interlude between 1779 and 1783 when the French seized Kingstown. In 1793 Captain William Bligh arrived from the South Seas with his 300 breadfruit seedlings. But the decisive moment came in 1795, when emissaries from Victor Hugues in Guadeloupe brought news of the slave insurrections there and in Haiti and promised to furnish arms and leadership for a grand assault on the English cane fields and fortified positions.

Joined by the French still resident on the island, the Caribs set fire to the outlying great houses and cane fields and, in two skillfully deployed forces, defeated the reinforced English time after time, holding Kingstown in a pincers for almost two years. The turning point came when General Abercromby seized St. Lucia from the French, cutting off the Caribs' most convenient source of arms, and descended upon St. Vincent in force. The Caribs lost a great battle, and on October 27, 1797, 5,080 men, women, and children surrendered to the British. Only two small villages of Indians, Sandy Bay and Morne Ronde, were permitted to survive in the wild north end of the island and then only on condition that sugar would never be cultivated there. The 5,080 Caribs who had surrendered were taken to Bequia, and from there were loaded on transports and shipped to the uninhabited Bay Islands off Honduras and the Central American coast of Belize, where their descendants intermarried with escaped Negro slaves.

Aspects of Kingstown

Most of this history, and as much contemporary lore, we had from C. G. Huggins and Fred J. Dare of the St. Vincent Tourist Board, who deposited us at the Blue Caribbean Hotel on the waterfront, and from two remarkable Vincentians with whom we made friends the following day. Edgar Adams, a sometime optometrist and all-time Caribophile, is the island's most articulate intellectual. Ken Punnett, a businessman from one of the island's most influential planter families, was our host after we returned from Bequia.

What a relief it was to be in a run-down commercial travelers' inn again! For the Blue Caribbean, like the Sea Side on St. Kitts, has character enough to compensate for its discomforts. There was rain on the roof and a high wind whipping through six unclosable windows and two rattling transoms. There were lots of mosquitoes and, to take care of them, on the bedside table an inflammable device labeled "Fish Mosquito Destroyer. Courtesy Blood Protection Co., Ltd. of Hong-Kong. Enjoy eight hours of peace awake or asleep!" We never could make the shower work, though its controls were equipped with abstruse directions. I read them aloud to Bill:

To Use the Simplex Shower

There is a switch on the outside of the bathroom door. When this is OFF the knob should be upward and must be brought down to switch on the current. FIRST pull the lever of the shower down to the middle—the water will flow COLD. SECOND. Pull the lever away to the opposite end—the water will then become HOT. Pull the lever *gradually* back until you get the desired warmth. When you are through ["Call an electrician with medical training," Bill interjected]—the water becomes COLD again. Pull back the switch. The water will turn OFF. But THEN—after *please* turn the switch OFF, that is, UPWARD.

Messrs. Huggins and Dare had taken us to this bizarre establishment reluctantly, and they insisted that we take a tour of St. Vincent's gold coast the following morning. We asked Huggins, on the way to Fort Charlotte, where a Canadian group is about to launch a major development (Ottley Hall), what distinguishes St. Vincent from the other islands.

"Quiet," he said.

As he said it, we passed a waterfront spot with the intriguing name West End Nitery. It had been St. Vincent's only nightclub, Huggins said, and it had closed down. There was once a nine-hole golf course, he added, and it closed too. Passing fields of arrowroot, the starchy tuber that is St. Vincent's second export crop, we detoured a bit to survey the Marriaque Valley, with its red-earth fertility, contoured hillsides, and rushing river. This brown torrent, the Mesopotamia, takes its name from a town at a confluence. Toward the sea it becomes the Argyle, and there, driving beside the black-sand beach, we caught an ugly glimpse of the brutality that poverty always engenders. A score of peasants were waiting by the roadside for a truck and cracking coconuts with a machete. The truck arrived, but it was already so full that only half of them were able to scramble abroad. One lanky ten-year-old boy with nothing on but a short ragged shirt failed to make it and fell to the road screaming. He must have yelled out that his knees were injured, because he was immediately seized and spread-eagled—presumably to "straighten" his legs. Those in the departing truck roared with laughter. Those left behind comforted him but also laughed. He clung to his mother's neck, sobbing hysterically, but, when we offered her money for medical attention, she laughed too. We left feeling guilty, not so much for being better off as for having witnessed their humiliation and having failed to soften it.

Almost immediately we were plunging through the hotel strip east of Kingstown, where nobody laughs but everybody smiles and all comforts are available at a price. The Sugar Mill Inn is cozy, with a marvelous view and a pool ingeniously constructed in an old molasses vat, but it seemed to be empty. Perhaps it was suffering from the same problems as the Blue Lagoon Guest House, whose driveways were a wallow of mud and whose tiny beach under the cliff was strung with barbed wire. It seems that a gentleman named Steen Nanton, who lives just beyond it on the point, doesn't want white interlopers next to him—or hopes to take the hotel over if it fails. It is he who has kept the road from being paved and the beach from being used. When a guest got mad and cut the wire one night, Nanton sued the hotel for trespassing and won. His brother, Newton Nanton, is a lawyer to whom the government is said to be heavily indebted.

The same government (in return for what? we wondered) rents the most desirable tourist site in St. Vincent, Young Island, to an American ex-Hiltonite, John Hauser, for the incredible monthly fee of B.W.I. $50. Young Island is a towering rock a few hundred feet off shore with a white, sandy beach below and the Young Island Hotel in the middle. "Charter your own Private Island in the Caribbean," says the brochure, "a twenty acre tropical paradise of fragrant flowers and fruit trees . . . a tropical village for twenty guests with all the comforts and conveniences, swimming, snorkelling, water-skiing, and a handsome 42-foot schooner to sail the fabulous Grenadines or the coast of St. Vincent. And a second island, Fort Duvernette, with its ancient cannons and embattlements, is yours too."

It's no exaggeration, either. We crossed over to the larger island from the dock after Mrs. Polly Hauser had shown us her gift shop, which carries the usual basketry, Dominica rugs, and cute paintings. (Two unusual items are white-duck jackets, frogged to buttons of bamboo stick, and shifts of flour-meal sacking printed with rampant cocks in faded colors.) The layout of Young Island is a demonstration of what can be done with half-a-million U.S. dollars, if you have the taste—and a way with self-governing island bodies. The Hausers evidently have all three. The dozen or so cabanas already built are reached by climbing steep stone stairways. On the beach are a dining pavilion, a beautifully designed bar with long clouded-glass lanterns and other lights in wicker baskets, a salt-water pool, and a shallow basin for the chef's fresh fish and lobsters. We had a memorable lunch, featuring banana bread hot from the oven, with an American couple staying there with their three children for the off-season rate of U.S. $75 a day. Next time, they told us, they intend to take advantage of the special $2,800 a week rate, which may be shared with twenty friends when you charter the pair of islands in the off season, ocean-going yacht included.

Tom Johnston's Moon Hole

We had to settle for the milk run in the dilapidated schooner *Whistler* that takes off at the Kingston pier for Bequia every afternoon at 1:00. Where the channel suddenly sinks to 200 fathoms, the sea boils in a rocking cross rip. It often rains too. The two-hour trip is not recommended for those with any tendency to *mal de mer*.

Bequia (pronounced *Bek*-wee), the northernmost of the Grenadines and second in size and population to Carriacou, the southernmost, is one of many "peaks" of the submerged volcanic mountain range into which the Windwards tail off. It is six miles long. Its width varies from a mile to a few hundred feet. It belongs to St. Vincent, as Carriacou belongs to Grenada, but for a long time all the Grenadines were privately owned by absentee landlords, who used them only occasionally as sheep preserves or duck blinds. Most of the smaller islets are still so owned, and there is a brisk trade in them as canny hotel magnates snap up one after another as hedges against the larger islands' diminishing privacy. But what drew us to Bequia even before we had reached the Caribbean was the growing fame of Moon Hole.

Elsa Voelcker, a friend who was having a "cave" transformed into a "house" (sight unseen) by the uncompromising proprietor, Tom Johnston, had procured for us an invitation to spend a night with Johnston and his wife Gladys at Moon Hole. Wild rumors of what we might expect

had already come to our ears in Kingstown. Johnston was a "Little Caesar" who might push us over the cliff if we criticized any part of his architectural fantasy. Johnston was such a "moody genius" that he probably wouldn't speak to us at all. Our conventional American friends at Young Island had seen the circular hole in the cliff, as they passed by in the hotel's yacht one day, and they described the eccentric structures beginning to crowd the opening as "a do-it-yourself nightmare." A wit at the Blue Caribbean had remarked, "I'd heard of a hole in a wall, but this was the first time I'd seen a wall in a hole." A lady at the Sugar Mill, who said that she was a friend of the Johnstons, told us more charitably, "It's really livable, ingenious, and quite delightful—if you don't mind dampness, salt spray, and the feeling that a hundred tons of rock may bury you any moment."

Our arrival was not auspicious. The note with the date of our coming had not been delivered. It was only by chance that a Land Rover was at Elizabeth Harbor and was able to drop us at Paget Farm (Bequia's other town), where we transferred to a rowboat with an outboard motor, which took us to an improvised pier six feet above the choppy water, onto which we hoisted ourselves and our gear. From the beach a narrow flight of flagstones embedded in cement circles the cliff to the towering natural bridge that gives Moon Hole its name.

It would be an exaggeration—and a defamation of his character—to say that Tom Johnston received us with open arms. But, considering the fact that he had had no notice of our sudden intrusion and that his wife was engaged in frantic preparations for dinner for a dozen guests to whom two uninvited interlopers had to be quickly added, his restrained welcome to us was an act of signal generosity. "Take the room at the base of the Hole," he said brusquely, "and spend an hour poking around for yourselves. Cocktails will be served at seven."

We scrambled down the stone catwalks to our lower berth, the one we surely would have chosen if given the choice. We found out later that it is called the "Whale Room" because you can sometimes see a whale spout in the distance without lifting your head from the pillow. Two of the three sides of this shelter have been cut into the cliff a few feet above the breakers; the third and largest is wide open to the sea. Directly below, a small swimming hole had been gouged out of the cliff's base, its "running" water supplied by the pounding waves. Turning, one is obliged to look straight up to see the stupendous jagged arch through which the moon peers. Climbing up and passing through it, we took the path across the island's narrow neck to Elsa's house in progress. There is a beach on this shore, and the doorway faces it. One of the half-dozen houses that Tom Johnston has built here in the last year or two, this one will be larger than most. Costs average between $5,000 and $7,000, about equally divided between labor and imported materials. The rocks are quarried at the site and shaped by hand. The water pipes and plumbing fixtures are the simplest. Tables, furniture, doors, and window frames are made of local woods, though occasionally bleached purple-heart from Guiana is used. The windows, some very large, are of rippling plexiglass. "Sofas" are carved out of the corners of the rock wall and then covered with foam rubber, Mexican blankets, and bright cushions. The railings are of bone from the whaling station across the bay at Petit Nevis. The narrow walks and steep steps connecting the various houses and their patios are protected against the dropoffs by stone pillars linked together with anchor chains salvaged from the sea. Capstans thrown up on the beach and fish-trap markers of green Portuguese glass enclosed in webs of rope are used as decoration; sometimes they are embedded in the door frames. There is no electricity. The powerful beams of Coleman lamps are sufficient and plentiful. The planting in and around the rock walls is attractive: varieties of fern and ivy, epithytes in loblollies, wild-pine parasites with orange berries, figs and frangipani, portulaca and sea grapes. There are wild hyacinths in rock pools, but there is a limit to what can be done because Bequia is dry—at least a lot drier than Peter Brand's Dominica.

Moon Hole is neither a tourist hideaway nor an artists' colony. Its inmates are neither sybarites nor those who like to rough it. It is not a place to save money in or to get a "quickie" sun tan (going to and from it alone is expensive and time-consuming). Its appeal is to people who are a little surfeited with "good taste" and want to get close to nature without going native—interior decorators; professors of English and art history; *aficionados* of folk crafts, marine biology, and the like. Above all they must be people who like the Johnston style and defer to it. Even Johnston's wife, the first time she came, exclaimed: "Take me away! I'm never coming back!" But she came to accept Moon Hole and finally to love it.

We had plenty of time to talk with Tom Johnston the next morning. We caught him at breakfast playing chess with Gladys. His chess is non-conformist too: The instant his opponent moves, he moves. The game was over in five minutes.

Nothing in his past prepared Tom for Moon Hole—except temperament. At Princeton (Class of '33) he played football and wrestled. Back in Illinois he wrote advertising copy. He had no particular interest in architecture. He was not mechanical. "In fact," Gladys said, "he couldn't (or wouldn't) even fix a storm window. The only thing I can remember his building was a horse stall, and the horse kicked the walls down a day later. Even here," she added, "you couldn't say that Tom is interested in the *mechanics* of Moon Hole. The last thing he puts in a house is a door latch, sort of as an afterthought, or when begged to do so; and he isn't interested in leak-proof roofs either. If they leak, he just keeps patching until they're waterproof."

Tom, who is a big bear of a man, shaggy-maned, crusty, almost truculent, put it this way: "If these friends I've built houses for here had given me *plans* I'd have called it quits. It's a friendship deal—the friends

have to trust me. . . . Engineering? Hell, no. I build by rule of thumb—
my thumb. When I put these reinforced-concrete beams up, I allow one
inch of depth for each foot of span. Probably it's too much. But I prefer
to err in strength, if only because these native boys who build for me
are no more experienced than I am. For the same reasons I use a stronger
cement mix than customary."

He paused, scanning the horizon through a hole in an unfinished wall
like an old salt in a crow's nest. "It's a great help not to know too much.
For instance, I've been told *never* to use salt water in the mix. Too late.
I'd already used it. And it works."

"Do you have any fears," I asked, "that the great stone arch may cave
in one of these days?"

"Sure, sure," he said. "Why not? Everything caves in sooner or later.
You know the saying, 'Dig yourself a hole in the wall, and pull the hole
in after you.' It's all a risk, and that's what makes it interesting—for me.
For most people it would be impossible. The cruise ship *Meteor* comes
by regularly, just to show tourists what the crazy American has done.
We amuse ourselves by saying that we'll arm the boys with spears and
shields and, when the ship passes again, have them leap out of the
bushes on top of the arch and drop a dummy riddled with arrows across
the opening. Another idea I toy with is to have a gigantic lamp with a
shade set up in the opening, so they'll be reminded of their picture
window back home."

His Bequia boys, Tom added, cotton very much to his method of
building without an exact image of how things will turn out. "It gives
them ideas of their own. Some of these ideas are very good. Of course,
once in a while there's a window here or a niche there or a closet behind
that abutment I don't like. I don't say anything, but a few days later it
disappears. If there's a tree, a stalactite, or a view we like, we build
around it. We're all creating together. If it weren't so, and we weren't
having fun doing it, it would never work." And it does work!

Tom came to St. Vincent first in 1939 after four years in the advertising business. He'd worked on a British ship carrying freight among the
islands and liked St. Vincent. During the war he was in the navy in the
Pacific and in Trinidad briefly. By 1961 he was thoroughly disgusted
with life in the United States, especially with keeping in step socially,
and made his first visit to Bequia. One day on a walk he saw Moon Hole.
Two years later he bought the twenty acres of land in the narrow neck
of the island; his land varies from 70 to 200 yards sea to sea. "My hedge,"
he interjected, "is a 105-acre farm in Virginia thirty miles out of Washington, which I've never farmed but which goes up in value constantly."
I asked him about taxes in Bequia.

"Once the tax assessor came with a tape measure to measure the 'four
walls.' Since he couldn't find four anywhere, at least no four that made
a square, he laughed and said, 'It's not a house!' and went away. Anyway, the Bequia District Council is now so proud of the whole damn

layout, it says, 'No house taxes!' The tax on land is 75 cents an acre."

At noon, after we had been swimming and snorkelling over the reef in front of Elsa's house, Tom picked us up in the tender to his ketch-rigged motor-sailer and ferried us to Port Elizabeth, where we had lunch with Phyllis and Mike Sprange, a Canadian couple whom we had met at the pier the previous day. They were operating the Bequia Beach Hotel, which shares the modest tourist trade with the somewhat larger (twelve rooms) Friendship Bay. We had time before catching the schooner back to Kingston to visit one of the best hand-craft and shell-work shops in St. Vincent, Linda Lewis' The Crab Hole.

The World of Ebenezer Joshua

We were to meet Edgar Adams at the Kingstown Library that afternoon. He wanted us to see its collection of Carib artifacts, but we exhausted it in the ten minutes that elapsed before he arrived. Some pieces were scattered on tables, others shoved under a wooden stage. There was not a single complete piece, but several indicated skill in ceramics and painting. Edgar told us bitterly that one Swedish museum has 3,000 pieces from St. Vincent, all in good condition. He was also bitter about the fact that there is no book press in the West Indies. "Publishers in the United Kingdom," he said, "print only what they want to hear about us. Eric Williams'[2] *Capitalism and Slavery* had to be published in the United States. The British didn't like the idea that they had abolished slavery for economic rather than humanitarian reasons."

We walked to a bar, talking on the way about what happens to intellectuals once they have had a taste of power. I kidded Edgar about his beard: "The first time I saw you, I thought you were a Ras Tafarian."

"I have nothing but contempt for that cult," he said.

"Why?"

"Because they're free-loaders. They think the world owes them a living."

"We're free-loaders at the moment," Bill said with a smile. "Tourists, at least, pay their way."

"You have a job to do," Edgar said charitably. "The tourist oscillates comfortably between the past and the future. He likes to be shown the suckers from Captain Bligh's breadfruits at the Botanical Garden. He is reassured to hear that the Beatles enjoyed Young Island and that Princess Margaret swam on the beach at Bequia they've now named after her."

[2] Eric Williams, chief proponent of the abortive West Indies Federation, is Prime Minister of Trinidad and Tobago. The book was written when Dr. Williams was Professor of Political and Social Science at Howard University, Washington, D.C. See Chapter V.

We asked him which of the island's political parties he belonged to.

"Neither," he said. "They stand for the same thing, basically—themselves. The important thing is that we get on our feet and realize our potentialities within our limitations. What has politics got to do with that? It is only an encumbrance. We really can't afford the obsolescent luxury of fighting over the spoils. Our real problems—how to balance exports with imports, how to control our growth—can only be solved within federation. Deciding how many bananas or how much arrowroot or copra to grow is absurd without regional planning."

Ebenezer Joshua, St. Vincent's Chief Minister, is the Vincentian counterpart of St. Kitts' Robert Bradshaw, and, like Bradshaw, Joshua came to power via his island's monolithic trade union, which he bosses. His People's Political Party (P.P.P.) has been in office ten years. In the last election it polled only 48 per cent of the vote, to the opposition Labour Party's 52 per cent, but it has remained in power through its control of the districts, seating five of its representatives on the Legislative Council to Labour's four. There are actually eleven members, two of whom are nominated by the Queen (as in St. Lucia). In the past these two were traditionally a planter and a businessman and could exercise veto power over "extreme" legislation, but at present the Queen is permitted to act only subject to the Chief Minister's recommendations, with the result that Joshua controls these two votes as well. As one of the P.P.P. seats was won by a margin of only four votes, the Labour Party has demanded a second round of voting. If it wins, it will control the government.

This change is what people like the Punnetts—and doubtless many others—are praying for. Ken and Phyllis, with whom we spent our last night in St. Vincent, are gentle people, very "English" in the sense of abhoring that peculiar combination of stupidity and ruthlessness that goes hand in hand in the Ebenezer Joshuas. They would have no objections if the black ruler of the island *practiced* socialism, they said. "What we object to is his *preaching* it as a means of despoiling the industrious, and then, instead of throwing the spoils to the impoverished, giving all of it to his affluent henchmen." Mrs. Punnett, a model of the prudent, principled, respectable middle-class housewife, seemed especially shocked by the "brazen" conduct of the Chief Minister's wife, recently appointed Minister Without Portfolio by her husband. We had already heard of Ivy Joshua's reputation as virtual dictator in the backlands district she represents in the legislature. I asked Phyllis whether or not it is true that Mrs. Joshua is illiterate. She laughed. "If one were to charge her with illiteracy, her constituents would rally to her support even more. After all, they're illiterate. Would they want to be represented by someone who wasn't one of their kind?"

Part 3. Grenada and Carriacou

Travelers who have "discovered" Grenada and made it their home away from home rest their case for calling it the most desirable of the Lesser Antilles on two grounds. First, it is the small island with the greenest mountains, the whitest beaches, and the prettiest capital. Second, its people are the friendliest and the least spoiled. All three parts of the first ground are matters of opinion. Dominica's mountains are higher and more generously watered; those on Montserrat and St. Lucia are as deeply viridian. The beaches of Antigua, St. Kitts, Barbuda, Anguilla, and the Virgins are as dazzlingly white and far more extensive. The architecture of Curaçao's capital is more distinguished than is Grenada's and more colorful, though some may prefer the bucolic charm of St. George's, steep winding lanes to Willemstad's busy canals. But, on the second ground, we could find nothing to quibble over. The friendliness of Grenadians, rulers and ruled alike, is overwhelming, and it seems to rub off on tourists, even to affect those who come to snap up bargains in hotels, transportation, and land. We could never have sampled in two days the incredible variety of what Grenada and its environs have to offer had it not been for the fact that everyone we met insisted that we miss nothing—and meet everybody else. Yet all this hospitality was conveyed with such a combination of relaxation and gusto that, instead of leaving in a state of exhaustion, we had to force ourselves to board the plane to keep to our schedule.

We drove from the north-side airport over the mountain pass to St. George's on the south coast—the usual full hour's drive, costing B.W.I. $14. Halfway over we passed the rather forlorn Grand Étang, which lies in the crater of Grenada's inactive volcano. The steel-gray lake is in a 3,816-acre forest reserve, a commendable and probably unique piece of conservation in the improvident Indies. The road was being repaired, and crushed stone was being brought up entirely by women's head power. We almost had a collision with an oncoming car. A peasant woman was standing in the middle of the road on a curve, splitting bamboo for a hat. She refused to budge. Our driver leaned out and said to the other driver: "Up to now, dat lady hasn't move yet!" and they both roared with laughter.

Mrs. Grenada

We drove into St. George's. There was a double feature playing at the local movie house: *Thug Island* and *The Face of Fu Manchu*—nothing out of the ordinary there. We drove on a long search for Gertrude Protain and found her—everything out of the ordinary there. She is big, buxom, bountiful. We had hardly introduced ourselves before her handsome black face was wreathed in smiles at the thought of the predicaments our two-day visit might get us into. "So the thing you want to do first is play tennis?" Laughter brought all the curves of that curvaceous body into play. "That's wonderful. I like that. Today at five you'll play with my son, who's quite a chahm-pion, and his girl friend. Tomorrow you'll play with the Minister from Trinidad and the wife of the Chief Justice. You boys'll *need* that exercise to limber up for the rest of what I'm planning for you! Get rid of that cab. He doesn't drive fast enough. I'll drive you myself. Throw your bags in the trunk. We won't get you to where you're staying at the Spice Island Inn until long after dark. Denny and Daisy Gilmore are giving a party at the Ross Point; they don't know it yet, but I'll be taking you—will the other girls be jealous! And then maybe we'll stay for some of that calalu soup and lambi. I'm phoning Dr. Watts to meet you at the Spice Island later."

"We'll *need* a doctor," Bill gasped.

"Dr. Watts is our leading social scientist. The only reason he isn't Chief Minister is that he's outspoken and offends people. He'll probably offend you. Then you will sleep—"

"Are you *sure*, Gertrude?"

"Not at all," she gurgled, "but you better, somewhere, somehow, because tomorrow we'll drive to the waterfall at dawn, getting back in time to attend the opening of the Legislature, visit the Willcoxes—."

"Take in a *shango* ceremony—?"

"Right, right! It may have to be tennis under the lights that night. The day is used up already. But the *next* day we'll relax on the beach to be ready to sail to Carriacou Friday."

"Friday! You forget we're leaving Thursday."

She wrung her hands in dismay. "Then you'll *never* see Carriacou or talk to Mr. Redhead."

It was our turn to do some positive thinking. "Don't worry," I said. "We'll get to Carriacou. We'll slip in that six-hour sail before Thursday. Gertrude, if you think we're leaving this island without talking to Mr. Redhead, you're crazy."

How the Nutmeg Brought Freedom

"The profligate disorder swells with sap juice, seed, pod, frond, raceme and spore: the island sinks with richness, barely stable. Dark opulence over us, spice in our nostril and under our feet the wealth of deaths that hangs on air the bright and heavy fruit." [3]

We'd done everything on the Tuesday-afternoon part of Gertrude's agenda—and a lot of other things—by the time we reeled in to Alan Krassner's beach-side hotel and were assigned to a cottage a sand flea's

[3] Josephine Jacobson, *The Nutmeg Factory*. Courtesy of the author.

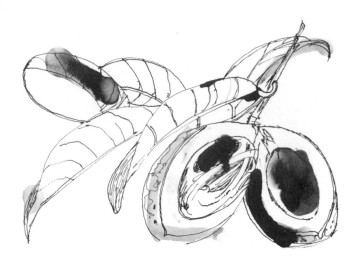

hop from the blue water. Krassner is another of those talented refugees from Madison Avenue—television in his case—with a lobby full of Haitian paintings and a head full of island lore. His Spice Island complex, with a splendid view of St. George's and its fort across the bay, was designed by Colin Laird, an English architect who is presently turning Trinidad upside down.

"What's for dinner?" we asked gauchely.

"Dinner's over. Where have you been?"

"With Gertrude."

"That figures. What'll you have?"

"Anything to sober us up for Dr. Watts. Who *is* Dr. Watts, by the way? Did we dream him up?"

"Dr. Watts," Krassner explained patiently, guiding us to a table in the empty dining room and sitting down with us, "is the founder of the in party.[4] He is able and self-assured but too bumptious to dispute the leadership with Herbert Blaize."

"Blaize?"

"Chief Minister. He's a self-taught accountant from Carriacou, but conservative, the kind of man who wants a 'paper' prepared on the height of every hydrant. His crowd wear halos, like the Anglican Presbyterians they are. But this is a Catholic country, and Blaize wouldn't dare advocate what Grenada needs most—birth control—before genteel poverty gets out of hand. He wouldn't go against the pattern of West Indian man, the drone who fathers the children and leaves them penniless with the dominant matriarch. Blaize is an ineffectual ruler. Gairy at least can say yes or no."

"Gairy?"

"Okay I'll go back a little. You've noticed the naturalness of the Grenadians? They have the least built-in prejudice. Why is this so? Because

[4] It became the out party again early in 1967, when Eric Gairy succeeded Herbert Blaize at the helm.

there has been no white ruling society to speak of for two hundred years. In the eighteenth century the French and English made a shambles of the place. In 1795 news of what was going on in Haiti and Guadeloupe reached the slaves, and with the news Julien Fédon—"

"—came straight from Victor Hugues?"

"Precisely. Fédon took over the whole island except for St. George's. Then the English under Abercromby struck back. Fédon disappeared! Naturally he became a legend, half hero and half monster. Well, the English who came back for good (militarily speaking) had lost everything economically. When the slaves were freed in 1836, that did it; the few planters left packed up and went home. The ex-slaves wouldn't cut sugar, and the Maltese imported from Trinidad to cut it turned into shopkeepers. The Negroes made a good thing of cocoa for a while, but in 1843 the first nutmeg trees were brought from the Dutch East Indies and planted on the same Belvedere estate where Fédon's rebellion started. The land was already in small parcels. Tending nutmegs was a family affair involving little labor; you sent the kids out at noon to pick the nuts and remove the mace. It was only in 1951 after Hurricane Janet—the *only* hurricane Grenada has ever had, by the way—uprooted most of the trees, that there was this shift to bananas. But the new nutmeg trees are already beginning to bear. Before '51 the average wage on Grenada was forty-eight cents a day. The economy was controlled by a tight little group, and there were bloody riots that year when the first union was established. Eric Gairy became the island's popular leader. Up to then it had been Theophilus Albert Marryshow, Grenada's George Washington, editor of *The West Indian* and intellectual leader of the middle-class anticolonialists. Marryshow never married, but he had ninety-six children; even the few who weren't intimately connected with him loved him."

We had already heard Gairy described as "two parts opportunist, one part crusader" and as "the Adam Clayton Powell of Grenada." We had also heard that federation with Trinidad was the current burning question. I asked Krassner where the two leaders stood on it.

"Up to Janet we balanced our budget," he said. "Grenada was one of the few, if not the only, island to achieve this miracle—but ever since the union took hold and wages multiplied we've needed massive aid. Blaize's solution—and it's a will o' the wisp, and the more people realize this the shakier his hold gets—is federation. You'd think that Eric Williams, whose power base is the black majority in Trinidad, would be in favor of federation with us, but Williams fears adding 80,000 indigent black Grenadians to his disciplined political machine as much as the old Negro bosses in Harlem fear the Puerto Ricans." The Grenadians, Krassner added, have insular prejudices of their own: They tend to call Bajans (people from Barbados) "sly mongeese" and Trinidadians "thieves." Gairy's comeback bid would seem to be well anchored in his opposition to union with Trinidad.

We'd taken in so much that first half-day that it was a relief to receive the message that Dr. Watts wouldn't be calling on us till the following night.

Blaize, Gairy, and the Willcoxes

I must have been dreaming of Grenada's predatory neighbors, because it struck me at breakfast that the beady-eyed black grackles that fought over our trays had the capitalist mentality. When Bill threw a whole piece of toast out on the beach to get rid of them, one grabbed it in his talons and flew to a tree. Now, if those greedy birds could learn to save and bank . . . But Gertrude Protain, whose contrary impulse is to share the wealth, was already at the door.

The meeting of the Legislative Council came to order promptly at 10:00 that morning. A huge silver mace was brought in by the Sergeant-at-Arms

and placed on an upholstered cradle. The Speaker (F. J. Archibald) and the Deputy Speaker (Dr. Watts) took off their wigs. The former intoned an abbreviated Lord's Prayer. On a dais under flags were the portraits of the Queen and her Consort. The chair for the Queen's representative was vacant. Bobbies in white jackets with silver buttons, blue trousers with a broad red stripe, and silver spiked pith helmets strapped under their chins stood at the doors. The proceedings were genial. The members, chuckling from time to time, seemed to be enjoying themselves. When asked a repetitious question about "unitary federation with Trinidad," Blaize won a laugh by answering, "He who has ears to hear, let him hear." Presently Gairy strolled out, and I buttonholed him on the gallery. "Why do you oppose union with Trinidad, Mr. Gairy?"

"Because," he replied, rolling his "r' "s, "Dr. Williams and his crowd are not in a position to solve our problem. After all, we're not much smaller than Barbados, and *they're* doing all right alone. With hard work we'll get along. Why should we denude ourselves of this Legislative Council and our other offices? Why should we become a county of Trinidad?"

"Do you favor independence?" I asked him.

"Not right now. We must try the new constitution we're getting in February and see how it works. You realize, I hope, that my party won a big majority in '62. The elections were rigged. They removed 17,000 names from the electoral lists and put 10,000 nonexistent ones in."

"I've heard that Blaize's party favor's birth control. What is your party's position on it?"

"That's an insidious, controversial question," Gairy said. "The answer to it is good housing, industrialization, the best use of the land, encouraging investment."

I asked Gertrude on the way to Annandale how she sized up the two leaders. She thought Blaize was a good man and extremely honest but overcautious. His party represents the rising middle class, which claims that Gairy "ran the island into bankruptcy with his squandermania." Gairy's is the party of the little men, the masses; at least, it claims to be. Gairy, I gathered, was a man with more charisma and less judgment, though Gertrude agreed with Krassner that he was to be admired for stating his views forthrightly.

Annandale Falls is on a private estate twenty minutes out of town. There is a deep pool at the base surrounded by silk-cotton and saman trees. We had a swim and drove back into town to meet John Benjamin, a local painter whose work, so similar in its meticulous detail to that of the Haitian Philomé Obin, I'd admired at the Spice Island Inn. I looked at his new work in a restaurant and asked him why he was now painting in such a variety of "modern" styles, none of them understood and all of them inferior to his own. "I went abroad to study art," he said, "so I feel I must experiment and take risks."

On the way to Westerhall Point, where the Willcoxes had invited us to have lunch with them, we noticed a cow in a field with its head painted blue and "Merry Christmas" scrawled in red paint across its belly. Such decorating is done, it seems, when any domestic animal strays into a neighbor's yard. We stopped at l'Anse aux Epins to inspect a house that Gertrude was building as a hedge against her retirement from the Tourist Board. She had been the first woman legislator in Grenada, she told us, after teaching school for a pittance for years. "But I couldn't afford public office at $120 B.W.I. a month—even the First Minister only gets $600." In her maiden speech, I was told later, Gertrude had not hesitated to cross the formidable Marryshow on the topic of slum conditions at the Children's Hospital. She'd gotten action too, my informant said. The house Gertrude is building will rent for U.S. $60 a week in and out of season. I counted sixteen men at work on the three-bedroom bungalow. The building costs would come to B.W.I. $15,000, and the half-acre of land, far from the desirable ocean, had cost B.W.I. $6,000.—A total cost of U.S. $12,000–$15,000: not cheap. Land and labor must be paid for in cash; a mortgage covers the rest.

Westerhall is a long, narrow 110-acre peninsula that Beresford Willcox, an English architect, and his Norwegian wife Kari, also an architect, bought in 1959, when it was covered with jungle. For four years they employed forty men to plant trees and shrubs—"including 800 flamboyants, probably a greater number than existed in the whole island"—and such exotics as cyperus grass, Australian callistemon, and several varieties of the Brazilian rubbery-pink kalanchoe. Conservationists as well as botanists, the Willcoxes became concerned about the near extinction of the green turtle—"which lives on nothing more than seaweed yet could feed the world." The survival factor of these "cows of the sea" is only 1 per cent. So the Willcoxes have been picking up 300-900 eggs a year on the beaches of their little marina and releasing them "fully armored" nine months later.

In between these life-giving labors, the Willcoxes have designed, landscaped, and built twenty-five of the sixty-five very unusual houses that their development will ultimately contain. People of many nationalities have been encouraged to move into them and have done so. The average house costs U.S. $30,000 with one-half to two acres of land included. Each is imaginatively designed and *different*—in the Peter Brand sense. None is air-conditioned or mosquito-wired; they need not be. They are built to catch the steady trade winds off the ocean. The pitched roofs cross the walls with a good six inches to spare for cross-ventilation all the way around.

There is no way to describe the Willcoxes except to say that they are beautiful people—physically, intellectually, spiritually. After lunch, to the accompaniment of a Mozart quintet, they showed us their pre-Columbian collection, the finest Arawak-Carib pieces I have ever seen, comparable in the sensitivity of their modeling to Totonac work from Mexico. It seems that when a bulldozer was clearing the jungle it struck a midden; all work was stopped dead for two weeks while the Willcoxes re-

moved each artifact carefully. They also showed us a remarkable piece of folk art: a crucified Christ and ladder in a cod-liver-oil-bottle. They had bought it from its maker in the town of Gouyave up the coast.

Back in town we visited a first-rate gift shop, Tikal, which specializes, oddly, in Guatemalan folk arts, and then had a drink at Carl Schuster's Nutmeg Bar & Restaurant. Schuster is a Dartmouth man, Class of '27, and another of those refugees from advertising. He exchanged, as he put it, "security [Young & Rubicam] for paradise." When he took over the restaurant, it was grossing $30 a day; now it grosses $300. One of the things he had to do was teach the local cooks not to pound steaks with pop bottles. On Friday nights a combo (vibraphone, bass fiddle, guitar, bongos) plays. Schuster charters his famous sloop, the *ZigZag*, winner of many races on Long Island Sound and the Caribbean, for trips through the Grenadines and beyond. I told him bluntly that we had a problem.

"We have one day—tomorrow—to see Carriacou and no funds to charter yachts."

"I'll take you," he said. "Be at the dock at dawn."

Dr. Watts Speaks His Mind

Dr. Watts arrived at our hotel after dinner. He had seen me talking to Eric Gairy at the legislative session. When I told him what the opposition leader had said, he looked outraged.

"If there was electoral fraud, why didn't he complain officially? He says this only for foreign consumption. When he was in power, he was investigated for misappropriating funds. There was an independent inquiry in 1962. For the first time in our history the Constitution had to be suspended by the Colonial Office in London. Blaize could have had him prosecuted, convicted, and jailed, but Blaize is a decent fellow. Since 1956 Gairy has never polled more than 11,000 out of 40,000 registered voters. When the voters turn out, he always looses. G.U.L.P. isn't a party at all; it's a one-man cult. Gairy just happened to be the man who took advantage of the rioting in 1952. There was a bad situation. The plantocracy was paying estate workers a little as 20 cents a day. Gairy organized what he called "The Manual and Mental Workers Union"—he's totally illiterate, I suppose you know—but it wasn't a union at all, not affiliated with either the T.U.C. or the A.F.L.-C.I.O."

I was more surprised by Dr. Watts' comments on Haiti. He had attended the same meeting of the Caribbean Tourist Association to which Mary Pomeroy had flown unannounced, and he'd been chosen President for the coming year. He'd met François Duvalier, and he'd been impressed. Duvalier had told him that he should be "proud that Henry Christophe, the first and only king in the West Indies, came from Grenada."

"Is that what impressed you?" I said with a smile.

"I have an open mind," he said. "I found him interesting. He complimented me on being the first black President of the Association."

"You mean," I said to the political leader, whose skin is several shades lighter than Gairy's or Blaize's and not much darker than mine, "that every past President had been *white?*"

"Well," he admitted reluctantly, "not exactly white but much lighter than I am. Besides," he asked as a happy afterthought, "as an American, you should like Duvalier. Wasn't he the first to take a stand against the communists in Cuba?"

I gagged and changed the subject to Grenada. The reason Grenadians were friendlier than the other islanders, Dr. Watts said, was that there were more small landholders there than anywhere else. (There are at least 1 million more in Haiti, but the point was well taken, for only Haitians could be called as friendly.) "We don't have a one-crop economy. The country folk are organized into producers' cooperatives—nutmeg, copra, bananas, et cetera. These are statutory bodies protected by government ordinance. The man in the street is friendly because he's satisfied. Workers in the field are also often employers. This is a reason why unions don't thrive here. And why tourism takes root slowly. We want hotels and tourism, but we don't want foreigners taking over our country. Have you noticed that there are six access roads to this beach? They had to be put in before the hotel could start business. So that Grenadians could get to the beach if they wanted to. Not that they'd ever intrude on you—they're not that kind of people. But they want their national rights. We're unique in this respect too: There's never been a racial problem here. Barbados had to pass a law against discrimination. St. Vincent has its Caribs."

I asked him about birth control. "The Planned Parenthood Association is active," he said. "We allow contraceptives in free of duty. What more can we do?"

"And unitary federation?"

"We're negotiating with Trinidad. They need our agriculture and tourism. We need their industrial power. It's better to be a big fish in a pond than a little fish in an ocean. What the hell we need a Prime Minister for?"

Carriacou and the *Shango*

The *ZigZag*, built in Huntington, Long Island, in 1956, is a thirty-five-foot auxiliary sloop with a lead keel; mahogany topsides; fittings of bronze and stainless steel; sails, sheets, and halyards of Dacron; and a Gray Seascout four-cylinder engine with a 6.5-knot speed. Under sail alone the *ZigZag* once maintained a speed of 7.6 knots for seventy miles. Schuster charters her at U.S. $70 a day (plus food at cost) for cruises ranging from one day to two weeks in duration. To date, his longest charter cruise has been to St. Thomas in the Virgins.

That day at the dock there was a crew of one and two other passengers beside ourselves: a distinguished liquor importer and reputed smuggler from St. George's and a shy but slim wisp of a thing from La Paz, Bolivia, who never opened her mouth during the eight-hour expedition. She had no need to, for Schuster is an entertainer who combines the best features of Johnny Carson, Alexander King, and Groucho Marx with a devouring curiosity and an encyclopedic knowledge of everything Grenadian. The monologue ranged from Catholicism to Columbus, Shostakovich to *shango*.

For example, he told us that the Church (all churches, as a matter of fact) is concerned that only 10 per cent of Grenadians with children ever marry. One reason that they don't is that a "decent" marriage party costs $100 or more. A sign that went unheeded at a recent church fair read: "Legitimize Your Children!"

At Dyke Island to the north an unmarried property owner with a large family has taken the precaution of building an enormous cross with slots in it for the deceased.

At Hillsborough, Carriacou's capital, a priest whose assistant had said to him, "But Father, we *have* no Holy Water," responded, "Take some ordinary water, and boil the hell out of it!" In a sermon another priest described paradise as containing cows; when asked why, he replied, "If you were reincarnated as a bull, you wouldn't ask."

A man in St. George's built furnished honeymoon cottages to let at £10 the night—"including bride."

To illustrate the saw that Grenada is a man's world, our liquor mogul told us what happened when he intervened once to stop a man from beating his wife; the badly beaten woman protested: "No! No! He beat me sweet-sweet!"

We asked him whether or not the tiny corner of Carriacou that belongs (by a geographical fluke) to St. Vincent facilitated smuggling. "I asked a native of the island the same question once," he replied, "and his answer was 'Hell, no, we don't need it.' "

Ed Link, of Link Trainer fame, has sailed with Carl, and they share a theory about Columbus' first landfall with which Admiral Samuel Eliot Morison (for whom Carl expresses considerable scorn) doesn't agree. According to Schuster and Link, all Columbus' descriptive phrases about the first island sighted—bean-pod-shaped, with a harbor capable of holding all the ships of the world and a beach alive with iguanas—fit Cacos, and *none* of them fits Watlings. Morison simply sat at the tiller like the professor he is," Schuster said, "with that copy of a copy of Columbus' log abstract in his lap, and sailed from the Canaries this way and that, three leagues to port, twelve to starboard, et cetera. He has the gall to say, when the great navigator mentioned seeing an island that didn't appear on Morison's horizon, 'Perhaps he mistook a cloud for an island'! *Our* theory respects Columbus' navigation."

We had good reason to respect Schuster's navigation as he guided us in alternating squalls and dead calms past Ronde, Diamond, and Kickem Jenny into Hillsborough's ample harbor. We swam ashore, and at the dock I split my big toe open on a submerged coke bottle. It was repaired according to ancient island custom in the corner grocery with a bottle of Jack Handle (raw rum), and we proceeded by car to explore as much as we could of this lovely island, inhabited by 8,000 prosperous fishermen. From the French fort on the high point there is a fine view of three more Grenadines: Petit Martinique, Petit St. Vincent, and Prune. (The last has been tastelessly rechristened Palm by an American hotelier who has just bought it.) We had a drink with Linton Rigg, the American who operates Carriacou's only hotel, The Mermaid Tavern. Rigg deplores the fact that Carriacou can't be reached by plane: "My God, even *Saba* has a strip!" We had a nonalcoholic drink with the Papal Volunteers from Kansas and Wisconsin, who manage Carriacou Handicrafts across the way. (They themselves make the "folk arts"—mostly out of driftwood and shells.) Then we had tea with Wilfred Redhead, the island's administrator, and his wife. I'd always been curious to compare the Grenadine *shango* rite with Haitian voodoo, and Redhead was reputed to be one of the two men in Grenada with a intimate knowledge of African dancing, drumming, and religious practices.

Redhead differentiates the tribal dances of Carriacou—as many as twenty-five different ones may occasionally be seen at a single big drum dance: Ibo, Yoruba, Arada, Corromantee, Mandingo, and so forth—from *shango*, which is a ritual. The ritual is still practiced, but very rarely now, in a *chapelle* at the southern end of the island. He referred us to Dudley Slinger "back on the mainland" (as Carriacouans refer to Grenada) for a description of a rite he had seen. The dances are not ritualistic and are danced in long, white, pleated petticoats, usually just before the spring planting. They have no connection, he said, with the goat sacrifices that often accompanies a boat launching here. The Arada dance is done to a slow 6/8 beat, "antiphonic singing in the Pentatonic Mode," to quote Andrew Pearce, a Trinidadian authority. Non-African dances seen here are in the Old Creole and New Creole styles. "Sugar" Adams, from the island's south end, is the most famous performer on the goatskin drums, which are used in batteries of three, as in Haiti. Each man dances waving a towel in each hand. Men and women never dance together.

Back in Grenada next morning we made a deal with our taxi driver to stop at Dudley Slinger's hotel, The Islander, before crossing the island to the airport. The Islander is the oldest (opened in 1948) and cheapest of the seaside hotels that can't be classed as guesthouses. It is nearer town than are the Spice Island, Grenada Beach, and Silver Sands, and it sits higher on a promontory overlooking the red tile roofs of St. George's. Slinger rented the eighteen acres in 1946 on a ninety-nine-year lease for B.W.I. $120 a *year*. He had "escaped" from England in 1933.

Slinger characterizes *shango* as the dance part of the three-day, three-night ritual known as *saraca*. The priestess of this cult is known as a "mamao." (Voodoo's priestesses are called "Mambos"). Baptisms are performed with the blood of beheaded cocks. Slinger had attended a ceremony in 1952 held by a large group in Tivoli, near Grenville. There were about sixty girls in highly starched print frocks, and red kerchiefs. The dancing and drumming began. Suddenly a girl wearing a blue kerchief bounded among the chanting participants. She was grabbed and bound by her wrist to a plank. "I looked at her closely. Her flesh was *writhing*." The drumming stopped, and she quieted down. But, as soon as it started again, she was rushed into the mamao's hut. "It was clear that this time they didn't want me to see her." He invited the group to come and "perform" at the variety show in his hotel. Only the older ones came. But shortly after the drumming had started, a girl from the audience was "seized," began writhing, and was carried out of sight high over the communicants' head in a rigid state. The ceremonies are held, Slinger said, to invoke aid for various causes and to forestall evil. Again, there is a similarity to voodoo. The counterpart of the Haitian water goddess, Maîtresse La Sirène, is Grenada's Maman d'l'Eau, whom *shan-goites* invoke by night on the shores of the "fathomless" Grand Etang. As in Jamaica, the big difference from voodoo is that "possession," instead of being the object—identification with the deity—just "happens."

In St. George's, at various functions, the British West Indies Ballet puts on a cleaned-up version of these rites, with simulated trances, lift-ups, and so on. The previous night's show at the hotel had featured a limbo dance, with a fiery hollow rod substituted for the solid one when the level reached eighteen inches from the ground. At that point a shirtless dancer in skin-tight pants, with a girl clasped to him, made it under the flaming bar.

As our taxi barely missed the last of a half-dozen kids skipping across the road on a narrow curve, we asked the driver about accidents. "We have none," he said. (But on the plane later I sat next to a Trinidadian insurance agent, who volunteered the information that Grenada has the highest accident rate in the West Indies.) The last thing I asked our driver was what the letter "Y" and "W" signified at either end of the fanciful names painted on the gaudy Grenada buses. "Dat simple," he said. " 'Why Worry?' "

Part 4. Barbados

More than one history buff in the islands had solemnly sworn to us that George Washington was Alexander Hamilton's father. Wasn't Alexander an illegitimate child? Didn't his mother Rachel leave Nevis to visit Barbados escaping from her unhappy marriage with Levine and just before she started living with James Hamilton? Weren't there unusually close ties between Barbados and the North American colonies? And wasn't it at about that time the Father of Our Country made his only trip outside the States—to Barbados? The clincher was always that the older man had "fathered" the younger one like a "son," refusing to let him expose himself to gunfire, and that Hamilton had responded by cordially detesting the great man.

The parts of the puzzle fit nicely. There *were* "unusually close ties"— South Carolina was settled by Barbadians, and many Virginia planters owned land in Barbados. Washington *did* visit Barbados for several weeks, and Hamilton *did* reject the role of overprotected son. All of the parts fit except one—Washington's Barbados excursion took place in 1751; Hamilton was born in Nevis January 11, 1757.

Visitors: George Washington and Patrick Leigh Fermor

The details of Washington's visit are interesting enough but characteristically unromantic. He had come with his ailing half-brother Lawrence, whose lungs were in bad shape, for the "cure"; the trip was a failure, for Lawrence died soon after their return to Virginia, leaving Mt. Vernon to George. Major Washington had found "lodgings" in Bridgetown (there was no hotel then) for the stiff price of £15 a month—"exclusive of liquor and washing—at the home of Captain Crofton, Commander of Fort James. (The house where the two young men are reputed to have stayed is now an office for the sale of sweepstakes tickets.) The Major kept a journal of the whole trip, a dull piece of writing enlivened only by his account of contracting a severe case of smallpox, which left his face pitted for life. But this illness did, as one of his biographers points out, give the future General immunity in the swamps, camps, and barracks of the Revolution: "The ancestral fever could not strike him down."

Tourists two centuries later come to Barbados (*if* their smallpox vaccinations are in order) not for the "cure" but to sample the fine beaches, excellent hotels, and temperate climate of the most "British"of the West Indian islands. Barbados is almost round, almost flat, and almost out of the Antillean chain entirely, lying seventy-eight miles due east of St. Vincent in the unprotected Atlantic. Unvolcanic, it is built up of coral secretions. From the air it looks almost uninhabited, for the villages are well concealed in trees and almost everything else is covered with sugar cane. Actually, Barbados' 250,000 people, crowded into 166 square miles, make it the most densely populated country in the hemisphere, with the possible exception of Haiti.

Though the great majority of "Bajans" are black, they are extremely proud of having named a Trafalgar Square and erected a monument to Nelson in it before England did. Ruggedly individualistic, they boast of being without beggars and of having but one shoeshine boy in Bridgetown—a full-grown man. Their government, headed by a Negro hero of the R.A.F., appears to have none of the ugly racist tendencies that neighboring islands have picked up and reversed from the white-supremacist "Buckras" and "Bims" who once ruled them. But this appearance is probably deceptive. A Bajan is close-mouthed, touchy, burnished with a veneer of proper provinciality—nothing if not respectable. But the racial trauma, however deeply buried, must be there. To be sure, Barbados was the *only* British island never touched by the Arawaks, the Caribs, the French, and the French Revolution and one of the few islands with no place for an escaped slave to hide. Even so, slaves *did* escape, and they *did* hide—in shallow caves in the wooded gullies of the comparatively hilly north end of the island, now populated by a surprising number of the same species of West African monkey that prowls St. Kitts. And these slaves emerged so energetically to prey upon the lordly great houses that hounds had to be imported by the sporting gentry to flush them out. This treatment must be part of the black majority's racial memory, and a much fresher irritant must be the club system of the nineteenth and early twentieth centuries, under which the whole machinery of discrimination was camouflaged after emancipation. As late as 1946, when Leigh Fermor described the (then) colony as "a shire drifted loose from the coast of England" with "the social and intellectual prejudices of a golf club in our outer London," white members of the ubiquitous clubs (which then included all restaurants and places of amusement) explained without embarrassment that, except on official and business occasions, no social contact between whites and blacks ever took place and that the latter "liked it that way." The club system, Leigh Fermor concluded:

> segregates the two races of islanders as effectively as the most stringent colour discrimination in the United States, and not half as honestly. There, at least, loathsome as the American colour laws appear to me, Negroes know exactly where they are. There is none of the mean juggling with the written word that prevails in Bar-

bados, where, on paper, no colour bar exists. It is a pretty state of society when any white Barbadian or English pup can bounce in virtually where he chooses, while the elected head of the Government, who is the island's equivalent of the British Prime Minister, may have to hesitate and draw back. It must be one of the most disgustingly hypocritical systems in the world.[5]

Hosts: Sam Lord and Kenneth Coombes

Leigh Fermor loved Barbados and spent all his time there exploring, with an antiquarian's fervor, its parish churches and sugar palaces, for which efforts he apologizes with the explanation that he and his party were guests of an ancient island family with as keen an interest in architecture and history. Sam Lord's Castle (which he mentions as one of those segregated "clubs") was our base in Barbados. Though long since desegregated, it has a clientele that is predominantly upper-class white, and it tended to isolate us in the same subtly seductive way. Now a full-fledged hotel, with the usual swimming pool, tennis courts, shuffleboard, and perfectly trained corps of black domestics in brass-buttoned white livery, Sam Lord's Castle is so overcharged with old-world charm that only a paranoiac Negrophile could escape having the batteries of his social conscience temporarily disconnected. The magnificent early nineteenth-century great house, with its gleaming white walls and machicolated roof, majestic ballrooms, chandeliers suspended from ornately carved plaster cartwheels, has now been enriched by its proprietor-manager, Kenneth Coombes, with the finest collection of paintings by the masters of English aristocratic portraiture outside a museum. The hotel's beach and seaview looking west to distant Bridgetown are hypnotically relaxing. Its aloe pits—Coombes told us that his nanny had rubbed bitter-aloe dust on his thumbs as a child to keep him from sucking them—are filled with exotic flowers under the front windows of one's individual cottage. From the back window one can, in the early morning, watch a mongoose chase a lizard along the white parapet that guards one's private lawn from the stares of domestics. Only a Dutch windmill, imported from Holland and reassembled amid the fountains of the terraced gardens that slope to the sea, seemed out of key with this carefully nurtured atmosphere of Anglican good taste.

Following an exhausting but pleasantly self-indulgent afternoon devoted to all the sports the hotel offers, we had dinner with Thelma and Kenneth Coombes and Eugenia Bedell, a travel writer justly nicknamed "Miss Caribbean." I thought it best to lay the ghost of Sam Lord first, and the amiable Coombes cooperated. According to the legend dominating all the Barbados brochures, the founder of the house hung lanterns in

[5] Patrick Leigh Fermor, *op. cit.*

the palms to make mariners mistake his reefs for the roadstead of Bridge-town; when their ships broke up, he hauled their furniture and other effects ashore to furnish his home. Sam Lord was a rake and a ne'er-do-well, Ken said, and no doubt he scrounged furniture from what wrecks there were, "but otherwise, as you Americans say, it's baloney." It was amusing to discover that Coombes' partner, George J. Stewart, made *his* fortune *insuring* ships. I asked Ken whether or not the hotel makes money. "Not yet," he said. "You've noticed that we have fifteen guests? Well, we have 150 servants to pay. And don't forget that we'd spent $2,-500,000 B.W.I. restoring the Castle and an initial $200,000 for the dilapidated mansion and the 100 acres that went with it. But, after only five years, the value of the land has increased to $3 million. We can compensate for our losses by selling a bit of land now and then." Stewart, I gathered, finds it relaxing to leave his gigantic corporate headaches in New York to fly down and settle a problem in plumbing or social precedence. Coombes and his wife have been amply compensated by the fun of art-collecting and knowledgeable restoration. Between visits to Sotheby's and Parke-Bernet they direct cabinetmakers and visit the local auctions looking for cut glass, black Wedgwood teacups, and old rectory lecterns.

"Other islands," as Ken put it, "may be more exciting to visit, but this is the only one to live in. Lord Avon found that out the hard way, finally moving here from Bequia last year. We have the best medical facilities, education, and roads of any island, and our two political parties stand only for 'better government.'"

"I've heard that the planters still own 75 per cent of the land," I said. "Isn't that, coupled with Barbados' total dependence on sugar, still a problem?"

"Not if the planters don't turn on their help by reverting to the old colonial ways out of fear," he replied. "But I see no chance of that. The absentee owners are selling out to local groups or to the government—which just bought Scotland Estate. Cane cutters make $12 a day or more. It's a fact, though, that they work only three months a year, and it's a helluva way to work. The great thing holding people and institutions in Barbados together is *respect*. If I don't sack a man who's neglecting his work, he despises me. If a man's house burns down, all the neighbors chip in, and he winds up better off than he was before. One must remember, too," he added reflectively, "that one reason there is relative peace here is that in the old days the planters were *not* absentees and that they treated their slaves well. A master had many concubines, but in his will he provided for all his bastards."

"The cheife fudling they make in this island," says on old chronicle of the Barbados colonizers, "is Rumbullion, alias Kill Divill, and this is made of Sugar cones distilled, a hott hellish and terrible liqour." Well fortified with the pleasant modern version of this famous native product, we took a long taxi ride back into Bridgetown to see what kind of night life there might be. We told the driver about a white woman we'd seen on the bridge the day before, shamelessly throwing pennies to naked adult male divers. "Canadians," he said with disgust. "They come here, with their pills, to get laid. If they don't make it at the bridge, they go to Harry's Nitery."

By the time we arrived at Harry's the floor show was almost over, and the Canadian girls, if they'd ever come, were gone. Guests sit in a circle, and four scrawny, naked black girls bounce from lap to lap. If the girls were attractive, they'd never get around. Finally, while they demonstrate "Lesbianism" on the floor, Harry gives a straight-faced "scientific" lecture on this and other forms of perversion that is by far the best part of the show.

In Search of the Redlegs

The next morning we set out for a complete circuit of the island.

We began with the "covered wagon" Barbados Hilton, which was just beginning to be built. Perhaps appropriately, only the bar was finished, it was fully air-conditioned and at 10:00 in the morning it was already jumping with uniformed bartenders shaking martinis for parched customers. One of them discarded a copy of *The Morning Advocate*, and we noticed the headline:

> *UK Plans $96 M Cut in Overseas Aid*
> *Restraint Regretted*

We noticed another item, which quoted St. Kitts' Robert Bradshaw as telling a conference at the Hilton: "My country will not throw off the shackles of British colonialism only to have them reimposed by some territory in the West Indies." He was referring, the bartender said, to a proposal by a Jamaica representative for a West Indies trading bloc.

We continued on into the interior of Barbados, which is a great deal hillier than it looks from the air. Aside from a few great houses tucked away in stands of noble trees, the principal features of the landscape are the fields of waving cane, which make tunnels out of the roads, and the homes of the poor. These homes are diminutive, built of frame with peaked roofs and usually standing several feet off the ground on pitted limestone blocks, perhaps rollers from the old mills. When the family is large enough to require more space, an identical second house is built. ("We divide our families by sex," our driver Noel Smith interjected; could he have meant multiply?) When two houses are not enough, a third is added at the rear, with its own complement of dingy colored glass and shutters, and (if the family can afford it) grace notes of jigsaw under the eaves and a tin sunshade over the windows. This last adornment resembles the smoke shield that used to cap the iron kitchen range in an American farm house.

We proceeded north along the west coast as far as Cherry Tree Hill, where the monkeys creep out at night to hunt for potatoes. Signs along the road reflected Barbados' 99 per cent Protestantism (which may or may not have a connection with its 99 per cent literacy): "Barbados Faith Tabernacle," "Church of the Nazarenes," "Pentecostal Church," "Pilgrim Holiness Church," "The Golden Egg—Trust and Try Friendliness." At Turner Hall Woods we passed through alleys of mahogany, then cane again, broken only by windrows of tilted, long-needled Australian casuarinas. From Hackleton's Cliff (1,100 feet), the island's summit, it is said that one can see St. Lucia's Mt. Gimie on a clear day. Then came cane fields, varied by eddoes a leek-like vegetable, and corn, all being hoed by rows of women. Men do only the "heavy work" here, Noel remarked, "like cane cutting and home building, and they don't like to do that." (Who does?) Near Less Beholden we turned off the road to see The Potteries. Two potters were at work. The clay is beautiful but sensuous only when being shaped wet on the wheel. The sensitive ancient forms are gone. The color is dead. There is no decoration save perfunctory scalloping. Could folk-art specialists reintroduce taste and style? we wondered. It would be worth risking when an art has sunk this low.

Coming into the "Redleg" St. John Valley, I asked Noel if mosquitoes were a problem in Barbados. "No, man," he replied. "If yo' don' keep yo' yard clean, if they find larvae—two weeks in jail, man!"

The Redlegs, we discovered at the grocery store at the next crossroad, sell Black Flag to those who miss the larvae. At any rate it stood there on the shelf next to Cafenol, Peter Paul Mounds, Palmolive Soap, and Johnson's Baby Powder. We bought a lunch of six bananas and three bars of chocolate from the dour blonde lady behind the counter, who complained that it was her first sale of the day. We couldn't elicit anything else to add to what we already knew about this enclave of miserable whites. They are descendants of Irish indentured servants, brought over after commutation of death sentences following the Monmouth Rebellion under James II. Their plight was worse than that of the Negroes, it seems. In the 1660s, when sugar suddenly made the imports from tiny Barbados five times as valuable as those from all the North American colonies combined, it was discovered that a Negro could do five times the work of an Irishman, and the small Irish farmers were promptly dispossessed. After manumission or emancipation, the planters felt a personal responsibility for the Negroes but not for the Redlegs. Even the charm of the Irish brogue forsook these "mean whites," as the Negroes contemptuously call them. They play no part in the island's political life and have nothing but their jealously preserved "racial purity" to comfort them.

"On top of this tower," said the warden of St. John's parish church to us at our next stop, "you'll be as high as you'll ever be in Barbados." He added a consoling homily on the subject of the slaves, who were obliged to sit by themselves in the balcony: "They were properly seated because they were nearer to God." We descended to walk through the nave and admire the black-marble tombs with crests and armored helmets incised on them and the monument to our guide's most illustrious predecessor:

Ferdinando Paleologus
Descended From Ye Imperial Lyne of Ye Last Christian
Emperor of Greece Churchwarden of This Parish 1655-1656
Vestryman Twentye Years Died October 3. 1679.

I recalled with awe Leigh Fermor's learned account of the tortuous paths by which this ultimate descendant of the last of the Caesars came to rest in this remote West Indian village, and I recommend it to anyone with a taste for romantic history sumptuously evoked.[6]

An Evening with Frank Collymore

We spent our last night in Barbados most enjoyably, talking to Frank Collymore and his wife Ellice. Frank is a poet, short-story writer, and expert on the Bajan dialect. Until his recent retirement, he taught school for forty years in Bridgetown. George Lamming, the novelist whose *In the Castle of My Skin* was the first fiction in a pioneering style to come out of the Indies, was one of Frank's pupils. Another was Hilton Vaughn, a distinguished member of Errol Barrow's Cabinet, who is also a poet and historian. Still another was Austin Clarke, whose brilliant stories Frank published in the literary magazine *Bim*. "His gift is for the comic," Frank said, "or was until he began to see himself as a sort of savior of the oppressed colonials."

"But our culture," he added deprecatingly when I complimented him on his progeny and wide influence on literature throughout the Indies, "is very provincial really. No theater. No fine arts to speak of. Only dancing and singing—most of the singing being the singing of hymns."

"The real provincials," I said, "are those who can't criticize their own culture. Did Lamming seem a great talent in school?"

"He wrote a bit for the magazine, but on the whole he seemed an average, fun-loving kid, a bit lazy but interested in books. He didn't really begin to develop until he went to Trinidad in 1945. There's a youngster of twenty-one, Timothy Callender, retiring and self-effacing but with one of the finest gifts for reproducing the Bajan rhythms in his stories."

"I'm glad to hear that," I said, "because I was told yesterday that the

[6] Leigh Fermor, *op. cit.*, pp. 145–9.

younger generation is so impatient with the past it would like to sweep out all of it—including the Bajan dialect."

"It's true," he said with a smile, "but they won't. A culture has to grow out of something, and if ours is going to amount to anything it will have to be stoked with native wood as well as sparked by rebelliousness."

"To what extent is Protestantism the root factor of Barbados' unusual calm?" I asked.

"To a great extent," he answered. "Bajans are hard-working, God-fearing people. It may be of interest that the small but growing Trinidadian colony tried to introduce their carnival in Bridgetown. It sputtered along without any real popular support for two or three years and then quietly expired."

Frank Collymore is a genial man, cultivated, with a love of books, of his island, and of all the islands. I had hoped that he would throw some light on the real issues separating Errol Barrow's Democratic Labour Party (D.L.P.) and the opposition Barbados Labour Party (B.L.P.), from which it split off, but that might be asking too much of any man. Barrow himself is an enigmatic figure. His father was a minister and his mother the daughter of a prosperous plantation- and sugar-mill owner. As a boy he won a scholarship in the classics. After his years in the R.A.F. he became a barrister. He married the daughter of an Episcopal minister from Montclair, New Jersey. He lists as his hobbies "sailing, swimming, skin-diving, flying, fishing, yachting, lawn tennis and photography." It sounds more like the background of a scion of the establishment than of the man who led the most overcrowded of Britain's Negro colonies to independence! But the leader of the B.L.P., Sir Grantley Adams, is elderly and even more conservative, they say. It was he who headed the ill-fated West Indies Federation as a compromise between the two leftist leaders of the "Great Powers," Eric Williams of Trinidad and Norman Manley of Jamaica. I asked Frank why Barrow's D.L.P. had won only fourteen of twenty-four seats in the last election.

"That surprised everybody," he said. "The significant reason, probably, was because he frightened Bajans with visions of one-man rule when he claimed he'd win all twenty-four seats."

"Then is the opposition party a little bit more liberal?" I asked.

"I'd be hard put to it to define how," he laughed. "Not more liberal. Just different."

"Different in favoring federation?"

"No. Oddly enough, Barrow's party today is more in favor of federation!"

V

TRINIDAD AND TOBAGO

I remember a road, brown as a snake
sometimes breaking its back in the bog
sometimes shining like the cry of a flute
and a mist full of diamonds.
I remember the metal screeching of parrots
and the earth exhaling the fume, the engine of morning
and the kettle of sunlight, boiling with vapour
when I set my foot down on the changing earth. . . .

So writes Derek Walcott in notes for an unpublished play, *The Dream on Monkey Mountain*, which Bill and I read at his home our first morning in Trinidad, after the poet had driven us from our hotel in Port-of-Spain to that address—Duke of Edinburgh, Petit Valley, Diego Martin—that seemed to symbolize all the historical catalysts in this most mixed-up, heady brew of an island, but lacks both of the basic ingredients: African and Oriental.

West Indian Poet: Derek Walcott

The union of Derek, part African, and his wife Margaret, part Oriental, already blessed with two children, may be part of a cosmic process reconciling these now-contentious racial strains and a harbinger of the ulti-

mate salvation of Trinidad, its coming of age. But even to suggest any such conscious intention on the part of the poet and his wife would be to strip them of all the natural beauty, spontaneous humor, and uncomplicated ease that is theirs and to reduce the creative process to a biological rut.

Derek was born in St. Lucia in 1930 and went to Jamaica's University of the West Indies on a scholarship in 1950. "I was almost tossed out," he told us, "for writing a paper answering a series of silly questions with silly answers. Like, for instance, 'What is the difference between a ruler and a philosopher?' which I answered, 'A ruler is a foot long, but a philosopher can go to any length.' But I got a degree, finally; married a Jamaican girl; and in 1954 I was back in Castries teaching English at St. Mary's College. Then I came to Trinidad, and in 1960 I married Margaret Mayllard—"

"—as in duck," said Margaret.

"It sounds teddibly English, I said.

"People used to evade their non-Caucasian backgrounds," she said, "by saying 'My grandfather was Dutch' or 'my great-grandfather was Spanish.' We're all mixtures here. I have an East Indian grandmother, along with an African one. Derek has English and Dutch."

"Negro is the only only thing we have in common," said Derek.

"I'm low-caste Indian," said Margaret. "The Negroes lowered the caste."

All was said casually; we were laughing in a way that would be difficult among Americans of different complexions.

"Negro women straighten their hair here," Margaret continued, "or else they wear wigs. The wig business is big business in Port-of-Spain. Even the low-salaried wear them."

The talk shifted to Carnival, architecture, painting, politics, and mutual friends like Frank Collymore, John Hearne, and Robert Lowell. Derek's son Peter was out in the street batting a ball around with neighborhood kids. Derek showed us the proper stance with the cricket bat and how to throw curves underhand; he had some amusing things to say on the subject of Trinidad's passion for this sport. Soon it was time for lunch.

On the way to Maracas Beach, Derek asked me if I knew the painter Roland Dorcély in Haiti: "I always liked his line, 'You have in your eyes a Sunday in black.' What ever happened to him?"

"Dorcély went to Paris and hasn't been heard of since," I said.

"Well, if he's disappeared," Derek said, "I suppose I can take the line."

At the beach Margaret was joined by several other beautiful African-East Indian women, who looked especially stunning against the white sand.

"I've discovered at last the advantage of white sand over black," I said.

"The white sand can vote," said Derek.

It sounds as if we were preoccupied with the racial question. We weren't. If the subject evoked the most merriment, it may have been because it was the natural way of expressing our ease with one another. No doubt there was, too, the unconscious recognition that race *is* the single most unsettling, divisive, and explosive question in Trinidad and that to avoid it entirely is to evade it.

It all began between 1833 and 1917, when Britain imported 145,000 East Indians to work the sugar fields to which the emancipated Negroes refused to return. V. S. Naipaul, the brilliant Trinidadian novelist, goes so far as to maintain that Trinidad "teeters on the brink of racial war" because the Negro and the East Indian, lacking any real respect for their own races, take out the frustrations of their particular rootlessness on each other. The greatest damage done to the Negro by slavery was to teach him self-contempt. "Twenty million Africans made the middle passage, and scarcely an African name remains in the New World." Until recently news films of African tribesmen on the screen evoked hoots of laughter. Ads in Port-of-Spain still show men and women with exaggeratedly Caucasian features—slightly tinted bronze. The Indian, for his part, despises the Negro for not being Indian. He has "taken over all the white prejudices against the Negro and, with the convert's zeal, regards as Negro everyone who has any tincture of Negro blood." Indians who have visited their homeland have returned to Trinidad "disgusted by the poverty and convinced of their own superiority." Nor did political independence, mostly the work of the Negro majority, help much; the politician "soon to be rewarded by great wealth, bared his pale chest and shouted, 'I is a nigger too'"[1]

[1] V. S. Naipaul, *The Middle Passage* (London: Deutsch, 1962).

None of this hatred, of course, is reflected in the attitudes of people like the Walcotts. And it seemed to be belied in a sign we passed as we left the beach: "Happy housewives Use Texagas," with seven smiling portraits representing the racial potpurri for which Trinidad is famous: Indian, Chinese, Lebanese, African, Mulatto, Spanish, and English. On Saddle Road, winding down through the jungle-clad valley, with its immortelles blooming in parasols of a delicate Chinese red and the grapefruit trees heavy with their golden globes, I asked Derek what kind of man Prime Minister Eric Williams is.

"Dedicated and incorruptible," he said, "which his party isn't. Obsessed with his own powers of leadership. His charisma is great but difficult to explain. His speeches are dry, fact-laden, academically delivered lectures, almost sermons, but they impress the masses with his knowledge and the seriousness of his concern for their welfare. He is humorless, and without any interest in culture as such or at least in aesthetics."

I asked him about Rundranath Capildeo, the leader of the East Indian minority, which is nearly a majority.

"He's a brilliant mathematician," Derek said, "but a political nut. Though he later denied it, he once promised his followers champagne for breakfast if they'd vote him into power." Capildeo, I gathered, was a mild man and weak; the East Indians picked him as their leader mainly to counter the popular "Dr. Williams" with a genuine "Dr." of their own.

Hiltonisms

Be My Guest is the title of Conrad Hilton's autobiography, which graces every bedside table at the Trinidad Hilton, in lieu of a Gideon Bible. There are many features of this stainless-steel-and-plate-glass pleasure dome, luxuriously insulated against the city it dominates, that could easily—too easily—be made sport of. Our hearts sank when we found that we had been assigned to it, but there is no denying that this particular Hilton (the franchise of which the government owns) is superbly appointed and run or that its physical situation is breathtaking. Perched on a steep hillside—the lobby and swimming pool are on the *top* floor, a circumstance that leads to endless confusion and guffawing in the elevators—our room looked directly down on the Savannah, an oval greensward the size of six football fields or twelve cricket pitches, with a racetrack running around it and, at the far end, Maraval Road, lined with baronial mansions in bizarre East Indian Victorian, capped with jigsaw cupolas and minarets, one of which serves as Trinidad's White House.

Our pace was slowing down. We had too much time in Trinidad (comparatively speaking, of course) so we tended to idle, reminding ourselves indulgently that this country is too big to absorb except by osmosis. We played tennis. We went shopping. Then we sat in the Tourist Board office while Oliver Burke set up appointments for us with Drs. Williams and Capildeo for later in the week. ("He's clever until he's almost mad," was the way a secretary characterized the latter.) Then we had lunch in a Chinese restaurant with Andrew Carr, an authority on folklore who works for Dr. Williams' party and is Chairman of Judges for the Carnival Development Committee. We asked Carr about *shango* in Trinidad. It isn't what it used to be, he told us, but there are still more than 100 "compounds" on the island, some in the environs of Port-of-Spain. *Shango* is a Yoruba cult, as distinguished from the Arada one that is basic voodoo, but both have invocations, prayers, drumming, sacrifice, and possessions. "It's not as pure as in Haiti," added Carr, who studied with Melville Herskovits [2] at Northwestern University. He also said of Grenada and the Grenadians: "Blaize beat Gairy twice because those people *want* federation with us. Fifty per cent of their families have relatives here. So the feeling between us is mutual. Economically, though, Grenadians would be the gainers. We have to think about what would happen if 40,000 of them descended upon us to add to the 22 per cent of our work force that is now unemployed.[3] We have the industry (34 per cent of our revenues come from oil alone) and the agriculture (sugar is by far Trinidad's biggest employer of labor) and even the tourism (Tobago is bigger in that respect than Grenada). The important thing about tourism is not to develop it too fast. After all, why do people go to Tobago and Grenada? Because those two islands are still unspoiled."

We stopped on the way back to the hotel to let Bill make drawings of some of the fantastic structures bordering the Savannah. The Queen's Park Hotel, Alec Waugh's "Barracuda," described by Leigh Fermor as

[2] Herskovits is the author of *Life in a Haitian Valley* (an in-depth account of voodoo) in the village of Mirebalais, which has been undeservedly out of print for many years.

[3] Opposition leaders claim that the figure is as high as 50 per cent; 125,000 of Trinidad's 1 million people live in Port-of-Spain, where unemployment is concentrated.

"dominating this town-locked prairie like a giant dentist's chair for the painless extraction of dollars," is even more dilapidated than when those two writers saw it. C. C. Stollmeyer's house at 31 Maravel Road is said to be patterned on a Rhine castle, though others call it "Scotch baronial." It was built in 1902 at a reputed cost of $60,000—a fortune at the time. The jigsaw extravaganza belonging to a Dr. Pow, which faces the Savannah on Queen's Park West, is smaller and lovelier. Prince's Building was put up in honor of the visit of Queen Marie of Rumania's father, a visit that never took place. Nearby is a giant *saman* or monkey-pod tree, whose "wingspread" must cover an acre. Close by is one of those orphic Trinidadian signs: "Nero Brings Unity."

After a typical Hilton dinner—barbecued suckling pig followed by British trifle, a concoction of wedding cake, whipped cream, grapes, plums, peaches, and rum that must have played a part in giving the Empire the *coup-de-grâce*—we staggered with the rest of the guests to the entertainment shell behind the pool to see the floor show. The *limbo* and everything that led up to it were truly Hiltonian. First the master of ceremonies came out and told everybody how happy everybody ought to be to be there. "And is there any little lady or gentleman who happens to have a birthday on this happy occasion? I see one—you, dear, come forward; don't be bashful. We want to make your happiness our happiness, and the steel band will now play 'Happy Birthday'"—which it did in its tinkly fashion while the audience drowned out the more euphonious frogs and cicadas in the well-kept shrubbery. Presently two painted "savages" appeared, unrolled a piece of cloth containing some broken bottles, and proceeded (with ugliest imaginable posturings and pirouettes) to walk through it, roll in it, stomp on it, caress it, and kiss it. After this piece of masochism, a single painted "savage" came out with two lighted kerosene torches and licked, chewed, chomped, and gargled the flame. Two more of these characters took his place, carrying high jumper's equipment; they were joined by two of the ugliest young Negresses we had ever seen (and ugly Negresses in Port-of-Spain are collectors' items). One was fat, and one was skinny; both sported sunglasses with "diamonds" set in the frames. The fat one tried to get under the crossbar but succeeded only in executing an unfunny prat fall. The skinny one made it. "The grand finale, the climax of climaxes," roared the master of ceremonies, "is over, ladies and gentlemen, except that *YOU* are our Absolute finale! Your climax is our climax, so—" And, unbelievable as it seems, the crossbar was raised slightly and snuffed out, and an aging, paunchy Middle West businessman went under, paunch and all, to the gleeful hysteria of 300 sub-Hiltonites.

Be my guest.

Pitch Lake and a Hindu Temple

Derek and Margaret came to the Hilton the next morning. We transferred their gear to our car, chauffeured by the Tourist Board's incomparable 300-pound Edward Joseph, and set out for a grand tour of the interior.

Our first stop was San Fernando, Trinidad's second city and the center of its clustered oil refineries. I had already "collected" so many signs that I was running out of paper:

> *Ju-C*
> *Drive-in Roti*
> *Heart-Shaped Hot-Dogs*
> *Fly-in Barber* [*over a bridge*]
> *Esoterica Face Cream*
> *Snackettes Air-Conditioned*
> *Coterie of Social Workers*
> *Learn To Drive* [*and next to it*]
> *Guides Funeral Home*
> *Ishmael J. Kahn, Markuk*
> *Shindig De Noel*
> *Sno-Kones*
> *Moulin Rouge Hotel* [*in bright blue*]
> *Gold Bond Stamps*
> *The World's Most Evil Vampire Lives Again*
> *Haberdasher, Stationer, Broiler*
> *Contention Street* [*and on an outhouse*]
> *4 U 2 P*

"Here's an interesting sign for you, man" said our black mountain of a driver, whose wit is quite the equal of Derek's and Bill's:

> *Men at Work.*

"What's funny, Edward?"

"See any men working?"

Derek insisted that we stop at Sangre Grande to buy us some roast corn. It was tough. "How old do you think that corn is?" he asked Edward.

"As old as the old woman who sold it to you," Edward replied.

We stopped at a deserted outdoor theater, the Naparime Bowl ("Aeschylus slept here," Derek said), to eat our sandwiches on the stone benches and then we drove back to San Fernando, where Derek and Margaret wanted to be left to do some Christmas shopping. Edward drove us twenty-five miles beyond to the famous Pitch Lake. It is surprisingly small and looks like a beat-up parking lot with puddles here and there. A few bulldozers were poking around in the middle, and at our end a train of hand cars was being loaded with chunks of the asphalt, which looks like black gingerbread. At the far end of the "lake," which can't cover 100 acres but which has disgorged more than 13 million tons of pitch over the past seventy-five years, the government is beginning to compete with a smaller excavation of its own. The lake's level is said to be dropping six inches a year, but, as the pitch is removed, the surface "settles" so that the change is not noticeable. All around, in fact, the earth's crust is compensating for man's greed: The road is full of ripples, and, as one stands on the rubbery surface, one leaves deep footprints—and moves on quickly.

A current story we had from one of the unloaders was of a man who sank in almost to his neck and had to be pulled out with ropes. He had ventured out there at night to make love to a woman. She had run away, leaving him there. "He'll never make love in *that* position again," said our informant. "Over there is better," he added, pointing to an asphalt tennis court with no net or lines.

"They have asphalt balls?" I asked Edward.

"Judging by the number of children in this neighborhood," he said, "they must have."

We drove back to San Fernando past flaming clumps of poinsettia and windbrakes of newly planted teakwood with enormous leaves. Faded flags on long bamboo poles are put up by the Hindus to mark their feasts of thanksgiving. Picking up Derek and Margaret in the traffic-clogged main street, we drove next to something that none of us had anticipated— almost driving by it, in fact, as we passed through Moose Bhaget. There above the roadside it stood, a small Hindu village temple, erected in 1904, with astonishing wall paintings that caught my mural-conscious eye. The painting was done by the grandfather of the present sadhu, Ramjattan Das, who received us at the gate and presented us to a much older seer, Mir Singh, aged eighty-seven. Singh had withered brown arms and legs, an almost transparent body in floating white robes, a wild mane of snowy hair, and deep, almost black, pits under his burning, faraway eyes. It was clear that these grotesque paintings of Hanuman Rama, Sita, Garu, and the other holy men—some triple-headed, some dog-faced and attended by heraldic animals—were in the great tradition of Indian painting. I asked Ramjattan Das how the murals retained their vivid hues. "We repaint them every two or three years, very carefully," he said. They are on the inner wall of the gallery that runs around the temple, and on the outer wall of the inner shrine that forms the building's core.

The sadhu in his dirty white shirt and tunic put on a string of prayer beads to have his picture taken. They are made of the stalk of a common weed, which he showed us, cut into sections. Each necklace contains 100 or more beads. I asked him how long it took to tell them.

"Four and three-quarters minutes," he said.

"The prayers are that short?"

"One word or phrase for each. I take a long, deep breath, and away I go."

This temple is for devotions only; there are no marriage or burial services. I asked him if the cult was dying out.

"I'm afraid so," he said. "The children go to school now and come away speaking English. They don't want to speak Hindi any more. It's too great an effort for them. Besides," said Ramjattan Das, who used to drive a taxi for a living, "our religion says no sweets or meat or liquor, and they don't like that."

Bill asked Margaret whether or not the East Indians still cremate their dead in Trinidad.

"Sometimes on the Caroni River," she said. I had a quick vision of suttee being performed on the banks of that flamingo-haunted stream.

"Does the wife throw herself in the flames?" I asked.

"Not here," Edward said. "She throws herself into the arms of her next lover."

"The wife gets the insurance these days," said Derek. "She can't afford to die."

out of earshot of the sadhu,
[...] about the three painted

repainted
s."
r temple,
kled holy
until his
ke to see
esting de-

away.
known," I

u see him

ence. How
nd, intact but

e Penthouse that night—and
be convinced that American
perhaps the impresarios are
x 12′ stage and a hundred
mphasis of the performance
and sex.
a in which the Trinidadian
s are "fundamental" and "in-
stanza by The Mighty Spar-
Post advice on dating:

Tell your sister to come aon, boy.
I have something here for she.
Tell she is Mr. Benwood Dick,
The man from Sangre Grande.
She know me well. I give she already.
Mm. She must remember me. Go on, go on,
Tell she Mr. Benwood come.

And Naipaul goes on to distinguish between that bastardization called "culture," for which Trinidadians, in their compulsion to catch up with American modernity, "are as much to blame as anyone" (try dancing in costume and steel bands which we were reassured to find him detesting as much as we did)—and the entertainment in hotel night clubs.

The *calypso* singer at The Penthouse delighted us by treating every-one in the audience as fair game. The Terror's extemporaneous shafts were directed at one man's bald head, another's big belly, a girl's prom-inent breasts; one unfortunate, sitting next to this girl and ogling her a little too obviously, was asked about his married life and why he was holding his hand between his legs.

The *limbo*, performed here by three men and two women, was a thing of beauty, sustained (with the racketing drums and trumpet directly behind it) in unflagging intensity. How these five flailing gymnasts kept out of one another's way, without knocking over the posts or falling off the cramped stage, was astonishing. They rolled under the bar—three together when it was twenty-four inches up, one at a time when it was aflame and supported on two coke bottles. This part was the finale, of course. In between the *calypso* and the *limbo* there was a series of pre-paratory numbers, two of them memorable: a hip-swiveling *banda* danced, by a woman dressed as a butterfly with big "eyes" on her wings, to the tune of "Haiti Cherie" and a belly dance by a girl with a golden "sun" in her navel and silver "stars" spattered across her back. After going through all the motions of copulation, this solar Venus had a pro-vocative way of stopping directly in front of one, slipping her hand down under the triangular pad of her G string, and thoughtfully stroking her sex.

A Day in Tobago

We flew out of Piarco Airport at 8:00 in the morning, with instructions from Edward to look out for his opposite number in Tobago, Tall Boy Hercules.

"How do we recognize him?"

"He's tall all right, but the rest is strictly a family name."

Tall Boy made it easy by finding us. He said we must see the beauty of the "underwater gardens" at Buccoo Reef and drove us directly to Pigeon Point, where a glass-bottomed boat was waiting. We chugged out and then went overboard to have a closer look. Perhaps Tall Boy had oversold us on this attraction, for the "gardens" struck us as having an evil look: sponge coral in folded piles like entrails gone out of control and a cancerous-looking olive-brown deposit with exposed yellowing patches here and there like decay around the gums or places where the "fillings" had been ripped out by the keel of a gunboat. The brain coral has a better claim to beauty, its patterns being more clearly marked and regular, but exposed brains are unlovely by the very nature of the associations to the name.

Forests of waving plants had ominous colors and rhythm of their own, some ocher, some lavender, and one chrome variety with holes in the tips—aimed at what? All these plants are "living," to be sure, but it is a fixed life, regimented to prey on what passes by—or be preyed upon as is the species exuding an acid craved by the parrot fish, which turns languidly on its side to scrape its horny host with razor-sharp gills. We liked the darting angels, banded butterflies, and squirrelfish better, wondering why. Because they are free?

Leafing through Commander Alford's *Guide to Tobago*, which Tall Boy had in his glove compartment, I was reminded of the previous night's belly dancer as I read the description of the mating of the birds of paradise on the island of the same name:[4] "Their bodies are covered with a golden mantle which they keep in a state of vibration. Then they proceed to strut up and down in a sort of side-step, cocking up their tails now and then and displaying their golden treasures to the full."

We had lunch later with the Commander's wife, Kitty, and with Anthony Bishop, a Grenada-born businessman (copra and cattle) currently serving on the Tobago Tourist Board. Bishop is irritated at the red tape that holds tourism in Tobago to a trickle, and he envies Jamaica. "If only they'd turn this island over to a John Pringle," he sighed. "If only they'd extend our runway for jets and start building hotels." Since the fifty-three-room Crown Point went up in 1956, there hasn't been a hotel bed added to the little twenty-seven-by-seven-mile island, which had 400 beds in that year. All of this slowness, he said, is caused by Trinidad's merchants and politicians, who want Piarco to be the sole terminal and

[4] It is also called Little Tobago and is an islet off the west coast; it is a bird sanctuary.

Port-of-Spain the only shopping mart. "Two-week package flights from the States give Tobago the last two days, which makes tourists mad as hell. They leave saying it should have been the other way around."

We asked him to show us Arnos Vale, Tobago's other first-rate hostelry, which lies across the narrow island from Crown Point and Scarborough, the capital. Arnos Vale is smaller than the Crown Point and more expensive, making up in atmosphere what it lacks in sporting facilities. Its situation, in a lush valley perched over a tiny palm-fringed, white-sand beach between rocky promontories, reminded us of Frenchman's Cove on Jamaica. It was built in 1954 by Clifford Dibben, an Englishman of good taste, who brought with him from England all the roof tiles for the main house and cottages. Two per cent were lost in passage, we were told and 22 per cent when the shipment passed through Port-of-Spain. Dibben built out of local woods and coral, and he built well.

Bishop took us to his attractive house, made out of one of those circular stone sugar mills that crumble forlornly on most of the sugar islands, and then for tea to the home of Sir Richard d'Oyley Carte's widow—Tobago is rich in distinguished "retirees" from the mother country. Bishop was full of interesting political folklore. For instance, the Governor-General of Trinidad-Tobago is of Chinese extraction because a Negro would be intolerable to an East Indian and vice versa.

Prime Minister Williams (with whom Bishop attended Queens Royal College) had his antiwhite propensities understandably shaped by a series of "unfortunate incidents," as Bishop put it. At Oxford, for example, there was a popular don who used to invite his students to his country seat. The brilliant Williams was duly invited, but when he arrived at the front door the butler looked him up and down and said, "I'm afraid there's been a mistake." There were similar incidents, inevitably, in Washington, D.C., during the period when Dr. Williams was preparing his doctorate (*Capitalism and Slavery*) at Howard University. Also the American courts slapped an alimony judgment on Williams that prevented his setting foot in the United States again, lest he be seized by the police. Considering all these experiences, it's remarkable that the London *Times* can now describe the Prime Minister as "a right of center conservative."

Capildeo, who might be similarly described, though he calls himself a "democratic socialist," differs from Williams in many ways, Bishop continued—his sense of humor, for one thing. He enjoys his nickname, "Caput," and he is full of fun. But one reason that he won only twelve seats in 1966—the same number that he won in 1961—was that he earned much criticism by referring, immediately after his return from England, to his well-paying lectureship there. "He has promised not to again," Bishop added, "and so far he hasn't. As a mathematician Capildeo is reputed to have refuted Einstein's theories, at least in part. . . . He has a phobia about voting machines. In a recent speech he said; 'Ian Smith should accept Harold Wilson's terms for a Rhodesian settlement—and then install voting machines.' Ask him about that when you see him tomorrow!"

Rundranath Capildeo

On the way to the opposition leader's gingerbread cottage on Carlos Street the next morning, we asked our driver if he would pass through some of those parts of Port-of-Spain that had acquired an aura of romance in our minds from Naipaul's and Samuel Selvon's fiction: Laventile Hill and Miguel Street, for instance. Edward had been indisposed, and his replacement lacked his liveliness. "I call Laventile Hill off limits," he said cautiously. "Squatters and all that. Few police. Full of lawless. A few decent people lives everywhere, of course. 'John-John' is the nickname. I suppose Miguel Street up there."

At our destination we were received by a plump, gray-haired woman, with bare feet and wearing a soiled dress. We shook hands. Her hands were wet from wringing the mop. She took our coats and hung them on wire hangers from a book case in the living room. On the shelves books had been shoved in on their sides and were covered with dust. Two Goodyear rubber-tire ashtrays, a wax rose under a glass globe, two china tigers, and a half-dozen diminutive ivory elephants on a table with a faded lace doily completed the *décor*. A smell of cooking curry drifted through the bead curtains at the back of the room. The maid padded back, plugged in a rusty fan, and told us that we wouldn't have to wait long. In a couple of minutes Dr. Capildeo arrived, and, after maneuvering him into the chair that would give Bill the best light in the dark room, I asked him about the voting machines.

"Mind you," he said with a smile, "I haven't any criticism of voting machines as such. It's simply that here, instead of being supervised by an impartial agency, they're controlled by the government under a law of the government's own making. At Bolingbroke Jail our party is permitted to *look* at the machines but not touch them! Only civil servants have access to the keys to the twenty locks. Dr. Williams promised to have this law amended but has never kept his promise."

"I've heard that you intend to boycott the next election," I said.

"That is correct. We refuse to participate in any further fraud until the law is changed."

I asked him if the voting went along racial lines.

"It has so far," he said, "but I've been doing everything in my power to break this down. We expected—and indeed won—twenty-three out of thirty-six contests in the last election, but of course that isn't the way Dr. Williams' party counted it. Several of our candidates were Negroes, *and not a single one was declared victor*. That could not possibly have been accidental. As for the government's candidate, a few were Indians, three were elected—and we claim all three of those seats! Their Minister of Health, Winston Mahabir, was an Indian, but he has now broken

with Dr. Williams' party and calls its racial policy 'apartheid in reverse.'
Mahabir's comment on his service in the Cabinet was 'I felt used, com-
promised, and deceived.' " White expatriates in Trinidad, Dr. Capildeo
added, were cruelly persecuted—"and by the very man who invites them
and their kind to invest in Trinidad."

I asked Dr. Capildeo what real principles separate the two parties.

"Principles?" he said bitterly. "Dr. Williams has none. Nor does his
party appear to have any program at all."

"A writer without a program, an intellectual without principles?"

"Dr. Williams' first book was a doctoral thesis. It's really his only book.
The others have been scissors-and-paste jobs. He even boasts that he
wrote the *History of Trinidad and Tobago* in a fortnight. My name appears in it just once. I'd have preferred deregotary treatment to censorship by omission. But, to come back to your original question, *our*
program begins with the demand that Trinidad's present $100 million
B.W.I. imports bill be cut to $20 million. We *must* move forward toward
self-sufficiency in foods. From here on out, who cares if we starve? If
Trinidad were to be suddenly destroyed tomorrow, how many days
do you think that would be front-page news in the world press? Ten at
most. Then—nothing. We have simply got to cut down these ruinous imports. We must build schools of local materials, like impregnated tiles,
not of galvanized sheet metal.

"The second big concern of our party," Dr. Capildeo continued, "is
unemployment. Even *they* call it the 'number-one problem.' By now 66
per cent of all youths between the ages of fifteen and nineteen are job-
less and 80 per cent of those twenty to twenty-four. Dr. Williams is accelerating this dangerous trend by keeping his party oldsters in their
jobs. We would use the educational system to teach the young initiative—to help themselves and to work out small business ventures. We
also emphasize cooperatives."

I asked Dr. Capildeo whether or not he anticipated violence when the
Indian minority becomes the majority ten years from now.

"More than anticipate," he said. "I'm holding violence back with difficulty. I've been told that, should I pull out of the party leadership, there
would be an explosion in Trinidad within three months. That, incidentally, was one reason I left Trinidad in 1963 to teach at my alma mater,
the University of London, for two years—I was under the mistaken impression that my absence from the scene would contribute to a cooling
off. The other reason was that I was offered that lectureship while spending several weeks abroad for my health and saw a way of supporting my
family. It's quite impossible on my parliamentary stipend, B.W.I. $430 a
month after taxes. And I might add that the University here wouldn't
dream of offering me a job. I applied for one once, and my letter wasn't
even answered. But, to come back to my principal motive for staying
abroad so long—my belief that my presence in Trinidad was inflammatory. It was exactly the reverse. When Dr. Williams was holding his vic-

tory parade, for example, the leader of a band of hot-headed youngsters in our party came to me and asked, 'Would you like us to turn this into a funeral parade?' Had I said 'yes,' they would have done just that. The situation is very bad. Indians who come to the police stations to make complaints are frequently turned away without even a hearing. And Dr. Williams has his hooligan gangs, though he'd never admit it. The contemptuous word 'coolie' is hurled at us—and at me personally—by the Negroes."

"Do the East Indians," I asked, "hurl back epithets like 'nigger'?"

"Of course. The ignorant element does. But less frequently, because the African is stronger, not only in numbers but physically."

"Physically?"

"Yes. He is better fed. The Indian eats less, saves his money. But this is changing."

"Does the Indian participate in Carnival?" I asked.

"On the fringes. What a tragic waste of Trinidad's energy and resources Carnival is! Do you know that nine months of the year are spent preparing for those two days? The costumes are discarded forever on Easter Sunday—some of them costing thousands. Can you imagine what this time and money and effort could produce if directed into, say, food chemistry or building an administrative capital like Brasilia?"

"Or on Tobago," Bill said, "which we hear Dr. Williams loves dearly."

The opposition leader squeezed out a smile. "He loves it—empty. Empty for him. Our party would develop Tobago for tourism. But we'd place the hotels in the *interior*, building fast ten-minute access roads to the beaches, which would then be preserved in all their natural beauty."

"How do you stand on federation with Grenada, Doctor?" I asked.

"We're opposed to it," he said. "We believe in economic federation for the entire Caribbean area, political federation to follow." Federation with Grenada now, I gathered, would only create more unemployment and swell Dr. Williams' ranks. I asked him why the Indian element was growing faster than the African.

"That's hard to say," he answered, "except that most Indians are on the land and have a stronger family sense."

"By the logic of politics, you should be opposed to birth control," I said.

"Yet we're in favor of it," he replied. "See our party platform. *They* ignore it."

Was it true, I asked Dr. Capildeo finally, that he had "refuted" some of Einstein's theories?

"Not 'refuted,'" he said. "One scientist must stand on the shoulders of the preceding one. But I've posed a credible alternative to the Special Theory, one in which the universe is regarded as a turntable." He went on to point out weaknesses in Einstein's concept of time, in "the untenable proposition that you'd grow younger if you moved far and fast enough," and in the concept of gravity, "which neither Newton nor Einstein really accounts for but which I think I've explained a little better.

"The difference between politics and science," he continued, "is that in politics you don't have the data, but you know what the answers are or should be. In mathematics you are given the data, but you don't know what answers you will get—if any."

I remarked that, when scientists like Einstein and Bertrand Russell dabble in politics, they are regarded, with some justice, as crackpots. He laughed. "Einstein was a child when he got away from science. Russell's ego overpowers his judgments. Maybe I'm a crackpot too, but I'd like my critics to point out where the pot is cracked!"

Prime Minister Eric Williams

It would be difficult to imagine a greater contrast than that offered by Dr. Capildeo's dingy parlor, with its dust catchers and Oriental aromas, and Dr. Williams' big sunny office at Whitehall, with its uncluttered desk in a corner, unless it is the contrast between the men themselves. Rundranath Capildeo's soft, dreamy eyes; his relaxed physique, with one leg thrown over the arm of an overstuffed chair; and his easy humor were still very much in our mind when we sat down in our straight-backed chairs to confront the trim Eric Williams.

Glancing at his wrist watch the Prime Minister leaned back in his swivel chair. He was wearing a long-sleeved white shirt with a battery of gold pens in the pocket, a black silk tie neatly knotted, a white hearing aid in his left ear, and sunglasses. Behind those two lenses, it was

difficult to tell whether one's questions were being received with re-spect, contempt, or indifference; he has a disconcerting way of occasion-ally glancing at one sharply over the rims. A cigarette dangled from his thin, pursed lips.

I decided not to mention Dr. Capildeo, but I did ask about the racial problem.

"It's not a problem, really," Dr. Williams said. "It's a question. Only a problem for those who choose to make it one. We do what we can. We appoint a Hindu, a Moslem, a Chinese, a Syrian, whenever the right in-dividual is at hand. We never appoint a man for racial reasons, as cer-tain countries that I could mention do. That is not our way."

I mentioned Dr. Winston Mahabir's resignation and "apartheid" charges. The Prime Minister sniffed and then, with just the flicker of a smile, purred, "Dr. Mahabir left us to have a better life in Canada."

"Do you think there is a healthy two-party system at present in Trini-dad and Tobago, Mr. Prime Minister?" I asked.

"Our party is healthy," he replied. "It is not our business to make theirs healthy. It is hard enough to keep one's own party in good health. Of course we do what we can to help them. We give them offices and stationery and even a special salary for the leader of the opposition. What you hear from them, of course, is what you hear."

I mentioned the complaint we'd heard in Tobago about that island's underdevelopment.

"We are developing Tobago," he said, "but in our own way. We don't want to make it exclusive like Montego Bay, where you have to be a foreigner who can afford $50 a day for a hotel room even to get onto one of the beaches. The roads we are building across the island will help. And so will the 150-to-200-room hotel that is being built by the same syn-dicate that is now laying out the eighteen-hole golf course."

Dr. Williams spoke with more enthusiasm of his government's effort to save money on imports by assembling automobiles (456 this year) and refrigerators, and his plans for a port and industrial complex on the south coast of the island. But the quality of the Prime Minister's mind is seen to better advantage in his writings than in his guarded conver-sation.

Capitalism and Slavery is a determinist tract in the impressive trad-dition of Marx's *Capital* and Lenin's *Imperialism: The Highest Stage of Capitalism*. Though lacking the magisterial dialectics of the first and the inexorable prophetics of the second, Dr. Williams' book is more convinc-ingly "researched" than either, less dogmatic in tone, and more urbane and witty in style. The thesis is that, under the mercantile system that preceeded the Industrial Revolution of the nineteenth century, slave labor alone could make profitable the operation of those large plantations that were the keystone of the "triangular" trade among Europe, Africa, and the North American colonies; that, while this need prevailed, all the components of the Great Powers' ruling classes—royalty, aristocracy, statesmen, merchants, the church, the press, and even the poets—praised slavery or acquiesed in it; and that, once the mercantile system was destroyed (by the American and French Revolutions and the Napoleonic wars), the abolitionists won their campaigns for an end to the slave trade and emancipation, ostensibly motivated by their "humanitarianism" but actually riding the wave of the economy's shift from sugar to cotton, from the West to the East Indies, from a "closed" labor market to the new steam-driven factories' and mills' insatiable demand for "free" wage slaves.

> The sugar planters charged that distilling from corn tended to raise the price of bread. This concern for the poor consumer of bread was touching, coming as it did from extortionists who wanted the poor to spend more money on their sugar. . . . In 1783 the captain [of the ship *Zong*, which was short of water] had thrown 132 slaves overboard, and now the owners brought an action for insurance alleging the loss of the slaves fell within the clause of the policy which insured against "perils of the sea." Damages of thirty pounds were awarded for each slave, and the idea that the captain and crew should be prosecuted for mass homicide never entered into the head of any humanitarian.

Regardless of whether one considers Dr. Williams' single-minded pursuit of his thesis "realistic" or "cynical" and however much he may judiciously have selected those sources and quotations that support it, few would deny that the weight of evidence presented is impressive. It is not the kind of writing, however, that indicates qualities a ruler of Trinidad will need in the long hot summers ahead: flexibility, tolerance, warmth.

Nor was Whitehall, we thought as we walked down its marble steps (with those oddly juxtaposed open fireplaces and whirling fans), exactly the symbol of that total emancipation from the white man's world that one would expect the author of *Capitalism and Slavery* to demand. As the French say, "plus ça change, plus c'est la même chôse." Or, to quote Sparrow's mocking calypso:

> *Well, the way how things shaping up*
> *All this nigger business going to stop.*
> *And soon in the West Indies*
> *It will be "Please, Mr. Nigger, please."*

Trinidad's Two Souls

Trinidad, it was becoming clearer, has two "souls" struggling for ascendency. The one we had glimpsed in Whitehall was a denial of what makes Trinidad different from all the other once-British islands—its community of all races, its exuberant flouting of Western dress along class lines, its "tolerance for every human activity and affection for every

demonstration of wit and style" (to quote Naipaul), its eccentric anarchy, its carnival spirit. Whitehall was a denial of Trinidad's history.
In 1783 there were only 300 English administrators, planters, and soldiers to take over from the French and Spanish settlers, who had never
been able to make a go of the island; the number of slaves was minus-
cule. The slave trade was abolished fourteen years later, and emancipation came twenty-seven years after that. Obviously there could be little
of the deeply suppressed resentment that the other islands labor to exorcise. By the time the African population began to multiply, shiploads
of foreign labor were being brought in from all over the world in a vain
attempt to catch up with the sugar prosperity that was already a mirage—labor in which the Negroes refused to participate. Those lines sung
by the Trinidadian Harry Belafonte—

> *This is my island in the sun*
> *Where my people have toiled since time begun—*

harked back to a past that never was, a state of mind that had to be
artificially created. What John Hearne calls "the pathetic nostalgia that
corrupts so many Negroes: the retreat into apologies for their condition, their endless 'historical' explanations and their lack of any direction . . . the sentimental cameraderie of skin which provides the cheap
thrill of being 'African' "—began to take hold *politically*. There arose the
Trinidad that the expatriate Naipaul found on his return, "where the
weak were humiliated; where the powerful never appeared and were
beyond reach; where no one was allowed any dignity and everyone had
to impose himself; an uncreative society where war was the only profession." Was Stokely Carmichael about to return to the place of his birth?

Though we couldn't, unhappily, be in Trinidad for Carnival, we caught
glimpses of Trinidad's other "soul" during our last two days on the island. Those glimpses rounded out the solid impression we had already
acquired. Two of them came on what we thought was going to be our
last day in Trinidad—at the National Museum of Art on Victoria Square
and in a chance encounter with John Craig on the Savannah.

We visited the Museum in the company of Sybil Atteck, a painter, and
M. P. Alladin, Director of Culture and also a painter. The pictures in the
current exhibition, sophisticated and primitive alike, would not have
made the grade in Haiti's least discriminating gift shop. The "folk arts"
were almost as pitiful: coconuts carved with "cute" monkey faces, figurines of drummers beating drums, a few indifferent baskets, and an un-
skillful copy of a Dominica straw rug. But what a contrast were the
Carnival costumes, gathering dust and "faced" with peeling tin foil! They
were far from the best, by Alladin's admission, but still outstanding in
their imagination and originality. Here is where the true creativity of
Trinidad expresses itself—and disappears, save for these few moldering
relics, two days after its appearance.

Joined by Minister of Education Donald Pierre, we repaired with our two perceptive guides to the Film Center to see reels of the 1964 Carnival and others. For those two glorious days the typist becomes a titled lady and the dock worker a Watusi warrior—and then, pouf! The same abundance of visual vitality that assumes permanence in Haitian art vanishes in all its evanescent splendor. The Bullshit Ballet; The Golden Age of China; the Ku Klux Klan in *black* carrying "Down with Slavery!" signs; the Saga Boys in their pleated trousers, wasp waists, and crossed Coca-Cola bottles, the Mayan priests and Roman senators; the witch doctor's office, a thatched kraal on wheels, with skulls; the U.S. Navy in white face riding "tanks" and brandishing "machine guns"; headdresses with "logs" on which giant "butterflies" perch; Satan Kingdom; stray bats—the parade of imagination is inexhaustible.

Bill was sketching a coconut vendor's cart, and Edward was sitting with me in the car when a tall, skinny Negro with gray hair and wearing nothing but a loincloth of rags came up the street.

"Who is he?" I asked.

"They call him the "Town Crier," Edward said. "His name is John Craig. He's quite mad. Some time ago he came back from years and years in Venezuela across the bay. He'd been sending his savings home to be banked, but when he arrived there wasn't a penny to be found. He's been this way ever since. He writes letters to the Legislature criticizing the bills—and his criticisms are almost always sound."

"What does he live on and where?" I asked.

"If you hand him a penny, he refuses it with an 'I don't beg,' but if you give him 10 cents he'll take it. I saw a man offer him a dollar once, and he turned it down indignantly. He lives at the Hilton. No, I'm not kidding. He sleeps by the toolbox just up the driveway from the Savannah. He keeps a pan there for cooking and builds a little bonfire every morning and evening. No one disturbs him. He's very popular. He's very proud of the Queen and of Solomon Hochoy, the Governor General who represents her, but if you say 'Dr. Williams'—"

"I'll try," I said, "and see if he'll let me take his picture for Bill."

I intercepted John Craig, introduced myself as a visiting reporter, and asked him if he favored the programs of Dr. Williams or Dr. Capildeo.

"Party leaders do what is good for their party," he said. "What this country needs is a country leader. And what the world needs is a world leader. My thoughts on this subject," he added, in the most cultivated tone, "are on record. I've written a book, and Cambridge University Press has it."

"When will they publish it," I asked.

"That's up to them. I've done everything I can. I'll talk to you, and I'll talk to anyone who will listen. What more can a man do?"

When I reviewed V. S. Naipaul's *Miguel Street* for *The New York Times* ten years ago, the story that made the greatest impression on me was "B. Wordsworth." It is about a man "whose English was so good it didn't sound natural," who asks the little narrator of the story if he can watch his bees:

> I said, "What you does do, mister?"
> He got up and said, "I am a poet."
> I said, "A good poet?"
> He said, "The greatest in the world."
> "What's your name, mister?"
> "B. Wordsworth."
> "B. for Bill?"
> "Black. Black Wordsworth. White Wordsworth was my brother. We share one heart. I can watch a small flower like the morning glory and cry."
> I said, "Why do you cry?"
> "Why, boy? Why? You will know when you grow up. You're a poet, too, you know. And when you're a poet you can cry for everything."

When B. Wordsworth suggests to the youngster that he persuade his mother to buy "a poem about mothers" for 4 cents and when the mother upon being approached, replies, "You tell that blasted man to haul his tail away from my yard, you hear," the boy tells the poet that his mother doesn't have 4 cents. B. Wordsworth says mildly, "It is the poet's tragedy." But what makes the protagonist more than a man living out a fantasy to cover a deep hurt is the universality of his yearning to create—in this yearning B. Wordsworth is the incarnation of Trinidad's other "soul." "He did everything as though he were doing it for the first time in his life," Naipaul says. "He did everything as though he were doing some church rite."

When the Town Crier shuffled off down Maraval Road, I thought of B. Wordsworth.

Bill joined us, and we drove into town by way of Wrightson Road, which used to be called "The Gaza Strip" in the years when the U.S. Naval Station was the noisiest and spendingest thing in Trinidad and all the night spots were on this street. Now only the Miramar, across from the railroad station, remains. The rest have been dispersed to St. James and San Juan, and even Laventile Hill is being spruced up, with real-estate speculators moving in for the kill. Only Independence Square (formerly Marine Square) is as it was, with its statue of Captain Arthur Cipriani, the father of Trinidad's independence, on a column in the center. We asked Edward if this World War I veteran, now dead, was a Negro or an East Indian. "Neither," he said. "He was a mixture, what we call "French Creole."

We drove on toward the airport, and Edward pointed out an empty field enclosed by a high fence. The gates were gone. "It was bought by a local merchant," he explained, "who had to leave the country. I guess he fenced it because he thought the land itself might be stolen. Well, they got even with him. They stole the gates."

When we discovered that our flight was scrubbed and that we wouldn't be leaving until early the following morning, we decided to take in the Miramar with a friend from the hotel, Martin James, who had been urging us to accompany him.

Derek agreed to go along. "You realize it's sinful," he said jokingly, "but what the hell." (Margaret had a migraine headache from taking the children to see Santa Claus at the Hilton the night before.) Driving in Derek's car through the dark, almost deserted streets, the four of us were silent. Derek's remark began to prey on me, and I conjured up a *Walpurgisnacht*. To break the mood I asked him whether or not he thought Naipaul's harsh criticisms of Trinidad were exaggerations arising from an expatriate's guilt.

"For instance?"

"You know. That Trinidad is an 'uncreative society,' that on the highways you drive without dipping your lights 'to make your opponent swerve,' that 'everyone in Trinidad knows that to run over an Indian in an Indian village and to stop is to ask for trouble,' and so on. True or false."

"You saw my column in the *Guardian* yesterday," Derek said, "the one on Walt Disney's death? I have a less critical temper. Maybe I'm soft."

I'd seen the column: "He was not a great artist. He lacked savagery, his satire was saccharine, inoffensive. He could sweeten all the savagery out of nature. But. . . he educated a century in the appreciation of the living line. . . . His morality was Franciscan, because it imbued every creature with reverence. . . . The world he made for us was as real as that in the fable of the creation. Tenderness, after all, looks like an easy kill, but it is natural and indestructible."

"Isn't it too easy," I persisted, "when you have as much sensitivity, honesty, and talent as a Naipaul, to pack up and live abroad, leaving this dirty little world with its hypocrisies and provincial pretensions behind? Could you leave Trinidad?"

"I could once," he said, "but never again. This is where I belong. This is where my roots are. All the criticisms he makes of Trinidad are true—true but irrelevant."

We had expected to compare the Miramar's floor show with the one at The Penthouse. But, despite an electric sign reading "Six Hours of Continuous Entertainment," there was none. Or perhaps it meant another kind of entertainment. The only thing that was continuous was the efforts of the slinky black whores to lure us to their adjoining "hotel." They danced with us, sat on our laps, drank our rums, fondled every part of our torsos they could reach without sawing the seats out from under us.

"I salute your detachment," I said to Derek, who finally managed to get a bench to himself.

"I can't do it. Soft again! It makes me feel too guilty the day after."

"There goes another broken prejudice," I laughed. "I'd always thought we whites had a corner on the guilt market."

"Look at Martin," Derek said pointing to our companion, knotted with the most African of queens. "He has no qualms about his Countess Dracula!"

But we finally managed to untangle ourselves, reel down to the street, and say a most reluctant farewell to our friend. Back at the hotel I was still sober enough to read Bill that most unsoft of poems, Derek's "Nights in the Gardens of Port of Spain":

> *Night, our black summer, simplifies her smells*
> *into a village; she assumes the impenetrable*
>
> *musk of the Negro, grows secret as sweat,*
> *her alleys odorous with shucked oyster shells,*
>
> *coals of gold oranges, braziers of melon.*
> *Commerce and tambourines increase her heat.*
>
> *Hellfire or the whorehouse: crossing Park Street,*
> *a surf of sailors' faces crests, is gone*
>
> *with the sea's phosphorescence; the boîtes de nuit*
> *twinkle like fireflies in her thick hair.*
>
> *Blinded by headlamps, deaf to taxi klaxons,*
> *she lifts her face from the cheap, pitch-oil flare*
>
> *towards white stars, like cities, flashing neon,*
> *burning to be the bitch she will become.*
>
> *As daylight breaks the Indian turns his tumbril*
> *of hacked, beheaded cocoanuts towards home.[5]*

[5] Derek Walcott, "Nights in the Gardens of Port of Spain," *The Castaway and Other Poems* (London: Cape, 1965).

VI

THE DUTCH WEST INDIES

The canny Dutch, when they traded New York for Surinam, were no cannier than the French, but they wisely held onto their distantly separated island possessions in the Caribbean, and they are beginning to make a good thing of them.

The islands are too small, too isolated, too dependent upon the outside world, and too tightly controlled to have political problems—yet.

Nationalism is strong in Surinam, and Holland's "twelfth province" on the South American mainland may be a bellwether. There East Indians and "Bush Negroes" get along well with their former colonial masters from Amsterdam but would like *talkie-talkie*, the local dialect, to replace Dutch and become the basis of a new culture. As in the once-French colonies, however, economic subsidies and a strenuous effort to eliminate racial prejudice sharpen other antagonisms. Without either the French scorn for "primitive" or "provincial" cultures or that arrogant Frankish insistence on the primacy of their own, the Dutch, for all their tolerance and administrative incorruptibility, remain isolated from the Negro.

V. S. Naipaul, who visited Surinam in 1960, touched upon the cause of the *psychological malaise* with his usual acumen. The bewilderment and irritability of the Negro was an inevitable consequence of slavery in colonial times. "Racial equality and assimilation were attractive but only underline the loss, since to accept assimilation is in a way to accept permanent inferiority." Surinam had emerged from Dutch rule as "the only truly cosmopolitan territory in the West Indian region," yet, "The para-

183

dox is that Dutch idealism is leading to rejection, while out of British cynicism has grown a reasonably easy relationship between colonials and metropolitans." [1]

The Netherlands Antilles are divided into two triads of islands 500 miles apart. The northern triad, Saba, St. Eustatius, and St. Maarten, lies east of Puerto Rico, surrounded by the Virgins and the once-British Leewards. The southern triad, Aruba, Curaçao and Bonaire, lies off the northern coast of South America far to the west of Surinam and due south of Hispaniola. The northern triad is scenically the more attractive but culturally the less developed. The three northern islands are also poorer economically, and, although St. Maarten is beginning to compete with St. Thomas and Antigua in hotels, tourists are only now discovering them. Two decades ago, Patrick Leigh Fermor found the northern triad primitive and depressingly neglected; he ignored the southern triad entirely. At the turn of the century, Ober visited all six islands and found them moldering in almost total decay. But, in the last two decades, oil refineries at Aruba and Curaçao have brought so much prosperity to the southern islands that the Dutch have determined to make all six "desirable." Today only 'Statia seems to be having trouble getting its share of the Dutch bounty, though Saba and Bonaire (wisely) are reserved for those who like to travel with field glasses, scuba tanks, or knapsacks.

At the beginning of the seventeenth century, Holland was given trading rights in those parts of the New World not already controlled by Spain. This grant and the search for a secure supply of salt, which led from Portugal to the Venezuelan coast to the offshore islands, impelled Dutch traders and smugglers to think in terms of permanent bases on those islands not already firmly committed to the other three maritime powers. Curaço and St. Maarten had excellent harbors. St. Maarten, Aruba, and Bonaire could supply enough salt to keep all the meats imported by the Dutch West India Company from spoiling. 'Statia (then but not now) was rich in sugar, cassava, coffee, tobacco, and indigo. Saba, without harbors or even roadsteads, was a natural fortress.

By 1640 the six islands were secured. Following the Napoleonic wars their status was reconfirmed. After World War II the Dutch granted them autonomy in internal affairs and integrated them into the Kingdom of the Netherlands.

Part 1. Aruba and Curaçao

Unless you are an oil magnate or a refinery worker, Aruba has one thing and one thing only to offer: the Aruba Caribbean. It is still a lot, because this hotel has everything a luxury hotel is supposed to have—

[1] V. S. Naipaul, *The Middle Passage, op. cit.*

and most don't. It has a superb white-sand beach and a huge swimming pool right above it, surrounded by 200 foam-rubber sun-tanning couches. It has two green-on-red composition tennis courts, two shuffleboard courts, four cruisers for fishing excursions, two circular dance floors water bicycles, a night club, a gambling casino, splendid food and service, two nine-hole golf courses nearby, and doubtless many more facilities we never discovered. Furthermore, as luxury hotels go, the Aruba Caribbean is not expensive, and everything has been done to make it easy to reach: Trans-Caribbean's, $35 one-hour jet flight from San Juan, for instance.

Aruba of the Tourists

My wife and I arrived at Princess Beatrix Airport from Puerto Rico by this route and were met by W. Watti Chai, assistant to Mike Kuiperi of the Tourist Board, who drove us the fifteen miles to the hotel. The first sign we saw along the way was in English: "Flaming Dishes: Talk of the Town." Aruba is like an oval plate, its flatness accenuated by a single volcano shaped hill, which Arubans call The Haystack, and some hummocks and large boulders off to the southeast. All that we saw of Oranjestad, the capital, as we drove through it was docks, oil drums, warehouses, restaurants, and piles of dredged sand flanked by organ cactus and a few wind-blow divi-divi trees. The very limited rainfall, absence of fresh-water springs, and a constant trade wind combine to keep even the coconut palms low. But the cool temperature and almost invariably sunny days are conducive to tourism—especially among the kind of people who go to Miami, San Juan, or Montego Bay and want to venture just a little farther, if only to add a name (and a label) to the island bag.

Marcel Wortman, a Frenchman from Surinam and the hotel's general manager, had already greeted us in our rooms with a big basket of cut-up fruit enclosed in red plastic, and now he invited us to dinner. The hotel and its annex, both attractive architecturally, were full; there were 160 guests stuffing themselves as a prelude to seeing the floor show.

"This is more people than we can handle," he said. "In fact the building you see going up a hundred yards to the south of us will be a Sheraton, even bigger."

"What brings them?"

"We have the finest beaches in the Caribbean, free-port shopping, and the friendliest, most relaxed natives"—the usual answer.

I asked him whether or not his guests really like this kind of all-American entertainment, for that was what the orchestra and the Atlantic City-caliber song-and-dance teams were providing. (It was clear by the applause that they loved it.)

"Can't you give them any local talent?" I asked.

"Ah, but there is so little," he sighed. "You will hear our only good steel band at the pool tomorrow afternoon. If I gave them that alone, they'd be bored. Besides, as soon as any local talent appears in our islands, it is immediately snapped up by Europe where the pay is double."

"What about talent from Haiti, Trinidad?"

"Have you ever tried to book Latin-American entertainers?" he asked, "even from Mexico? They generally arrive three days to a week late. And then what happens if they see some girls in town who are prettier or cheaper than they are accustomed to? They take off. If they don't get those girls, they get drunk!" He threw up his hands. "They have what you and I like, but how can I book such people and expect to stay in business?" Aruba's 59,000 permanent residents, we gathered, provide a very small reservoir of talent, and its "culture" is peripheral, Venezuelan or Trinidadian.

We left the hotel early the following morning with Mike Kuiperi, driving south along the west coast, passing the Olde Dutch Windmill (imported from Holland) and the Hydroponic Farm. This experimental station is, with one exception, the only place on the island where vegetables are grown. The exception is on the way to Fontein on the east coast. It is probably the best-protected vegetable garden in the world, watered by one of the few wells on the island and entirely surrounded by eight-foot walls with broken bottles along the top. It belongs to a Chinese citizen who is (like all Chinese) reputed to have pots of money buried under his house.

After cutting back to Santa Cruz in the middle of the island, we drove due south to Sabana Basora, where some of the typical nineteenth-century houses are to be seen. These dwellings sometimes have "hex" signs in low relief (white on green, yellow, red, or blue) on their corner pilasters. The single steeply pitched gable over the door then slopes gently over the windows to the pilasters—no doubt to catch the annual seventeen inches of rain (compared to Puerto Rico's 117 inches). In the days before a desalinization plant was built at Spanish Lagoon, the lack of fresh water was the island's major problem. This ingenious plant, which was completed in 1959, not only supplies all the fresh water for the island (the water is filtered over coral to put back the taste, for in the original filtering all the bacteria are removed), but also, in the process of changing the water into steam to remove the salt, supplies Aruba's electrical needs as well. This effort became necessary as a result of two developments. By the seventeenth century the Spanish predators had destroyed all of Aruba's forest cover. As a result, only a population of 10,000 was able to survive on the rain water provided by roofs and cisterns. But, when the huge oil refinery was installed by Esso in the 1930's, 8,000 workers had to be imported to man the installations at St. Nicolas. They came to Aruba from every island in the Caribbean, and supplying them with fresh water from tankers proved to be an expensive business. Hence the desalinization plant. But, by the time it was finished, Esso had automated its refineries to such an extent that only 1,500 workers were required to man the huge installation. Tourism was promptly developed

to take up the slack, and it almost has. The Aruba Caribbean alone employs 300 people.

From Sabana Basora we returned to the Coastal road leading to the southern tip of the island and passed by the great refinery. It is an imposing sight, quite beautiful with its towering ovens, some painted blue and green and banded with catwalks, and its spindly stacks tipped with flame.

"Four hundred fifty thousand barrels of crude oil from Venezuela are processed daily," Mike Kuiperi observed.

"Why here?" I asked him.

"More political stability than on the mainland," he answered, "and cheaper labor."

The Esso executives have built themselves a fine yacht club, with a movie theater, tennis courts, and bathing facilities, and on the bluff behind it a modern hospital.

We decided to drive back to the capital by way of Fontein again and to have another look for the Arawak scratchings that had eluded us on the way down. In the caves at Guadirikiri, there was nothing but bats, but in those just before the lovely dunes at Boca Prins our lengthy search was rewarded. Unfortunately, later-day savages have covered every inch of the walls and roofs with their less-imaginative graffiti.

We had a lunch date with Ike Cohen, who runs the Coral Strand Hotel of Oranjestad and its Talk of the Town restaurant. He is also an art patron, very possibly the first in Aruba's history. We asked him about the paintings in an expressionist vein that crowd his walls and corridors. They are the work of J. B. Schweitz, a thirty-year-old self-taught artist of Indonesian extraction, and we were sorry to hear that the artist was in Holland—after a brief stop at New York to try to collect from a crooked dealer who had taken his whole output the previous year and had never sent him a penny. Schweitz has a flair for color, and if he learns to draw as well as he paints he may become the first distinguished artist of the southern Caribbean. In addition to his work, a few brilliantly painted old Spanish houses on Wilhelminastraat, the "hex" signs, and furniture made of the massive highly polished *kwihi* wood in the village of Savaneta constitute Aruba's aesthetic accomplishments—a beginning.

We had an all-Indonesian dinner at the Bali, a houseboat docked in Oranjestad's artificial harbor. The single-course specialty is *rijsttafel* (rice table)—"blended during the centuries of close relationship between Indonesian and Dutch housewives," the menu says. To one side of one's plate stands a mug of *sajur,* something between a soup and a stew; a dish of *krupuk,* a puffed-shrimp mash dried out into boat-shaped wafers; and *sambal,* a very hot sauce of red peppers mashed in onions and lemon. One of these dishes is mixed with the main dish, which consists of a ring of polished rice surrounded by a dozen or so small silver containers heated by the brazier on which they nest: roast pork on sticks, tiny meat balls, grated roast coconut, curried veal, chicken smothered in coconut milk, tomatoes, pork in soya sauce, pickled pineapples, fried shrimp, eggs, beef strips, and mixed vegetables. What a feast for $5!

After dinner we stopped in at the Olde Mill for a drink and at the bar discovered that we were chatting with Oscar Henriques, Lieutenant-Governor of the Netherlands Antilles; in Aruba, things are that informal.

Curaçao of the Poets

It would be hard to imagine a greater contrast to Aruba than Curaçao or a lovelier city than Willemstad, Curaçao's capital. Its harbor is as capacious and beautiful as any in the world, and its architecture far surpasses anything else in the Caribbean. One would have to go as far afield as Venice, in fact, to find anything as picturesque as this concentration of noble buildings, brilliantly colored, in a maze of inland waterways alive with sailboats. The Schottegat, a many-fingered deep lagoon, is connected to the ocean by a long narrow inlet, St. Anna Bay. Forts were built on the four points of this inlet, and were surrounded by satellite bastions well into the nineteenth century, making the Schottegat an impregnable naval basin. Around Fort Amsterdam, to the right as one enters the inlet, the city proper grew, expanding along the banks of a smaller lagoon, the Waaigat, parallel to the ocean. But across the inlet another city (or part of the same one), Otrabanda, also began to take shape, and to connect the two a bridge of boats was conceived in the mind of some poet-engineer. Not only was it built, but, to keep open passage to the Waaigat and the Schottegat, it was also hinged at one end; it swings back and forth as interminably as a camel's tail to this day, causing monumental traffic congestion at either end but adding another dimension of aquatic beauty to the Canaletto-like scene. Otrabanda has its own lagoon paralleling the Waaigat and its intricate drawbridges.

The houses, and even the stores, are like palaces. Violet, cerulean, Chinese red, lemon yellow with cornices, window frames, and doors of dazzling white. There are triangular pediments over the windows, fans over the doorways, projecting dormers, gracefully curved Rococo gables right out of Vermeer, steeply ridged roofs, galleries supported by circular piers, arcades with squat bulging columns.

The Penha store at Herenstraat 1 has a chrome-yellow four-story façade covered with exuberant flowers, scrolls, and figures in appliquéd gesso. The Fort Church in the Antillean Government quadrangle is a masterpiece of Dutch austerity, if you can picture austerity with a double-pavilioned grand staircase in front and a circular lantern sprouting from an octagonal cupola in the center of the high-pitched roof. The Portuguese synagogue is one of the great unsung religious structures of the world, inside as well as out—its brass chandeliers with "parfait glass" candle shields hang from the gleaming barrel vault in an explosion of sunlight. But only a poet could describe Curaçao fittingly, and fortunately a poet has:

> *I shall play a game with the houses of Curaçao,*
> *placing the sea on the left,*
> *and make gambolling bridges. . . .*
> *We are in Holland and in America*
> *and it's a toy island*
> *with decrees of a queen*
> *and doors and windows of joy.*
> *With the strings of the lyre*
> *and the handkerchiefs of travel*
> *we shall fashion sails for the boats*
> *that are going nowhere.*
> *The governor's house is too small*
> *for a Dutch family.*
> *Afternoons Claude Monet will come*
> *to eat electric and blue things,*
> *and through that suspicious-looking alley*
> *will march Rembrandt's Night Watch.*

Within an hour of landing in Curaçao, surrounded by ghostly Giacometti-like figures I was translating this poem by the Mexican Carlos Pellicér with René de Rooy, who dug it out of a school textbook for me, in The Yellow-Green Pad, the art gallery that doubles as his studio. I had read a short story by De Rooy, "The Precious Stones of Uncle Brink," a few weeks earlier, but I hadn't been looking for him; I simply stumbled into The Yellow-Green Pad, and there he was, writing a poem of his own—in English:

> *One earthly joy was granted*
> *and it was shared in pain*
> *because a curse was planted*
> *love grew a thing too vain*
> *And thus so separated*
> *each stood in separate fear*
> *longing unmitigated*
> *blind to what was created*
> *so near. . . .*

That was as far as the poem had progressed. He promised to send me its conclusion—"as soon as I've worked through the metrics and rhythms to the sense of what I'm driving at"—and I'm still waiting. I intended to go back the next day and find out how this strange and wonderful man from Surinam, who writes poems in Dutch, Spanish, French, English, and Papiamento (the island dialect), marshals his images in so many tongues and media, but my wife and I became entangled with other poets. De Rooy, knowing Curaçao, must have realized that we would.

We had had an equally strange encounter even before we arrived at The Yellow-Green Pad. Two other stories in the Dutch section of Barbara Howes' anthology [3] had impressed me. One was "The Monkey Weeps" by L. A. M. Lichtveld, and the other was by Boeli van Leeuwen; both authors were reputed to be diplomats in Curaçao. We were met at the airport by the Tourist Board chief, who introduced himself as Dr. Lichtveld, but he turned out to be a distant cousin of the author of "My Monkey Weeps," who is presently stationed in Washington. Herman Lichtveld tried to reach Boeli van Leeuwen on the phone. Nobody answered, so he asked us whether or not we would like to visit a 200-year-old *landhuis* out of town that had just been restored by an eccentric veterinarian-blacksmith named Dr. Diemont.

Dr. Diemont could be described as a mild, wild man—mild by the standards of our frentic society, wild in the Dutch context of stiff propriety. He *looks* rather like a retired dentist from Minnesota: Nordic, emaciated, overcharged with nervous energy, solicitous for the patient's comfort (in the wating room). Only the slightly bulging blue eyes and staccato wit suggest that the bouncy Doctor fancies himself a mad genius—which he possibly is. But there was no suggestion of anything go-go in the "waiting room" itself: the restored plantation house with its so-so antiques. The action was in the basement. The "dentist's chair" is a mahogany pillar supporting the roof of a combination wine cellar-bar that was once the slaves' prison.

There Dr. Diemont drops his Dr. Jekyll mask and becomes (a not malevolent) Mr. Hyde. Wine flows, the spirit of revelry takes over, and the Doctor's chisel flies. For three years the stout mahogany column has been taking shape as a daemonic Bacchus, "rubbing his navel three times for

---

[3] Barbara Howes, ed., *From the Green Antilles, op. cit.*

good luck" as the creator put it. Hopping about his sculpture with infectious enthusiasm, Dr. Diemont had already become transformed into the perennial artist; we could have been in Greenwich Village or Montmartre in their glory days. "When I feel in the mood," he exclaimed, "I work at it night and day like a demon, but for weeks and months on end I take no interest in it at all." And when he *is* in the mood, the Doctor is clearly a natural with the chisel, for this Bacchus is savage, "tasteless" in the right degree, utterly convincing as far as it goes—which may be just far enough.

I asked the artist if he was familiar with Haitian voodoo, for his Bacchus called to mind certain sculptures evoked by that uninhibited cult. He replied that many Curaçaoans, Negroes of the poorer class, go to Haiti when they can afford it to practice voodo. "It's a short cut to Africa. But, as for me," he added with a twinkle, pointing to a shelf in the corner on which some blackened candles stood, "I practice black magic right here."

Curaçaoans, Lichtveld told us as we drove away, have an even older intercourse with the other part of Hispaniola. The Dominican Republic, along with Venezuela, supplies them with almost all their food; this setup is a Caribbean oddity, because the Dominican Republic can't supply its *own* food needs; it imports meat, common vegetables, and even avocados, from the United States. And Curaçao has also traditionally been a sanctuary for revolutionary exiles from both food-supplying countries. Francisco de Miranda and Simón Bolívar from Venezuela and Juan Pablo Duarte and Buenaventura Baez from the Dominican Republic all licked their wounds, tried to recoup their fortunes, and plotted their returns to power in tolerant Willemstad. Lichtveld told us an amusing story about one of these exiles, General Urbina, who escaped from Caracas a step ahead of the Venezuelan dictator, Gómez, several decades ago. Receiving little active help in his attempt to mount an invasion of the mainland, Urbina vowed to return to Curaçao and to avenge himself for this neglect. He did, and sword in hand managed to storm the citadel and hold it for a few hours. Urbina was shipped back to Venezuela, where Gómez permitted him to return to his plantation provided that he stay there; which he prudently did.

On the way to the Piscadera Bay Club outside Willemstad, where we were to have lunch, I asked Lichtveld whether or not there were wild goats on the island, as on Aruba. "Wild?" he replied. "If they eat your garden, no one claims them, but just run over one and you'll find the owner right there with a warrant for your arrest!"

The Piscadera Bay Club was in a muffled uproar over the construction of the new Hilton next door. Why this almost beachless inlet in the rocky coast has been chosen for the site of Curaçao's status symbol of "mature" tourism is a mystery. But it is clear that the forced incorporation of the rich, native upper class's favorite eating place was arousing resentment among its captive proprietors and guests. Lunch was an interminable affair, with a deafening steel band drowning out most of the acid comments of the victims.

We then set out for our hotel. The Curaçao International is ingeniously built into the ruins of Fort Amsterdam on the edge of the city at the entrance of St. Anna Bay. But, as we approached to within sight of it, a Shell tanker beat us to the waterfront in Otrabanda, and the bridge of boats swung lazily away. Each time this happens, day or night, there is a twenty-five minute wait at the narrows. Pedestrians, we were delighted to see, receive favored treatment. Tiny ferries carry them back and forth free of charge. For drivers there is no pleasanter way to sit out a traffic jam. Things are jumping in every direction on sea and on land, and the view of the finest houses at the intersection of the Handelskade and the Breedestraat across the inlet is superb. I was already beginning to regret that we had talked Herman Lichtveld into flying to Bonaire the next day, but perhaps Boeli van Leeuwen would talk us out of it—if I could ever find him. Another call, from our room, went unanswered; I decided to walk directly to his house.

Boeli Van Leeuwen

The chapter from Boeli van Leeuwen's second novel, *The Rock of Offense*, that appears in translation in Barbara Howes' anthology had made as deep an impression on me as had John Hearne's two stories. It is about Aunty Da, who takes care of her invalid father until she is forty and then, after his death, goes to live with an equally tyrannical brother, who has seven children. She falls in love, at last, with a common welder from The Hague, and he wants to marry her; but Da's brother is not anxious to give up a housekeeper and a free nurse for his children, and he explains to her carefully why their class could never put up with such a relationship:

> . . . in Holland [he] would live on the third floor of one of those houses where the washing hangs behind the windows. . . . On Curaçao it won't be so bad, but imagine if he should decide today or tomorrow to return to Holland and take you with him, what then? Would you be happy in a cramped house among workers who sing about Sien, Sien, beautiful Sien, when they are drunk, and slap one another's wives on the behind. . . ?
>
> Aunty Da, crimson and deeply hurt, looked at her hands and thought of Karel's good-natured face and his awkward affection for her. She thought of the dreams which had come to her in her sleep, of a house where she could be alone with a husband who would fill his pipe after the evening meal and read the "Stock Exchange and News Reports," shaking his head over political affairs and knife fights in the Punda.
>
> And she thought of a cradle in which her child would lie with its

little fist in its mouth and grasp Karel's forefinger with its other hand. But she realized at once that she would never have the courage to defy her brother.[4]

The consummation of love is followed by madness with the same inevitability as in a Greek tragedy based upon the "taboo" of incest. In a novelette by another Curaçaoan · writer, Cola Debrot's *My Sister the Negress*, Curaçaoan society is drawn with the same Jamesian introversion, the same crippling gentility. "On the small island," Debrot writes, "all the whites were related either by birth or by marriage." And in his novella the Negro girl with whom the young aristocrat is about to find happiness turns out to be his father's child. "Saved" by the threat of incest this time! I had already formed a picture of Boeli van Leeuwen as a tormented intellectual, gnawing his nails in a dusty garret.

How different was the reality! If introspection is there, it is buried under a mask as aggressively masculine as Hemingway's, a façade hand-

[4] Quoted in Howes, *op. cit*.

somer and more self-assured than Fitzgerald's. The novelist bounded down a flight of stone steps to open the gate and then stood bareheaded in the sunlight, looking at me quizzically as I explained a mission that was as vague in my own head and as sure of fulfillment as a primed canvas about to be attacked with paint.

"You—*what?*" he said, not unkindly, seizing me by the elbow and guiding me up to the door.

"I have no more idea what I'll find in Curaçao," I said, "or even what I am looking for, than you have when you start a novel. Here's my last adventure." I handed him a copy of *The Road to Panama* and autographed it. "Judge for yourself."

He picked up a copy of the Spanish translation of *The Rock of Agony*, which had just been published in Mexico and scrawled across the title page:

> *To Selden Rothman, a visiting wasp*
> *from the North! May you penetrate*
> *beneath the surface.*

I could see that lots of sparring lay ahead before I would be permitted to penetrate anywhere.

"Where's your wife?" he said abruptly.

"Napping at the Intercontinental. Where's yours?"

"Picnicking with the children. The Intercontinental is one place where I never nap. It's my studio, you might say."

"Studio?"

"I do all my writing there."

"You rent a room?"

"No. I use the lobby. It's the perfect place to work. People milling around, day and night, anonymously. What could be more private? I take out my typewriter and go to work. No distractions. Who can work in the bosom of the family?"

"I can," I said. "My typewriter's on the porch, where the traffic is heaviest. The children flying in and out; delivery men at the door; rabbits, woodchucks, and juvenile delinquents racing around the pond. My kind of privacy. Tell me about Curaçao."

He had been pacing up and down the long, book-lined living room, stepping over kiddycars and half-deflated balloons, his six-foot-four frame slightly stooped. He flung himself into a chair, threw a leg over one of its arms, and brushed aside the lock of wavy brown hair that half-covered his long pointed nose, which made a Grecian profile. His blue eyes narrowed.

"Curaçao? Nobody respects a country that has no communists. We're too lazy to be that doctrinaire. We laugh. And if you laugh you can't be a communist."

"You don't appear to have any gnawing poverty or overpopulation to attract communists," I said, "like Haiti. But there aren't many communists there either."

"You won't go into that starving, bedeviled country and save it from Papa Doc—until there's a communist problem, will you?" he said sarcastically.

I had to admit that we wouldn't. He seized the advantage.

"Why are you in South Vietnam? Surely not to help the South Vietnamese but to 'save' them from the Chinese Communists."

We argued the pros and cons of that one for a while and then the controversy over the Kennedy assassination, which seemed to fascinate him. He'd read all the critics of the Warren Report and approved one of the counter-theories. Sensing my resistance to conspiracy weaving, he needled me with the most outrageous fantasies—without giving me any feeling that he believed them himself: Oswald went to Russia as a cover for his "rightist" activities, Tippet was an F.B.I. agent, Ruby was a gangster in the pay of the conservatives. I laughed and begged him to talk about Curaçao.

"We're the only people in the Caribbean," he said, "who have something to lose by disorder. We have the democratic sense of all being equals under the law. We have a very relaxed sense of racial relations. In the 1962 elections an advocate of Black Power got 600 votes—600 out of 40,000. Here's a story that may make the point. One night I had to go to an official function and was wearing my white tuxedo. In the back of my car was a Negro friend. We both knew the Negro at the filling station, whom I asked to handle the oil stick so I wouldn't get soiled. 'You wouldn't do that for *me*,' my friend said to the mechanic jokingly. 'Of course not,' the mechanic quipped back. 'For a stinking nigger—what you think I am?'

"For the white man here," Boeli continued, "there's something very special about a Negro woman. Perhaps because one had one as a nurse in childhood. But I have a sense of security in their company. When my wife and I were in New York to have my back treated in a New York hospital, we turned to Negroes instinctively for comfort. Perhaps it was the cold climate, but I think it went further than that. And sometimes the Negroes rebuffed us—as they wouldn't here."

"They will if they keep reading the news reports from the States," I said.

"I was going into the Concertgebouw in The Hague last year," Boeli said, "when a New York Negro pushed me rather brutally. I asked him what he was trying to do, and he suggested we go outside and fight. I said to him: 'My friend, you forget you're in Europe. This isn't Alabama.'

"But we have this rapprochement in this hemisphere only in the Dutch islands," he added.

"And the British?" I suggested.

"Maybe the British. But we aren't safe. We're close to South America, close to the corrosive ones. Can we maintain the Western norm? The sense of spiritual freedom, the ability to call those in power 'sons of bitches' openly, regardless of their skin color? You've lost it. You can throw a white man out of one of your restaurants if you don't like his expression or attitude, but you can't throw a Negro out any more. You're trapped by prejudice in reverse, by your guilt. We're not. Not yet, anyway. We have an expression here: 'From wine you make vinegar, but once you have vinegar you can never make wine again.'"

I mentioned Naipaul's observations on Surinam. He nodded in agreement.

"We have the best of it, tolerance, but also the worst of it under the surface, hypocrisy. Why? Because the subtle gradations of social and racial hatred—which exist in the various mulatto strata—are not vented openly, as they are in your Watts and Harlem riots. This neurosis shows itself in fear. Those who are neither black nor white don't know whether to look up or down. Why should God be white? But he is!"

Boeli has ambivalent feelings about the United States. He is proud of Curaçao for being so frankly and blatantly in love with everything American. "The Dutch islands alone have never demonstrated against your presence in Vietnam. A Cuban sugar ship comes here, and we refuse to unload it. How can it be otherwise? Every house in Curaçao has TV. Every radio carries American news, almost exclusively. Every child's hero is Gary Cooper or Wyatt Earp or Batman or John F. Kennedy."

"Is that bad?" I asked.

"No. It's good! I love Westerns and Tarzan myself. Perhaps Mickey Mantle isn't my hero, but that's because I don't go for any sport."

Yet a few minutes later Boeli was deploring the perversion of life and "the loss of the tragic sense of death," under the impact of such "purveyors of optimism and unreality" as "Walt Disney and Dwight Eisenhower and Lyndon Johnson and Forest Lawn."

"Only a handful of your intellectuals," he continued, "realize that the end of life is death, that the world is bent on self-destruction. Why, when the man who bombed Hiroshima went mad with remorse, he was regarded as a traitor to the American way of life! I gave a poem to an intern at that New York hospital. It was inspired by my fear or by the cold weather. It went: 'If you help someone without loving him, you debase him.' But my brother from Canada who came to see me the next day was more acclimated. He said to me: 'Cut out all this crap, shave your sideburns, cut your long hair, and stop writing poetry, or they'll put you in the psychiatric ward, man!' I followed his advice, and that intern congratulated me for 'rejoining the healthy, normal people of this world.'"

Boeli's wife, Dorothy, came in with the children. She said that Carole and I should visit those beautiful beaches and flamingos at Bonaire the next day. But Boeli had already convinced me otherwise. "Why is Curaçao so beautiful?" he had said. "Because here people, a few people anyway, have always been inspired to *make* things. You've seen Aruba. It's a cultural desert. So is Bonaire. I'll run a film for you tomorrow morning that will show you why Curaçao is different—without words."

That night Boeli came for us at the hotel and drove us after dinner to a bar on top of Fort Nassau. From the terrace there is a spectacular view of the Shell refineries, which look, at least at night, vaster than Aruba's Esso works. Nothing is more beautiful than a refinery at night, unless it is a steel mill, a square mile of city slums, a garbage dump, or an active battlefield—all seen by night, of course, and from as far away as possible. The trick is to make any of man's collective enterprises attractive in pitiless daylight. There aren't many places where the trick is successful. Curaçao is one of them.

We talked about painting on the way home and the dearth of it in the West Indies outside Haiti.

"The best school of painters in the world isn't worth that price in misery," Boeli said. "I agree with the French painter who said, 'If my best painting and the cat were in a burning house, I'd save the cat.' Would you?"

We both answered that it would depend on the painting. "A good one, and the cat would have to go. A baby—that would be different."

We saw a very different side of Boeli van Leeuwen the next morning. He is the head of the government's legal department. Dressed in a business suit, he was sitting behind a desk that didn't have a paperclip out of position. Back of his swivel chair hung a sterotyped painting of a mulatto working man.

He saw the surprise on our faces. "It is my pride to be a good lawyer," he said. "Unlike the other desks, you see no papers on mine. I keep this department humming. Nothing is put off for tomorrow. Especially because it is known that I am an artist, I must prove that I am a good executive. Of course," he added, "when I put on my artist's mask, I take that part just as seriously—because I love it."

"Then there's no conflict between the two?" I asked.

"T. S. Eliot was a pretty good banker," Boeli said, "wasn't he? It's not damaging to do something different from your art, but it's very risky to do something similar. As a novelist, it would be bad for me to be a reporter. But I owe it to my family to make a living. I want to send the kids to school in Europe, as I was sent—only hoping they don't suffer the great trauma I did when the Nazis shipped me into Germany."

"I agree that it's as dangerous for a novelist to be a reporter," I said, "as for a poet to be a professor; the first smother their readers with facts and the second with abstractions. But isn't there an equally great danger in dividing yourself into two parts? Look at Wallace Stevens at the Hartford Indemnity Co. To prove himself pure in art, he wrote verse so precious that only fellow poets can read it."

"I'm lucky to actually *love* this job," Boeli replied, "especially the subtle political tugs of war between our two almost similar parties, and watching the great artistry it often requires to get things done and to assist in this by understanding human nature. So I'll stay here just as long as we have absolutely free elections and judges who can't be bought. If it changes, I can always leave!"

He turned in his chair and pointed to the mulatto working man in the frame.

"Here is my real boss. When I have to make a decision, I turn to him."

Boeli's documentary gave us many insights into Curaçao and into his own sense of poetic fantasy.

It begins with bubbles rising through the sea. Then come fish, rocks, and creatures with claws gripping the rocks while the surf thunders; then iguanas, cactus, the characteristic Curaçao landscape; and, finally a man, a grizzled, serious Negro fingering a shark's rib cage and building a crude boat like it. But the big developers move in on him with their bulldozers and jackhammers. He tries to cut their chains with his machete, but his boat is destroyed, and he is taken to a government old-peoples' home, where he receives a certificate and a number. Meanwhile, the other protagonist, an old white man of the upper class, is also doomed to unproductiveness by "progress." He is first seen in his *landhuis* with insensitive tourists flocking through. He encounters the aged Negro, tips over his glass of milk with his cane, and takes him away from the institution to his home. In the final scene the Negro is showing the aristocrat's tow-headed grandson how to make a toy boat just like the big one that had been destroyed, and they are smiling at each other.

We spent our last afternoon in Curaçao photographing the more remote classic Dutch houses and talking to Cola Debrot in the largest and most classic of them. This novelist is not balancing between the life of art and action. He has become Governor of the Netherlands Antilles and appears to be the right man for the job. He was familiar with my books on Haitian art and eager to see the Dutch islands discover a cultural identity of their own. Gracious, knowledgeable, multilingual, he made it seem obvious that a politician would be out of place in this post. But a man like Boeli van Leeuwen would probably go mad from refraining from insulting 90 per cent of his visitors.

Part 2. St. Maarten, St.Eustatius, Saba

There are places that it is criminal to fly into, places that must be crept up on and savored slowly. Philipsburg, capital of the Dutch part of St. Maarten, is not one of them. From the air Philipsburg is transcendental, a landscape no landscape painter (not even Turner) could have imagined. From the sea it is just another array of trim beach houses and tidy hotels sprawled along an arc of white sand. From the land it is two avenues of traffic creeping in opposite directions, Front Street and Back Street, neither of them with an ocean view and only the first with a sprinkling of jigsawed bungalows. But from the air—what a spectacle! Only the female body (and not many of those) has so many enticing curves. First, there is a blur of lagoons, barely land-locked ponds, green hills, and rocky promontories highlighted from the deep seas by a dazzle of beaches. Then, as the plane banks to approach the runway arrowing into the double-tracked capital, the whole landscape suddenly locks into shape, and color completes the picture. The eye, feasting on various depths of blue defined by the reefs, is swept up by that scimitar of sand and whipped around the perfect curve of Philipsburg harbor. Immediately behind the thin dividing line formed by the beach and the two rows of white houses lies an immense semicircular pond laid out *in pink squares.*

It is the famous Great Salt Bay, once the only source of St. Maarten's prosperity and now threatened by "progressives" who would drain it and fill it with city streets—which would be a disaster. If the disaster ever comes, it will reduce Philipsburg to just another of a dozen virtually identical Caribbian harbors. Viewed from the hills back of the city, this pink geometry of traps and dykes is just as breathtakingly beautiful as it is viewed from the air on the sea side. Up to 1900—when British protective tariffs, the mining of salt from mountains, and its distillation from brine made St. Maarten's salt industry no longer economical—the Dutch simply let the ocean flow into the lagoon, closed the dykes, and waited for the sun to turn the salt into cakes. The dykes are still useful, for without them the heavy rains would cause the flooding of Back and Front Streets from the rear. The rest is beauty. (The pink color, incidentally, is given off by a tiny microbe that develops as the salt "matures"; when there are heavy rains, there is no pink.)

A Toast to Dutchman's Head

We spent our first night at the Sea View, a small hotel with the advantage of lying between the beach and Front Street. Julian Conner, the new Tourist Board chief, wanted us to see the more luxurious establishments, so we set out with him on a tour of the island the next morning. The tour began with 'Guana (from Iguana) Beach, which an American, Richard Soskin, is developing and where Benny Goodman has already built himself a house. The lower parts of the island are parched, rocky, and virtually treeless, a landscape similar to Antigua's. Like Antigua, Barbuda, Barbados, and the Virgins, St. Maarten is not volcanic. We climbed to one of the high points (the highest is 1,400 feet) and there interrogated Conner.

There are about 4,500 people in each of the two parts of the island; 90 per cent of them are Negroes who speak only English, though the Dutch and French schoolteachers *teach* in their own languages only. This arrangement is particularly mad, considering that there are only 120 Dutchmen in the Dutch part of the island and only 30 French-born inhabitants in the French part and that the economic future of *both* parts must rise or fall with American tourism. "*We* are independent," Conner said proudly, "and *they* are not." But could the boom in real estate and tourism that the Dutch part of the island is experiencing be equated with freedom? Having visited all the main French islands by that time, I was more inclined to think that the big difference is that the Dutch genuinely like Americans, whereas the French don't. "Take us or leave us as we are," say the French in effect, "but we shall change nothing to suit you." "Visit us," the Dutch reply, "and we'll make you feel as much at home as if you wcrc in the United State." The docility of the ex-slaves is also a factor. In the last election in St. Maarten, the opposition party voted to go along with the government's candidates, thus saving expenses by presenting "one list" for all three Dutch islands.

Conner told us a story that might be to the point. A good mistress of slave days decreed a half-hour recess after breakfast. Surprised to see the slaves still carrying rocks during the recess, she asked them why. "*This* isn't work, Ma'am," was the reply. He told us another story to illustrate the difference in the French and Dutch temperaments even a hundred years ago. French and Dutch officials were banqueting together when the French derisively presented the Dutch with a cheese full of wine, calling it " Dutchman's head." The French officers didn't think it funny at all when the Dutch politely drank the wine and passed the empty cheese back as "Frenchman's head"—in fact they challenged the Dutch to duels.

There are fine beaches all the way around Simpson Lagoon, which occupies most of the west corner of the triangular island from Philipsburg
to Marigot, the French capital. Most of the land belongs to developers
and hotels, but all beaches in St. Maarten are public. We visited three
hotels. Mary's Fancy is small, intimate, and arty. Even the swimming
pool's filtering pump has a thatched roof. This guesthouse, justly famed
for its gourmet cuisine, was built by Kit Osborne, a retired actress, and
Peter Byrom, a retired interior decorator. They now run the Windward
Island Shop in Philipsburg and have turned the little hotel over to an
American couple, the Vincents. The Caravanserai, near the airport, is arty
too but in a more substantial way. Its neo-Moorish inner court contains
an oblong pool, which achieved local fame recently when jolly Queen
Juliana was thrown in during a party. The *décor* includes Oriental-style
murals, wind flutes, Japanese wicker chairs, and Turkish hookahs. There
is a splendid beach within walking distance. The big hotel on the Dutch
side is the Little Bay Hotel, just around the western promontory that
guards Philipsburg harbor. It has an air-conditioned bar, a gambling
casino, movies, and American entertainers.

Our Unpaid Debt to 'Statia

If one-sixth of the $80 million the United States allocated as a virtual
gift to the six Dutch islands last year went to St. Eustatius, there is little
to show for it. In addition, there were several low-interest loans to the
Dutch islands for routine road building and repair, some share of which
trickled into 'Statia. There is a commemorative plaque at the ruins of
Oranjestad's fort; it was presented to the island by Franklin Delano
Roosevelt, who stepped ashore on the occasion of its presentation in 1939.
The plaque memorializes the first salute to the American flag by a foreign
land, a gesture that took place at Fort Oranje on November 16, 1776,
when our ship, the brig *Andrea Doria*, visited St. Eustatius.

That courageous salute, and the more important fact that during the
ensuing four years the then-prosperous island supplied the American
revolutionaries with most of the arms and ammunition that enabled them
to fight Britain, cost 'Statia dearly for two centuries. For in 1780 Admiral
George Rodney, fresh from his victory over the French fleet at the Saints,
paid a retaliatory call at Oranjestad. On the pretext that the fort had
failed to dip its flag or lower it in time, Rodney destroyed the fort, the
wharves, and the capital; carried away £ 3 million worth of merchandise
from the stores and warehouses before burning them; and set fire to
400,000 guilders worth of dyewoods. With devilish ingenuity, he left the
Dutch flag flying while he plundered, with the result that he trapped altogether 150 unsuspecting trading vessels in a month. 'Statia never recovered from this looting and arson. It may plausibly be argued that
supplying the American rebels was primarily a smuggling operation at
which the Dutch Governor winked, in support of his greedy constituents,

but it cannot be denied that the "illicit" trade saved the American Revolution or that the salute to the young nation's flag was a gallant gesture— or that our debt remains unpaid.

Perhaps the most shocking reminder of 'Statia's decay is the sudden apparition of St. Kitts as one rounds the crater of Quill's extinct volcano at the southern end of the island. St. Kitts, it will be recalled, is anything but prosperous. Yet there are fields of sugar cane billowing up Mt. Misery's slopes: In the distance verdant St. Kitts glows like an emerald. 'Statia is neither green nor glowing. Sugar once waved over every inch of the dipping saddle between Quill and Venusberg, the blunted cone at the opposite north end of the island; but today the saddle, with Oranjestad's open roadstead to the west and Concordia Bay to the east, is dun colored, and and so are the two mountains, almost stripped of trees. This stripping may account in part for the lack of rainfall, and it may be argued that the mass of Mt. Misery on St. Kitts deflects some of the rain clouds that would otherwise move north, but both these conditions existed in the eighteenth century. In the seventeenth century the island had been bounced back and forth among the great colonial powers (there were twenty-two changes of flag), but between 1696 and Rodney's raid in 1780 the Dutch were in almost continuous occupancy, and a million pounds of sugar were exported annually. As late as 1768 600,000 pounds were still being produced, but the island's fabled prosperity ("the Golden Rock," they called it) was mainly in trade. In that year 9 million pounds of sugar, and in 1779 (the last year) 25 million pounds, were transshipped, mostly to the embattled North American colonies. 'Statia was doing just as brisk a business in slaves and other commodities. As in Curaçao, Sephardic Jews from Portugal and Spain became the leading merchants. Their community Honen Daliem (He Who Does Well by the Poor) erected a yellow-brick synagogue only slightly less magnificent than the one in Willemstad. Today it is one of Oranjestad's many melancholy ruins.

Windward Islands Airways landed us in 'Statia, on the short hop from St. Maarten, a little after dawn. Guided by Jan Lens, the island's genial Administrator, we had breakfast at one of Oranjestad's two guesthouses (there are no hotels as yet) and then walked to the ruins of Fort Oranje. It overlooks the pumice works, 'Statia's only "industry." It also affords a good view of the rubble Rodney left strewn along the black-sand beach below. The island is subsidized by the Netherlands, Lens told us. Although its population of 1,100 is not self-sufficient in food, yams as well as meat and fish are actually exported to St. Kitts. "Politically there are no issues," Lens said. Ninety-seven per cent of the people are Negroes who speak English: 60 per cent Methodists, 20 per cent Seventh Day Adventists, and the remainder Roman Catholic. As in St. Maarten, elections have been by-passed by agreement to agree. The Dutch government is spending $800,000 on a new pier for Oranjestad—a considerable sum when one considers the handful of Dutch votes on the island.

We were joined after lunch by George A. Bauer, a retired master sergeant in the American army, who had bought a 300-acre strip of land in the central saddle, from which he has already sold fifty one-acre plots. This enterprising Michiganite will put 'Statia on its feet, if anyone can. With the profits he has already realized, he plans to build a hotel, develop the calm beach on the northwest coast for swimming, and introduce surfboarding in the Northeast, where there are suitable rollers. But Bauer considers 'Statia better suited to be a retirement haven, on the order of Montserrat, than to be a luxury spa like St. Maarten. Imports are costly because the big freighters won't dock between San Juan and Curaçao and the small interislanders can't come in directly as they do at such tolerable ports as Antigua's St. Johns and St. Kitts' Basseterre. Transshipping therefore requires a costly third stage: lighters. With the new pier and an expanded airstrip (the present one is unpaved) leading ultimately to a jetport, "things will be different," Bauer said. How different will depend upon how many pioneers of Bauer's caliber are attracted to St. Eustatius. Bauer took us to his small house in the wind-blown saddle to meet his wife. We passed three of his five children playing happily in the yard with neighboring Negroes: a promising beginning.

Saba's Miniature Paradise

There was a time not so long ago when vertical Saba, capped by a rain forest in an extinct volcano's crater, could be reached only by inching in toward the rocks from 100 fathoms of deep water all around and leaping ashore. But it was never true, as the Encyclopaedia Britannica once said, that Sabans built schooners atop the mountain, lowering them afterward to the ocean by block and tackle. Alec Waugh scotched that one. Saba has no large timber, and the only big boat building the inhabitants could remember was when movie makers, who had read that fanciful script, went through the absurd motions of hauling lumber up the cliffs and letting a reasonable facsimile of a schooner down. Small boats, however, have always been constructed at Saba, and they are occasionally carried down the steep rock steps by their fisherman builders.

Waugh received the impression when he visited Saba fifteen years ago[5] that the introduction of roads and jeeps after World War II had begun to undermine the islanders' fabled happiness: ". . . [T]he practice of holding regular dances at the Rest House has been abandoned. The young men do not think they are worth the cost of a jeep and the girls will not go without one. There is less fun on the island now. . . . What kept [Sabans] happy, occupied and healthy was the difficulty that was presented by every project. Everything had to be worked for. . . . The Sabans had always been entirely dependent upon their own resources." Romantic? Perhaps not. The lovely neat homes and gardens that the self-sufficient fathers and grandfathers built are still there, but we saw very few people

[5] Alec Waugh, *House and Garden* 1952. Reprinted in *Love and the Caribbean* (New York: Bantam, 1965).

of marrying age; children spoke of going abroad if they could, and most of the action seemed centered in the guesthouses that cater to a small but growing wave of tourists in search of something different.

For different Saba is. One no longer leaps overboard with one's gear to breast the surf amid the rocks, but the very airstrip is an experience. And until helicopters drop one directly atop The Bottom, it will continue to be so. The 1,000-foot strip is hacked out of volcanic rock across the only relatively flat promontory on the island. One end of the runway drops straight off the cliff to the sea—and so does the other end. It is precisely like landing on an aircraft carrier but hardly more hazardous, for Windward's three pilots are all "hot." We had already flown with Georges Greaux and Hippolyte Ledée. This time it was José Dormoy, who is hotter than either of them. "Le Pipe," as he is called, in fact takes a day off every few months to indulge in aerobatics. "If I didn't, I'd go crazy," he says. Born in Guadeloupe, he was flying Spitfires for the R.A.F. in the Battle of Britain at the age of seventeen. Later he flew P-51s and P-47s for the French. Later still he was a bush pilot in South America for ten years, flying anything that could get off the ground. After 15,000 hours of such flying, bringing in Windward's nineteen-seat twin-engined De Havilland and its six-seat Dornier—even on such a strip as Saba's—is a bore. The Netherlands Civil Aeronautics Board permits only such twin-engined STOLS (short-take-off-and-landing ships) to carry passengers commercially. It is for this reason that St. Barts' Rémy de Haenen, who pioneered this field before it was leveled and paved in 1959, has never been able to take commercial advantage of it.

From the strip, the road snakes up the mountain. Two of the three principal villages, Hell's Gate and Windwardside, could already be seen hugging the mountainside precariously high above us. But, as we ascended, a rain cloud, which we had watched from the runway as it swept in from the sea in a dramatic rainbow, caught up with us. Everyone in the jeep was drenched—and enjoyed it. But halfway up to The Bottom we were transferred to another jeep, with side curtains, and soon we were stepping out in bright sunlight at Bud Vass's Captain's Quarters in Windwardside. Vass is a West Virginian who lived in Brazil for a while and then managed the Pasang-grahan guesthouse at Philipsburg for ten years. Captain's Quarters, a luxury hotel on a very small scale, was understandably full. It boasts a bite-sized swimming pool and what looks like a bite-sized concrete tennis court (actually it is regulation size but with abbreviated surrounding space), giving one the impression that an inaccurate lob might fall several thousand feet into the ocean. The court is built over a 65,000-gallon cistern. The hotel's main building is a remodeled Saba home on a typically walled street. The open-air bar is attractively furnished with Vass's glass collection. After a drink, we continued on to our more modest quarters, one of The Bottom's three little guesthouses.

The Bottom does not lie, as most of the guidebooks say, in the bottom of an extinct volcano's crater. The whole of Saba's precipitous five square miles is an extinct volcano, and there are several craters, one close to the top of Mt. Scenery (locally called "The Mountain") nearly 3,000 feet above sea level. Saba was colonized by the Dutch in 1640, and Père Labat, who visited it shortly thereafter, described what saved it from the invasions that the other islands were then experiencing: The inhabitants simply rolled rocks down upon their unwelcome guests.

The Bottom is an English corruption of the Dutch word for bowl, *botte*, and a bowl is what Saba's capital lies in. It is almost in the center of the circular island. Its streets are steep but nothing like those of Hell's Gate, where houses actually have to be chained to the rocks lest they be blown into the sea. Hell's Gate, incidentally, is where "Spanish work" originated; Spanish work is a form of intricate embroidery introduced by Gertrude Johnson of that community after a sojourn in a Caracas convent. When antimacassars and embroidered pillowslips were in fashion, Spanish work (sometimes called "drawn work") took up some of the economic slack after sugar and indigo declined. Export of these embroideries reached a peak in 1928. Now only a few old ladies have the required patience and skill. In the 1930s there was a big exodus from Saba to the refineries in Aruba and Curaçao. So many men left that Saba came to be known as "the Island of Women." But the exiles sent their savings home, and in time many returned. Only in the last ten years have tourists begun to "discover" Saba: 200 a year so far.

The Caribbean Guest House, in which we spent the night, is run by a gargantuan Negro of imperturbable calm named John Godfrey Woods. His thin, bespectacled helpmeet, who wears hair curlers and a perpetual slight frown of Protestant disapproval, stands between him and his guests. An English couple who complained that the toilets never flushed was presented an hour later with a bouquet of roses. At the table, the lady of the house devotes her considerable energy to snatching plates from under the noses of diners when they converse and let their attention wander. "Either you eat, or you talk," she explains. We received iced coffee in teacups, heavily sugared and without ice, though there were three men with her in the kitchen beating something that *sounded* like ice for fifteen minutes.

After breakfast, we walked to the house of Saba's Administrator, Gerard van der Wal. He told us of Saba's plans: Three hundred fifty steps are to be added to the 850 that now lead from Windwardside to the top of Mt. Scenery. There, in the small cloud forest with its orchids and lianas, are three "domes" from which Windwardside, Hell's Gate, and The Bottom may all be seen. A fourth village, St. John's, contains the little island hospital. Land in Saba is not easy to acquire, not only because there is so little of it but also because there are so many "heirs" involved in the "undivided plots." There is no real-estate broker, and nothing can be accomplished by mail. Prices aren't quite as low as in 'Statia, but they are much lower than in St. Maarten or St. Barts.

I asked the Administrator, as he drove us along one of the narrow walled strips of concrete that snake up and down the peaks, whether or not sand could be imported to make a small beach in one of the more protected coves.

"Sand? The sea wouldn't allow any attacks on her territory. She would remove the sand in two hours."

Though he came here in 1964, Van der Wal is like all the Caribbean islanders in thinking his island has the most. "What is more, I have no desire to ever leave." Noting that we were in the January-April dry sea-

son, he added: "This year it has rained every month. I'm chauvinistic. If I were a cloud, *I'd* stop here!" He was also quick to point out that there had been plane crackups at St. Maarten, 'Statia, and St. Barts—"but never here. Our strip may *look* the most dangerous, but it's the safest."

We drove down to Fort Bay, where the fishing boats and supplies unload and where Queen Juliana had come ashore after the dunking party at the Caravanserai. The good fishing is four miles offshore over the Saba Bank (40-100 feet deep). As little as 500 feet offshore the depth can be as much as 300 feet. There is no lobstering at Saba, but moonfish and red snappers are plentiful.

On the way up again, I asked our friend who designed and built these extraordinary roads, many of which were dotted with rocks from recent avalanches but all of which seemed to be in good repair.

"They were designed and built by a local with only two years' high school," he said. "Engineers from abroad were beyond our means. Lambert Hassell stepped in and just started driving in pegs where common sense dictated they should go. The first paved road, Fort Bay to The Bottom, was finished during World War II. The first jeep arrived in 1947." (Patrick Leigh Fermor made his entry in it "up that ladder of a road . . . through a chasm of rock" until the final twist revealed "the center of Saba like the inside of a rotten tooth.")

The teaching of Dutch in the Saba schools goes back only twenty years and seems to have made no impact on the English-speaking population. Even American currency is used. Fifty-five per cent of the 1,030 inhabitants are Negroes. The races stay separate in Saba, rarely intermarrying, or even attending dances together, but they do attend the same schools and churches. Twelve and a half per cent of the 1,030 are Johnsons, and 25 per cent are Hassells. The Johnsons are white, and the Hassells are "mixed from way back"; a James Hassell was Vice-Commander of Saba in 1677. The inbreeding shows, inevitably; white Sabans have an anemic, almost haunted look. Bad blood would seem likely between these self-segregated whites and blacks, but it does not appear to be so. We saw children of the two races playing together amicably in the streets. There is no friction in the schools or churches, the Administrator told us. "Racial *pride* doesn't exist among either whites or Negroes." Considering the bloodshed and arson weeping our cities in the wake of legislated desegregation, perhaps we have something to learn from Saba's live-and-let-live seperatism.

At 3:30 in the afternoon we took off in the Dornier. One of Windward's three pilots was already ashore with a Saba girlfriend. "Le Pipe" was at the controls again, with a girlfriend in the copilot's seat. She yielded her place to me when I told Dormoy I wanted to photograph Philipsburg during the approach. I asked him jokingly as we lifted off, "How can you go on smoking that pipe when the sign here says—"

"It says 'Passengers No Smoking.' I'm not a passenger."

Nonconformity, *si!* Saba, *si!*

VII

PUERTO RICO

"We have a two-party system," the classic Latin American joke goes. "One party is in the palace; the other party is in jail."

In Spanish Cuba, where the joke is reality, it is repeated in whispers. In Spanish Santo Domingo it was whispered so often during the thirty-year terror of Trujillo that whispering became a habit. In Spanish Puerto Rico, where there was always a measure of personal freedom and where today freedom is complete, a way had to be found to rejoin the family at the Latin American weeping wall. To be free was bad enough, but to be prosperous was treason. The prosperity posed a dilemma. Even the most fanatical advocate of the Hispanic way of life could hardly campaign for poverty and repression. To those who complained that the same party had been in the palace for twenty-seven years, the answer was that votes had kept it there and that the opposition (now in the open) was making most of the noise. There were still, to be sure, big problems—economic underdevelopment and an expanding population—but they were soluble in any atmosphere except one of political chaos. There was only one way left to supply that chaos: to feed artificially an existing state of self-hypnosis. *Puerto Ricans are still not sure who they are.*

The Crisis of Identity

Puerto Rico's identity crisis began as a seedling with vestigial racial and national roots, both fertilized when Puerto Rico became an American dependency at the turn of the century. The ugly plant had broken surface during the three months we lived in Puerto Rico, while the island was preparing for the inconclusive plebiscite of July 23, 1967, to determine whether or not it wanted statehood, independence, or a continuation of the existing compromise called "commonwealth." [1]

Unlike any of the other Caribbean islands we had so far visited, Puerto Rico does not have (and never has had) a Negro majority. Under Spain and even during slavery, Negroes never constituted more than 14 per cent of the population. Spain never really developed its colonies in the Greater Antilles, and it used Puerto Rico and to a lesser extent the Dominican Republic as convenient dumping grounds for its "undesirables." In Puerto Rico these poor whites took hold and became small farmers. This development was possible because during the seventeenth and eighteenth centuries sugar did not dominate Puerto Rico's life as it did that of the other islands. The small farmer or peasant survived in the neglected, ramshackle colony and became the *jíbaro*, symbol and backbone of Luis Muñoz Marín's successful drive to bring Puerto Rico into the modern world with massive American assistance. The Negro population of Puerto Rico today is in about the same proportion to the white majority as in the United States, but there is a difference: Prejudice hardly exists in Puerto Rico. Clearly the "racial" root would need a lot of watering.

But what about the root of nationalism, which can flourish even in the deserts of Arabia? Nationalism was not a factor in Puerto Rico until the "liberating" Americans arrived in 1898 and imposed a more tyrannical military government than that of Spain. The aboriginal Arawaks had retreated in the sixteenth century to the spine of mountains that runs down the center of oblong Puerto Rico from west to east; there they intermarried with escaped Negro slaves and with the original *jíbaros*. The tiny white sugar plantocracy, with its wealth in the plains around San Juan, Ponce and Mayagüez, provided the tenuous link with Spain. The only serious attempt to invade Puerto Rico had come in 1797, when Sir Ralph Abercromby, fresh from his conquests of St. Lucia and Trinidad was repelled at San Juan by the guns of El Morro and La Fortaleza and by the *jíbaros*, who streamed down from the mountains to the island's defense.

In the nineteenth century, with coffee and sugar bringing a measure of prosperity, two political parties emerged. Conservatives spoke for the plantocracy and favored stronger Spanish ties. Liberals, led by Ramón Power Giralt, Ramón Emeterio Betances, and later Baldorioty de Castro, demanded a measure of autonomy and home rule. The island's only violent rebellion, the so-called "Grito de Lares" in 1868, was not nationalistic; led by an American and a Venezuelan, it was a labor protest against a requirement for work permits. The abolition of slavery in 1873 only

[1] The vote for commonwealth was 60 per cent, for statehood 39 per cent, for independence 1 per cent.

confirmed an evolutionary process that was already almost completed. So far Puerto Rico was unpromising terrain for hardy nationalism.

Luis Muñoz Rivera, sometimes called "Puerto Rico's George Washington," who began to come into prominence about that time, was anything but a revolutionary or a nationalist. Born in 1859 in Barranquitas, high in the center of the *jíbaro* country, he began his career as a poet (just as his more famous son was to do). Soon he became a pragmatic newspaper editor ("We are men of our century, eminently positivist in the noble and generous sense of the word; this is not the epoch for generating dreams and building vain mirages. Platonism has no destination in our times"). He was dismayed by the violence of the Cuban revolt against Spain. He succeeded Baldorioty de Castro in the leadership of the Liberal Party, talked the Spanish liberals into giving the island self-government, and became the first Premier of Puerto Rico. And then, when this promising development went up in smoke the following year with the Spanish-American War and Puerto Ricans cheered their new "liberators," only to find themselves saddled with a military government and a new set of economic overlords, Luis Muñoz Rivera turned his Autonomists into Federals and campaigned for statehood within the American system!

It was about that time that Puerto Ricans began to be confused about their identity—politically and culturally. Statehood was first championed by Celso Barbosa, Muñoz Rivera's political opponent, who modeled his American Republicans after the then dominant party in the United States and spoke for the men of substance in Puerto Rico. Muñoz Rivera steered his Liberals into the same course, the better to bargain, so he hoped, for self-government within the "federal" American system. But, as American control over Puerto Rico became at once more pervasive economically and more benign politically, in accordance with a shift away from imperialism toward liberialism in Washington, a new grouping of allegiances took place in Puerto Rico. Muñoz Rivera's son, Luis Muñoz Marín, who had broken with his father's political philosophy while living in New York, in the 1920s and who advocated independence, returned to Puerto Rico—and to the parental pragmatism—in the late 1930s. He and the American New Deal Governor of Puerto Rico, Rexford Guy Tugwell, devised the ingenious idea of limited autonomy with close economic ties that came to be known as "commonwealth." The violently nationalistic and anti-American course taken by the independence party under the leadership of Albizu Campos had been one of the factors that turned the gentle, humane Muñoz Marín to a middle road. Albizu Campos was the illegitimate son of a wealthy white Spaniard and a mulatto-Indian mother, from whom he inherited his color; running head on into American racial prejudice in the Army during World War I launched him on his desperate career of conspiracy, political murders, Marxism, and madness. Statehood, meanwhile, continued to be the ideal of most wealthy Puerto Ricans, who feared the growing leftism of the *independentistas* and wanted to see the ties with the United States become unbreakable; by 1967 the leadership of the liberal industrialist Luis Ferré had encouraged more than a third of the island's electorate to vote for complete union with the United States.

If we discovered anything from living in Puerto Rico those three months, it was that Puerto Ricans—even many of Muñoz Marín's supporters—are having a hard time accepting their destiny under the sensible compromise of commonwealth. Only a fool would deny that the twenty-five-years rule of Luis Muñoz Marín and his hand-picked successor, Robert Sánchez Vilella, has brought Puerto Rico into the industrial age and the modern world. An honest civil service, imaginative government planning, aid from Washington, and exemption from both Federal taxes and minimum-wage restrictions combined to raise the islanders' per capita income in that period from $120 to $905 a year. Puerto Rico's annual economic-growth rate of 10 per cent is one of the highest in the world. Compared with the rest of Latin America, Puerto Rico's prosperity is exceeded only by that of Argentina. Illiteracy has been virtually eliminated. Tourism brings $120 million a year into the country, and the hotel strip in San Juan rivals the one in Miami Beach.

But malcontents of right and left much prefer to look at the dark side of the picture. Both cite this contrary set of facts: The per capita income of Mississippi, the lowest of any state in the United States, was 80 per cent higher than Puerto Rico's in 1940, *and today is 81 per cent higher.* The average wage in manufacturing is $1.26, half that on the mainland. Eighty per cent of Puerto Rico's families earn less than $3,000 a year—"poor" by American standards—and 42.7 per cent earn less than $1,000 a year; 51 per cent of the total income goes to 20 per cent of the richest families, whereas only 5 per cent goes to the 20 per cent who are poorest. Almost one-third of Puerto Rico's 2,668,000 people receive surplus food from American relief agencies. Illiteracy may have been abolished, but the *educational level* of the Puerto Rican people is fifty years behind that in the United States and won't catch up before the year 2010—if the United States remains stationary. Higher education in Puerto Rico enables a few thousand people a year to become lawyers, professional men, and partisans of an almost nonexistent local Spanish culture. Elementary education tends to be by rote; the teaching of English is ineffective.

Already one of the most densely populated places on earth (with 686 people per square mile) Puerto Rico has a rate of population increase 50 per cent higher than those in the United States and the Soviet Union and 200 per cent higher than the average rate in Europe. Even with the present high rate of emigration to the continental United States, Puerto Rico's population is expected to *double* in thirty years. The Catholic Church has been permitted, at least until quite recently, to wreck any government birth-control program.

This dilemma of rising expectations in a setting of deteriorating urban decay is what most Puerto Ricans find themselves facing today. Their situation is in some ways like that of the American Negro, except that the American Negro is a full citizen with at least a fair chance of forcing a betterment of his condition. The Puerto Rican is a second-class citizen, and he resents it. Yet he finds his present political status an economic necessity. Practical people—and most Puerto Ricans are practical—believe the country can afford neither the cutoff of American aid that would come with full independence nor the obligation of American income taxes—the primary objection to statehood. Yet what do those who urge them to throw off the "bonds of neocolonialism" have to offer? The moderate *independentistas* hold out the false promise of retaining the economic advantages of the present association while breaking the political and cultural ties. The extremists can offer nothing but Castro-style collectivism and austerity; an end to political freedom; oil, heavy industry, and armaments supplied (meagerly) by the dictatorship in the Kremlin. At best there is the prospect of a steady decline into the underdeveloped somnolence of neighboring Santo Domingo, a return to the political instability of the old Puerto Rico. The *cultura hispánica* that the advocates of independence constantly talk about wanting to save from "anticultural America" is the biggest mirage of all. Puerto Rico has produced no major poets, playwrights, novelists, painters, sculptors, or architects. The island's only folk art, the diminutive *santos* once carved by aged *jíbaros*, is not considered worthy of mention in compilations of Hispanic religious sculpture. The charming but hardly original architecture of Old San Juan, far from being cherished by the chauvinists of independence, is being restored under a commonwealth program by foreign (mostly American) merchants; the University of Puerto Rico itself is replacing the older buildings with poorly built imitations of the glass-and-concrete modernism the *Bauhausi* invented half a century ago. The Spanish language, though it remains the predominant language of the schools and of all but the commercial classes, is a drag upon the Puerto Rican's effort to accommodate himself to the American world he has opted for in every other sphere; in the streets it has yielded to "Spanglish," a racy amalgam of the two great tongues.

When Muñoz Marín left Greenwich Village more than thirty years ago to revitalize Puerto Rico's moribund social economy, he seems to have left the poet in him behind. Industries, hotels, road builders, advertisers, competing oil companies, and purveyors of popular entertainment were invited in without control over the barbarities that they might foist upon the countryside and the native way of life. It was inevitable that they would bring with them, if unchecked, the cheapest and worst manifestations of the American way of life—and they did. Too late to have any effect on the deteriorating popular taste, Muñoz made three gestures. He saved Old San Juan by subsidizing its tasteful restoration. He invited Pablo Casals to Puerto Rico and subsidized a festival symphony orchestra, which plays classical music quite outside the cultural orbit of the Puerto Rican masses; presumably, the idea was to give Puerto Rico cultural "tone" abroad. He announced in the early 1960s; that "Operation

Bootstrap," the successful economic-development program, would be followed by "Operation Serenity"—a spiritual countermeasure to the invasion of frenetic American values. No one has been able to define what "Operation Serenity" is, much less to observe it in action.

It would seem that, in providing Puerto Ricans with a serious clue to their identity, statehood would have all the advantages. But proponents of making Puerto Rico the fifty-first American state seem singularly unconcerned. If they discuss the matter at all, they say that, "once Puerto Rico has become a state," there will be no problems. But there are two problems right now. One is a majority problem and the other a minority problem, and perhaps the minority problem is the more serious.

The American Congress will never vote to incorporate an embattled minority, even supposing that it could be persuaded to burden the economy with a new state twice as poor as Mississippi. How then does one go about making American culture attractive to that minority of Puerto Ricans who think Puerto Rico holds all the cultural cards? One would think that at the very least statehooders, who control a large share of the island's communications media, would be countering night and day day the image of the Ugly American that bodies forth in its Bermuda shorts on Ashford Avenue and in the advertisements of American manufactured products. One would expect dramas celebrating the revolutionary emancipators from Thomas Jefferson and Abraham Lincoln to Eugene V. Debs and Martin Luther King, readings and exhibits honoring such American culture heroes of world stature as Poe and Whitman, O'Neill and Frank Lloyd Wright. Even bringing in Walter Cronkite or Huntley-Brinkley by satellite might catch Puerto Ricans up in the rhymthm of our times. But there is nothing of the kind. The scene is left entirely to two types that dishonor the American image from Saigon to Port Said: The ruthless businessman and the prostrate tourist. And, finally, an art museum erected in Ponce by Luis Ferré, statehood's standard bearer is filled, not with masterpieces of American or even Pan-American art, but with the sugar-coated leftovers of European culture.

The second problem confronting proponents of statehood is more substantial, though time is likely to resolve it. It is the objection to statehood on the part of the Puerto Rican *majority* which doesn't care a fig for culture—Hispanic *or* American—but which continues (though in declining numbers) to vote for commonwealth. "Statehood?" says the street cleaner in Caguas, the shopkeeper in Mayagüez, the taxi driver in San Juan. "We can't *afford* statehood!" This Puerto Rican isn't concerned about the Americanization of the Condado—he'd like to see an Ashford Avenue in every village on the island. But he is concerned about taxes, and he is prepared to give up the special concessions Puerto Rico receives as a dependency. Sooner or later this Puerto Rican *will* vote for statehood, and when an overwhelming number follow suit Puerto Rico will have an identity (an *American* identity) just as the Oriental Hawaiian has.

But until that happens the Puerto Rican will continue to be very confused, and not at all happy, not knowing who he is.

Inside Puerto Rico

The day we arrived, the island's intellectuals were in an uproar over a casual remark dropped by Stuart Udall. The American Secretary of the Interior had told reporters at the San Juan airport that the hotels along Ashford Avenue constituted "a blazing strip of vulgarity." It was an understatement, yet some of the same people who claim that the serene face of Puerto Rico is being turned into an ugly, chrome-plated grimace by the morticians of the American tourist industry are offended when a high American official makes the observation publicly. The reason Ashford Avenue was allowed to develop as a continuous belt of low-lying, high-priced hotels, cutting off San Juan's beach from the city it might have graced, reflects the crisis of identity. Commenting on the snafu that led up to this situation, a former chief of the Tourist Board characterized Puerto Rico as "the only country in the world where schizophrenia is a government policy." To provide reasonable rates, plenty of trees and grass, and access to the beaches for city dwellers, the hotels would have had to be at least twenty stories high and spaced wide apart. The Caribe Hilton, the first and at that time the only tourist hotel in Puerto Rico, measured up to these specifications; it is beautiful to look at in its setting of pink ruined forts, green sloping lawns, and blue flamingo-dotted lagoons. What followed was a nightmare. The Caribe was Muñoz' baby, and, when critics fulminated against its skyscraper proportions and other "American" features, he retreated. In fact, he leaned over backward until he (and the rest of the hotels that sprang up along Ashford Avenue) crouched close to the ground. "Go ahead and build," he said, in effect, "but not too high—about the height of our Puerto Rican buildings." As a result, rents skyrocketed; the excessive *length* of the buildings precluded any space between them, and the adjacent beaches were as effectively denied to anyone but well-heeled guests as if barbed wire had been strung around them. Too late, the Tourist Board complains that the hotels and restaurants are pricing Puerto Rico out of the tourist market. In 1967, at a time when Puerto Rico was losing the advantage in lower air fares that it enjoyed in 1964, room-and-board rates far exceeded any others in the West Indies, Hawaii, or Mexico. The average daily winter rate for a room in a leading hotel was $42 *without food*. With no customs exemption on foreign merchandise, Puerto Rico was at a total disadvantage in shopping. A rum drink that cost 30 cents in Barbados and $1.20 in Hawaii was $1.45 in Puerto Rico. There were inexpensive hotels and boarding houses outside the strip, but tourist agencies in the United States that make their money on percentage of total price do not like to direct tourists to them. When we left, there was talk of filling in the Condado lagoon, which borders Ashford Avenue on the south and is its one remaining feature of natural beauty, to build moderately priced hotels there.

With the possible exception of the El San Juan, whose black, light-switching *décor* is billed as "a psychodelic experience," the most swinging of the hotels Udall was referring to is El Americana, on an extension of the Condado strip that now reaches as far as the airport. It was being remodeled when we visited it, but there was enough of its combination of Disneyland and Playboy Club visible to point up what is happening. The beach was already defaced with molded-plastic elephants, camels, and rhinoceroses in gharish pinks and oranges. Uncouth stained-glass windows of knights in armor with lights behind them winked in the lobby. A new neo-Moorish night club was being hung with imitation Spanish moss. Exterior mosaics of the most tiresome banality depicted the discovery of Puerto Rico. By the glass doors leading to the mammoth swimming pool was this sign:

> *You ask "What is it all going to be?"*
> *Would You Believe . . . Fiddler's Green*
> *The only 30,000-gallon Aquarium in Puerto Rico*
> *Stocked with Underseas' Lights ! ! !*
> *A 20-Foot High Waterfall*
> *Moats and Grottoes of Natural Turquoise Stone From the*
> *Mines of Colorado!*

We rushed out of San Juan that night for Barranquitas in the Central mountains, assured that here was one village and one hotel that the *norte americanos* hadn't tampered with. On the way out, signs bore witness to the islanders' impatience to catch up with what we had just fled from: "We Speak English, Spanish, and Spanglish Teenager," "El U-2" "Sign of Good Taste: Coca-Cola," "Bar Bunker Hill." But El Barranquitas Hotel, wholly owned and operated by the Commonwealth government, would surely provide a cushion to this anxiety. From its Olympian perch, fanned by temperate winds and shaded by giant tree ferns, it looks down upon the Commonwealth's shrine, nestled in a valley whose slopes are green with tobacco, bananas, and coffee: The village where Muñoz Rivera, and Muñoz Marín, and the Popular Democratic Party itself were born. As the only Puerto Rican hotel in the mountains—equipped, according to the brochure we carried with us, with a heated swimming pool, a golf course, a tennis court, shuffleboard, and ping-pong—surely it must have a waiting list of American tourists competing with the Puerto Ricans for its two dozen double rooms. How lucky we were to have made reservations weeks in advance . . .

When we arrived at midnight, the hotel was empty. When we woke up the next morning, we discovered why. As I had been invited to lecture on art at the nearby campus of Inter-American University and as there was no other place for my family to stay, we had engaged two double rooms. The price of the rooms alone came to more than my lecture fees, and

the meals were so stupendously expensive that we were obliged to live on canned food cooked over a two-burner hot plate. Such expense could have been considered our private dilemma, however, *if* the "luxuries" and "superb food" offered in the brochure had existed. American tourists had long since found out that they do *not* exist, which was one of the reasons we had the hotel to ourselves. All that remained of the swimming pool's heating plant was a dangling rusty pipe. The "tennis court" was a corrugated-tar wreck. The "golf course" had greens of shifting sand crisscrossed by cow tracks. The shuffleboard diagram had been erased by the rain. The ping-pong paddles and balls had long since disappeared. The view from the Hotel (on the few days that Barranquitas isn't enveloped in rain clouds) is offset by inane, tinkly music piped throughout the lobbies, salons, dining room, poolside, and children's playground day and night.

I remarked to the manager, a dour Pole who flings his arms skyward in despair a dozen times a day that Pablo Casals, that solitary hero of Puerto Rican culture, doesn't appear to be influencing music appreciation on the island. "Casals' audience," Mr. Choderowski groaned, "is almost entirely foreign visitors, and those who do attend his concerts go only to be seen. The man on the street wouldn't know good music if he heard it; in fact, were I to play any of it in this hotel, my Puerto Rican guests would instantly get up and leave." This comment underlines the other half of the hotel's dilemma, for 90 per cent of the clientele *is* Puerto Rican. But Puerto Ricans can't afford the American prices, so they come for the day on weekends only—by the hundreds. They dance a little, ride the spavined horses on the hotel's trails, listen to the tinkly music, and photograph one another endlessly by the pool, into which no warm-blooded islander would dream of dipping a foot.

Lecturing at the university was another disillusioning experience. (We had already heard a class in Basic English at the "Hotel School," which the Commonwealth runs to keep a section of the Barranquitas busy. "John spoke English," we heard the instructor intone; "John did *not* spoke English.") But at the university, where, I was told, my students had already had between nine and twelve years of English, only *one* of the twenty-nine understood a word that I was saying, and it became necessary to lecture to them part of the time in my own fractured Spanish and the rest of the time through the interpretation of that one student who could follow. If the students had had any background in art or even in history, this language barrier would have been a mere technical problem. But it soon became apparent that they were as much victims of the crisis of identity as are the San Juan taxi drivers and bellhops. They had been brought up to believe that the United States had no culture, but they had been taught no pride in or knowledge of Spain's culture, much less of Puerto Rico's. Not one of them had ever visited the museums in San Juan or Ponce. On a map of Europe only half were able to point to the Iberian peninsula. And the only artists any of them had heard of were Michelangelo, Van Gogh, and Toulouse-Lautrec—and only those who had seen the American movies about those three had heard of them.

I drove to Mayagüez at the western tip of the island to lecture on the Dominican Republic and Peru at the nearby San Germán campus of the University; there, I had been told, an American faculty was giving the student body a sophisticated understanding of the United States' role in world affairs and a pragmatic education, contrasting with the nationalistic "cultural orientation" served up at the much larger, state-financed University of Puerto Rico. Driving down the central spine of mountains and back along the south coast through Ponce was a revelation.

This is Puerto Rico! It is sadly neglected and virtually unseen by the tourist but rich in natural beauty and history. Whether one takes the northern route through Orocovis and Jayuya or the more southerly one through Adjuntas and the Toro Negro forest reservation, the scenery is spectacular: tobacco farms and coffee plantations; bamboo trees twenty feet high forming a continuous Gothic arch over the narrow, winding road; views of both the Caribbean and the Atlantic from close to 4,000 feet up with the fertile plains around Arecibo to the north and richly cultivated Ponce to the south. From Utuado, where the two roads join, to Lares and San Sebastián, where the road descends to the rolling fields of sugar back of Mayagüez, there are many points of interest. Adjuntas and Utuado are attractive hill towns, the former with a fine square shaded by banyans, the latter with streets of stone steps against a hillside. The island's major Arawak site is on Route 111 between Utuado and Lares. The so-called "Ball Court" ("arranged" and possibly misnamed, one suspects, by Puerto Rican archaeologists, who have left no written identification of anything to help the visitor) consists of river-rounded boulders and jagged monoliths surrounding quadrangles of sand. Some of the stones are incised with faces and full figures, one seeming to be the "X-ray" of a pregnant woman, very similar to the already-described Carib carvings in St. Kitts. A guide, had there been one, might have explained what kind of ball was played there. Unless the soldiers of Juan Ponce de León knocked down all the original walls, it could not have been anything like the *pelota* played in the pre-Columbian courts of Yucatán and Guatemala. There is something awesome about the site, notwithstanding; it is a little Stonehenge in a bowl-shaped valley surrounded by crenelated hillocks.

Lares, where in 1868 the rebels gave the *grito* (cry) that was a prelude to the movement for independence from Spain, is the site of more Indian pictographs (in the Cueva de la Pajita). Near the caves a sign reads (in Spanish) "Country Club: No Single Man Allowed," and amid the dripping stalactites there are a dance floor of sorts and a bar. There is also an immense abandoned hotel, which was begun in the 1930's but never carried further than its basements.

The preservers of pre-United States Puerto Rico have shown more taste in the preservation of the Church of Porta Coeli in San Germán. This little chapel, surrounded by steps on a hill overlooking a lovely valley, is, together with the collection of restored homes and convents in Old San Juan, the most distinguished relic of Old Spain on the island. One assumes that the hand-hewn octagonal piers, the black ceiling beams, the whitewashed walls of stuccoed brick, and the lavender tiles in the steps leading up to the altar are intact from the late sixteenth century, when the church (now a state museum) was built. Later additions, but still from the colonial period, include the stations of the cross (bottle-shaped figurines carved by a *santero*) and several almost life-sized devotional images—the Virgin in bridal dress and one spectacular mannequin with hinged knees and elbows and a bold head that could have been the prototype of all Chirico's "metaphysical" dolls. The severely handsome carved wooden altar screen of twisted columns in pale wood may be the original one, as the Puerto Ricans claim. The altar cloth, depicting the Last Supper in needlepoint, is a fine example of a vanished Puerto Rican craft.

Mayagüez is an interesting provincial capital. It has as many spindly-columned homes in the nineteenth-century Spanish style as Ponce has, but they are in more imminent danger of vanishing. The finest façade I saw, with iron grillwork, was being torn down the week I was there. The

Mayagüez Hilton, set above the town with a commanding view of the ocean, ranks with Laurence Rockefeller's Dorado Beach Club (west of San Juan), El Convento in Old San Juan, the Racquet Club near the capital's airport, and the Caribe Hilton among the tasteful luxury hotels of Puerto Rico. There are fine beaches all the way up to Aguadilla in the north and down to Boquerón just short of the island's southwest corner. But at Boquerón is another of those sad reminders of Puerto Rico's split personality. The Commonwealth government has erected a colony of several dozen vacation bungalows, completely equipped with bedclothes, cooking equipment, frigidaires, and even air conditioners. As no family is permitted by law to stay more than a week and as application for rental must be made weeks in advance in San Juan, American tourists are effectively kept out and Operation Serenity at last has a visible symbol. But the rub is that the $7-a-day tariff and the difficulties involved in traveling to this remote area are too much for those Puerto Ricans who need such facilities (and who never "vacation" except on weekends or holidays anyway). When I visited the development on a weekday, *not a single house was occupied.*

The student body at the San Germán campus of Inter-American University is almost as infected with the anti*gringo* spirit as is the student body at the University of Puerto Rico. At a conference on the Dominican crisis, every reference to "American imperialism" was applauded, and so were several suggestions that Castro had been prepared to take over the strife-ridden island when the United States intervened; it was clear that these students had no conception of the tragic poverty and the political authoritarianism in the neighboring Spanish-speaking Antilles. They represent a minority so far, these students, but they are the most vociferous and articulate part of the student body. I asked one them whether or not the United States would be expected to go on paying the bills for Puerto Rico's development following independence.

"Of course," he said.

"And if the American Congress balked?"

"We would turn to Moscow as Fidel has—you wouldn't want that, would you?"

An informal seminar of young faculty members and some of the brighter students from all over the West Indies discussed the roots of this attitude. An American professor of liberal persuasion thought that the ethical ambuiguity of the American presence was to blame:

"After all, we did come here to exploit Puerto Rico rather than to help it. Why is American business here? Because labor is cheap and the unions are weak and because there's no return tariff on the finished product. The richer Puerto Rico gets, the stronger becomes the Puerto Ricans' desire to run the whole show—with their culture and language predominating—even if it means economic ruin, which it surely will."

But a student from Barbados thought the traditional Hispanic lack of sense of individual responsibility for the general well-being was basic:

"That and the Catholic Church."

"Is there a connection?"

"The other day the Chancellor caught a small boy from San Germán in the act of stripping the movable parts from his son's bicycle—right on campus. When he asked the kid what he thought he was doing, the thief replied without even looking up, 'It's okay; I'll tell the priest about it in the morning,' and the Chancellor had to pull him away from the bike physically."

"They have an immense pride in their culture," a student from Curaçao agreed, "but no feeling of personal responsibility for what's happening to it."

I told him about the waiters at El Barranquitas, who invariably bring the wrong dishes rather than admit that what is listed on the menu isn't in the kitchen—or that they can't read English. I asked a Spanish-born music instructress from the Arecibo campus whether or not her students yawn and talk during her lectures as mine do—except when a nude is shown, which makes them giggle. She nodded regretfully.

"I thought it could be the language problem," I said, "Are they proud of Casals?"

"When Casals came to play for them, they didn't stand up and applaud," she said. "In fact, their only interest in him seemed to be the fact that at the age of ninety he's happily married to a Puerto Rican girl in her early thirties—and they regarded that as some kind of a perversion!"

The flat road from Mayagüez to Ponce was choked with sugar-cane trucks. It passes the immense industrial complex of refineries and the Union Carbide chemical works fronting the Caribbean near Guayanilla— Puerto Rico's Pittsburgh. Closer to Ponce it passes El Tuque, a moderately good public beach that would rank as one of the Caribbean's best if the municipality would pay to have the seaweed and refuse raked off now and then. Ponce itself is an attractive city. In a declining section, not far from the main square with its famous red firehouse, the typical West Indian town house of the turn of the century may still be seen at its best. This house consists of a square wooden or stone structure, sometimes on stilts, with a veranda cut out of one corner, ornate slender columns of wood or iron, transoms and balconies carved with a jigsaw, and doors partly of stained glass. One beautiful stone mansion is graced with a corner crown of marble supported by eight Ionic columns. Another outstanding house has twin arched doorways, with sunbursts of glass in the lunettes, separated by a richly carved pilaster topped by a plaster Greek head with a sea shell sprouting from its filet. But there are favorites for every taste.

The taste involved in Luis Ferré's Museo de Arte de Ponce, alas, can be commended only for its $1.5 million envelope. Edward Durrell Stone's prize-winning two-story structure of gleaming white stone, with its triangular recessed galleries, sculpture gardens, divided grand staircase,

and perfectly lighted hexagonal exhibition rooms, harmonizes beautifully with the traditional horizontal architecture of Ponce. But the collection, put together from a sum slightly in excess of the building's cost, is a disaster. In political terms, as already noted, its fails to concentrate on the best of either American or Hispanic painting; aesthetically, it fails through the initial decision to purchase quantitatively from every period rather than to exercise qualitative standards in buying a smaller number of pictures and sculptures of incontestable excellence.

The discrimination of those seeing painting for the first time can only be debased. A people brought up on religious chromos, calendar art, and commercial advertising finds its taste confirmed. The most vulgar pictures in the museum—Lord Leighton's saccharine *Flaming June* and Bouguereau's evocation of picturesque poverty, *Far from Home*—are inevitably voted the popular favorites. The only type of painting, in fact, that is adequately represented in the collection is late nineteenth-century genre: those weepy Pre-Raphaelite fantasies of Arthurian legend tidied up by Victorian squeamishness and academic realism, from the neo-classicism of such *petit maîtres* as Vien, De Troy and Girodet-Trioson to Ulrich's pseudophotographic *Glass Blowers*. Of the great names, only Rubens and Velazquez appear, and they are represented by pictures of poor quality and doubtful authenticity. There are good examples of Zuloaga, Lucas Cranach, Bronzino, George Inness, and José Gutiérrez Solana. The rest is kitsch.

From Ponce one may continue all the way around the island's eastern tip by coastal Route 3, which eventually strikes San Juan, or cut diagonally northeast across the island by way of Caguas, Puerto Rico's fourth city. The road to Caguas via Barranquitas is very winding, but the scenery is grand. From Caguas a four-lane speedway puts San Juan only an hour away. If one continues east, however, there are many points of interest on the way to Fajardo before the road doubles back to the capital. The island of Vieques, along with smaller Culebra, may be seen, from most of the eastern shore. Together with Mona, in the western passage separating Puerto Rico from the Dominican Republic, Vieques is the largest of Puerto Rico's satellites. Twelve miles long and already boasting two airports and good roads of its own, Vieques is rapidly being engulfed by tourism.

A spectacular luxury hotel with bowling greens and golf courses around it, El Conquistador, rests on the cliff's edge at the northeast tip of Puerto Rico looking toward the Virgins. A few miles beyond Fajardo and less than an hour's drive from San Juan is the magnificent palm-fringed beach, Luquillo. Just a little beyond Luquillo's entrance is the cutoff leading to El Yunque, a rain forest that the Commonwealth has turned into a national park with recreational facilities.

San Juan: Old and New

The curious tourist who is willing to move a few thousand feet east or west of San Juan's Ashford Avenue finds two clues to Puerto Rico's aesthetic creativity from the sixteenth century to the present. Very few will be likely to visit the University of Puerto Rico's art museum east of the strip, but hardly a visitor misses the ancient forts and restored Old San Juan to the west; Old San Juan has become a shopping center for curios and paintings, and most of Puerto Rico's artists live there.

Muñoz' program for rehabilitating the decaying colonial city has been farsighted and successful. A bill was passed making it illegal to destroy the old houses or to "improve" them without expert guidance; funds were made available for anyone prepared to buy and restore an old building.

A good example of what many merchants did to turn the ramshackle slum into a showcase of colonial Spain, with balconies of chocolate brown against gleaming white façades, is the Galería Botello on Cristo Street. Angel Botello Barrós is a Spanish artist who had lived in Haiti. He moved to Puerto Rico in the 1950s and began scouring rural Puerto Rico for the "three kings" and other religious figurines carved and painted by the old *santeros;* sometimes he had to rub off as many as eighteen coats of smoky paint to reach the original finish. From his almost monopolistic collection, he now sells pieces at his two outlets, one in the tropical garden of the Caribe Hilton and the other in the street-level gallery of his renovated home in Old San Juan. The restoration of this home, with little inside balconies overlooking a pebble-strewn patio and tiles on the walls, is a good example of the tasteful initiative the Commonwealth program is encouraging. Another is La Casa del Libro at Number 255, with its superb collection of rare books presided over by David Jackson McWilliams. The magnificent El Convento Hotel, a little higher up off Cristo, is the shell of an ancient convent restored with fidelity and furnished with period pieces and good copies of the old wainscoting and carved doors. If the spirits of the pious sisters are disturbed to have the guests dancing, drinking, and swimming over their graves, they haven't made their displeasure known.

A share of the credit for the restoration of Old San Juan must go to culture czar Ricardo Alegría, an archaeologist by profession, whose headquarters is in the Institute de Cultura below La Fortaleza. Alegría's critics call him an antiquarian with no sympathy for the living arts. Others accuse him of pushing whatever is "Puerto Rican" to the exclusion of what is good and universal; his Puerto Rican theater, without dramatists, is cited as an example. He would not consider producing O'Neill's *The Fountain*, with its Puerto Rican setting, and he shows no interest in the poetry of William Carlos Williams, though Williams' mother was born in San Juan across the street from Casals' mother. Although Alegría has given more encouragement to the production of lithograpic posters than to painting, it may be argued in his behalf that Puerto Rican posters, issued under the inspirational direction of Lorenzo Homár, are as good as any in the world. No one has faulted Alegría on the restoration of Old San Juan.

Puerto Rico has talented painters, from the primitivistic Rafael Tufiño and the Lebrun-like Rosado del Valle to such known practitioners of the varieties of international abstraction as Julio Micheli, Augusto Marín and Domingo García. I was impressed most by the prints of José Alicea and Marcos Irizarry, both of whom have moved to Spain; a large lithograph of a *baquiné* (village wake) by Irizarry was the one work I saw that combined effortlessly Puerto Rican subject matter with a strong personal style.

The humdrum architecture of the University of Puerto Rico has already been mentioned. What makes these low buildings of glass and concrete even more depressing, however, is their decay after less than two decades. Cheap concrete stains and streaks in the rain, and this concrete must have been the cheapest. Upkeep is something Latin America has never understood. You put something up, and then you forget it. A case in point is the bronze memorial to the victims of the Spanish Civil War by Spaniard Pablo Serrano—one of the two impressive monumental sculptures on the island, Lindsay Daen's *Boatman* at the Sheraton being the other. The former stands in a shallow reflecting pool in front of the university museum. But the pool has been allowed to fill up with green sludge, milk cartons, gum wrappers, and contraceptives, thus totally negating the sculpture's message that *somebody cares about those million dead.* The museum has a good collection of Arawak pieces, an Egyptian mummy, a case full of *santos* that look like fakes (and possibly are) in comparison with those at Botello's, three amateurish welded sculptures, and a huge academic canvas of a *jíbaro* wake by Francisco Oller (1833–1917). Rafael Hernández (1885–1965), not otherwise identified, smiles benignly in bronze at a bird on his shoulder whispering coyly in his ear. The work of the best of Puerto Rico's artists is not generally on view; it is necessary to visit such enterprising commercial establishments in Old San Juan as La Casa del Arte and the Galería Colibri to see their work.

Mari Bras and Independentismo

The day after Stokely Carmichael had led a parade protesting "American Imperialism" at the university, I had a 10:00 o'clock appointment to interview the most radical of the independence leaders. Juan Mari Bras has a law office a few blocks from the campus. When I found his door still locked at 11:00, I asked the grocer on the ground floor when he was likely to show up. The grocer laughed: "These rich *abogados* can afford to sleep it off mornings."

By the time I finally caught up with the leader of the Movement for Puerto Rican Independence, the campaign for a referendum on the island's future status was already in full cry. The official statehood party was boycotting the plebiscite. So were the three independence factions. I asked Mari Bras why.

"Because a referendum under Puerto Rico's present colonial status will produce only what the United States want to hear. We insist that the United Nations is the place to bring Puerto Rico's oppression to the world's attention. We will vote only under U.N. supervision."

"Suppose you do," I said, "and Independence wins 51 per cent of the vote. Do the 49 per cent who voted No lose their American citizenship? Can you disenfranchise them?"

"We didn't ask you to come here and make us American citizens," he said bitterly. "Those who don't accept will be foreigners. They can stay or leave, as they like."

"And if statehood wins?"

He dismissed the possibility with wave of his hand. "The U.S. would *never* accept Puerto Rico as a state anyway."

"Why not?"

"We're not like Hawaii or Alaska. We're a living nationality. In a *free* referendum Puerto Ricans will vote as all humanity votes—for their country."

"And the Muñoz solution?"

"The pressure for decolonization mounts throughout the world. A majority of Puerto Ricans favor it now, but Muñoz is taking advantage of the *fear of change* to keep us in a status which violates the spirit of the American Constitution."

I'm not a lawyer, so I didn't try to unravel that one. I asked Mari Bras instead how Puerto Rico would survive without American aid.

"Today there is a deficit of balance of payments *despite your aid*. Do you know that the average profit on U.S. investments here is 30 per cent—compared to 11 per cent on the mainland?"

"Don't glare at me," I laughed. "I'm not an investment banker. A poor *gringo*—"

"*Piti yanqui*," he corrected me with a smile. "You have to understand that the forced consumption of American goods via monopoly far exceeds what we gain."

"And you think Puerto Rico would grow faster under a Castro?" I said. "You *are* a Castroite, aren't you?"

"I am *allied* with Castro. American imperialism—your finance capital controls your foreign and military policies, you know—is too powerful to be countered by any small oppressed country acting alone. We must join with the peoples of Cuba, Peru, Vietnam, and so on. But we will maintain our own absolute internal independence."

"You think Castro has?"

He sidestepped that one. "Castro gives us no money. But his airing of our cause on Radio Havana is worth millions to us."

"You must have heroes of your own," I said. "Who are they?"

"Betances, de Hostos, de Diego, Albizu Campos . . . "

"Not Muños Rivera?"

"Perhaps. But he was a politician—though not as cynical a one as his son!"

Muñoz Marín Speaks for Commonwealth

"This July plebiscite," Muñoz said to me a few days later, "is a contest between labels and reality. Puerto Ricans have always freely voted for the present status, *knowing it has defects*."

"But," I said, "wouldn't you admit that *ultimately* Puerto Rico will have to be independent or a state?"

"No. No. No. I refuse to be the prisoner of a dichotomy. We invented a third way in 1940, and a third way can be found again. That is the difference between being creative and noncreative."

I asked him what he thought the independence movement had to offer.

"It's an absurdity: 10 per cent of the student bodies; 3 per cent of the electorate. And always declining. How can they even think of taking his American citizenship away from a single Puerto Rican? Statehood *is* a possibility, but it implies imposing a limitation on the people's economy, and it constitutes a distrust of their creative capacity to find a native solution. The Statehood Republican Party is a subculture. There are fine men in it, like Ferré, and there are S.O.B.s, but they all distrust Puerto Ricans."

"How?"

"By demanding this artificial expression of loyalty to the United States. It's *undignified*, this 100 per cent Americanism—and it creates a natural reaction of suspicion. Why should an American citizen have to boast of his allegiance? That's taken for granted—by everyone but a statehooder."

I had talked with the Commonweath leader before—at La Forteleza in 1948 and several times in Oakland, New Jersey, my home, where he sometimes visits our close friend, Roger Baldwin, the founder of the American Civil Liberties Union; in fact, Baldwin was with us during this interview. We were all sitting in our swimming trunks at a rustic table under a sea-grape tree in front of Muñoz' beach house near Fajardo. Doña Inez was in the beach house preparing lunch. Santiago Polanco Abreu, Antonio Colorado, and other cronies were chopping up coconuts with a machete and putting the milk in a tin pan. On the drive out, Roger had remarked astutely: "Muñoz' career illustrates a truth: great men in politics weaken a country's morale. The statehooders and independentists base themselves entirely on the artificial, obsessive concern with Puerto Rico's relationship to the United States. Muñoz refuses to demand that the island's legislature be empowered to accept or reject Federal laws. If he did, he thinks, the statehooders would call him an *independentista*." He had gone on to tell me about accusing his friend jokingly of shirking his duties as a Senator: "Doesn't your conscience tell you, Luis, that you should at least *attend sessions* to earn your salary?" he had asked. "But—but," his friend had replied a little sheepishly, "if I even *go* there they talk to me about this bill or that, and, even if I express no opinion, the opposition charges me with making the decisions and running the country as if I were still governor. They've got to learn to do without me. It's the only way." This dependence on the father image—and the basic Latin American hesitancy to take personal responsibility for an action—lies behind the decline of Muñoz' party. While Muñoz was at the helm, it was incorruptible and efficient but boss-ridden

in the lower echelons; as soon as the weak Sánchez Villela became Governor, it became unresponsive to public opinion. Its critics were able to charge that it had made Puerto Ricans believe that the world, the United States, and the party owe them a living, that they don't owe anything in return, and that the dole is preferable to earning money. The party's philosophy, these critics charge, is summed up in the dictum attributed to Dona Felisa Rincón de Gautier, San Juan's flamboyant perennial Mayor: "I don't *care* whether it's against the law to take this money; I'm giving it to the poor." The fact that Muñoz was now being forced out of retirement to save his party from defeat in the plebiscite was most revealing.

As we waded out into the choppy water, Muñoz asked me whether or not I was having language problems teaching at Barranquitas. I told him that I was surprised to find that college students couldn't speak English after ten years of instruction. I told him about a Puerto Rican friend in San Juan, Aidita Moylan, who married an American thirty years ago and can no longer read a book in Spanish—"with the short unsubtle sentence structure." She had told me that English was well taught in the schools until Muñoz' Minister of Education put the emphasis back on teaching in Spanish. I reminded Don Luis also that, when my friend Steve Banker, in an interview the week before, had asked him why he took longer to answer the questions put to him in Spanish, Muñoz himself had replied "Because English is a more precise and economical language." I wanted to ask him whether or not the fact that when you want to say "I dropped it" in Spanish you have to say "It fell from me" indicated linguistically an evasion of responsibility. But he was already answering my first question when a wave swallowed him up. I looked around, startled for a moment, and then he reappeared, gesticulating through the bubbles.

"Yes, it's pretty bad, the teaching of English today in the schools," he sputtered, "but remember that once our teachers became *free*—you know they *had* to teach classes in English before 1940—it was inevitable that they would swing in the other direction to emphasize Spanish. Our first good commissioner of education was Padín. He was brought in by Teddy Roosevelt, Junior, a pretty good governor, and left there by F.D.R. It was Padín, not me, who brought back the teaching in Spanish. A child *must* study in the vernacular, the language his family talks. Padín was called 'un-American'—as if it were un-American to be talking one's native tongue! And the U.S. Senate—led by Chavez, the Spanish-speaking New Mexican—kept insisting that the teaching of English must go on. It was our Rafael Pico who told them, "You are insisting that a Commissioner of Education must be either unpedagogical or a liar!" Finally, when I became the first Puerto Rican elected Governor I appointed my own commissioner, and F.D.R. approved him."

I asked Muñoz as we walked out of the surf whether or not he was disturbed by what American tourism was doing to Puerto Rico.

"I am disturbed. I don't agree with those who want to make tourism

Puerto Rico's number-one industry. We don't want to become a nation of caterers. Operation Serenity—"

"—is a success?"

"A limited success," he said. "The Casals Festival, the theater movement, Ricardo Alegría's rehabilitation of Old San Juan and other cultural landmarks are steps in the right direction. But it can't be a complete success until the economy grows *and becomes the servant of what people want life to be.*"

In this matter, as in that of education, Muñoz' dilemma is the dilemma of the Commonwealth. Serenity and culture (least of all Puerto Rican culture) are not natural by-products of an Americanized economy; they can no more be tacked on as afterthoughts with any hope that they will take hold than can the teaching of English survive in an educational apparatus emotionally oriented to recapturing the old Hispanic culture. Commonwealth has enough momentum to survive at least one more referendum, but it is aging too rapidly to eliminate its inner contradictions, and without Muñoz in the saddle, gallantly waving his *jíbaro* hat, the old gray mare is going around in circles.

Muñoz' essential greatness, everybody agrees, was in his capacity to make Puerto Rico wake up, stand on its own feet with *dignidad*, and accept the American presence as a means of raising the standard of living. Once the old *independentista* in Muñoz began to have regrets, however, the way was prepared for the other two parties to contest the future. There are many stories illustrating the style of the dynamic Muñoz:

For example, the last time he ran for governor the Catholic Church attacked him quite openly, and he won handily. But after the election the good politician in him journeyed to Rome. When reporters at the Miami airport asked him how he'd repaired the feud with the Pope, he replied:

"There was no feud. All Puerto Ricans are good Catholics, and so am I. We all love the Church. Of course, before the election, they made a little mistake. Nobody loves a mistake, but we all make them now and then." The little mistake of 1960 was that the Church, alarmed by its loss of control over education and perhaps by the falling birth rate, organized a party of its own. It received 8 per cent of the vote and elected two candidates, neither of whom was found to be legally qualified.

Just after the Caribe Hilton opened there was a rumor that a Negro had been refused service. Muñoz phoned the management: "I don't know whether it's true or untrue, but if I ever find out that such a thing has happened I'll close the hotel the same day and turn it into a hospital."

Earl Parker Hanson, who knows Muñoz well, works for the Commonwealth, and has written a knowledgeable panegyric on both,[2] has several stories about the naturalness and simple logic that characterized Muñoz the campaigner. There was the local party organizer who introduced Don Luis in 1940 as "one of us" because he had just had a drink of Coca-

[2] Earl Parker Hanson, *Puerto Rico: Land of Wonders* (New York: Knopf, 1966).

Cola from the bottle. "I appreciate your support," Muñoz replied, "but if you support a candidate who drinks out of a bottle instead of a glass, every political son of a bitch on this island will run around sucking on a bottle. You vote for principles which I will now explain to you, and that is why we will win." Over and over he would ask a farmer how many times he had voted.

"Eight times, Don Luis," one farmer replied.

"Did you ever see any change in your life as a result?"

"Never, except that things grew worse."

"Then, for heaven's sake give us a chance. You can take your vote and give it back to your old party if you don't like what we do with it."

Votes were for sale in the old Peurto Rico, and Muñoz didn't blame the poor for selling them, but he pointed out that "You can't have two dollars *and* justice." Vote selling vanished.

Then there was the old *jíbaro* who sold his last two chickens for bus fare to keep a promise to the Virgin that he would kneel at Muñoz' feet if the latter were elected. They knelt together, but when Muñoz' family suggested that he reimburse the old man for the 90-cent bus fare, he replied, "When a man offers you his soul, do you give him change?" He sent the old man home in his own car.

Today this great and good man obviously enjoys being back in the arena, but he looks tired of it all and quite old. He limped out of the shallow water, where he had been standing without swimming while Baldwin, who is ten years older, was snorkeling with Carole over the reef. He joked apologetically about the armed guard the island government has assigned to him, but, when we suggested that he give them the slip, he shook his head. He spoke of looking forward to a cruise in the Mediterranean with Rómulo Betancourt on the yacht *Bacardi*, which belongs to their friend, the rum magnate Pedín Bosch, who financed Castro when the Cuban revolutionary was in the Sierra Maestra. Muñoz features are slack, and his eye wanders during conversation. It was only when Steve Banker took out a tape recorder and placed a mike in front of him that the old political war horse came to life, as though electrified:

"I'm going to identify myself so much with this issue in the plebiscite," he barked, "that everyone who believes in me will vote for Commonwealth! 'Personalismo!' they cry—and why not? The statehooders are campaigning unethically. They are using fear to sway the voters—fear of a nonexistent threat of Castroism. I tell you that five months from now those of my party who now say they will leave us to vote for statehood *will vote for me!*"

Doña Felisa: "The Mother of Us All"

Banker, who was making recordings for the Canadian Broadcasting Corporation, accompanied me to a luncheon with the lady Mayor of San Juan. Doña Felisa Rincón de Gautier is seventy years old and as full of grace and energy as a lioness. Not that there is anything carnivorous about this *grande dame*. She was regaling a delegation of fifty Red Cross workers when we arrived at City Hall. We asked her social secretary, Saida Rosa, what accounted for Doña Felisa's surviving twenty-one years in this exacting job. "She is—and always was—the mother of us all," was the reply. "You know she never had any children. They say that even forty years ago when she lived near Arecibo it was the same. Sometimes as many as fifty people were being cared for and entertained in her father's house." It was Muna Lee, Muñoz' first wife and lover of all things Puerto Rican *and* American, who brought her closest friend, Doña Felisa, into the Popular Democratic Party shortly after 1940.

"Things were terrible that year," Doña Felisa told us at lunch, "and it was entirely *our* fault. The United States was pouring just as much money into Puerto Rico, but where was it going? Stolen? No, not exactly, but it was disappearing in—shall we say?—bad administration! If we hadn't taken charge of ourselves then, there would have been a communist revolution, a worse one than Cuba's."

Doña Felisa's father came to Santo Domingo from Salamanca in the 1860s with the Spanish troops who were trying to reimpose Spanish rule on the unwilling Dominican Republic; he migrated from there to Puerto Rico.

When I asked her if she thought "our" culture was crowding out "theirs," Doña Felisa denied vehemently that the United States had ever "imposed" anything on Puerto Rico. "If there is Americanization and bad taste, as you say, then that is because we asked for it and prefer it that way. Secretary Udall was right in deploring Ashford Avenue, but he exaggerated. We *have* saved the forts and Old San Juan, but every time I try (and I've tried ten times) to put a symphony orchestra in the city's budget, I have to cut it out. Always there's a hospital or a clean-water project or housing or just plain relief that has to come ahead of culture. When all these things the people need are taken care of, *then*—"

"Then let's hope," I said half-jestingly, "it won't be too late to save their souls."

"It won't be," she said with that irresistible smile and a toss of her regal, turbaned head. "Our soul is still our own."

Luis Ferré Speaks for Statehood

The Commonwealth position on statehood, perhaps in an extreme form, was relayed to me by Earl Parker Hanson long before I'd met Luis Ferré. "It's an absurdity," the choleric, cigar-chomping geographer had said over breakfast in San Germán one day. "The party represents nothing but Ferré and his fellow island tycoons, and even *they* can't be for statehood seriously when all it would mean would be that their taxes would be tripled. What they are really interested in is power. This is their only way of undermining Muñoz and his successor and establishing a minority power base to fight for their interests in the legislature."

"But didn't 26 per cent of the electorate vote statehood in the last election?" I said. "Surely there can't be *that* many capitalists in Puerto Rico!"

Hanson removed his black spectacles, lit another cigar from the butt of the last one, and guffawed. " 'Smiling Mike' Menshikov, the Soviet Ambassador under Khrushchev, raised the same point when he was here. I explained to him that the employees of these businessmen might be afraid of losing their jobs; also, that there *are* a few who'd like to feel the self-respect of being first-class American citizens; and finally that a party that has been in power since 1941 has inevitably made some enemies. 'After all,' I said to him, 'a stevedore who loses his job has got to go *somewhere*, doesn't he?' 'Ah, I see,' said Mike, smiling. '*You* have a one-party system, too!' "

Ferré was actually "made" by Muñoz, Hanson continued, when the government of Puerto Rico decided to sell to private interests the cement, glass- and clay-product factories and paper mills it had taken over as part of Tugwell's state-industries program. "When Muñoz was asked why he was turning over this empire to his principal political adversary, he replied with a grin, 'Because the facts show that Luis has a lot more brains for business than for politics.' And how right he was! Do you know that Ferré once said on a radio program, 'Anyone against statehood is a traitor to the United States'—as if Congress would accept Puerto Rico as a state even if the Puerto Ricans begged them to! Somebody raised that point with Ferré, and he was naïve enough to answer, 'Congress can make us a state and then declare us a stricken area!' They say Ferré wants to be Governor in order to place a sign on La Forteleza: 'Another Ferré Enterprise.' "

Whatever Ferré may or may not have said, the portrait was psychologically false. Ferré may be as naïve politically as he is aesthetically, but no one could meet him and not be convinced that the industrialist's motives are idealistic and pure. There is simply nothing self-seeking in Luis Ferré and not a grain of pretention or guile.

When I went to call on him at his home in a residential suburb of Ponce, this genuineness was borne in upon me even before he arrived for his appointment. The comfortable neo-Spanish bungalow, set amid lawns and fragrant fruit trees, could be in a modest part of Palm Beach. No man concerned about his public image and eager to cut a figure as a sophisticated patron of the arts would have a tile above his doorbell with a Disneyish caricature of a plumber, wrench in hand, creating havoc among machines over the legend, "Aqui Vive un Industrial." On a vase inside hangs another slogan, just like the ones in every middle-class parlor from Oakland, New Jersey, to Oakland, California: "El Hombre Reina, La Mujer Gobierna." The parlor furniture is garden-type iron, painted white. Five-foot propane tanks and air-conditioning equipment are unconcealed against the glass wall looking out upon the patio, where sprinklers were turned on. On the other three walls hang canvases of academic picturesqueness. The largest, depicting Mont St. Michel, might have been the blue-ribbon winner in the Paris Salon of 1900.

Ferré came in and apologized, like an American, for keeping me waiting five minutes. He is a handsome man, youthful looking, relaxed, gentle. He has none of the stuffiness of the usual self-made millionaire, none of the self-consciousness one would expect of a provincial banker and cement manufacturer who had become a television personality overnight. He comes of an old Ponce family, and his wife, who has been an invalid with a weak heart for some years, comes of an equally distinguished family from San Germán. Until the present campaign, Ferré's solicitude for his wife's health was a political handicap and gave him a reputation for lacking courage. The Statehood Party machine was in the hands of her brother García-Mendez, a know-nothing type with an autocratic temper; every time Ferré intervened to give the movement respectable direction, his wife would plead with him to keep peace in the family, and he would yield. But, when García-Mendez sought to withdraw the statehooders from participation in the plebiscite, that was too much; Ferré assumed the leadership, stopped acting as a figurehead, and was winning popularity throughout Puerto Rico as a leader with at least an outside chance of winning an upset victory.

I asked Luis Ferré whether or not he thought Commonwealth had been a necessary step in Puerto Rico's evolution.

"Yes," he said. "It was one of the trials, economic and spiritual, we had to live through on our way to becoming an American state. It can be a useful state of suspended animation for another five years at the most. Muñoz, who will be seventy-five then, has already outlived his usefulness. He will be remembered as a great man. But his weakness was that he was too much the politician and not enough the statesman. The political machine he created has made it impossible for a healthy, effective opposition to flourish in Puerto Rico."

"Do you think the United States Congress will accept Puerto Rico as a state?"

"Definitely. After we have made our own wishes known and," he added with a smile, "after six to eight years of Congressional hearings."

"Can you win in July?"

"I think so. The people have lost faith in Muñoz' infallibility, and they have no confidence at all in his hand-picked successor."

Puerto Rico's reading public (and twice as many more who never pick up a book) had been in an uproar over the publication of *La Vida* ever since we arrived. Like Stuart Udall's remark about Ashford Avenue, Oscar Lewis' book was regarded by most Puerto Ricans as casting uncalled-for aspersions on the Commonwealth's "honor." When the author was charged at a public meeting with overplaying the lurid sex life of the slums, he replied that he had omitted 60 per cent of it. I wondered what Luis Ferré would have to say about *La Vida*.

He hadn't read all of it, he said, but he remarked that the "culture of poverty" is something that exists in every developed or developing country. "Mr. Lewis does show that there is a reservoir of kindness and understanding even at the bottom of Puerto Rican society. If there were one crust of bread left on this island, the man who had it would divide it with his neighbor. That is why we have not had revolutions. The people are kind, hospitable, long-suffering, and they believe in evolution." It was the same observation that our Puerto Rican friend Aidita Moylan had made the week before. "I've noticed in my social work," she had said, "that there's none of the classic schizophrenia. Even in the poorest family, a child 'relates' to others. If a baby is left on the floor, the neighbors come in and 'talk' to it."

The United States has been luckier than it deserves to have had a man like Luis Muñoz Marín guiding Puerto Rico's destinies in the first stage of the island's coming of age. We shall be just as fortunate if Puerto Rico continues to accept Luis Ferré as its standard bearer in the march toward statehood. But somewhere along the way the more aggressive American culture and the warmer Puerto Rican social graces will have to merge. The genius to bring about that merger has yet to be found, and until the merger takes place the Puerto Rican will continue to be as unsure of his identity as he is about the island's future.

VIII

THE VIRGINS AND THE BAHAMAS

Is natural beauty a commodity? Can it be cherished, preserved, and sold or rented in small packages? The Virgins and the Bahamas, which have a superabundance of natural beauty and nothing much else, think so, and they are making, against considerable odds and in a variety of ways, vigorous efforts to live by tourism without being disfigured by it.

Even to consider natural beauty a "commodity" might be taken as one more proof that our age is the most materialistic ever—but is it? In all the centuries past, did it once occur to the European colonizers of these floating gardens of delight that they existed for any other purpose than to enrich the few materially? Were they ever cultivated for anything but fortunes in sugar—which brought, in the process, destruction to both the soil and those impressed to till it? If any planter looked with ecstasy upon that tideless, island-studded mirror; allowed the sun to caress his body while kneading the powdery sand with his fingers and toes; or swam over the reefs to admire the kaleidoscope of fish among the elk-horn and gorgonia, there is no record of it. Did even such men of vision as George Washington and Alexander Hamilton respond to the coral sunscapes of Barbados and St. Croix? There is no mention of either island in all their voluminous correspondence, once they departed. All this luxuriant visual poetry was left, it seems, for our "money-mad" society to cherish, preserve, and enjoy.

Which is not to say, of course, that all who come now are grateful or that poets, nature lovers, and conservationists are more numerous than real-estate promoters, merchants, and hoteliers. But there is a consensus that what these islands have to offer is beauty and that, if Aphrodite is turned into a tart, everyone will suffer.

Nor is it to say that the Virgins and the Bahamas are without economic and political problems. How to share the sudden wealth, how not to be victimized by the high cost of imports, and how effectively to curb the rapacity of speculators in land and hotels are as much problems here as elsewhere in the Indies. But there is no "crisis of identity" among the predominantly Negro native populations. The American Virgins will settle for nothing less than their present prosperous territorial status and nothing more than eventual statehood. The poorer, less developed British Virgins may quite possibly switch nationalities and follow the same course. The Bahamas, plagued for years by a minority of ruthless white promoters and gamblers, have opted for independence with Black Power overtones, but the islands' first Negro chief executive is a London-educated lawyer with no illusion that his 700 islands have a future without foreign investment and tourism.

Part 1. The American Virgins

Webster defines a "vignette" as ". . . in general, a picture, illustration, or depiction in words, esp. one of a small or dainty kind." These islands are small and in vignettes they must be described. But first a word about how they were discovered, named, and grew to be what they are: The discovery was brutal, the naming was poetic, and the growing was commercial.

The Virgins were discovered by Columbus on his second voyage, as he cruised northwest from Nevis on his way to Puerto Rico. Fresh from their violation of the Caribs on Guadeloupe, the Spanish sailors came ashore at Salt River Bay on St. Croix on November 13, 1493, and proceeded to butcher as many of the "barbarians" as they could lay their hands on. The Admiral permitted Michele de Cuneo to keep one of the Carib women as a slave. "Having taken her into my cabin," wrote Cuneo later, "she being naked according to their custom, I conceived a desire to take pleasure. I wanted to put my desire into execution but she did not want it and treated me with her finger nails in such a manner that I wished I had never begun. But seeing that (to tell you the end of it all), I took a rope and thrashed her well, for which she raised such unheard of screams that you would not have believed your ears. Finally we came to an agreement in such a manner that I can tell you that she seemed to have been brought up in a school of harlots." The males who resisted conquest did not fare so well.

When Columbus sailed on, expecting the many elevations he sighted to cohere into one continent and finding instead that each was a separate island, he decided that they were uncountable and named them after St. Ursula's 10,999 virgins. According to one version of this ecclesiastical legend, Ursula, the daughter of a king of Brittany, took ship rather than marry in the pagan rites; was joined by all the virgins of the faith; sailed to Rome, where the Pope himself joined the company; and, along with her followers, defended their maidenhood against the soldiers of Attila the Hun. According to a less poetic source, Ursula was accompanied by a single companion, Undecimilla, whose name was later misread as the numeral *un decim millia* (11,000). But still another scholar identifies Ursula with the Norse goddess Freya, patron of the souls of dead maidens.

In the centuries that followed, the islands changed hands several times. Between 1755 and 1801, they enjoyed great prosperity under Denmark; many fortunes in sugar and rum were made. But a British occupation, the tariff imposed by the United States to protect Louisiana's sugar growers, and finally the emancipation of the slaves by Denmark brought on a long decline. There was a revival in the 1840s, when Charlotte Amalie became the third largest Danish city by virtue of its position as the best trans-shipping port on the trade-winds route. But the steamship put an end to that pre-eminence. And beet sugar dealt the islands a second blow. The Negroes, who had forced their emancipation by rioting, rioted again in 1879 against the planters, who felt no responsibility to feed them. Finally, in 1917, when the United States was concerned to deny the Virgins' ports to German U boats, Denmark made what was considered a very good bargain, selling St. Thomas, St. John, and St. Croix to the Americans for $25 million.

In the beginning, American rule appeared to be the culminating blow to the islands' economy. Prohibition eliminated the rum trade. Sugar continued to decline. There were no tourists. The natives subsisted on a dole. But, beginning in 1936, when Congress passed the Organic Act (Constitution) for the Virgin Islands, things began to pick up. The United States subsidized and bought the sugar. Later it phased out this crop entirely, which made more sense. Generous tax concessions lured light industry into St. Croix, and several plants were built. The hotels of St. Thomas began to rise. Laurance Rockefeller bought up the better part of St. John and presented it to the Federal government for a national park. Tourists started flocking to all three islands—some from the mainland, many by cruise ship, the greatest number on round-the-clock shuttle flights from Puerto Rico forty miles away.

Today the American Virgins boast a per capita income of more than $2,000 a year—more than double Puerto Rico's, five times that of Mexico. There is no unemployment. The multimillion-dollar "shopping bag" retail sales of Charlotte Amalie dwarf anything similar in the Caribbean. St. Thomas is the fastest-growing area in the world and ranks second only to New York in the number of alien arrivals annually. Only from these three islands may the American traveler return home with a duty-free gallon of liquor and $200 worth of goods—*every thirty days*. Progressive island governors have engineered this boom without defacing either the scenery or the charming Danish architecture of the towns and without a single gambling casino or superstar night club offering. The annual budget for the 50,000 inhabitants [1] is $45 million—twice that of Haiti, whose 5 million half-starved peasants never receive a cent of their government's take.

The drawbacks—prices on "American" necessities 25 per cent over those on the mainland [2]; domestics asking $100 a month and getting it; electric bills averaging $45 a month; a modest home on an acre lot selling for $75,000; a total lack of cheap hotels; poor roads and left-side driving —hardly affect the native population. Very few would exchange the benefits for the privilege of voting in American elections. Still fewer, perhaps none, would exchange their lot for the anarchy of independence.

Tram Combs: Poet of the Virgins

Ten years ago I received in the mail a slender volume of poems entitled *Pilgrim's Terrace: Poems American West Indian*. It was my introduction to the Virgin Islands and to Tram Combs. I liked the poems so much that I reviewed them for *The Saturday Review*. Here was a new voice out of a new world:

> *as God made the world*
> *I take it I am;*
> *and in its seizures*
> *cycling quiet*
> > *fires and riots,*
> *I find my being*
> *springs adorations,*
> > > *planned and chance*
> *falls to wintering like the dead*
> *casts, dies of rebellions revels reveries,*
> *I—yi—yi—yi! . . .*
> *of the urgencies*
> *and luxuries of being*
> *human I shall sing*

So the book began, rather like Walt Whitman but with a tincture of the extravagant verbal mysticism of Father Hopkins and the clipped, nononsense middle-class mysticism of William Carlos Williams. I wrote Tram Combs and talked about visiting the Virgins because I wanted to

[1] St. Thomas has 25,000 people, St. Croix 23,000, and St. John 2,000.
[2] The *per diem* allotment for U.S. government workers assigned to the Virgins is $30—the highest in the world.

see this landscape, so outrageously sufficient unto itself, and to know whether or not any poet could live on it long, where

> *in apricots the sky burns and the lights*
> *of town come burning gold*
> *in life's august and bronze a lizard*
> *swarms onto a brown stone and enters*
> *rites of thrust-ups to the west of flames*
> *hibiscus fold in pink spirals*
> *and papaya trees sail the wind green*

Williams, with his Puerto Rican background and nostalgia for the Caribbean, had been "soothed" and "delighted" by this poetry. And Kenneth Rexroth, carrying on his long war against obscurantist trickery at a time when "anything except corn-belt imitations of John Donne found publication almost impossible," warmed to its intaglio lucidity. Less a purist than these friends—with their contradictory gregariousness—professed to be, I doubted that even a lyric poet could detach himself from the mainstream of contemporary life, live as a beachcomber, and write only about the observed moment on an island in the sun without soon running dry. (Remember that these poems were written long, long before "dropping out" of society, embracing Zen Buddhism, and facing up to nothing but one's alienation had become the fashion.) I even thought I detected in one of Tram Combs' odes to Father Nature his own doubt:

> *when you first rub up against God's own skin*
> *He turns out to be rougher than Christ's men most expect,*
> *like a wood-rat, rasp or ravenous*
> *connoisseur with tender grapes! a rough trade!*
> *yet this seduction and adoration*
> *of Him we must get done, dangerous*
> *though it go; poetry's ways're*
> *strewn with the early-de-railed, -ridden, -filed who*
> *heard its sirens; and rose to go*
> *singing, but couldn't make it, hammered*
> *and strove but with beats unsuccessful*
> *to get on to come on with*
> *the real jazz and sea   for one's*
> *self, to reach follow-, fellow- father-*
> *ship with Him!*

Years passed, and I forgot about Tram Combs—until I came to the Virgin Islands at last, and there he was, middle-aged and surrounded by rare books up to the ceiling but still with his cats, still in love with the islands, and still writing with the same zestful detachment:

the beauty of the many colors of your skins, St. Thomas,
lights me.
on any casual corner
i watch ever delighted the passage
of Indian - copper Borinqueños; black-black, purple-black
& brown-black Negros from down islands; native Euro-africans;
eggshell-pinks of pallid continents &, subtly swart, Semites
from Portugal & Spain, Poland & Brooklyn;
palest, "the poor whites of the Saints,"
& scatterings of Arabs & Asians.
•

a rill of jewels in a stream of Ind.
scent of jasmine
on the steep streets, & far be • low
black water under blue stars
•

! nights of Charlotte Amalia ! [3]

I asked the Alabama-born poet why he had come to St. Thomas after the war. The war, during which he circled the globe, and its aftermath on the West Coast, with its waterless defenselessness on the leading edge of Russia's expected firestorm, had been factors. "The Virgins' incredible beauty took hold of me," he said, "and its easy race relations, where so many different nationalities live in harmony. Do you know that between 1920 and 1950 *thirty* books of verse were published here? With an adult population of no more than 8,000! To be sure, none of them were exceptional—but what a typical Latin American drive for culture is represented in that statistic!"

Tram is lean and sinewy, his wiry black hair crew-cut. He is a bookish man who supports himself by supplying mail orders from his 20,000 Latin American books, but he is at the same time an outdoorsman with a profound knowledge of everything relating to the Virgins—and a surprising lack of experience in the other Caribbean islands. His mind is as orderly as his card index, and he speaks slowly, meticulously, and to the point. He is a compulsive bachelor, and he has a compulsive interest in keeping up with the preoccupations of the younger poets. He has smoked pot, and he intends to take a "trip" with LSD on his next visit to New York, where he keeps a flat in Greenwich Village. But he enjoys introducing the urban poets to the simpler pleasures of island living too; when Lawrence Ferlinghetti visited St. Thomas, Tram did some genealogical research and surprised the California poet by disclosing to him that he had an unknown aunt who owns an offshore island.

[3] Tram Combs, *St. Thomas: Poems.* (Middletown, Conn.: Wesleyan University Press, 1965).

I am a later Thoreau, perhaps—
my pond the Caribbean,
my bean-rows bookshelves
making love
with particulars of God's humming [4]

Up and Over St. Thomas

Tram took us to lunch at the Mountain Top Hotel, from which a splendid view unfolds. One of the unique fascinations of the Virgins is the constant sight of other islands: The sea is never empty. From Signal Mountain, Jost Van Dyke is in the foreground, and beyond, due east, are St. John and British Tortola; the passage between the latter two separates the American and British Virgin Islands. Forty miles farther down passage lies Virgin Gorda, pictures of whose boulder-strewn beach had figured in my dreams for years. Anegada, farther to the northeast, is too low to be visible; its reefs were a terror to seamen in the days of sailing ships, and many a galleon still lies there waiting to be looted. Directly below the hotel's terrace is Magens Bay, with a swatch of sand so neatly tucked into its square pocket that it looks like the work of an interior decorator. Tram, who had majored in meteorology and physics in college, told us that St. Thomas and its satellites are composed of a granitic rock called "blue bit," or "bitch." It is a hard porphyry edged with accretions of coral and limestone. St. Croix, behind us far over the tops of St. Thomas' mountains, is not, geologically speaking, a Virgin at all or even a member of the West Indian volcanic chain; like Barbados it is a coral pop-up and is separated from its sisters by a trench 15,000 feet deep.

The people of St. Thomas traditionally distrust and dislike the people of St. Croix, Tram remarked, "and vice versa." In St. Croix itself, he added, the people of the two towns, Christiansted and Frederiksted, also distrust each other. He chuckled. "It's a matter of precedence signifying nothing, since everything in the Virgins is imported—including the people."

From another vantage point on the winding road we had a fine view of Inner and Outer Bras and of Hans Lollik, which was sold five years ago for $500,000 to Walter Marlowe, another of those architect-contractor-idealists like Peter Brand. He intends to plant a hotel there, with housing and a golf course—and to ban the internal-combustion engine. On our way to Coki Beach we had our first view of Tutu, the fertile interior valley of St. Thomas, already beginning to sprawl with Levittowns. Tram prefers Coki to the more celebrated and fluorescently named Morningstar on the Caribbean side or Sapphire on the Atlantic. Coki was happily deserted, except for a boy at the gate, who collected a 50-cent

[4] Combs, *Briefs: Poems*, with illustrations by D. Clark (Franklin, N.H.: Hillside, 1966).

admission fee—a low price for privacy. We swam toward the sunset in the cool, green waves.

On the way back to Charlotte Amalie, I told Tram that I'd recently read that the British consider their Virgins a drag on the Exchequer. "What prevents us from acquiring them?"

"Congress," he said, "and the political consequences of taking in 'colonial' Negroes with disturbing politics of their own. Example: The present dominant party, the Democrats—formerly the Unity Party, with racist tendencies—has *by law* effectively prevented the opposition party from continuing on the ballot."

"I've heard that the same thing is happening here," I said, "but I won't embarrass you by asking whether it's true. My interviews with the politicians should take care of that, but tell me one thing: Will the white population ever be in a majority?"

"With Puerto Ricans included, it probably is now, excluding resident aliens," he replied. "But perhaps it won't be for long. Negroes are especially fond of children. In this mother-oriented society, where the men rarely live in the house and the children are apt to be fatherless, there's some security in a high birth rate, and the birth rate here is ridiculous!"

St. John's Peacock Paradise

The very, very rich and the very, very poor are conspicuous by their absence. But if middle-class America may, like all Gaul, be divided into three parts, the lower middle part has found its playground in St. Thomas, the middle middle part in suburban St. Croix, and the upper middle part in St. John. St. John's superior beauty is insured against contamination by the difficulty of getting there—by motor launch from St. Thomas' Red Hook Bay, private seaplane, or yacht only—and by the princely price of a pad in Laurance Rockefeller's Caneel Bay Plantation.

The question, though no one is impolite enough to ask it, is What was Laurance Rockefeller trying to prove? Fifteen years ago he bought the inner two-thirds of the irregularly shaped island and its best beaches. He gave the better part to the U.S. Government as a public park and wild-life preserve. He is clearly a philanthropist and public benefactor, laying the ghost of rapacious John D., Sr., as the old man's son and all the other grandchildren have also done. But then he built this luxury hotel, the Frenchman's Cove of Caribbean America, which charges prices only the rich can afford [5] and caters, with its exaggerated personal service, to that peculiar combination of snobbery and underkeyed taste that the upper middle class demands. Here, in their "uniform"—solid-color Bermuda shorts and knee-length stockings for men, cashmere cardigans and sober muu-muus for their wives—they live, cut off from one another

[5] It costs $65 a day per couple, which, added to a minimal $50 in extras and the $250 round-trip first-class air fare from the United States, comes to about $1,450 for a two-week vacation.

and the world, waited upon by handsome, obsequious blacks. They sleep, eat, and drink unobtrusively far from the raucous fleshpots of San Juan and the bargain-basement honky-tonk of Charlotte Amalie.

Caneel is the old Dutch word for cinnamon. Our particular guest house was a good ten minutes walk from the cinnamon-colored main building. Others are farther still. The distance problem is solved by running buses from the cottages every half-hour, but this solution has the drawback of turning the guests into commuters: One is constantly watching the clock, missing connections, sitting on the waiting bench. By the time we'd made it to the main dining room, we were obliged to race through a superb lunch. Tortola-born Edward Sullivan, one of the managers, was waiting to drive us to Cruz Bay.

We drove over the ridge, from which there is a fine view of St. Croix forty miles to the south. Then we stopped off at Islandia, a gift shop that specializes in Finnish *objets d'art*, pins designed after Haitian *vévérs*, and The Little Devil Do It Yourself Voodoo Kit (For People Who Don't Like People), complete with "pain pins," a smartly dressed doll to stick them in, "life-like effigy wax," "spotless brand jumbie beads," and an empty flask labeled "one live jumbie (invisible)." The price for the kit is $6.95. One of the shop's co-owners, Suzie Sheffield of Wyckoff, New Jersey, showed us some of the pretty little abstractions that she paints on the insides of calabash shells—further testimony to Haiti's influence.

We climbed again to a spot in the mountains where orchids bloom from May to July. From there tourists can take a two-mile downhill walk to Reef Bay, where a boat waits to pick them up. In these reforested 1,000-foot hills, which were once covered with sugar cane, a few deer and wild pigs still roam. There are traces of the cobblestone road the slaves built and, of course, many sugar mills in ruins. From another lookout we could see Tortola and Virgin Gorda, Norman and Ginger Islands, and Dead Man's Chest, where Blackbeard is reputed to have marooned the "sixteen men" of the famous song. Poisonous manchineel and aromatic bay rum trees lined the descent to Maho, Cinnamon, and Trunk Bays. At Cinnamon Bay's campsite we talked to Mrs. John Woodside, wife of the Interior Department's concessionaire there. She told us that a Christmas crowd of 228 campers had strained the camp's capacity. There are thirty-five four-man tents, which rent for $25 a week, apiece, and twelve cottages (each housing four to six people), at $10 a day. This one Virgin Islands gesture toward the unaffluent is so popular that tents must be reserved a year in advance.

At heart-shaped Trunk Bay, which has been described as the second-best beach in the Western Hemisphere (and except for its quarter-mile size it could be the best), we watched snorkelers floating face down to read the underwater markers "squirrelfish," "parrot," "banded butterfly," and so on along the trail. The fish apparently respect the signs. The name "Trunk" probably derives from the trunk turtle, the largest species (up to nine feet and weighing as much as 1,000 pounds) and now threatened with extinction.

We had drinks before dinner with Charlotte Dean Stark and her husband, Gustav. They have lived in St. John since the 1930s, and she has become its chronicler. Land sold for $10 an acre when the Starks moved to this lovely beach not far from Caneel; "The same land now brings $8,000 an acre—if you can find an acre." The Starks sold their two acres with a house for $106,000 and are now renting the nearby cottage that belongs to the widow of the great physicist Robert J. Oppenheimer. Another neighbor is Colonel Julius Wadsworth of upper New York State and Washington, D.C., an eccentric millionaire who has religious impulses. Mrs. Wadsworth is a pupil of Carl Jung and a believer in Zen. The Colonel had a twenty-one-foot *Christ of the Caribbean* cast in concrete on the bluff above us and is perennially working on a book about peace. Mrs. Stark was asked to provide ghostly sponsorship for this undertaking but begged off on the grounds that her fee (which she purposely set high at $10 an hour) would be too steep for the Colonel. "Not at all," said he, and they went to work. One day, as they were getting nowhere, she asked him, "What is this 'God in Finance' you keep mentioning?" and he pulled out a handful of coins and repeated over and over "In God We Trust" till Gustav walked by and interrupted irreverently "All others pay cash." That seems to have broken up the seances permanently.

"We were all a little crazy," said Mrs. Stark with a laugh, referring to the eight original white intruders of the 1930s. Most, if not all, of the old-timers, she added, think Laurance Rockefeller "ruined" St. John. "The natives once did everything for themselves and were self-sufficient in food. Now they are money-mad, lazy, and a prey to the common cold."

What St. John was like in the old days is recreated nostalgically by Mrs. Stark in her *Souvenir of St. John*. In a dozen "short stories" based on a lifetime of sympathetic observation, the natives' idiom, superstitions, and stubborn but hapless resistance to white intrusion come to life. Until recently, pride was more important to an islander than money, and, although the invader might be regarded with "amusement, resignation and distaste," hate was accorded only to those of all races who were hateful. In a second booklet, *Some True Tales and Legends about Caneel Bay, Trunk Bay, and a Hundred Other Places on St. John*, Mrs. Stark suggests that the self-sufficiency of the Negroes can be traced back to slave, and even to Arawak, times. The Arawaks found the by-passed island a good place to hide from Caribs and Spaniards; the slaves, who revolted in 1733, used guerrilla tactics effectively to keep their Dutch, French, English, and Danish masters at bay.

St. Croix: Politics in Perpetuity

I had begun to think, in tourist-happy St. Thomas and St. John, that the American Virgins were moving onward and upward to the tourist nirvana in a political vacuum. It took Roger Baldwin, back in politics-ridden Puerto Rico, to disabuse me of such a notion. As I took off, with my older daughter Oriana, for a weekend in St. Croix, he advised me to talk to Dr. Aubrey Anduze, leader of the "in" Democrats in Christiansted, and to Ron DeLugo of the Independent Democratic opposition. "I think you will find out," he said, "that the delegates-at-large system plays into the hands of the majority party, giving them almost total control." This dangerous state of affairs, he added, could only be overcome by returning to island representation, for, although the Independent Democrats hold six of the fifteen seats in the unicameral legislature, they have no power.

Frank Luce, a Yale classmate who practices law in St. Croix, and his wife, Bobbie, met us at the Caribair desk and drove us down island to the Beach Hotel. Oriana was happy to be left on the hot white sands of this neighborly establishment, run by two old friends from Haiti, Ron Southerland and Andy Andersen. I set out for the capital at the other end of the island, accompanied by Sally Kramer of the Tourist Board.

Dr. Anduze—he is a dental surgeon as well as a member of the Senate and Lieutenant Governor—has his office in the handsome Government House, which dates from 1747. He is a mulatto with small features, a trim gray moustache, and the manners of an omniscient bureaucrat. He scoffed at Baldwin's analysis. "I'll agree only that town government should relieve us of some of our onerous functions—such as garbage collecting; but the old system of minority representation was un-American. A thousand votes could make a senator. We'd have splinter parties and coalition government. The majority's only function would be to appease the minorities."

"What *is* the main quarrel between the two parties?" I asked him.

"It sounds silly," he replied, "but their principal beef is that *they* are the real Democrats. Yet they asked for Republican support and were elected under the Republican symbol; the Republicans oppose even an elected governor, claiming that the Virgins aren't 'mature' enough to govern themselves. They're great letter writers, the Independents. They flood the offices of congressmen opposed to the elected-governor bill, giving an impression of chaos here. DeLugo claims our election was 'fixed.'"

I had a late breakfast at the attractive Old Quarter Hotel on the waterfront with Victor Gilbert, a Republican, who denied flatly that his party opposed the elected-governor bill. Gilbert runs the successful Cruzan Moon discothèque, which had had 1,000 customers when we visited it the previous night. "The Democratic Party," he said, "is so deeply entrenched by patronage that very few dare vote against their meal ticket. Out of a population of 45,000, 12,000 work for the government—the highest rate in the world. There is a room in the Registry of Deeds where one man does the job; he has thirteen secretaries he doesn't need or want, reading comic books. Our government *is where the natives work*. All the so-called 'menial work' for the 'white masters' is done by bonded aliens. This is a Virgin Islands special! Officially there are 6,000 bonded aliens here, but in reality there must be 16,000, almost all of them here illegally. Bonding—a thirty-day pass to find a job or return—simply doesn't work. When one gives a job to one of them, one 'gives bond' that he'll work for you six months. At the end of six, he 'hops the Goose' to Tortola and re-enters the same day. At the end of a year the alien has to go home— for forty-eight hours; so the hotels pay for this expensive junket rather than lose a waiter. Since there is no unemployment in the Virgins, there is no labor pool. The result is our absolute dependence on bonded aliens." I had already discovered that our waiter at the Beach Hotel was from Antigua, the headwaiter from Haiti, and the bus boy from St. Lucia; the skipper of the next day's cruise turned out to be from Nevis.

DeLugo was not to be found, so I walked over to the Ford agency to talk to David Hamilton, a senator of the Independent Democrats. Hamilton is a tall, handsome white resident in his thirties, who has lived here ten years. In addition to his automobile business, he is prominent in banking and insurance. I asked him whether or not DeLugo's charge that the election was "fixed" was true.

"Not fixed," he said, "but determined. Determined by the preventing or refusing of registrations prior to polling. Six hundred of our voters were disqualified—more than enough to give us the majority. The American Congress never dreamed that a legislature would appoint election boards—it's legal, but not done in any American state—and thus be able to perpetuate itself in power. To rectify this, Congress would have to change the Organic Act, our basic charter. May I go back a little in history?"

"Please do."

"In 1932 the Republican Hoover called the Virgins 'The Poorhouse of the Caribbean.' Perhaps he looked down his nose at us because the Democrat Wilson had bought us from Denmark. Our revival began when F.D.R. established C.C.C. camps here. Eisenhower was the first President to propose that we elect our own governor. *All* our parties are now in favor of this. As to statehood, we only have a population of 50,000, almost a third of whom are bonded aliens or 'illegals.' St. Croix's population is 23,000. Eight years ago the Independent Democrats were the 'in' party, and their leaders included Anduze, DeLugo, Paiewonsky. The split came when De-Lugo challenged this closed club and took the national committeemanship away from Paiewonsky. Paiewonsky countered by joining with the Unity Party to form the present Democrats. The Unity Party had been radical—though it backed Nixon against Kennedy. Then and now its boss was Earl B. Ottley, who is both President of the Legislature and boss of the Virgin Islands Labor Union."

"What solution is there to the bonded-aliens problem?" I asked Hamilton.

"Lowering or eliminating quotas—as in Jamaica and the other once-British islands."

"And real democracy?"

"Under the tidy, prosperous surface," he said, "there are the same problems here as everywhere: nationalism versus union, racism versus integration, bossism versus democracy. There is a tremendous resistance in these black matriarchies to governing themselves; you must have seen it in the other islands. Very few will accept responsibility. Power becomes heady. You've seen Anduze, that mild one; you wouldn't believe it was the same man if you saw him in the Legislature. He goes haywire, bangs his gavel, dissolves the session when he doesn't have his way." He laughed. "I never thought I'd want to be black, but believe me, being white is a real handicap here. Over 35 per cent of us are white, 15 per cent having moved here in the past ten years; but, to accomplish anything, one black always has to be balanced off against one white."

"Don't any Negroes from the mainland ever settle in the Virgins?" I asked.

"They're not tolerated here. They're resented—usually because their competence shows up the locals. White continentals just can't find enough competent Negroes for supervisory jobs."

It was my turn to laugh. "It sounds like you're all ready for independence—if you can decide who's going to be independent from whom."

"There's no independence movement yet. But nationalism is very strong. A Virgin Islander is that first and an American second."

Christiansted, Frederiksted, Buck Island

Senator Hamilton, who is no relation of his illustrious namesake, left me in front of Alexander Hamilton's hardware shop on the waterfront, where I had to make arrangements to take Oriana snorkeling at Buck Island the following day. It was in this store that the future Secretary of the Treasury had begun to show his genius for finance, shortly after his mother obtained her divorce for "abandonment" in the St. Croix courts. It was then the counting house of Nicholas Cruger, and at the age of twelve young Hamilton was left in charge of the business while his employer was abroad. It was his impressive description of the St. Kitts hurricane of 1772 that led to his being permitted to go to the North American colonies to complete his education. In that dispatch to the *Royal Danish American Gazette* Hamilton observed that the rain tasted salty and that, at the climax, there was an odor of gunpowder in the air, but otherwise he wrote in the "Gothic" style of the day and with religious overtones:

> Good God! . . . fancy meteors flying about in the air—the prodigious glare of almost perpetual lightning . . . sufficient to strike astonishment into angels . . . Where now, oh! vile worm is all thy boasted fortitude and resolution?

Preparing for college at Elizabethtown, New Jersey, Hamilton chose Princeton University, but Princeton wouldn't permit him to move from class to class as soon as he was qualified, so he entered King's College (Columbia University); his studies were soon interrupted by the Revolution, through which he rose to fame and fortune.

Joined again by Sally Kramer, most knowledgeable and charming of guides, we drove to Frederiksted by way of Whim Great House and Laurance Rockefeller's Fountain Valley Golf Course. Whim is probably the finest of the plantation houses still standing. Its beautifully rounded bay of buff-colored stone and the dry moat that once screened it from the slave quarters are its unique features. The nearby windmill was being restored during our visit. The eighteen-hole golf course borders a strip of low rain forest, complete with mahogany, tree ferns, mangoes, and lianas, that is part of Rockefeller's 4,000 acres on St. Croix. The course was designed by Robert Trent Jones. Even the fairways are kept emerald green through a system of underwater irrigation. A fleet of surrey-fringed "golfmobiles" convey from one lie to the next those customers who can afford $7 for eighteen holes, an $8 greens fee, and the usual accessories.

Frederiksted is a pretty little town, mostly rebuilt after a devastating fire in 1879, its wooden houses decorated with ornamental lattice and bandsaw work. Life is informal. Mushrooms are sold in the paint store and eggs in the hardware shop. We had lunch at the Royal Dane, inspected the nearby Magic Island Beach Club, and then drove back across the twenty-eight-mile-long island to the Beach Hotel.

> *Under the mackerel cloud pack where*
> *this vestal in her watered silk*
> *shapes up, a green half mile offshore,*
> *and dusts her décolletage with talc,*
> *a reef of razor coral skulks.*
> *Sea urchins prune and strop their spears,*
> *those spines athwart each crotch and stalk*
> *that warned Columbus once, beware. . . .*[6]

Buck Island's 283 dry acres, with empty beaches and teeming reefs, are where Cruzans would go to to get away from the tourists—if it weren't the place to which the tourists go first. It is a pleasant two-hour sail,

---

[6] From Maxine Kumin, "Ballade for the Virgins, Christiansted, St. Croix," in *The Privilege* (New York: Harper, 1965).

tacking against the wind, from Christiansted wharf and an hour back downwind. Our "authentic West Indian sloop" was provided by Bill Miller, and its able "native skipper," Sam Wilson, was from Nevis, as already noted. The beach faces Christiansted. The underwater trail is east of it, within view of St. Thomas and the British islands. The trail, over forests of antler coral with purple seawhips and waving fans, far exceeds in richness the one at Trunk Bay. With so much mobile vegetation and so many streamlined fish flowing under one's mask, one sometimes forgets that the coral itself lives. The reefs are the stony skeletons of the dead. The live organism colonizes algae and minute plants within them, which manufacture oxygen from the light to help feed it. Though immobile, the coral is carnivorous, feeding on small floating creatures, which it stings and then covers with a slimy secretion. None of this activity is apparent to the naked eye, of course, but there is a pervasive sense of pursuit and escape in these depths, of ambush and anxiety, death and resurrection, that makes any eavesdropping over a reef an exhilarating experience.

The word for St. Croix itself is not "exhilarating" but "comfortable." Its flatness and its eighty-four square miles (compared to St. John's twenty and St. Thomas' twenty-eight) give it the brightest future of the three U.S. Virgins. It already has industry. Harvey Aluminum and Hess Oil between them employ 1,000 people. Its major harbors, jet strip (which can be expanded to 15,000 feet), beaches, and empty spaces give it a potential equal to that of any middle-sized Caribbean island. The fairly safe assumption that it could never cut loose from the United States, as Puerto Rico might, lends stability. Compared to St. Thomas, St. Croix is not a swinging island where blacks and whites make merry together. Even Christiansted and Frederiksted have little intercourse with each other. But there is something in St. Croix that appeals to the pacifist, the hedonist, and the *voyeur* in every man. It may be the middle-class heaven.

Part 2. The British Virgins

Forty-one islands, thirteen of them sparsely inhabited and three of good size, make up the British Virgins, which lie east-northeast across the Sir Francis Drake Channel separating St. John from Tortola. Tortola, with the chain's capital, Road Town, is the largest of the three larger British Virgins; the other two are Virgin Gorda to the east and Anagada much farther to the north. Diehard Anglo-Saxons credit Drake, rather than Columbus, with discovering and naming the Virgins, claiming that the tactful pirate so honored the Virgin Queen before she knighted him. There is no question at all, however, that the Spaniards, after a short, frantic exploitation (and exhaustion) of the copper mine on Virgin Gorda, retired from the scene and that by the second decade of the sixteenth century pirates and beachcombers marooned by marauders were in undisputed occupancy. Among them the British predominated and gave most of the smaller hideaways their romantic, piratical names: Dead Man's Chest, Fallen Jerusalem, Little Dogs, Norman, Beef, Salt, Prickley Pear, Rum, Peter, Sombrero, Seal Dogs, Cockroach.

Two-thirds of the 9,000 people (mostly Negroes, from the days when slaves took care of the poor pickings in sugar on the larger islands) live on Tortola. It is twelve miles long, fairly high (Mt. Sage reaches 1,710 feet), and fairly well patched with forests and farms. Tortolans are real peasants, living on and off the land, and paying little attention to the dozen white administrators and merchants. Those who have succumbed to its bucolic charms have dubbed Tortola's society "Black Elizabethan." One such was Glanville Smith,[7] who found the pace of all the smaller West Indian Islands to his taste; he wondered why St. Thomas' Camille Pissaro ever left to paint Impressionist landscapes or Virgin Gorda's William Thornton never returned after designing Washington's Capitol and organizing its Patent Office. In Road Town, when Smith was there, the men were still grinding sugar and women doing "drawn" needlework, and the owner of the one tourist hotel occupied all three bedrooms because he didn't like tourists. As in Haiti, the clearing of bush and planting of yams were done *en masse* to the accompaniment of lilting work songs. Smith looked for the turtledove after which the Spaniards had named the island, but found few that had escaped the gimlet-toothed mongoose imported to all these Indies from India in order to keep the rats out of the cane. Then as now, the crowing of cocks was the dominant bird cry; at the table peppered fish and conch stew were the *pièces de résistance*, and the coffee tasted like cough medicine.

Today, a Road Towner told me, the British islanders are swept by irrational enthusiasms as the prosperity of tourism blooms all around them. "One year it's batting averages in the majors, another year it's 'Hate those whites; they're buying up all the land,' another it's 'Join the Americans before it's too late!'" There was, it seems, strong sentiment a few years back in these islands, which are neglected by the crown, to change nationalities. The currency in use is still exclusively American. But no answering note of welcome came from St. Thomas, where the idea of sharing the Federal largesse with these poor squatters to the east was anything but appealing. Belatedly, but perhaps in time, London earmarked $1 million for roads and announced a ten-year tax holiday and duty-free imports. A tourist resort started going up on Beef Island, an appendage of Tortola and connected to it by a bridge where the little airstrip is. Laurance Rockefeller had already bought 500 acres on the

---

[7] Glanville Smith, *Many a Green Isle* (New York: Harper, 1941). Until Tram Combs acquainted me with this delicious rarity, I had been secretly planning to use Shelley's opening words from "Epipsychidion" as the title for the present book.

northwest corner of Virgin Gorda and had started to build his Little Dix Bay Resort.

Little Dix and the Baths

So far, tourism in the British Virgins *is* Little Dix Bay. Gorda, the Fat Virgin, has been twice blessed: She has the most distinguished luxury hotel, architecturally speaking, in the Caribbean, and in the Baths in her southeast corner she has perhaps the most poetic swimming hole in the world. Rockefeller was well advised (or had the good taste) to build as far from the Baths as possible. The arc of white sand in Little Dix was already faultless. A few hundred coconut palms, those swaying symbols of *mañana*, with their immaculate flesh and cloudy nectar, provided a conventional transition from $70-a-day living to the cactus-spine aridity of Virgin Gorda's characteristic terrain. But the design of the main pavilion was anything but conventional. Its three conical shingled roofs of varying pitch and altitude are anchored at the base points on low blocks of mortised yellow stone. Walls would be superfluous, and there are none. The terrace extends on all sides, so that one can walk or recline in the shade or the sun as one chooses. The fifty guestrooms, of red cedar, with cantilevered balconies facing the bay and individual terraces, are scattered about the slope. Whoever it was in that New York firm of Tippetts-Abbett-McCarthy-Stratton who designed this wingéd complex had looked at the birds and soared with them.

Whoever designed the Baths—God, Nature, or perhaps some Plutonic colossus who tossed up these house-sized boulders from the fiery depths as if they had been pebbles—"arranged" them on the beach with a flawless eye for gradations of scale and color, shining smoothness and ruffled texture, rondure and jaggedness,

> *smoothing the raven down*
> *Of darkness till it smiled . . .*

No conscious artisan, bent upon evoking the mystery of the haphazard, could ever have managed it.

The boulders begin on the hill out of sight of the ocean, appearing one at a time, menhirs of black basalt rising huge and menacing out of the scrub. They begin to combine into dolmens on the descent but still, masculine, thrusting, hardly touch one another. But, as the ground begins to level off and cactus gives way to sand, the shapes of the immense stones change utterly. White crystalline granite predominates, and the shapes begin to billow and flow as if in response to the waves that lap against them. There are breast-like boulders and hippy ones, shadowy secret orifices, some with smaller rounded rocks wedged and locked within them, some opening into deep caves where inlets of sapphire water kiss the golden sand. Sometimes one is forced to penetrate through lips of stone so narrow that only the dampness keeps one's back and belly from being scratched. Crawling deeper and deeper into this nest of caves to photograph (sometimes neck deep in warm water) the wedge-like apertures in the ceilings, through which patches of blue sky are occasionally visible, I got lost and had to call cavernously to Carole, whose faint answering cries guided me to daylight. When I found her, she was standing half submerged like some goddess of the sea in an enormous chamber, lit by a shaft of sunlight that dropped a flickering star around her as it fell from a single jagged opening in the rock vault above. We staggered out into the blinding light and sank exhausted on the hot sand, somehow reassured to see white sails on the horizon and a boatload of tourists coming ashore with sunglasses, black-rubber fins, and bottles of beer.

Part 3. The Bahamas

Bill Negron and I spent our first night in the Bahamas at the Montagu Beach Hotel, one of a dozen luxury establishments that make Nassau, along with San Juan in Puerto Rico and Charlotte Amalie in the Virgins, a rival of Miami Beach as the tourist mecca of the United States' eastern seaboard. New Providence Island, on which the capital squats, is only one of the 700 Bahamian coral chips. The larger ones—Andros, Eleuthera, Great Abaco, the Exumas, the Inaguas, and Grand Bahama, with its "made" city of Freeport—are already stretching to compete in hotels and housing complexes. But most of the 140,000 Bahamians live in Nassau, and, as the seat of the newly independent government headed by Lynden Oscar Pindling, Nassau is the focus of the most dramatic racial-political

confrontation in the West Indies—a confrontation tempered but by no means blunted by the tolerant good manners inherited from four centuries of British rule. The first government ever to represent that part of the population (85 per cent) that is black faces a narrowly defeated and predominantly white opposition party (the so-called "Bay Street Boys"), which had, with paternalistic efficiency, in one generation turned the islands from a modest watering place for the very rich into a multimillion dollar carnival of giant hotels and gambling casinos. So the problem is how can all this affluence and power be subjected to the black majority's control "without killing," as the new Premier puts it, "the goose that laid the golden egg?"

The Montagu Beach is on an extension of Bay Street that sweeps eastward around Nassau's harbor. The plush part of the capital on both sides of Bay Street, the only part most visitors ever see, is separated from the wooden cottages of the Negroes in the sector known as "Over the Hill" by a perceptible bluff. The predominating color of the large hotels is pale strawberry. The predominating style is "no style." The Bahamas have no culture of their own. The British simply imported their own Greco-Roman stereotype for the handful of public buildings and let it go at that. They made no effort to educate the mass of the Negroes. There is no Bahamian art or literature, very little folk mythology or distinctive idiom, and no tradition of slave uprisings. Mr. Pindling's party constitutes the first real expression of native Bahamanism, and his government will have to start from scratch if it hopes to develop an island personality independent of both colonialism and tourism. Present plans for more primary and secondary education along Western lines will not be sufficient. There are already disturbing signs that pridefully aggressive Black Power attitudes, picked up from the United States, with its ugly history of racial prejudice, are filtering into the cultural vacuum. But there are also signs that the new leadership may be too intelligent to settle for another uncreative import, and also that it realizes that the prosperity of an economy 90 per cent dependent on tourism could be shattered overnight if investors lost their confidence and visitors their sense of being wanted. After sitting in on several sessions of the Assembly, visiting some of the out islands, and talking to leaders of both parties, we left with more hope than confidence that the Bahamas will meet the challenge.

Black Tuesday and Murky Monday

We were lucky to arrive on a Monday. The Assembly was meeting for the first time since Pindling's Progressive Liberal Party (P.L.P.) had lost the by-election for the seat vacated by Sir Stafford Sands of the United Bahamian Party (U.B.P.). Sir Stafford, the promotional wizard responsible for raising the annual influx of tourists from 40,000 to 800,000 in ten years, had left the islands in the wake of P.L.P. charges that his acceptance of $1 million in "consultant fees" had covered the awarding of lucrative contracts to his friends among the "Bay Street Boys" and that the gambling casinos in Nassau and Freeport were being taken over by American gangsters. The U.B.P. struck back by rewinning Sir Stafford's seat in the only way it possibly could—by running a black candidate. Until that Monday, when Cleophas Adderley took his seat, the all-Negro P.L.P. cabinet, facing the all-white U.B.P. opposition across the narrow Assembly chamber, had been careful to keep the racial angle out of its charges of malfeasance. But Adderley's presence was too much. The suppressed resentments of centuries of colonialism and slavery were bound to erupt.

The august chamber, presided over by the "impartial" Speaker and his clerks in their white wigs, came to order against a background of excited whispers from the visitors' gallery. Under the glazed stares of Edward VII and George V, those beefy bourgeois Teutons in their scarlet coats and gold braid, and Victoria in aquamarine satin, such a scene was about to be unveiled as this chamber had not witnessed since "Black Tuesday," April 27, 1965. Had that day not coincided with the climax of the Dominican Revolution,[8] the world might have taken more notice. Representatives of the P.L.P., then in a minority, had been expelled from the Assembly for talking too long. But Lynden Pindling had served notice that the Bahamian majority was no longer to be thwarted by technicalities. Seizing the golden mace, symbol of parliamentary impartiality, he had hurled it through the window; masses of his followers in the street below, singing *We Shall Overcome* and other civil-rights songs, had broken it into several hundred pieces to carry home as tokens of their coming of age.

Monday's session began mildly enough. The embarrassing question of how best to deport the refugees from Papa Doc's Haiti, thousands of whom drift into the friendly Bahamas on small boats, was tabled until the next day. Was the Bahamian coat of arms being abused? It could properly be used, a cabinet minister explained, "for tourist souvenirs and for blazer insignia, with proper government authorization, but *not* on tableware or car stickers." The fledgling ministers were obviously enjoying themselves. They chuckled over the opposition's little barbs about phone bills, private cars, and traveling expenses. They even laughed good-naturedly when taunted with having voted themselves big salaries—both sides knew that these salaries were a proper answer to the pernicious system of elected officials with *no* salaries, a system under which quasi-legal "fees" had been accepted for awarding contracts. "Who are you," the P.L.P. members seemed to be saying to the U.B.P. adherents, "to be accusing us of legal petty larceny when your palatial homes on East Bay Street were built out of legal grand larceny?" Once the presiding Speaker gently cautioned a cabinet member who had barked "Shut up!" to a shaft from the opposition bench: "I know, I know. You're all back from vacation with feelings running to exuberance. I went to school myself once and remember how the first day back feels"—and both sides smiled

[8] See the discussion in the last section of Chapter IX.

appreciatively. But, when Basil Kelly, the U.B.P. representative of Crooked Island, invoked the testimony of Cleophas Adderley, the proprieties were suddenly forgotten.

"This is double talk!" shouted Minister Without Portfolio Clarence Bain. "When you put your arms around that black boy [he pointed to Adderley, a fifty-two-year-old electrician], you don't mean him no good!" Another minister joined the attack, leaping to his feet and taunting Adderley with "not being man enough to stand up to the men who once whipped and brutalized the Negroes." Adderley stood up to defend himself. He was not being used, he said. "The United Bahamian Party is trying to *unite* the people! [laughter and jeers from the government bench]. You are trying to separate them." Minister Wallace Whitfield asked Adderley if he'd forgotten that the forefathers of his sponsors on the opposition bench had "enslaved the Bahamian Negroes prior to 1834." He recalled that, during the election, Adderley had charged him with having two wives, a black and a white one. "It is the U.B.P. that is prejudiced! I have roots in both races. We unite flesh and flesh, but the U.B.P. discriminates against colored people.They think it a *crime* that I have a white wife and that the Honorable Arthur Hanna has one!"

We would be talking to Messrs. Pindling and Kelly later in the week, and it would be interesting to see whether or not they privately deplored this public airing of racial antagonisms. Meanwhile, on the way to the airport, from which we were flying to some of the out islands, a taxi driver, the Reverend Albert Thompson, pastor of the Church of God Incorporated, reminded us that the Bahamas' real problems are economic. His sect, he told us, ranks after the Baptists, the Roman Catholics, and the Anglicans numerically. "*All* denominations supported the P.L.P. Why? Because gambling was the big issue. That brought Pindling to power." "Has he stopped it?" Bill asked.

"No. Not yet. But the million dollars Wallace Groves in Freeport paid to Sands to keep his casinos open now goes to the government, where it will be used for education, our major need." The second big issue, he added, was agriculture for home consumption. "Importing our food only profits the Bay Street merchants, whose stores refuse to buy home-grown oranges and pineapples." This last observation was more in line with another view we had heard: that the Bahamas' real hang up isn't mobsters and casinos but businessmen with total control over the gigantic tourist industry. If this view is correct, Pindling's job is to tax these untaxables to obtain the funds he needs for low-income housing, education, and social services. Is there any other way?

Packaging the Out Islands

Evidently the Premier still thinks that there *is* another way, for his Freeport speech about not killing the goose has reassured Freeport's impresario, Wallace Groves, and the flow of development dollars to the other out islands is rapidly converting their wild beauty to the pattern of super comfort that Americans are supposed to demand. Paradise, nearest to New Providence and smallest of the wooded sandbars, is an extreme example. Densely planted with Australian casuarinas when it was the private fief of Axel Wenner-Gren, the late Swedish munitions king, it is now connected to New Providence by an ugly $2 million concrete hoop, and its forests are being mangled by arterial highways hacked out of the limestone at right angles to one another, with steep shoulders of white detritus. When we visited the minnow-shaped islet, it was crawling with bulldozers slurping up a mammoth parking lot for a skyscraper hotel directly in front of the bridge and in sight of Nassau. Huntington Hartford, during his brief suzerainty, had given the island its corny name. It was previously called Hog. After building tennis courts and importing Pancho Gonzales to play with him, he put up a pavilion of bleached wood with covered walkways surrounding an outsized ping-pong table. Presumably he also selected the following "poem," whose eight lines (half their letters now askew) frame the octagonal bar:

> Oh 'tis sweet to rest in Paradise
> A singin' in the breeze
> With a store of good tabaccy
> In a hammock 'neath the trees
> With a gentle lass to fan you
> As you listen to the roar
> Of the breakers on the outer reef
> That never reach the shore.

Freeport, on Grand Bahama Island ninety miles from Florida, is the $400 million creation of a man with still less taste but much more know-how—Wallace Groves. The former Wall Street financier acquired his 150,000 acres of scrub land ten years ago. His Port Authority licensed six luxury hotels, a drive-in movie theater, a commercial complex of 800 licensed businesses, golf courses, a marina, two gambling casinos, and a jetport to receive gamblers flown in from Miami. Fifteen miles away at West End, Jack Tar Enterprises has just taken over another behemoth hotel, which boasts the world's largest Olympic pool and has a drive-in theater and jetport of its own. Evidently these competitors are not on speaking terms, for the road between them was filled with potholes when we drove over it.

Freeport was bracing itself for a crisis that might never come. The Lucayan Beach, at which we spent the night, was rumored to be facing bankruptcy. It had lost its casino (one of Freeport's two) following the Pindling government's doubling of the half-million-dollar tax, and its English desk clerk felt certain that the P.L.P.'s real aim was to drive every white man off the island. "They've made a good start," he complained darkly. "We're left at this echelon only because the Negroes don't know yet how to *greet* people without *grimacing*." At the marina a yachtsman in a trimaran was battening down the hatches against Hurricane Enid. "We're pulling out ahead of the storm," he growled, "—both storms." A taxi driver, pointing out Groves' opulent home, remarked that "not so long ago this man ruled the island with an iron hand. A sleeper would be waked at 4 A.M. and put on a plane at 6 A.M. with the words 'Never come back here if you know what's good for you.' Maybe things have changed. We aren't sure yet."

The formidable Mr. Groves, with whom we chatted for an hour later in the day, exuded only confidence. Smiling like a Buddha, he reminisced about the happy days he had once spent "on the 100 acres of Little Whale . . . spraying the fruit trees and protecting the birds." It was with considerable difficulty that we prevailed upon him to say a few words about the change in government. "Sure, the Bay Streeters did wonders for the Bahamas," he said, "but times change. Their successors will do greater wonders. Next year will be bigger than last year. We're expanding all along the line. We have complete confidence in Mr. Pindling and his able associates. Black Power? That's political talk and means nothing. They're conservatives! Sure, one casino had to go when the government tax was increased to a million. There are only so many visitors. But soon there'll be enough for two again. No Bahamian is permitted to gamble, which is as it should be. The government is getting $10 million out of Freeport, more than a quarter of its revenues. Naturally the Premier says he won't kill the goose. Taxation *would* kill it, so why should they tax? Every year they get more out of the wealth we're creating here out of nothing. Twelve years ago Grand Bahama had 2,500 souls. Today there are 40,000, half in Freeport; the half out of Freeport are Bahamians all." Clasping his hands over his stomach and tipping back in his swivel chair, Wallace Groves invited us to come back in a year and see whether or not his confidence was justified.

Everything in Freeport is imported; nothing is authentic. "Come see the Crown Jewels," a sign reads, "in exact facsimile!" The Lucayan Beach has larger-than-life troubadours, with floppy hats and lances carved out of wood, to guard the dining salon. Off the lobby one can buy "bosun's mates" in painted clay mounted on wall plaques or paintings on velvet of children crying in dark alleys—highlighted orange tears coursing in simulated elevation out of the corners of sweetly anguished eyes to roll down candle-lit limbs. "The grandeur of the Taj Mahal in a lush Tropic Isle," says a poster advertising the casino. "Home of the elegant El Morocco and Kasbar Show Lounge—Largest in the World."

We drove there dutifully after dinner. It sprouts, sure enough, like a gaudy mosque, detached minaret and all, amid "Chinese" pagodas on the main square. The roulette and crap tables, flanked by batteries of illuminated one-armed bandits, are in a gaudy salon the size of Grand Central Terminal's main waiting room. We lost our money too quickly and thoroughly to take in the belly dancers in the Kasbar Lounge.

The Exumas, which we visited next, have been spared most of this commercialism so far, and so, presumably, have Andros, Eleuthera, and the smaller, more remote islands. Great and Little Exuma, connected by a bridge, are the southern extremities of a chain of cays ninety miles long stretching south-southeast of New Providence. Bahama Island Beach on Little Exuma is billed as "the finest beach in the Caribbean," and it may well be, but it is only one of dozens. The vegetation is surprisingly lush, considering the seventy-foot maximum elevation, and bananas (an oddity) are grown in circular natural pits forty feet deep. The hotels—Two Turtles Inn, Pieces of Eight, Peace 'n Plenty, and others at George Town, across the bay from Stocking Island, on Great Exuma and the Red Hill Plantation on Little Ex—are small and reasonable though not cheap. A third of the land is still held in commonage. Nature has provided a hydroponic system of agriculture in the region around Mosstown: citrus fruit, guavas, mangoes, sapodillas, and sugar apples abound. Peacocks, once privately owned, have taken to the bush and roost in the fig trees. Land crabs are a delicacy. Bonefish are plentiful in the shallows across the cay from Rolletown. Deep-sea fishing is as good as it is anywhere. There is only one policeman, for there is no crime in these islands. A hand-crank telephone connects Stevenston in the north with George Town, where native craft compete in a world-famous regatta.

It can't last, of course. The Exumas are poised on the crest of a land boom that threatens to turn them into insular beehives. The visitor fights his way through a blizzard of real-estate promoters' brochures from the moment he steps off the plane. It is said that 90 per cent of the buyers of quarter-acre plots have never seen the Exumas and may never see them. Speculators are conducting a whopping mail-order business. You buy "your home or holiday retreat" on the installment plan, "$15 down, $15 a month" for "unimproved sites." Come and get it! "*No* income tax. *No* land tax. *No* purchase tax. *No* gift tax. *No* business tax. *No* real estate tax. *No* capital gains tax on land sale profits. *No* death duties. *And many other tax advantages!*" Still worried? "We offer an unconditional money-back guarantee if you change your mind for any reason whatsoever within 60 days!"

How can you lose? How can the Exumas win?

Views from the Top: Basil Kelly and Lynden Pindling

Basil Kelly, the United Bahamian Party leader, whose constituency is Crooked Island, received us in the upstairs office of his hardware store on Bay Street. I asked him what changes the P.L.P. had brought about so far. "Changes? The salaries they have voted themselves, and those retroactive taxes, like the million-dollar one that forced the Lucayan Beach's casino out of business. You saw Groves? Certainly he made a contribution to our party's campaign fund—and they called that a 'a pay-off' for gambling! Obviously investors will stop putting money in the Bahamas if they think this government will tax retroactively every time it runs out of money."

We asked him whether or not he thought the Premier had associated himself with Monday's racial attack on Adderley. "Not directly," he replied. "He was careful to stay out of it so that the papers couldn't quote him. But did you see his face while the Works Minister, who is their real merchant of hate, was letting Adderley have it? He was smirking and jeering with the rest of them. If you'd seen him campaigning against me in Crooked Island, you wouldn't have believed it was the same man. He was like a wild man!"

"But why is it," I asked, "that only this late in the game your party comes up with a black candidate? It does look rather opportunistic, doesn't it?"

He sighed. "If we could have gotten colored candidates to run before, believe me we would have. It wasn't for lack of trying. The fault was theirs. They *wanted* us to run the country. They were lazy. We're all lazy. The Assembly was a plush club in those days. But, by the end of the year, you'll see; there are enough intelligent, right-thinking Negroes here to join us, and they will. Ideally, we'll have two Negro parties—which would be good. The Negroes love politics. Let them fight it out in the democratic way. I'd like to retire from politics and devote my spare time to these sailboats you see on the wall, and I'm sure the other white leaders of our party would too—*if* a colored party dedicated to serving the best interests of the Bahamas were in office."

I liked Basil Kelly for not being apologetic about the Bay Streeters and for having no qualms about seeing his kind of world administered by a race that had not been consulted in establishing its values. I liked Lynden Pindling for his optimism in thinking that those values could be left undisturbed and for his honesty in not attempting to conceal his emotional resentment of Cleophas Adderley's "defection" from the Negro camp. I asked the Premier whether or not Monday's outburst indicated that the P.L.P. wanted the races permanently separated.

"Certainly not!" he bristled. "Some of our ministers pointed out good-naturedly that Adderley is a 'Tom,' that's all. And he is!"

"But the very word you are using has racist connotations," I objected. "Aren't you borrowing it from the race war in our race-conscious country?"

"Well, yes," he conceded, "but we use it differently. We're saying that *politically* Adderley is a 'Tom.' He plays the game for the old white ruling class that is on the way out and that must never be allowed back in. And he started it all in the campaign by referring to his 'two black wives' and taunting our Minister of Works with having a white one. These are revolutionary times. We're the party of the people; they're the party of the colonial masters."

"Well," I said, "if they're changing the racial complexion of their economic domination by running a black candidate successfully, what's to prevent you from running a white one in one of your districts?"

"We did run four in local elections," he replied. "They all lost. Their color must have associated them in the public's mind with the corruption of the U.B.P."

"How do you propose," I said, "to keep the P.L.P. from becoming just as 'corrupt' as the U.B.P. once you've had the same temptations of power?"

"Our government has published a code of ethics. It forbids conflicts of interest. Also we *pay* our cabinet ministers and pay them enough so that they won't be inclined to steal. Also we're educating the masses; $7,316,000 of our budget goes to the schools this year, as against $4,867,-000 last year. Next year—"

Pindling is a handsome man, short, stocky, his very dark skin contrasting dramatically with the whites of his restless eyes. He has a good sense of humor. His father came from Jamaica. He was trained as a barrister in London. His closest boyhood friend was Sidney Poitier, who campaigned for him last year. He has traveled in the United States and England—in circles where prejudice is remote. As our friend Ted Doyle of the Government Information Services put it, "What the Bahamian people have known, racially speaking, is friendly familiarity under an umbrella of colonial superiority." Pindling's experience of the Caribbean has been confined to these Bahamas and possibly enlightened Jamaica.

I touched on the cultural vacuum, mentioning the creative upsurge in Jamaica and Haiti. He didn't appear to be familiar with either. "I came back on the plane from Freeport yesterday," I said, "with a Haitian escapee in charge of one of your policemen. He told me that you were sending him back to Port-au-Prince, where Papa Doc would have him shot. I realize that the Bahamas can't cope with all these refugees unassisted, but is deporting them to certain death the answer? Isn't Haiti more than a Haitian problem? Isn't it a Caribbean problem? Or a Negro problem?"

He shook his head. "Revolutions are not made by color but by oppressed people. We haven't been oppressed to that extent. We've been used, but we're changing that. Perhaps if we can bring justice to our own people, we'll have enough energy left over to help those who are really oppressed. But for now my responsibility has to be to my Bahamian brothers."

IX

THE DOMINICAN REPUBLIC

"Two revolutions ago," said a Dominican lady at the turn of the century, "my son took a gun and went into politics." Sixty-five years earlier, when the Republic had been free from Haiti and Spain just one decade, the remark would already have been appropriate. Sixty-five years *later*, when United States troops were coming ashore for the second time to restore some measure of internal stability, political issues were still being decided with guns.

In the climate of endemic revolution that has existed in Santo Domingo from 1822 to the present, there has been no chance for a native culture to take root, no opportunity for the country's vast resources in arable land and scenery to be enjoyed, no time even to think of tourism. Heirs to the Spanish misrule that began with Columbus' genocide of the peaceable Indians and ended with Madrid's bloody "Restoration" of 1861, idealistic Dominicans like Duarte, Espaillat and Juan Bosch never lasted in the palace more than a few months at a time, and constructive politicians from Cáceres to Hector García Godoy and Joaquín Balaguer have had to devote all their energies to patching up the patient and spiking the guns. Only tyrants have had time to *build*. So the traveler is perforce reduced to exploring the unhealthy symbolism of forced growth—and to expressions of pious hope that a people so resilient will learn to govern itself without inviting further therapy from its friends abroad.

Dictatorship Unlimited, 1930–1960

On a hilltop commanding San Cristóbal, birthplace of Rafael Leonidas Trujillo Molina, there stands a building that resembles a cheap, three-story parking garage set beside a filling station and capped by an archaic airport control tower. A dozen years after its construction it had already fallen into decay; its concrete had moldered, the pavement of its patio was split by cracks, and the elaborate gardens were choked with weeds and cactus. Entering by a massive door and crossing a parquet floor flanked by carved mahogany wainscoting, one is confronted by a stair-case that appears to rest upon a dung-colored doughnut the size of a bomber wheel. Six gigantic bedchambers, to which this staircase and a brace of stainless steel elevators lead, stand empty. These chambers, with recessed, half-domed ceilings—"supported" by pink, blue, and green pil-asters appliquéd in gesso with military emblems, victory wreaths, and imitation Grecian urns spouting blue foam—are lighted by cheap plastic chandeliers that would have been rejected by the interior decorator for an automat. There are fifteen outsized bathrooms. Walled and floored in imported mosaic featuring octopuses and other tropical fish, they are equipped with six-foot blue mirrors. The bidets and washstands are of red porphyry. The revolving toothbrush racks resemble gold. And the closets, like those in the bedrooms, not only are lined with aromatic cedar but also contain hundreds of empty, perfectly fitted drawers and drawers within drawers, hand-made—one's guide is proud to explain—of a precious wood forbidden to common use by constitutional edict. A smoking room, with sculptured Buddhas leapfrogging across the ceiling and Oriental lettering in bamboo relief on scores of safe-sized humidors, is not at all out of key with the prevailing décor. The mammoth kitchen, with its functional stainless-steel sinks, spits, ovens, mixers, fans, electric washers and driers, king-sized freezers, and air-conditioning blowers, is saved from violating the canon of bad taste by a tiny electric clock in the form of a red teapot, which winks high and naked on one wall. Spiritual and aesthetic needs are supplied by a chapel of imported marble that re-sembles a Victorian bathroom and a mural of rustic Dominican *chiquitas* (all white) being presented with roses by simpering *campesinos*.

This atrocious palace was never occupied, even for one night. No one seems to know why. There was never any furniture in it. Two or three typical parties were thrown, at which the elevators presumably ran and the gigantic bars groaned with champagne and caviar—and that was all. As those who paid for the millions of hours of sweated labor that went into its construction were never intended to enter it, its purpose and cost are not a matter of public record. The architect, who had previously built himself a landlocked "cruiser" complete with blue-concrete "waves" a few blocks from the National Palace (which he also designed), declined to take credit for providing totalitarian dictatorship with its perfect visual symbol. He was modest enough, in fact, to insist that the *real* creator of El Cerro (the word with one "*r*" fewer spells "zero" in Spanish) and of other eyesores that now disfigure the country—from the Peace Monument at Santiago to the Altagracia Cathedral at Higüey—was "The First Architect of the Nation: Rafael L. Trujillo Molina, Benefactor of the Fatherland."

This book is not the place to trace the dictator's rise as a protégé of the marines or the methods by which he diverted a large share of the profits of every private enterprise in the country into his own pocket. The Machiavellian skill with which he forced the government of Haiti to honor him for massacring 15,000 of its peasants and the way he hoodwinked Franklin Delano Roosevelt into supporting him as the bogus champion of Latin American democracy are now well known.[1] What should be noted is that almost every man-made thing in the Dominican Republic today—the sugar mills, the roads, the power plants, the public buildings, the docks, the monuments, the fairgrounds, the churches, the hotels, even the lids for the sewer mains—bear Trujillo's stamp and that every bit was paid for out of the pockets of the worker, the farmer, and the small businessman, crushed under a burden of hidden taxation.

It would be a mistake to think that the meaning of such a phenomenon as the Trujillo dictatorship can be conveyed in terms of its political economy alone. The savagery, cynicism, and vulgarity of its ambiance filtered down from the top, infecting the whole of Dominican society. A servile press, a controlled school system, and a spy apparatus without precedent in the Americas were the instruments through which the gross vanity of the tyrant and his family were foisted upon a terrorized, demoralized population. The drive for self-deification, which had begun in his early thirties with his assumption of the titles "Generalissimo" and "Benefactor of the Fatherland"; the changing of the capital's name from Santo Domingo to Ciudad Trujillo; and the renaming of time-honored provinces after assorted ruffians of the blood exceeded a burlesque. Bronze plaques, carrying Trujillo's picture in color and manufactured in Mexico for $2 each, were forced upon every merchant in the land for $30 each. "Men are not indispensable," thundered *La Nación*, "but Trujillo is irreplaceable!"

The dictator's family was apparently irreplaceable too. Ramfis, the eldest son born in 1929, was commissioned a colonel at the age of four. Polite refusal to admit a fourteen-year-old daughter as an "Ambassador" to the coronation of Elizabeth II was the cause of a British minister's framing and ouster. An older daughter, after four notorious marriages, was given an official post in Washington from which to court the depraved good will of American café society. The tyrant's third wife satisfied some atavistic literary ambition by having herself proclaimed "the First Lady of Caribbean Letters" and (as if it were praise) "the equal

[1] The story was told for the first time in Selden Rodman, *Quisqueya* (Seattle: University of Washington Press, 1964), the only complete history of the Dominican Republic. Some passages from that book have been adapted for the present narrative.

of Norman Vincent Peale," following publication of her ghost-written *Moral Meditations* and a "play" that even the cringing Dominican drama critics felt willing to review only in terms of its elegant costumes. One sister, married to a chief of staff, gave birth to another chief of staff. A brother made a quick fortune in Paris selling passports to desperate Jewish refugees. Another brother commited suicide after a paranoiac army career and the fathering of an idiot son. A third brother waxed rich upon the the control of prostitution. A fourth ran a lawsuit racket and a charcoal monopoly. A fifth hid under his mother's bed after an abortive plot against Big Brother but finally settled down with a gambling casino, radio and television stations, and a lieutenant-generalship. A sixth, the dim-witted Hector, emerged from his vast estate, Engombe, to front for Rafael in the Presidential chair.

The sign over the lunatic asylum in Nigua—"We owe everything to Trujillo"—seemed to indicate that the dictator had suppressed the people's sense of humor along with its pride. But there was a popular saying of the time to refute this assumption: "The brothers export, the brothers-in-law import, the head of the family deports." Although the thirteen-foot, gold-plated statue that stood at the entrance to the largest monument ever built for a living man was overtuned and pulverized by the infuriated mobs of 1961–1962, the monument itself—inhuman, funerary, preposterous—continues to dominate the center of the fertile Cibao like a petrified phallus.

The International Fair of 1955–1956, dedicated like the Santiago monument to "peace" and "brotherhood," took tangible shape in a complex of seventy-nine buildings, a complete Coney Island imported from the United States, and a tawdry million-dollar fountain of lights and music. Expected to bring in 500,000 tourists, the fair attracted 24,000, most of them flown in, expenses paid, as part of an enormous publicity campaign to counteract the increasingly ugly image of Trujillismo abroad, following the dictator's kidnapping and personal strangulation of Dr. Jesús Galíndez. The fair's symbolism was best revealed in two "golden albums" of morroco-bound rotogravure, carrying as frontispiece a tinted portrait of the dictator in gold braid and largely devoted to the rites attendant upon the coronation of "Her Gracious Majesty Angelita I," Trujillo's youngest daughter. In her $80,000 Italian gown, diamond-studded tiara, and pony-tail (which reportedly cost $1,000 to invert), the "precious" queen was pictured a hundred times passing through orgies of ribbon cutting, speech making, champagne swilling, and pig kissing, while her father, in several dozen of his thousand suits and uniforms, was shown greeting the few foreign dignitaries—President Kubitschek of Brazil, the special envoy of Generalissimo Franco, Cardinal Spellman, and the ambassadors of Cuba, Venezuela, and the United States—who could be lured into fawning upon his apotheosis.

Near the gateway to his estate Fundación—by 1960 spilling over from its original 3,000 acres into adjoining provinces and guarded at checkpoints along the wall by machine-gun nests—Trujillo built an "informal" home, calling it after his favorite wood, La Caoba. There everything remains as it was: the closets with row on row of uniforms made to order in Washington; the racks of $100 painted neckties; the tricolor sashes and jeweled identification bracelets; the pottery ashtrays molded to resemble catcher's mitts, the wine decanters blown into grape clusters; the American calendars ("Fine Cattle Produce Fine Milk"); the cheap chromo snow scene behind the desk, with its legend, "Christ Is Supreme in This House"; the private bedroom carpeted two inches deep with the Dominican flag, its bed so arranged that Trujillo's companion would have to be watching a chromo of the Virgin and Child.

It was toward this bed and its latest occupant that the old lecher was driving lightheartedly on the moonlit evening of May 30, 1961. At 10:30 two carloads of armed men intercepted the dictator's unescorted vehicle just behind Angelita's fairground. All of them were members of the establishment who had been humiliated or bankrupted by one or another of the tyrant's whims; some could be described as patriots, others as disgruntled mobsters. They had received minimal assistance in procuring arms from the C.I.A. (Trujillo had outlived his usefulness to the United States once the O.A.S. made a *cause célèbre* of his bungled attempt to assassinate Rómulo Betancourt in Caracas). Trujillo jumped out of his car, fired a few shots from his automatic, but went down with twenty-seven bullets in him.

Dumping the body into the trunk of one of the cars, the conspirators sped to the home of General Román Fernandez, Secretary of State for the Armed Forces and Trujillo's nephew-in-law, who was in on the plot. Unfortunately Trujillo had just ordered the General to leave town, and stupidly he had gone. The other members of the conspiracy panicked. In a second blunder they took one of their wounded to a private clinic, and four of them hid in the home of Dr. Roberto Reid Cabral. The secret police, alerted, closed in. The doctor and his patient were put to torture, and the patient talked. Several of the conspirators were gunned down in the streets. Only two, Antonio Imbert and Luis Amiama Tió, escaped into hiding.

On May 31, Ramfis, who had been playing polo in Paris with his former brother-in-law, Porfirio Rubirosa, when his father died, chartered a $27,-000 private flight and flew home to supervise the inhuman torture of the conspirators. On June 1, unable to suppress the news longer, *El Caribe* appeared with the following headlines:

> *Vilmente Asesinedo Cae el*
> *Benefactor de la Patria*
> *Su Muerte Llema de Luto*
> *la Sociedad Dominicana*

And underneath a eulogistic obituary by the newly named President, Joaquín Balaguer, concluded: *"Por Trujillo y por la Patria, pido a todos la colaboración y la conducta austera de que debemos dar prueba en esta hora suprema de dolor."* A poem of mourning consolation that appeared in the paper several days later was found to contain a more truthful message; alert readers discovered that the first letter of each line, read from top to bottom, spelled "Asesino y Ladron."

Hotels: Luxuries Without Necessities

The first time I visited the Dominican Republic, in the year immediately after World War II, Trujillo had just started to build hotels in his characteristic style; consequently there were still inns left from the disorderly old days, homey places with good food and friendly atmospheres. By the time I returned in 1962, the Benefactor's body had already been shipped to Paris, but the legacy he left behind him included a chain of unmanageable "luxury" establishments in the oddest places.

For instance, there was the Nueva Suiza, a fifty-nine-room affair at Constanza, down in the valley with no view of Pico Duarte (formerly Pico Trujillo, Hispaniola's highest mountain) or any other high mountain; its *piscina* was two kilometers away, and the hotel was empty. Two hours beyond was another mountain resort, Buena Vista, which advertised a scenic waterfall; the Salto de Jimenoa had unfortunately long been turned into an unsightly trickle by one of Trujillo's hydroelectric plants. Buena Vista's luxury hotel, the Montaña near Jarabacoa, which also looked out on nothing, boasted "an Olympic swimming pool"—filled at that time with yellow-green sludge.

At Barahona the imposing Guaracuya, instead of standing on the good beach of the country's westernmost Caribbean port, was at dockside, with polluted water from the sugar *central* lapping its lawns and nothing but the city's salt and gypsum factories in view. When I stayed in it on several occasions, the Guaracuya had boiling hot water running day and night from both taps—and the taps couldn't be turned off. The immense foyer occupying the ground floor was "dead space," and I remember vividly how it was flooded with sudsy water one day after breakfast and a waiter carried me across to my room pickaback.

Memory of a night my wife and I once spent in the country's easternmost hotel, at Higüey, is more vivid still. Equipped with the usual chromium-plated balconies, louvered windows, and sparsely planted atrium, this hotel also had nothing but boiling water in the taps, as well as unflushable toilets. Its larder was so badly stocked that nothing but a can of cranberry juice could be found for breakfast. About 2 in the morning, we had been sleeping fitfully when two men walked into our room without knocking and started arguing at the foot of our netted bed. When I asked them what they wanted, they said it was "absolutely illegal" to be sleeping in a room without locks on the doors. When I pointed out that during the evening the desk hadn't been able to locate a room that did have a lock and suggested that they move us or find us a key, one of them shouted, "This hotel will take no responsibility for you in an unlocked bedroom!"—And left, opening and slamming every other door in the corridor as they scolded their way back to the lobby.

But none of Trujillo's provincial hotels was good for as many laughs as the capital's Embajador, the biggest, most luxurious, and most bizarre of them all. It was not always so. In the 1940s and 1950s the gangsters and bullies in their dark glasses congregated at the Jaragua, the dictator's first bid for cafe-society approval, and an airport was built an hour from town to bring the traveling mob directly from the Stork Club. But, when the Jaragua was sacked following the assassination, the unemployed executioners and ghouls moved west to the Embajador, and in the country's first free election Juan Bosch dubbed the glittering fun factory "La Casa de los Tutumpotes" (House of the Filthy Rich). The Embajador achieved a second footnote in history when its lobby was strafed during the first days of the 1965 revolution, becoming in the months that followed both landing pad and check point for the U.S. Marine Corps and headquarters for the press of the world.

Having known this hotel intimately in war and peace, I can testify that nothing substantial ever changed. From the day Trujillo built and bugged it, the Embajador was a throbbing dynamo of scuttlebutt and snafu. Its site—far out of town and far from the Caribbean—is said to have been determined by Ramfis' polo requirements. Its neighbors are the German Embassy, the Jewish synagogue, and the heavily guarded mansion of one of Trujillo's two surviving assassins. Its *décor*—Louis XV modern, with chandeliers and soft pink lighting in the gaming salon, night club, and penthouse—bespoke a belated sophistication in the aging Caesar.

Our first night in the Embajador was memorable. My wife, who detests air conditioning, ordinarily turns it off the moment she enters a hotel, but she had reckoned without the Generalissimo, or, rather, he had anticipated any such obstructive nonconformity by providing no controls in the rooms—his listening devices were in the airshafts. Carole spent her first hour in the room attaching cardboard menus to the grill with Scotch tape. We never did find out exactly what role in the Great Eavesdropper's precautions the radios built into the bedside tables played, but it was impossible to turn them off. There would be silence for an hour or two, and then sleep would suddenly end with that maddening tinkle; as no plug had been provided, we finally took care of this plague by yanking the device out of the wall.

There was no political motivation for the inconveniences of the dining room; obtaining food was simply expensive and time-consuming. At a time when there were twenty waiters to a guest, being served a small orange juice (forty cents) never took less than a quarter of an hour; when there hadn't been any orange juice for several days and we asked why, we were informed that the electric squeezer had broken down. A suggestion that the man whose sole function was to replace hibiscus blossoms in the patio fountain twice a day might squeeze a few oranges was not well received. One day the paging waiter, with his bicycle bell and little blackboard, came by intoning "Señor Blanco! Señor Blanco!" On the blackboard the gentleman's correct name, Mr. White, was printed in capital letters. "If the Dodgers' Negro relief pitcher, Joe Black, ever comes here," Carole observed, "there's going to be a crisis in race relations."

Roads to Nowhere, Beaches for the Birds

Trujillo's roads, not surprisingly, led to his business enterprises and country estates. As he had businesses in every part of the country, this system was not too bad: There are few Latin American countries with better roads. From a visitor's point of view, however, the tyrant's road net is deficient: The best beaches and the highest mountains—no doubt for self-protecion—he left inaccessible. But there are advantages. Every trip is an adventure in exploration. One is strictly alone, and one always returns with some objective still to pursue.

A case in point is the great salt lake, Enriquillo, knifing into the rugged, fortress-studded Haitian border. I have driven around it twice without seeing any of the alligators or flamingos it is reputed to harbor. But once, dipping down in an open-cockpit plane over the lake's one island, where the courageous Arawak Prince Enriquillo had forced the Spanish ruffians to sign a treaty granting the remnant of his people asylum at Boyá, I saw an unforgettable sight—a flock of the great pink birds, each seeming as big as the plane itself, flying in formation below us against the deep blue of the unruffled water. The only alligator I ever saw was being escorted on a leash through the streets of Jimaní, but it may very well have been captured in the Étang Saumâtre across the border, where alligators (caimánes) abound.

It is the same with the beaches. The longest and best one is at El Macao, facing Puerto Rico, twenty-nine kilometers east of Higüey on a dirt road. It was not easy to find, but when I finally reached it I had fifty miles of perfect, reef-protected beach fifty feet wide entirely to myself.

The smaller beach at Sosua, the colony of Jewish cheese makers on the north coast, is prettier. But Dominican friends insisted that the best beaches of all were strung out east of Sosua and to the north of Nagua. Trying to verify this claim almost cost my wife a miscarriage in 1964. With two friends, we drove on and on past San Francisco de Macorís until the road became a cow track and finally a checkerboard of potholes. Reluctantly we turned back. Later we flew very low along the whole coastline, but it is hard to tell whether or not beaches are as glorified by aerial perspective as are city slums. We spotted dozens of beautiful little beaches in coves on both sides of the Samaná Peninsula and others on tiny, heavily wooded offshore islands. In a decade this whole region could become a tourist paradise. The time to savor it in its unspoiled grandeur could be *now*. And this statement applies as well to the inviting beaches along the Cabo Rojo south of Barahona, the westernmost Dominican city on the Caribbean, all undeveloped and quite easy to drive to.

The beaches promoted for tourism under Trujillo are predictably shoddy. Monte Cristi and Puerto Plata on the Atlantic are filled with seaweed and rum ads. At Boca Chica near the capital, the water is so shallow one has to wade out hundreds of yards to wet one's shoulders.

We had our best view of the central part of the country (the Cibao) driving north from the capital to Santiago de los Caballeros, the Republic's second city, by way of La Vega. In prosperous, progressive Santiago, which the dictator hated, all the splendid arcaded palaces and warehouses I had admired in 1946 had been torn down; in their place Trujillo had left a suspension bridge leading nowhere and the "peace" monument already described dominating the Cibao. From La Vega a little train with one passenger car tootles daily through the Yuna River delta to the coffee port of Sánchez at the base of historic Samaná Bay; if all goes well, it returns the following day. At Samaná there is a ferry across the bay to Sabana de la Mar, from which a good road returns to the capital via Hato Mayor, San Pedro de Macorís, and Boca Chica. The train ride may be noisy and dirty, but it's still the best way to see one of the richest agricultural valleys in the world. Seeing it first from La Vega, Columbus christened it the Vega Real, and it has astonished everyone who has seen it since. "There, at the Santo Cerro, where the Admiral watched his armored men and bloodhounds massacre (with "Divine intervention" the Church claims) the helpless Indians, the Vega Real may be seen stretching eastward in endless fertility, pink-blossoming *amapolas* shading the coffee bushes and fruit trees that grow abundantly out of the fabled fifteen-foot-deep loam. The miserably poor capital of the Vega Real, San Francisco de Macorís, bears witness to the country's economic problems; its decapitated statuary, which once glorified the Benefactor, testifies to the peasants' resentment of their victimization by absentee landlords, all symbolized by 1960 in the person of Trujillo. But the ruins of Columbus' brick fortress and church eight kilometers north of La Vega, between the old and new roads to Santiago, were unaccountably spared. We were taken to see them by a band of Negro urchins with blond hair. They didn't know what they were showing us, but they were proud of it and of our interest.

Trujillo also destroyed the romantic charm of the island's oldest edifice, Diego Columbus' palace (incorrectly called "the Alcázar") on the Ozama River east of the capital. When I first saw it in 1948, it was a dove-haunted ruin. Trujillo restored it tastelessly with period pieces from Spain. Earlier predators did their best to uglify the noble cathedral by cluttering up the nave with a Victorian "tomb" for Columbus. But the plateresque façade, dating from 1540, though stripped of its sculpture, remains, as does the rib vaulting of the thirty-three-foot-wide columned nave and the gilded baroque high altar.

A very short drive east and west of the capital we discovered two places as delightful to explore and picnic in as any in the West Indies. Just to the right of the road to Boca Chica and not far from the Duarte Bridge is the series of underground pools known as Tres Ojos (Three Eyes). As we descended on dank steps through vault-like chambers festooned with ferns, lianas, and bats' nests, shafts of sunlight from the limestone roof disclosed a deep pool of salt water of a perfect aquamarine transparency. Once again a band of urchins were our guides, showing us niches on the wall from which to dive; taking us a to a second subterranean pool, sulphurous but not hot; and warning us at the brink of a third (fresh water) not to swim, lest we be sucked into a tunnel leading to a boiling lake from which there is no return. One of the boys showed us a wonderfully carved head of orange travertine, which he said had been dug up nearby; but later, in the capital, we learned from Émile de Boyrie Moya, who has a superb collection of these pre-Columbian pieces, that they all come from the extensive caves called Los Paredones back of Boca Chica.

The other notable site is a ruined colonial hacienda on the 5,000-acre estate that once belonged to Trujillo's brother Hector (El Negro). The ruins are on a hill overlooking the Rio Haina back of the gigantic sugar *central* that the dictator built. There are extensive redoubts and fortifications, powder mills, sunken gardens, mosaics, and one mighty wall with tiers of arches lying flat on the ground, which must have fallen during an earthquake.

A Revolution Without Revolutionaries

I visited Santo Domingo before, during, and after the revolution of 1965, and what strikes me most in retrospect about those sixteen months, which began with the overthrow of Donald Reid Cabral on May 24 and ended with the withdrawal of American armed forces in the fall of 1966, was that there were no real revolutionaries. All the principal characters seemed to have been drawn into the malestrom against their wills. Every-

one was looking for a messiah but no one wanted to be one, except, perhaps, the leaders of the various communist functions whose participation was ruled out by the United States as soon as the shooting began.

Consider the mild man whose threatened "dictatorship" the Revolution was mounted to forestall. I had met Donald Reid Cabral for the first
time in 1962, when he joined the Council of State that organized shortly
after Trujillo's assassination to prepare the sick country for elections.
A frail, blue-eyed young man who sold automobiles, he had been drawn
into the chaotic situation by his outrage over what the *Trujillistas* had
done to his brother for sheltering the wounded conspirators in his clinic.
He was a patriot and an idealist, with no experience in politics. He
showed me a submachine gun under his desk and declared with flashing
eyes that he would fire it until they killed him if any attempt were made
to subvert the Council's role as peacekeeper. The Council did its job,
and the elections took place freely and fairly; Bosch won, did none of
the things that were expected of him, and six months later was exiled
after a bloodless coup that few seemed to resent at the time. Donald
Reid Cabral returned to the Palace as provisional President, not seeking
power but with the laudable motive of keeping the *Trujillista* army
officers, who had masterminded the coup, from dragging the country into
a facsimile of the Trujillo era. I came to see him again, and I'll never
forget the waiting room, that antechamber to the Presidential office
where Dominican time stands still. There were four occupants, all male.
One sat at a cluttered desk combing his hair and riffling through the ads
in the telephone book. A second occasionally added a line to the docu-
ment in his typewriter by the hunt-and-peck system. A third, in full
colonel's uniform, spent the hour reading *El Caribe*. The fourth, obviously
top man, in an impeccable white suit, stared into space or walked up and
down as if in deep thought. Toward the end of the hour several teen-age
characters dropped in, and one of them showed me his stamp collection;
but, just as he removed the stamps from a greasy envelope, the air-conditioning system suddenly came on and blew the little images of Trujillo
all over the room. For the rest of the hour (and perhaps the next) everybody in the room had something to do. By the time President Reid
arrived he was so exhausted—perhaps from doing the work these clerks
should have been doing—that he fell asleep in his chair while I was talking to him. I had already summed up his program on the back of an
envelope: "Keep business happy, and if the money runs out the Americans will provide more." Could Donald Reid Cabral be blamed for accepting our guidelines?

Juan Bosch, who had just been overthrown and in whose name the
next *coup d'état* was already being plotted, had operated just as ineffec-
tually in accordance with the contrary dogma. Any program that the
United States supported must be tainted. Jaime Benítez, Chancellor of
the University of Puerto Rico and Bosch's close friend, put his finger on
one decisive weakness while driving me to the Dominican leader's com-

mand post in San Juan during the 1965 revolution. "All Latin American intellectuals," he said, "are caught in the vise (you can spell it "vice") of their own rhetoric and linguistic image. They are not makers of policy. They are thinking: 'How will I look to history? Will I be called somebody's puppet?' " Bosch, who had spent all his mature life in exile, had theories to explain everything—and no stomach for action. Tall, blue-eyed, with craggy features and a white thatch, he exercised great personal charm while holding the center of the stage. He was vain, and, like many writers and professors, he did not care to listen to others. His intolerance made enemies, even within his own party. He got along with the American Ambassador, John Bartlow Martin, who shared many of his qualities, but Martin was in no position to save a president whose secret ambition was to die a martyr in the cause of resisting Dominican salvation at American hands.

Bosch had been elected President for two ironic reasons. The vast array of those who had served Trujillo were frightened into his camp by the threats of the ultra-right candidate, Viriato Fiallo, to bring them to trial. The peasants were won over by the promise that there would be a social revolution involving the division of the big landholdings. When this promise wasn't kept, it was inevitable that Bosch would be overthrown. But it was unfortunate that the *Trujillistas*, rather than the peasants and the urban unemployed, overthrew him. In exile, as the figurehead of the 1965 revolution, Bosch seemed a patriotic figure. Had he returned in May when Reid was overthrown, the American intervention would not have taken place; from his hideaway in Puerto Rico he generated only deeper division and ill will. And, when he finally did return after the revolution, to run for the Presidency a second time, he was equally impotent, issuing statements from his guarded home in the capital while the frail Balaguer barnstormed the provinces.

The other major figures in the revolution—Wessin and Imbert on the Right, Caamaño and Aristy among the rebels—were *papier mâché* revolutionists too. Wessin, obsessed by communist bogeymen, came close to misdirecting the armed forces to an early defeat at a time when he controlled all the heavy weapons. Imbert made a belated effort to rally the Dominican people to the rightist cause but had no social-economic program to offer them. Caamaño, Bosch's stand-in behind the barricades, was an admirable figurehead but not clever enough to sense that the provincial masses wanted no part of a solution imposed by class war in the capital. His spokesman, Aristy, an opportunist gifted with agility and glibness, barely succeeded in holding together the motley array of disaffected intellectuals and soldiers of fortune holed up in Ciudad Nueva.

The real heroes of the revolution were the two men who brought the Dominican Republic out of it relatively unscarred: Hector García Godoy and Ellsworth Bunker. The three Dominicans who have it in their power to transform the tragically embattled country from its historic self-

destructive stance to one of self-reliant democracy are José Francisco Peña Gomez, Fiore Marra, and Joaquín Balaguer.

President Balaguer has already proved himself, redeeming himself for his passive role in the Trujillo past by reconciling the warring Dominicans with one another, reducing the political power of the armed forces, and giving the builders a chance to build. Peña Gomez, heir to Bosch's fragmented P.R.D. and most enlightened of the revolutionaries, can decide by his actions or even by his powers of restraint, whether the Dominican Republic shall advance as a two-party democracy or regress to a police state. Marra, equally young and idealistic and educated in the United States, created the Office of Community Development, the first organization ever to help the peasants to help themselves. He started it on a shoestring before the revolution. He kept it alive during the fighting because he was protected by his wife's family (related to Caamaño) and his own (related to Imbert). Then, with $10 million of A.I.D. funds, he began to teach a quarter of the landless to use the abandoned Trujillo lands, not as small squatters but as cooperative *producers*. With four times as much help, the minor miracle of a successful pilot project could escalate into an economic revolution capable of transforming the Dominican Republic and spreading to the entire "underdeveloped world." [1]

[1] These developments, as well as the causes and results of the American intervention, are examined at length in the author's "Balaguer—The First Nine Months," *The New Republic*, March 25, 1967; "Why Balaguer Won: Anatomy of a Revolution That Failed," *The New Republic*, June 18, 1966; and "A Close View of Santo Domingo," *The Reporter*, July 15, 1965.

Dominican Traits

I asked a Dominican friend on my last visit why no Dominican girl of the middle or urban working class ever appears in public without a headful of hair curlers. "Very simple," he said. "She wants to straighten out the Negro kinks, and, even if she doesn't have any, she thinks those 'status symbols' will offset her dark complexion." This antipathy to the Negroid has deep historical roots. Haiti (where hair curlers are not worn) occupied the Spanish part of the island for two decades early in the nineteenth century and brutalized it. Trujillo's massacre of Haitians in 1937 was in part a retaliation for the earlier occupation, and Trujillo went to great lengths to convince foreign visitors that he, his dark-skinned brothers, and the nation were "white" and therefore "civilized." Dominican Negroes have never been segregated or denied high political and military office, as in the United States, yet this unspoken prejudice persists. Haitians are widely regarded as animals, and very few Dominicans have ever visited their island neighbor—or would dream of doing so.

I asked my friend, whose enlightened frankness typifies a growing number of intellectuals who have been abroad, what he thought were the characteristic Dominican traits. His ready answer—"violence and generosity"—confirmed my own findings. During the revolution I had asked Buenaventura Sánchez, Bosch's Minister of Education and one of the founders of the P.R.D., why he believed the American intervention was justified. "Because we are a violent people," he said. "Before your troops arrived, more people were killed here than in Castro's whole take-over in Cuba, and if it had continued as it was going there would have been a blood bath from which we might never have recovered." At a recent baseball game, a knife was drawn by a pitcher against his own second baseman, who had criticized him for throwing the wrong pitch. Even for Latin America, the number of obscenities used in ordinary speech is astonishing. Boorishness is a mark of the urban (not the rural) Dominican. The word "thanks" is almost never heard in the city. I have seen an uninvited guest at a reception demand a glass of water and when it arrived say curtly to the host, "por fin" ("at last").

If you're down and out, however, or even lacking cash momentarily, the Dominican will empty his pockets for you—and look stunned if you pay him back the next day. The generosity, but not the violence, is a peasant characteristic that seems to have permeated the whole society.

Artists Without a Cause?

Very little of this generosity, or even of the Dominican physiognomy, is reflected in the arts so far. Trujillo, an *arriviste* without taste, looked down on any form of folk expression—and especially on the wearing of carnival masks that might have concealed hostile looks; he imported *pompiers* from abroad to paint his tawdry glory in the most retarded of styles. By the time he was assassinated, Dominican talent had either emigrated or was experimenting clandestinely with the various abstract modes. Two painters, Jaime Colson and the late Paul Guidicelli, deserve particular praise for resisting the blandishments of the dictatorship. Colson kept alive standards of good draughtsmanship. Guidicelli experimented with new media.

The 1965 revolution had an electrifying effect on the arts. It even spawned the Republic's first "primitive," Justo Susana. Susana lived near the Duarte Bridge then, and he painted with inventive gusto a series of pictures showing rebel commandos under the piers firing at Wessin's tanks and the American helicopters. Ambassador-at-Large Ellsworth Bunker became his first patron and one day showed me the pictures that he had collected. His favorite title, he said, was the one the artist had given him, El Pato Macho de los Manganeos, which he translated for me freely as "The Male Duck of the Wheeler-Dealers." But two years later, without anyone to give him a sense of direction, Susana in green pants and a red corduroy shirt was hawking bargain "repeats" of his better pictures in the lobby of the Brazilian Embassy.

Whether or not the revolutionary *élan* of the more sophisticated artists will survive the pragmatic Balaguer era, no one knows. Will Ramón Oviedo continue to be imbued with the mystique of the noble worker who carries his burden of cane triumphantly up the hill on his head? Will Cándido Bidó go on mourning for the poor with such appropriately somber magentas and purples once the poor have come out of their wretched hovels? Will Lepé (Leopoldo Peréz) become altogether bemused by the elegantly swirling black lines that already tend to obscure his message? The paradox is that what is good for the country may stifle these artists, whose creativity was born of a freedom close to anarchy, and, to some degree, of a fierce, doctrinaire anti-Americanism. What will they have to say if Fiore Marra is given enough American money to help the Dominican poor to help themselves?

But what will happen to the Dominican Republic if the Fiore Marras fail? [2]

---

[2] In 1968 Fiore Marra was removed from his post and replaced with a loyal bureaucrat. The Dominican Republic seemed to be reverting to type.

X

HAITI

Haiti. What does the name conjure?

A nation of sorcerers and *zombis?* Blue-black mountains and blue-black people? A nation of artists? Overpopulation and underdevelopment in a tropical paradise? Catholic priests in jeeps distributing prayer beads or priests of the *loa* making *vevers* out of flour, ashes, and raw rum? French-speaking surrealist poets? African drumming with a beat stronger than Africa's? Jean Jacques Dessalines ripping the white stripe out of the tricolor? King Henry Christophe's Royal Dahomeys or Papa Doc's Tonton Macoutes?

Overlooking the cactus desert, the *coumbite*, accompanied by bamboo *vaccines*, is burning off last year's millet. Only the birds are watching the waterfalls. The sweetish smell of sweat, charcoal, and crunched cane floats over the *camion* dubbed Malgré Tout, topheavy with pigs and fighting cocks. The market women carry their head burdens by day like the abandoned dancers they are by night. A beggar with yaws reels through the street carrying the mask of a werewolf. The taxi driver is quoting Catullus. Under the flickering street lamp the schoolboys memorize their Bossuet. Why are peasants in flour sacks with ten undernourished children and yam fields the size of Cadillacs more turned on than the hippies? Why do they laugh more easily than Hiltonites?

It was all there when I visited Haiti for the first time thirty years ago —though the famous painters and the infamous Tonton Macoutes hadn't surfaced yet. Nothing else seems to have changed. To be sure, the government is more repressive and has virtually eliminated the hereditary aristocracy, that mulatto *élite* that once exploited the black masses through its business wiles and legal guiles, supplying the capital in turn with its French culture, a pride of poets, and a gross of Sorbonne-trained technicians. The concomitant withdrawal of American aid completed the debacle of primitive husbandry and perfunctory road repair and frightened away most of the tourists who promised in the 1950s to give Haiti an escape hatch of sorts from its economic purgatory. But, when Bill Negron and I visited Haiti in April of 1967 and again in October, we looked in vain for that pervasive climate of despairing evil that Graham Greene had come looking for in 1965 (I was in Haiti that year too) and found. Evil exists, of course, at the center of Haiti—in the Palace and the palace guard; in the "bogeymen" who have become the tax collectors, as well as the informers and executioners; and in that handful of unprincipled entrepreneurs who become *nouveaux riches* on the fringes of any entrenched mafia. But the center of Haiti is not its heart and never has been. A maximum 5,000 people, out of a population of 5 million, take advantage of the misery of their neighbors out of weakness or fear. The shopkeepers have not changed. The taxi drivers have not changed. The *hôteliers* have not changed. The *houngan* in the voodoo *tonnelle* has not changed. The situation of the artists has not changed—as with every nation's artists, some have "sold out," and some are better than ever. Above all, the peasantry has not changed.

The weakness and strength of Haiti are in the immutability of these peasants on their tiny plots of abused land. The division and subdivision of the farms in the century following the expulsion of the French strengthened their proprietors' conviction that all evil comes from the city; that all government is bad; that tax collectors, lawyers, even doctors and educators are to be shunned like Baron Samedi of the cemetery. No wonder the communists steer clear of Haiti—except to encourage chaos. There are no large estates to be broken up, no landless army to appease with land, no wage slaves to lead on strike—for who works for a wage? We talked to peasants "falling out of their corn fields" in the towering mountains behind Kenscoff. We waded with them among the carp in the rice paddies of the Artibonite. We stopped them on that caricature of a road between Léogane and Jacmel. We surprised black Susannahs beating their clothes with clubs to time-honored rhythms in the stream beds between Cap-Haïtien and Ouanaminthe. The answers were the same ones I had been hearing for thirty years. The words were the same. "Times are bad, worse than ever, M'sieu. Certainly we can imagine a better government and even hope for one, but nobody expects it. The *bon dieu* provides us with black children, not black saviors." Even the proverbs were the same: "If work were a good thing, the rich would have grabbed all of it long ago"; "The fish trust the water, and it is in the water that they are cooked"; "To nod your head yes won't break your neck"; "When black hurts black, God laughs."

Inside Haiti: Hotels and History

Robert Baussan is the proprietor and architect of the Ibo Lelé Hotel, a medium-luxury chateau in Pétionville, the residential suburb of Port-au-Prince that perches 1,500 feet above the incandescent capital. With its exquisite pool framed in crimson blossoms, its murals by Antonio Joseph and Rolland Dorcély, and its multilevel patios commanding views of both the magnificent harbor of Port-au-Prince and the sugar-green Cul de Sac stretching eastward to the great lakes on the Dominican border, the Ibo Lelé was a work of art before Rockefeller's Little Dix, Peter Brand's Island House, and Arthur Leamon's Golden Lemon were dreamed of. (And consider that it is closely rivaled by the Villa Créole, El Rancho, the Oloffson, the Sans Souci, and a dozen smaller hotels with pools and that in all Santo Domingo there are only *three*.) Ibo Lelé is a *loa* (spirit) of the Ibo tribe in West Africa, the tribe that chronically wars with the government of Nigeria for its independence. Ibo rites are still practiced among the descendants of the Ibo slaves whom the French imported in the eighteenth century to work their plantations. For more than five years the Ibo Lelé hotel has been virtually empty, but Robert Baussan, along with the proprietors of most of the other hotels, has doggedly refused to let bankruptcy affect his accommodations, his cuisine, or his spirit. He

and his family do most of the work, and he has developed a small beach for swimming and spearfishing on little Cacique Island, hugging the harbor's northern rim. In lieu of guests, he drives out parties from the occasional cruise ships that stop for a day; plays tennis with those who are up to it (he was Haiti's champion forty years ago and still wields a formidable racket); snorkels for the fish and crabs he serves; discusses poetry, history, and political philosophy; and serves the best Barbancourt-rum punches in Haiti. But this great gentleman has one serious fault, a typically Haitian fault: So great is his hospitality that guests who are old friends must fight to make him accept even a share of the bill.

Carmelle Hereaux, who runs the immaculately clean little Quisqueya down the hill a piece, with a pool the size of a big mango, has the same fault. And so does Harold Busenius at the Mont Joli in Cap Haïtien, to which Bill and I flew next in one of the Haiti's three remaining DC-3s, ancient but still expertly piloted.

Philomé Obin was giving a party for us. With his brother, Sénèque, who shares his talent, and his artist son Antoine, the great painter escorted us up the rickety stairs to his parlor. At seventy-eight Obin looks precisely as he did when I first knew him in 1946. "Precise" is the word. His appearance and the *décor* of his tiny house have always been as meticulous as his painting—those vibrant evocations of Haitian life and history, with their scores of fully individualized figures in buildings put together brick by brick. Obin's face is sensitive, ascetic. He weighs less than 100 pounds. His small feet, bony long-fingered hands, and taper-thin wrists contribute to his bird-like appearance. The white shirt and suit, the white straw hat with a black band, and the elegant cane are in keeping with his passion for order. In 1946 the feature of his parlor was a triumphal arch constructed of match boxes, each drawer containing a single treasured object—a collar button, a safety pin, a feather, a smooth stone. Today the feature is a grapevine. Originating as a thick purple rope in a pot of sand in the corner, it branches like a star from the center of the ceiling with leaves of green paper, carefully veined, and clusters of *papier-mâché* fruit; some branches even go out the window and festoon the balcony.

After seating us around the table and motioning to a girl, who poured a sweet liqueur into glasses the size of thimbles, the old artist announced that his *fête de coeur* would begin. To our astonishment, a choir of eight black children in white suddenly materialized on the balcony and proceeded to serenade us with Baptist hymns. When it was over, I asked Philomé how he was spending his money these days—he now receives several hundred dollars for a picture, a bracket in which only Rigaud Benoît and Antonio Joseph approach him. "Supporting my thirteen children," he said, waging his head, "in their constant troubles, education, business ventures, marriages and funerals. I've bought land to build a

house in the country, but I'm too busy with painting commissions to build it." With his brother, who also sells everything he paints, Philomé Obin is obviously the *grand seigneur* of the neighborhood, and, although the bourgeois Capois do not buy his pictures or even exhibit them in their hotels, they do take a sneaking pride in his world fame and have slowly come to regard "primitive painting," however grotesque, as one of the more lucrative professions.

The city of Cap-Haïtien is as unlike Port-au-Prince as the Haitians of the North are unlike the Haitians of the South. Le Cap is much poorer than the capital, but it is cleaner, and its buildings are painted and kept in tolerable repair. The South is traditionally "African": self-possessed, easygoing, exuberantly religious, caste conscious, and submissive. The North, where resistance to oppression is always smouldering, does not look to such ancestral conventions. The Spaniard, with his fiercely held beliefs, his political inconstancy, and his flair for the theatrical, has left a faint but unmistakable imprint. The iron balconies hanging over the narrow streets and the pastel bungalows whose jigsawed cornices protrude over the whole sidewalk are "Spanish," and Sénèque Obin's paintings—of dead bulls being devoured by dogs and funeral cortèges in front of Masonic lodges—are Goyaesque in spirit if not in style.

From the Obins' studios on the outskirts of the city, past the still-unidentified site of Columbus' ill-fated first colony, we drove to Milot, where Henry Christophe had built his palace.

The great slave insurrection of 1791 broke out along this road, following a voodoo ceremony at a place called Bois Caïman. Saint-Domingue,
as Haiti was then called, was France's richest colony, and a very large
part of the sugar and coffee consumed in Europe was harvested there in
the fabled Plaine du Nord. The mulatto freedmen had lighted the match
by demanding the political rights that the French Revolution had promised but failed to deliver. When the mulatto leaders were broken on the
rack in Cap-Haïtien, the 500,000 black slaves started a more uncompromising revolt of their own, burning the plantation houses in the Plaine
(only the stone gateways along this road still stand) and driving the
20,000 terrified white masters into the city. For ten years the struggle
continued all over Hispaniola with unprecedented ferocity. In 1801 Toussaint L'Ouverture, the brilliant black tactician, managed to bring the
whole island, including Spanish Santo Domingo, under the sway of the
ex-slaves and even, by Draconian methods, to revive the island's burnt-
out prosperity. Napoleon equipped and sent against him a large ocean-
going invasion force. His brother-in-law, General Leclerc, captured the
Negro general by guile and defeated the ex-slaves—only to lose both his
army and his life to yellow fever. Then the savage Dessalines, who had
already massacred most of the mulattos, completed the rout of the
French (who had been joined briefly by the English). Having proclaimed
himself Emperor for life, Dessalines was assassinated after a drunken
orgy by his own disgusted palace guard.

It was then (1805) that the country was divided between north and
south. General Christophe seized the North, General Pétion the South.
Henry Christophe was ruthless, hard-working, immensely ambitious, and
friendly with the English, who served as his advisers for a while. He
forced his subjects to work, made the North prosperous, created a
nobility, had himself crowned in Cap-Haïtien (Cap Henry he renamed
it), and started building the palace at Milot and the awesome Citadelle
on a mountain peak behind it. General Pétion, a mulatto who had been
educated in France, set himself up in Port-au-Prince. Being tolerant and
democratically inclined, he started giving away the land to the people,
thus inaugurating the pattern of a self-sufficient, indigent, isolated, non-
political peasantry without ploughs or wheelbarrows under which Haiti
vegetates to this day. Pétion is said to have died when he finally became
too indolent to eat. But when the tyrant Christophe was finally overthrown by his overregimented subjects, all Haiti accepted the lazy
Pétion's philosophy.

Pétion's memorial is "timeless" Haiti: the Haitian people still dancing
and laughing exuberantly over the right he bequeathed them to be
poverty-stricken in freedom. Christophe's memorial, built of blood, sweat,
floggings, and creative passion, is the ruined, still stunning palace and
the defiant, useless fortress.

Even in ruins Sans Souci dwarfs in imaginative *brio* anything that the
white man has erected in the West Indies. Those who saw it floodlit when

the Magloire government celebrated the sesquicentennial of the expulsion of the French on January 1, 1954, with Marian Anderson singing from the grand staircase, while "Christophe" and his dukes and lords in full uniform paced the battlements above, will pray that the greatest stage set in the hemisphere remains untouched in its crumbling, golden glory. Built of brick overlayed with stucco, four stories high, and covering twenty acres of sloping ground—from the sentry boxes flanking the regal steps to the royal stables that once housed the King's £700 English carriage and the giant star-apple tree under which Henry dispensed judgments (where now cigarettes, postcards, and coffee are dispensed by a little old lady who might well be a descendant of the hard-driving but pleasure-loving monarch)—one may still read above an arch, on a sun of black wood, the lordly inscription, "Je Vois Tout et Tout Voit Par Moi Dans l'Univers."

Completed in 1813, Sans Souci in Christophe's time had floors of marble and mosaic, walls of polished mahogany, tapestries and drapes imported from Europe. It also had bathrooms. Under the floors, conduits carried a cold mountain stream—ancestor of air conditioning—which emerged below as a fountain.

Poets of *tourisme* say that, as your horse mounts the steep trail to the Citadelle behind Sans Souci, you can pick a fruit salad as you pass. If your horses are anything like ours were, you will be much too busy even to look at the oranges, bananas, cashew nuts, mangoes, grenadines, avocados and coconuts lining the way. Coffee will be found in front of the *ti cailles* rimmed with bougainvillea, and mahogany trees provide shade. Just as you begin to think you will never arrive—and in the tropical downpours for which the region is famous, it is not unheard of for a traveler to disappear in a murky ravine whose matted floor must contain the bones of many an unfortunate royal hod carrier—the Citadelle is upon you, its menacing prow knifing the air at 3,000 feet.

They call the red lichen that covers the 140-foot walls "Christophe's blood." The walls themselves are ten to twenty feet thick and were built to house a garrison of 15,000 men, a modern division. Four gun corridors, each 270 feet long and 30 feet wide, with ports for firing, contain most of the 365 giant cannon that were originally dragged up that trail. English, Spanish, and French in origin, some bear such Roman names as Scipio, Romulo, and Remo; some the motto of the French Revolution, *Liberté, Egalité, Fraternité,* and some the *Honi Soit Qui Mal Y Pense* of the Knights of the Garter. Hundreds of smaller guns and cannon balls litter the battlements.

A section of forty rooms was originally set aside for Christophe, his family, and his staff. The King's billiard room, with two sentry boxes at the entrance, was equipped with an open fireplace. The water problem was solved by building catch basins and cisterns in the walls. Ammunition and powder rooms, dungeons, and treasure chambers, many of them sealed and still unexplored, make up the nether regions. But, although the Citadelle La Ferrière on which tens of thousands toiled for sixteen years, began as a safety measure, it ended as a monument to vanity and pride. Whether or not it is true that the King ordered a platoon of his Royal Dahomeys to march off the parapet to impress a visiting dignitary with their loyalty to him, it is a fact that Christophe in his last years had to have his entire border patrolled to prevent desertions to Pétion's happy-go-lucky South. The end came when the monarch, after suffering a paralytic stroke that prevented him from mounting his horse, was deserted by his army and most of his courtiers. He is said to have shot himself with a silver bullet at Sans Souci, following which the Queen and one faithful retainer dragged his huge body up the precipitous trail to the Citadelle and dumped it in a vat of quicklime. His tomb on the ramparts bears the epitaph:

Ci-Gît le Roi Henry Christophe
Né le 6 Octobre, 1767, Mort le
20 Octobre, 1820, Dont la Dévise
Est: Je Renais de Mes Cendres.

Inside Haiti: Waterfalls and Wagon Trails

All but one of the great waterfalls of Haiti are in the South. The exception is Basin Zim near Hinche in the Central Plateau. The beauty of the Haitian waterfalls perhaps impresses itself upon one the more because of the aridity surrounding them. One rides to Basin Zim through an interminable desert of eroded ravines, asking the way of every peasant in sight, for this road has lost even its wheel ruts. Suddenly it is there!— a bridal veil barely concealing the bride's curves and crevices as it falls out of a jungle the size of a double bed—a jungle with every delectable fruit and even a cave "signed" by the Arawaks. The pool below the diaphanous falls is deep, milky green, and cold; after the number of tires one has changed in getting there, its coldness seems blessed. I remember the last time I visited Basin Zim. It was in 1954. I was with John Hersey and Robert Théard, a Haitian writer who had just read us his "Bismark," a touching story about an eight-year-old peasant "slave" who dies for love of his cruel Syrian mistress.

"You must put a picture of François Duvalier in your new book about Haiti," Théard said, as we rattled down the road to Mirebalais.

François *who?*" I asked.

"No one has heard of him, but he's going to be the next Haitian President," Théard said.

The upshot was that the next week Théard did bring the obscure Michigan-educated country doctor to my house in Bizoton, and my picture of the two of them appeared in the first edition of *Haiti: The Black Republic.* I recalled the incident to Théard's attention while he was serving as Duvalier's Ambassador to the Dominican Republic in March 1967.

"What do you remember about him?" Théard asked, looking at me curiously.

"I only remember feeling that he loathed me for being American and white—something I'd never experienced in Haiti before," I said. "Do you have any qualms about serving him, Robert?"

He looked at me with an expression of anguish, then smiled and changed the subject. Two months later, recalled to Port-au-Prince for a routine report to Papa Doc, Théard and his wife packed their belongings and fled to Spain.

The southern peninsula of Haiti, stretching almost 200 miles in the direction of Jamaica, is full of surprises. Jacmel, the Caribbean port at the peninsula's base and only fifty-five miles from the capital, is the first. The trip to it by car is always a six-hour adventure. Passing Léogane and Carrefour Fauché, the road descends into a stream bed. The trick is not to lose the road, which fords the shallow stream constantly, sometimes following the stream itself for several hundred feet at a time. As everywhere in Haiti, there will be peasants to show the way, help change a tire and, if necessary, carry riders through a flood. The town, made famous by the diagrammatic paintings of Préfèt DuFaut, a native son, will remind you, if you have been in Italy, of hill towns like San Gemignano and Urbino. Pink houses with iron balconies (imported from Germany during the coffee boom at the turn of the century) are piled one on top of another, with roof gardens. Some of the narrow streets are ramps with steps eight feet wide and 4 inches high. As recently as 1965, on my last visit to Jacmel, the old Vitale house on the square, whose balconies and gardens overhang the Grand' Rue, served as a splendid *pension;* meals were served by a fragile ancient retainer in white uniform and *gloves.* If Jacmel has survived three more years of Duvalier and the two hurricanes that reputedly blew off most of its roofs, it remains the place from which to visit the palm-fringed beach at Carrefour Raymond and the Basin Bleu four miles above town; the latter is a series of natural swimming pools separated by cascades. Blue-green from the dissolved limestone, veiled in bolts of maidenhair fern, and haunted (they say) by Maîtresse La Sirène, these unforgettable glens must be approached via an arduous horseback ride and finally a climb over boulders. The sweetest fruits (to invent a Haitian proverb) don't fall in your lap.

Source Mathurin, farther down the southern peninsula in the *massif* behind Les Cayes, is harder to reach only because of the degeneration of the main southern highway. It is Haiti's grandest waterfall, and it is only a short horseback ride from Camp-Perrin, once the summer resort of Les Cayes' *élite.* When you are ready to hook up the hill to the right leaving Camp-Perrin, you have already covered fifteen of the sixty-five miles to Jérémie, the town at the peninsula's tip; but of the eight hours you should allow for your four-wheel-drive vehicle to cover this most bone-rattling but exalted of Haitian excursions, you have ticked off only *one.* The road, if such it may be called, was built under the marine occupation; having been hacked out of solid rock around mountains 6,000 feet high, it is a piece of engineering to be marveled at. But, if any repairs have been made since, there is no evidence of them. In one place, appropriately named Gouffre Effrayant, the road is exactly a foot wider than a jeep: A cliff juts above, and below yawns a chasm 2,000 feet deep. Nothing that drops off that precipice is ever seen again, for at the bottom is a mysterious river, the Glace, which ends its icy five miles of turbulence in a black hole in the cliff just below the dropoff. Descending into the Jérémie plain, prepare for the flooding terrors of the Roseaux, the Voldrogues, the Guinaudée, and the Grand Anse! I forded the first three once but hesitated at the fourth, where peasants assured me they could pull my vehicle across by ropes. They did, but it disappeared completely in the middle of the stream, and we had to wait two weeks for it to dry out on the far bank.

Émile Roumère, the *Créole* poet who makes his home in this city of poets, once told me that visitors marooned in the tin-roofed, triangular dovecotes covered by abnormally possessive frangipani have been known to go mad. Quite a few of the local citizens *are* mad, and they will give you the most far-out reasons why they stay in this most far-out city. But the average resident spends most of his time complaining of his fate or inventing ingenious ways to escape to the "paradise" of Port-au-Prince. It is a fact that in Jérémie flowers grow from the cracks in the walls, people paint pictures on ancient Victrola records, and the principle café is called the Nirvana. The town is (or was) faintly illuminated at night by a venerable private diesel plant, and there is a movie house; but, when the picture is showing, the rest of the town blacks out.

Visitors to Haiti are more likely to settle for the capital's immediate foreground and background. In the foreground lies Gonâve Island, larger than Martinique, completely roadless and a wonderful place to explore if you can rent a boat. Gonâve made the news in the 1920s, when an ex-marine sergeant named Faustin Wirkus published a memoir covering the time when he was in "command" of the island and its voodoo-worshiping inhabitants "crowned" him king in appreciation of his sympathy and kindness. Off Pointe Fantasque, facing Port-au-Prince thirty miles to the east, lies the tiny island of Petit-Gonâve, with a fishing village on the channel; its pitted limestone surface is inhabited by iguanas. A mile off the point are several curious square islands built of discarded conch shells and covered with fishermen's *cailles*. In the channel between Gonâve and the southern peninsula are the Rochelois Banks, on which the famous ghost ship *Mary Celeste* foundered January 3, 1867. In the channel between Gonâve and the northern peninsula lie the three uninhabited Arcadin Islands, miniature fairylands for swimming and skin-diving but guarded by wicked reefs.

Back of Port-au-Prince and connected to Pétionville by the one good road in Haiti is the *élite* mountain resort of Kenscoff (altitude 5,000 feet). Beyond Kenscoff, up a road that would not tolerate a car in 1967, lies Furcy (altitude 6,000 feet), from which a direct mountain road to Jacmel may some day descend. Furcy is worth the climb for the view alone. The stillness is awesome. At first there is no sign of human habitation. But slowly, as the eye and ear become accustomed to the tremendous scale of nature, the landscape comes to life. Far to the right, across a distant ravine where banana plants punctuate the red clay with their green sabers, a figure in blue denim threads his ant-like way. A thousand feet straight down, where it seems impossible that even a Haitian goat or *bourrique* could find a foothold, a woman with a crimson bandana on her head is bent double over her potato patch. Miles to the left plumes of smoke behind a cluster of white *cailles* in a stand of mangoes indicate the preparation of new fields for millet or the smothering of charcoal pits. The stillness is accented but not broken, first, by the wild notes of an African work song, plaintively falsetto; then by an even more distant melody played on a bamboo flute or a conch shell; and, finally, if one is patient and lucky, by the chorded whistle of the almost extinct singer of the cloud-forest dells, the *oiseau musicien*. One is aware, if one has brought a camera to this spot, that the scene is inaccessible to photography. It is, in fact, beyond the powers of any machine or any organism but the human eye—and one is glad.

Voodoo: A Living but Doomed Religion

Have you ever taken your seven-year-old daughter to a voodoo ceremony? Unless you are a Haitian (peasant or intellectual) the chances are you haven't. I did in 1959, and only now that she's sixteen do I risk telling the story without embarrassing her—at least I *hope* I won't be embarrassing her. It was some time before her mother in the United States would speak to me, after receiving a postcard from Port-au-Prince that read in its entirety: "Dear Mommy, Guess what! I saw my first voodoo ceremony yesterday. Twelve chickens had their necks twisted. Then they killed the bull. The blood was passed around in buckets. Love, Beebe."

Oriana (Beebe) was sensationalizing but not greatly; voodoo isn't for the squeamish. This particular rite, a *service caille* (home ceremony) was being held at the *houmfor* of Tonton Cheriza, a *houngan* in the village of Croix des Missions whose *la place* (assistant priest) is now André Pierre, one of the outstanding self-taught painters of Haiti. Pierre officiated at a ceremony in the same *houmfor* in 1967, when Bill Negron and I visited him, but the rite in our honor was tame compared with the 1959 extravaganza, perhaps because sacrificial animals are scarce after seven years of Papa Doc's "austerity." (In 1959, splurging after one year at the public till, Duvalier had just given his daughter a birthday present of a bullet-proof Cadillac with her name on the licence plates.) Beebe and I were taken to the ceremony by Odette Rigaud, foremost Haitian authority on the symbolism of the cult, who promised that this one would be a little special.

It was, but it began very slowly, as ceremonies always do. For two hours the *houngan* drew an extraordinarily beautiful and complex *vever*, a bull surrounded by symbols of the various *loa* to be invoked.[1] There was an outer border of linked arrows and an inner ring of what looked like propeller blades with rosettes at the hubs. The letters J.A.S. appeared under the bull and above him the familiar Masonic compasses. There were prayers to the Ogouns, with chanted responses, and an intensification of "interludes" from the battery of 'Rada drums. But it was only after a dozen cocks and two male goats had been sacrificed that the *tonnelle* began to rock. Six major and many minor *crises de possession* took place as everything vibrated with the drums' now-explosive percus-

[1] Voodoo—"vaudou" or "vodun," some scholars spell it—is a West African cult propitiating the forces of nature (*loa*) by prayer, music, sacrifice, and most particularly renunciation of the defiled "self" in an ecstatic, involuntary identification (*crise de possession*) with the deity invoked. The origin of the *vever*, a free-hand drawing of traditional symbols with flour or ashes, is not African. It may have been picked up by the earliest slaves from the aboriginal Indians, receiving its "Masonic" and "Catholic" iconography later. After the design has been sifted through the *houngan's* expert fingers and blessed with rum and sacrifice, it is obliterated by the dancers' feet. The Catholic component of voodoo is of course a nineteenth-century additive. It has been said that 90 per cent of Haitians are Catholics and 100 per cent Voodooists, but many, including the 10 per cent who are Protestant, will have nothing to do with either cult.

sion. *La place* amputated the testicles of a goat and was "seized," as they dangled in their sack from his mouth, by whatever spirit that animal represented. One *hounsi* climbed the striped center post reserved for Damballa, the Dahomeyan snake god; tore most of her clothes off before her fellow maidens-in-waiting could reach her; and was overpowered only as she bolted through the door to the altar room on all fours. In the thunderous, barely controlled bedlam, the vessels containing the blood from the necks of the sacrificial victims were upset.

It was too much for Beebe. She shed some tears and asked to go out, muttering as I led her into the sunlight, "I hate the Haitians because they're so cruel to animals." A motherly peasant woman, seeing her distress, took her into her *caille*, peeled an orange for her, and comforted her on the dirty bed that also contained—I discovered just in time, before sitting on it—a three-week-old baby under a piece of frayed mosquito netting.

"Well," Beebe said, after a few minutes had passed, "when do we go back?"

"Go back?" I asked incredulously. "Why?"

"Because they'll be killing the bull, and we'll miss it."

I walked back thoughtfully with her, not sure whether this experience was a useful baptism in reality or a damaging exposure of innocence to blood lust. I noticed, on the way, that the *houngan*'s sweaty shirt had been tossed casually over an arm of the wooden cross planted in the center of the courtyard. I thought of that most disturbing of crucifixions, a recent picture by Enguérrand Gourgue, which the Episcopal bishop had acquired. An enormous cross occupies the foreground, with the body of Christ attached to the far side, barely visible. It is night. In the background an oily river crosses the canvas, and on it boatloads of Haitians carrying torches peer at the martyr we do not see. We "see" voodoo similarly, not the living religion it is but the spectacle. Maya Deren, the dancer, claims to have been possessed; those who haven't been possessed gain as little from voodoo as they risk.

The sacrifice of the bull was oddly anticlimactic. Perhaps all passion had been spent. Perhaps the unmanageable nature of the beast simply did not permit any foreplay or afterplay. The body could hardly be brushed across our faces, as the bodies of the birds had been, with hypnotic effect. *La place* jumped aboard, guided the partially hobbled animal to the *houngan's* machete, and it was all over. One *hounsi* broke loose, began to "bellow," and was handled by her sisters with the customary gentle solicitude. It was dark now, the drummers were leaving, and some of the younger children present had dozed off. The meat of the slaughtered animals, we were glad to hear, would feed this poor community for some time to come. We drove back to the capital past thousands of *cailles* illuminated by flickering wicks in dishes of kerosene.

Freud would have made much of Beebe's excited description, at the Hotel Quisqueya's breakfast table next morning, of the incident of the

castration of the goat. "There was the priest," she said, "leaping around and around with the milk bottles in his mouth!" But what would Freud have made of Haiti, where voodoo provides the only therapy for mass frustration? The one Haitian trained abroad to administer Freudian psychoanalysis wound up in Papa Doc's cabinet. And the dictator himself, it is widely believed, practices in the Palace that variation of the cult that every reputable *houngan* frowns upon: *magie noire*.

Where Did All These Artists Come From?

The customizers will end up like those poor bastards in Haiti, the artists, who got too much, too soon, from Selden Rodman and the other folk-doters on the subject of primitive genius, so they're all down there at this moment carving African masks out of mahogany —and what I mean is, they never had *an African mask in Haiti before Selden Rodman got there.*

It's true. No one in Haiti had ever heard of an "African mask" when DeWitt Peters opened the Centre d'Art in Port-au-Prince in 1944—or when I joined him in 1946 and encouraged the artists at the Centre to paint murals and directed the painting of the Cathédral St.-Trinité in the years that followed. And it's true, too, that gift shoppes in Port-au-Prince have been turning out "African masks" of mahogany and selling them to gullible tourists by the thousands ever since. But it is also true that no reputable Haitian sculptor or painter has ever made anything remotely "African" and that, if anything so grotesquely derivative had ever been brought into the Centre d'Art, we would have treated it as a joke in poor taste and sent it back where it came from. Haiti's self-taught painters and sculptors—"popular" is the word for them, not "primitive" —*painted Haiti from the start* and were consistently encouraged to paint nothing else. A case in point was Jason Seley's discovery of the sculptor Jasmin Joseph in the ceramic factory near Arcahaie. The American sculptor, then in charge of the sculpture workshop at the Centre, took his own pieces—at that time strongly influenced by Henry Moore—to the factory to be fired. One day he was approached by a boy in the yard, who said to him, "I make figures too." In Jasmin's *caille* Jason was astonished to see dozens of fired figurines, acrobats, farmers, fantastic animals, all in a style that the boy had invented in his own fertile imagination. The American bought some of them, borrowed others for a show at the Centre, and urged the boy to make more pending his return to the factory in a month. But when he returned to Arcahaie he was horrified to see that the boy, eager to please him, had fired a dozen new pieces in Seley's own sophisticated style. Seley explained to the talented, illiterate boy as best he could that an honest artist is a man who makes images out of his

[2] Tom Wolfe, *The Kandy-Kolored Tangerine-Flake Streamlined Baby* (New York: Farrar, Straus, 1966).

own *milieu,* his own life. And Jasmin Joseph, who became one of Haiti's great sculptors in the decade that followed and carved the splendid open-work blocks for the choir screen at St.-Trinité, never deviated from his own vision again.

The other great Haitian sculptor, Georges Liautaud, never deviated at all from the original style of his hammered and pierced iron work, for Liautaud was a mature artist when he started, albeit a blacksmith in the village of Croix des Bouquets; his "commissions" before 1960 had never gone beyond crosses and *vever* symbols to top off an occasional grave. When he went on to flatten Esso drums for the two-dimensional pieces that now grace such institutions as the Museums of Modern Art in Paris and New York, it never occurred to Liautaud to make anything "African," if indeed he had ever heard of Africa. When DeWitt Peters commissioned him to execute two figures for above the folding doors leading to the pool of a new house he was building, Liautaud's double image of Maîtresse La Sirène, the voodoo water goddess, was a natural choice; natural, too, were the clusters of looped holes he cut into the two bodies with his shears—to simulate the jewels such a goddess deserves and to let in sunlight.

The spiritual roots of Haitian art are most certainly African: How could they be anything else? But it is an Africanism filtered through the persistent, pervasive cult of the Dahomeyan religion, the transplanted Africanism of a black man's society, his facial structures and gaits, his work songs and market ways, his thatched huts and grain mortars, his love potions and wake games, his characteristic proverbs and jokes.

The particular roots of Haitian *painting* are elusive. Before 1944 there was the decoration of drums, the stippling of the snake posts in the *houmfors,* and much more rarely the symbology of the *mystères* over the altars or on the exterior walls of *cailles* in remote districts. When my photographs of some of the last appeared in *Life* and other magazines in the late 1940s, knowledgeable Haitians professed to be seeing them for the first time. One sees what one is prepared to see. Travelers criss-crossed Africa for centuries without ever noting the existence of one of the world's great sculptural styles. But, to bring Haitian painting into the open, a demand had to be created. It was created when the Centre d'Art opened its doors and began to offer "popular paintings" for sale.

Two circumstances were crucial. The late DeWitt Peters was "the right man at the right time." He loved Haiti and the Haitians, and the nascent artists responded by accepting his sound advice to pursue their personal styles. The fortuitous appearance of three painters of very great talent, who had thitherto practiced what amounted to a hobby in total obscurity, was just as crucial. For it was the initial *réclame* of Hector Hippolyte, Philomé Obin, and Rigaud Benoît that stimulated such gifted youths as Castera Bazile, Wilson Bigaud, Enguérrand Gourgue, Micius Stéphane, and Toussaint Auguste to embark upon their careers. Sénèque Obin in Cap-Haïtien and Préfèt DuFaut in Jacmel rose to prominence in the early

1950s and Gérard Valcin, Salnave Philippe-Auguste, Seymour Bottex, and André Pierre in the early 1960s.[3] These artists have been the consistent performers, but Louverture Poisson, Robert St. Brice, Fernand Pierre, Adam Léontus, and others have painted occasional pictures of notable originality.

Hector Hippolyte, who died in 1948, was a voodoo priest in the village of Mon Rouis, who came to prominence after Peters, passing through the village one day, noted floral decorations on the doors with the prophetic name Ici La Renaissance. When the Cuban artist Wifredo Lam and André Breton, father of Surrealism, bought some of Hippolyte's pictures at the Centre d'Art and took them to Paris, they caused a sensation in the 1947 international exhibit sponsored by UNESCO. Hippolyte's brief career was launched. Just before he died, the artist confessed:

> I haven't practised *vaudou* for a while. I asked the spirits' permission to suspend my work as a *houngan*, because of my painting. Also, you know, there are so many false priests around today that it saddens me. The spirits agreed that I should stop for a while. I've always been a priest, just like my father and my grandfather, but now I'm more an artist than a priest. When people ask me now what I am, I say that I am an artist. . . . Both *Maîtresse La Sirène* and St. John help me. *La Sirène* helps me to earn money and St. John gives me ideas for my paintings.[4]

It was probably the artificial division of his life between the priest who occasionally painted and the painter who occasionally conducted rites that gave Hippolyte's work its uneven quality. His technique was never wholly adequate to translate his visions into effective plastic images, and, as his life as a medium gave way to his life as an artist, he tended deliberately to forsake the central content of voodoo for the peripheral subject matter of folklore, *zombis*, and black magic, which seemed to offer material for a freer exercise of his sense of visual fantasy. But Hippolyte enjoyed one triumph that probably no painter since the early Italian Renaissance has experienced: He lived to see one of his religious canvases born aloft through the streets (of Port-au-Prince) by a cheering mob.

The more restrained and disciplined vision of Philomé Obin has already been commented on. It was at about that time that Obin's two paintings of Franklin D. Roosevelt came to the attention of the Centre. In one, the

[3] These four and on occasion most of the other artists of the Centre d'Art are now handled by the competing Galerie Issa in Port-au-Prince.

[4] Quoted from Selden Rodman, *Renaissance in Haiti* (New York: Pellegrini & Cudahy, 1948). In the present book I have drawn upon subsequent magazine articles—"The Serpent and the Cross," *Art News*, September 1948; "The Christ of the Haitian Primitives," *Harper's Bazaar*, December 1950; "A Mural by Wilson Bigaud," *Magazine of Art*, October 1951; "Murals for Haiti: From the Centre d'Art Jeep to 'The Miracle at Cana,'" *Art in America*, December 1951—and from the chapter on painting in my *Haiti: The Black Republic* (New York: Devin-Adair, 1954; revised edition, 1961).

American President was depicted at Cap-Haïtien on a battleship, lifting the marine occupation of Haiti; in the other he was presented more symbolically, rising from the grave to cement the "Union of the Americas" under a sky containing angels and the Eye of God. Two of Obin's other early masterpieces were tributes to Charlemagne Peralte, the leader of the guerrilla resistance to the Occupation. *Funeral* contained no fewer than 750 individual figures in a small picture that remained remarkably uncrowded. In *Crucifixion* the martyr's body is lashed to a door, with the weeping figure of his mother in black standing by.

Rigaud Benoît's more factual pictures are addressed to the unmomentous present. His market scenes record in radiant detail the way rural Haiti "looks." Now married to Hippolyte's daughter, this former taxi driver has recently painted several versions of an *Interrupted Marriage.* The bizarre interior of a church combines the best elements of a mosque and the ribbed hold of a sailing vessel. The bride's clothes are being ripped off by an enraged rival. The groom is fainting. The white priest at the altar is scratching his head. The organist continues to play. And the bridesmaids are being propositioned by interlopers from the streets quick to take advantage of the general confusion.

It was in 1949, concerned over the "flight" of Haiti's artistic capital abroad (for Haitian pictures are rarely prized by Haitians), that I brought the artist William Calfee from Washington to the Centre to give a course of instruction in mural techniques. Deciding on egg tempera as the medium, Calfee divided the artists into two groups. Sophisticated artists of the *élite,* who were beginning to paint in academic or far-out styles, were given the walls of an upstairs library. The self-taught took over the stairwell and the basement. Obin, who disdained to work with anyone, received a small chamber of his own. Upstairs one of the "advanced painters," as they called themselves, worked with a projection machine.

Another erased his initial drawing five times and finally gave up. Another would descend from his ladder and ascend to correct with dizzying regularity. A fourth had a nervous breakdown. Only one, Antonio Joseph, survived to become a fine painter after years abroad. All leaned heavily on Calfee for technical advice and moral support.

Downstairs the "primitives," once coaxed into the initial effort, attacked their wall spaces with abandon. The briefest of charcoal sketches —then on with the paint! Talent separated the sheep from the goats. The untalented produced some real horrors. But Benoît, Bazile, Bigaud, Lévêque, and Obin simply translated to the dimensions of the wall space the images of those easel pictures that had been monumental in their simplicity. That month there appeared on the wall of the Centre d'Art privy a derisive pencil scrawl in a primitive hand: "Les artistes de l'étage qui se disent des avancés ne sont pas même des préliminaires primitives."

The following year, unable to get the Estimé government, which was then building dozens of exposition buildings along the waterfront, to commission a single Haitian mural, I turned to Bishop Alfred Voegeli of the Protestant Episcopal Church. (The Catholic Church had already expressed the view that "popular art" was an amalgam of voodoo and satanism.) Bishop Voegeli, who had begun to collect Haitian art at his residence, was delighted with the idea of having his barn-bare Cathédral St.-Trinité filled with joyous renditions of the Christian story. I arranged to have the scaffolds built; bought tempera supplies in the United States; assigned the four sections of the apse to Obin, Bazile, Benoît, and Lévêque; and gave them sacks of charcoal and an icebox full of eggs.

Keeping the eggs from being *eaten*, seeing that the artists showed up every day to paint, and making it clear to these Catholics [5] that the familiar religious "chromos" with which Catholicism flooded Haiti were to play no part in their iconography were my only real tasks. When Bishop Voegeli returned from a trip abroad a month later and looked at the finished apse, he turned to me and exclaimed, "Thank God they painted Haitians!" But to a deacon who expressed his surprise over such confidence, in an atmosphere of artificially stimulated public outrage, he added, "It only shows that it sometimes pays to be a little crazy."

By the time the second year's work in the Cathedral began, the apse had already been reproduced in *Time,* and money for the painters to supplement the church's funds had been donated by a generous American patron. Obin shifted effortlessly from his central *Crucifixion* to *The Last Supper* on the three walls of a chapel; Bazile moved on from the *Ascension* to the *Baptism* (in a Haitian stream, of course); and several new painters were given walls. But the glory of the second year's effort was the twenty-two-year-old Wilson Bigaud's *Miracle at Cana,* which covered a wall of the transept measuring 528 square feet and pierced by two windows. Bigaud completed this Brueghel-like extravaganza, with its moonlit graveyards, cock thieves chased by policemen, slaughtered pigs,

[5] Obin alone was a Protestant.

vaccine players, and bourgeois guests, in less than six weeks, though interrupted at one point by a deranged rival, who smeared his and an adjacent mural with black oil. But it was Bigaud's tragedy, and that of several lesser *populaires*, that he was not able to cope with the temptations that followed in the wake of sudden fame and fortune. First he went heavily into debt, and then, painting frantically in desperation, he lost focus and listened to the blandishments of unprincipled dealers and would-be critics who counseled him to mount the band wagon of "modernity." He emerged from a mental hospital finally, still searching for the style that was once so decisive and matchless.

What is most surprising about the phenomenon of Haitian art is that this corruption has occurred so seldom. Now wholly dependent upon the whims of tourists—and a mere trickle of tourists, at that—it seems inevitable that Haitian art will founder, starve to death, or be swept away in a final conflagration with the rest of the tormented country. That it has not happened so far is partly a tribute to the Centre d'Art, which survives under a dedicated new management; partly because such great new talents as André Pierre and Philippe-Auguste have kept the standards high; but most of all because of whatever it is that makes the Haitian spirit unconquerable.

Envoi: Three Haitis

Visitors to Port-au-Prince unacquainted with the history of the city's *fin-de-siècle* architecture—those weird, half-timbered castles of fantasy, with their stately hinged doors, gingerbread cupolas, and lacy spires—could be forgiven for assuming that it was the product of a happy collaboration between Saul Steinberg and Charles Addams. Actually, the style is closely related to that Victorian neoromanticism that ranges all the way from Aubrey Beardsley's effete Gothicism to Antoni Gaudí's Barcelona bravura. It was triggered, no doubt, by the Paris Colonial Exposition of 1900, where Oriental pagodas nudged Mohammedan mosques, for the finest of these Haitian residences still to be seen in the foothills of the city between the Vieux Mansion on the Pétionville Road and the Hotel Oloffson to the south, were the work of a group of sophisticated *élite* architects trained at the École Supérieure Polytechnique in Paris. One of them was Robert Baussan's father Georges, who designed the lovely house restored by Lawrence Peabody, presently director of the Centre d'Art. Others were Léonce Maignan, Léon Mathon, and Eugène Maximilien, who designed the orange and buff Cadasco confection near the Oloffson. The celebrity-haunted Oloffson itself—where James Jones was married, Graham Greene wrestled with Satan, and Malcolm Lowry once walked for a noon interview, fully dressed and martini in hand, into the swimming pool—was built entirely out of mahogany for that President Guillaume Sam whose dismemberment by the mob was the immediate cause of the marine occupation of July 28, 1915.

Unhappily, the *élite* grew ashamed of their gorgeous rookeries and let them fall into decay while moving up the hill into reasonable facsimiles of Miami Beach modern. Unhappily, too, fires will account for the rest— at least judging by one I witnessed in the Canapé Vert some years ago. As a tragicomedy of life among the city folk, the scene deserves to be memorialized.

It started when two repairmen failed to stop a leak in a gas stove; irritated at being recalled, they strolled back insolently with cigarettes dangling from their mouths—and were blown into the street. Long after it was too late to save the burning house, the *pompiers* arrived and began attaching their hoses to the almost-pressureless water main. A crowd was now enjoying the spectacle—and stepping on the hoses. Finally one hose was disentangled, and a tentative jet of water burst from it, to the applause of the crowd. Alas, the fireman's aim was so bad that the stream overshot the building, drenching those on the far side. Meanwhile the Haitian next door (whose house was never touched by the flames) was frantically lugging his worldly possessions—an armoire of clothes, two trunks full of faded photographs and newspaper clippings, and a complete dining-room set—down three flights of stairs to the pavement. While he was engaged in this operation, one fireman drenched him with water, another pushed a burning wall with a crowbar so that it fell directly on his salvaged furniture, and a third collided head-on with him just as he emerged from the door with a tray of glassware held high. A Canadian diplomat watching this Mack Sennett tableau was so convulsed that a policeman felt obliged to admonish him: "Ce n'est pas drôle, M'sieu." This scolding in turn convulsed the crowd—and before long the policeman too.

Policemen, even in countries that count them as part of the armed forces, have an *esprit de corps* of their own. When Bill Negron and I made our second trip to Haiti late in 1967, we noticed unusual traffic snarls and soon discovered why. It seems that the day before a police-man had stopped the Defense Minister from driving the wrong way down a one-way street. The Minister brusquely revealed his identity, but the policeman was not impressed. Fortunately for him, the Chief of Police happened by just as the Minister was taking the stubborn law enforcer to the Palace and insisted on accompanying them. Face to face with Duvalier, the Chief stood firm. The dictator, who had just put down the latest conspiracy against him by shooting a dozen officers in the army and driving his son-in-law into exile, was enraged at the prospect of los-ing another top loyalist. "Remove *all* the traffic signs in the city!" he screamed.

In the first two years of his presidency, before several assassination attempts had brought out his latent paranoia, Duvalier had the makings of a program for Haiti. He had it in mind to transfer the economic power of the mulatto and Syrian business class to the black majority. As the *élite* had never done anything for the black majority, this program was bound to be popular; it was the failure of the exiled leaders to appreciate this point that led to their inability to arouse any popular opposition to Papa Doc. Unfortunately for him (and for Haiti), Duvalier had no idea what to do with this economic power once it fell into his hands. In fact his henchmen used the tax money extorted from the businessmen, who were left in nominal control of their businesses, to feather their own nests in the traditional way. What had always been done legally and politely was now done openly, with blackjacks. The wife of a cabinet minister, whose bureau had just exacted an exorbitant "tax" from a jewelry store on the Rue de Quai walked to the counter one morning and priced a wristwatch at $100. She declared the price excessive. That afternoon the Minister returned with her, extorted another $100, and with the cash he had just received from the frightened merchant bought his wife the watch. That same week I watched officers of the militia playing poker on the sidewalk in Pétionville. When a big loser was wiped out, he sent a private across the street to collect the grimy one-*gourde* notes that barefooted peasant *marchandes* coming into town from a village three days' walk away had been forced to put in the box.

What the President-for-Life in his *Catéchisme de la Révolution* calls "the remission of our economy from the hands of the bourgeoisie into the hands of the people" now stands exposed as a gigantic grab. Those who pay up receive in return what is called "L'Extrême-Onction Duvalieriste." It will be administered "by the popular army, the civil militia, the Tontons Macoutes, and the Haitian people under the command of the chief, the Honorable Doctor François Duvalier, to the accompaniment of grenades, mortars, Mausers, bazookas, flame-throwers and other utensils." That's what the *Catéchisme* says.

The third Haiti is neither farcical nor mad, though like everything poetic it contains a measure of both qualities.

When I took Truman Capote to see Hippolyte in 1948, he remarked on the naturalness of this most unusual man's environment and how the painter's personality dissolved one's sense of isolation. Later he wrote that he found Hippolyte's art admirable because there was nothing in it "that has been slyly transposed; he is using what lives within himself, and that is his country's spiritual history, its sayings and worships." Later still, Truman overheard an old man on a bus, who wore a carnival mask like raven's wings, claim to have made the sky. When another passenger observed scornfully "I suppose you made the moon, too?" the old man replied, "and the stars, they are my grandchildren." A rowdy woman clapped her hands and announced that the old man was crazy. "But, dear lady," he responded, "if I am crazy, how could I have done these beautiful things?"

"If to be a bragging liar is to be an artist," wrote Herb Gold five years later, "then the Haitians are the nation of artists par excellence. . . . The brag confesses all, delusion and dream, giving a large and lyric perspective on experience and saying furthermore: Life is worth the trouble! Many Haitians excel at this sort of brag—the sort that should lead straight to glory." And the novelist goes on to give this account of a man at a Sunday cockfight:

> His bird has just had its eyes pecked out and its skull fractured. This expensive, highly trained, meat-fed battler upon which he has lavished so much love is now good only for the frying pan. He accepts the glass of consoling rum but shakes off the sympathy of his friends, wiping his eyes with his sleeve and crying out: "Listen, you!" (A hush comes over the huddle of men.) "Listen, let me tell you what has just happened to me, otherwise you will not know. . . . I came with my cock in a sack to win lots of money. I promised my girl a trip to the Cap. You know what women are. Well, I spread this cock's wings and I sprayed it with rum and I licked its beak in mine and I bet everything I had. My old father's money too! My cock fought, friends, it lost, yes, you know it, but I don't go home empty-handed, not me. No, dear friends, I still have the sack!"
>
> With the roar of laughter and applause that rewards him, he is no longer defeated. All of these men have lost and know what failure means. He has communed with them. He has made a work of art of his defeat and therefore a triumph.[6]

No, Haiti is not for the connoisseur of beaches nor even for the tourist who finds what he is looking for in Old San Juan or at Caneel Bay. And it is equally baffling to the idealist with a sense of mission who wants to *do* something. The problems besetting Haiti are so nearly terminal that serious do-gooders have been heard to propose resettling the whole population in the Sahara Desert or on the Amazon. Even fanatics of planned parenthood and the communists, who profess to be ready to tackle anything, turn pale at the spectacle of 5 million undernourished, moneyless illiterates jammed into a maze of scrabbled mountains the size of Vermont. But, as Arnold Toynbee says, "The destiny of our Western civilization turns on the issue of our struggle with all that Madison Avenue stands for more than it turns on the issue of our struggle with Communism." So perhaps there *is* hope for Haiti.

The poets think so. They find in Haiti what sustains their hope in the human race.

[6] Herbert Gold, "The Arts in Haiti," *Mademoiselle*, February 1955. Truman Capote's observations are from "Haitian Notes," *Harper's Bazaar*, December 1948.

INDEX